PATTERNS OF ARTISTIC DEVELOPMENT IN CHILDREN

COMPARATIVE STUDIES OF TALENT

This book traces the development of artistic talent from early childhood to adolescence through a series of studies that look comparatively at development in talented and less talented populations. It presents a model of artistic talent that attributes individual differences to the figurative abilities of talented children. The model proposes that artistic talent results from the continual coordination of heightened figurative abilities with conceptual processes throughout a period critical in semiotic development. The studies focus on the development of form, spatial relationships, and composition in children's artwork. Milbrath's theory is richly supported by original examples of children's artwork.

Constance Milbrath is Assistant Professor in the Department of Psychiatry at the University of California, San Francisco. Between 1989 and 1995, she was Resident Scientist at the MacArthur Program for Conscious and Unconscious Mental Processes. She has written extensively on child development and on the origins of artistic talent in children, and is a member of the Jean Piaget Society, the Society for Research in Child Development, and the American Psychological Association.

PATTERNS OF ARTISTIC DEVELOPMENT IN CHILDREN

COMPARATIVE STUDIES OF TALENT

Constance Milbrath

Photographer: Tom Houston
Research Assistant: Ana Caminos

CAMBRIDGE
UNIVERSITY PRESS

PUBLISHED BY THE PRESS SYNDICATE OF THE UNIVERSITY OF CAMBRIDGE
The Pitt Building, Trumpington Street, Cambridge CB2 1RP, United Kingdom

CAMBRIDGE UNIVERSITY PRESS
The Edinburgh Building, Cambridge CB2 2RU, UK   http://www.cup.cam.ac.uk
40 West 20th Street, New York, NY 10011-4211, USA   http://www.cup.org
10 Stamford Road, Oakleigh, Melbourne 3166, Australia

First published 1998

Printed in the United States of America

Typeset in Sabon 10.25/13 pt., Penta Software Inc. [BV]

Library of Congress Cataloging-in-Publication Data
Milbrath, Constance, 1943–
Patterns of artistic development in children : comparative studies of talent /
Constance Milbrath.
p. cm.
Includes bibliographical references and index.
ISBN 0-521-44313-X
1. Child artists – Psychology.   2. Creative ability in children.
I. Title.
N351.M54   1998
704'.054 – DC21   97-32148
                                                                  CIP

A catalog record for this book is available from
the British Library.

ISBN 0 521 44313 X hardback

To Claire, Daniel, Hondo,
Joel, Kate, Michael, Peregrine, and Tara
and their families

CONTENTS

TABLES

ACKNOWLEDGMENTS

This book grew out of a genuine interest in individual differences in human potential. Although part of me will always cherish the ideal that with enough effort anyone can succeed, the decade or more I spent studying talented children and their artwork opened my eyes to a larger reality. The potential for exceptional talent in a domain is likely to be inborn. This is not meant to diminish in any way the years of hard work that go into developing a talent, because without effort potential remains just potential. The eight children I studied over time put a tremendous amount of time and energy into their art from a very early age. Their art appeared critical to their self-definition, and although today only a few of them define themselves primarily as artists, in early adolescence their identity was closely linked to their outstanding artistic ability.

Could this potential have been developed at any age? I think perhaps in part but not to the same degree. There is something unique about the childhood years, a uniqueness that is especially apparent when we compare the facility with which children learn a language or a musical instrument to the more laborious training an adult must receive. The childhood years are also unique in allowing the time and space for free exploration of a domain. In the arts this leads to the coordination of imagination with a rich graphic vocabulary and the development of technique. Moreover for children with artistic potential, formal training appears unnecessary for mastery of basic technique. The children I followed over time received little or no formal instruction until high school, after they had already demonstrated their mastery of techniques such as figure rotation and perspective. The rules to map their understanding of the view-specific features of a scene onto a drawing were derived from experimentation and diligent practice, procedures that began at a very early age.

I am most indebted to the eight talented children I studied over time and to their families for teaching me about artistic practice and how children with exceptional potential develop their talent. These children were remarkably articulate and insightful about their own artistic development and generous with their time. The families were exceptionally supportive of my research efforts, allowing me continual access over many years to their children and to their thoughts and ideas about their children's development. It was the inspiration of these children and their families that convinced me to continue and expand my research on artistic development and it is to them I owe the greatest thanks for this volume.

I also wish to thank the many children who participated in the cross-sectional studies and the schools from which they were recruited. I owe a great debt to Wildwood Elementary School, Piedmont Middle School, and Piedmont High School, in Piedmont, California; the Arts Magnet School and the Berkeley Child Art Studio in Berkeley, California; the California College of Arts and Crafts in Oakland, California; the Museum School at the De Young Museum in San Francisco, California; and the University of Toronto in Scarborough, Ontario, Canada. The principals and staff at all three Piedmont schools were especially generous in allowing me the physical space and the time to take the children from their classes to test their composition abilities. I would also like to give special thanks to the art teachers at the schools who allowed me to study children in their classes and who took the time to identify the talented children. Some of the teachers also allowed me extended time to interview them on a variety of topics that provided me valuable insights into the artistic process. Others actually participated as subjects in the composition study. The art teachers were Michael Benedict, Helen Brainerd, Kathy Glazier, Allan Stein, Chris Johnson, Miriam de Uriarte, and Tom White. I am also indebted to the art students in Chris Johnson's and Tom White's classes at California College of Arts and Crafts, who gave up their class time to rate the original compositions generated by the children.

Two colleagues were especially important in carrying out this research. Ana Caminos generously gave her time and advice as an artist to the development of a coding system for spontaneous drawings and to the actual coding and testing of children. Tom Houston photographed the children's drawings. Tom willingly went anywhere, with very little advance notice, to take the photographs and slides that documented the children's artwork. He also provided continual inspiration over the many years of the project and was a critical sounding board for my ideas.

I am also grateful to the many students of Piaget who participated in the Piaget reading seminar at UC Berkeley over the decade or so I attended. With them and through them I learned all that I know about Piagetian theory and its application. Those I especially remember from their own insights into Piaget are Valerie Ahls, Keith Alward, Allan Black, Phil Davidson, Julie Gerhardt, Charles Helwig, Carolyn Hildebrandt, Melanie Killen, Linda Kroll, Marta Laupa, Ageliki Nicolopoulou, Barbara Scales, and Cecilia Wainryb. I particularly owe much to Jonas Langer, our expert guide. He carried the light that kept us on the steep trail.

I am also greatly indebted to Jonas Langer, Sue Parker, and Gerald Cupchik for reading and commenting on parts of the manuscript for this book. Julia Hough, my editor at Cambridge University Press, helped me immeasurably to shape a rough manuscript into the finished book with her editorial comments, her patience, encouragement, and support. Conversations with Elizabeth Saenger, Emiel Reith, Claire Golomb, Ellen Winner, and Gerald Cupchik, as well as their written works, were very important to the formation of my own ideas about artistic development. I also owe a great debt to the imaginative and enduring research of Norm Freeman. Don Hutchins, Jerry Lovelace, Bernie Lubell, and Ross Fink contributed their knowledge as artists to the project. They designed and made the composition block sets, constructed the composition stage, and generated the original compositions used in the composition studies. Just as significant were their contributions to my thinking on art and the creative process.

I could not have undertaken or finished the research or this volume without the continual support of my family. My parents encouraged scholarship in all three of their children and have been particularly supportive of my interests in the arts and of this project. My husband, Oscar, was himself a talented young artist. His "inside" knowledge allowed me into the drawing process from the perspective of the artist. Our daughter, Enion, an accomplished violist, showed me firsthand the degree of commitment necessary to excel in the arts. My son, Max, himself an enthusiastic young artist, was born midway through this project. He has shown great patience and unusual understanding while waiting for his mother to be finished with her book.

PART I

THE REPRESENTATION
OF FORM AND SPACE

PERSPECTIVES ON DRAWING

DERIVING A DEVELOPMENTAL MODEL FOR ARTISTIC TALENT

> To achieve progress (in art), nature alone counts, and the eye is trained through contact with her. It becomes concentric by looking and working. I mean to say that in an orange, an apple, a bowl, a head, there is a culminating point; and this point is always – in spite of the tremendous effect of light and shade and colorful sensations – the closest to our eye; the edges of the objects recede to a center on our horizon (Cézanne, letter to Emile Bernard).
>
> (Chipp, 1968, p. 20)

In this letter Cézanne directs us to a fundamental aspect of artistic "seeing": the artist's vision of objects as visual surfaces. I was first struck by the meaning of his words when I was drawing with friends who were accomplished visual artists. As we drew, I realized that we were "seeing" objects quite differently even though we were all looking at the same things. As I struggled to outline a form, the artists used light, shade, and details to define a visual surface. Where they saw edges, light, shade, and texture, I saw an orange, apple, or bowl. I had always believed that it was education and training that taught this "trick" of seeing to an artist, but several of these artists reported drawing with this skill as children with no special training beyond their own obsession to draw. This suggested, as did Cézanne's letter, that perception, and its natural education by looking, played a major role in their artistic development. Yet when I read accounts of artistic development, including

Piaget's, the message was quite different. Mastering artistic milestones, such as form, apparent spatial relationships, and perspective, was largely dependent on cognition and its development. Little was said about the role of perception.

Missing from most accounts, however, was the developmental story of talented children, those most likely to become visual artists. This omission seemed important because a convincing theory of artistic development should encompass talented children as well as those of normal ability. Most of what I did find to read about talented children concluded that they traversed the same stages as less talented children but more quickly. What I should expect, therefore, was that talented children would develop along the same trajectory as less talented children, but simply get "farther faster." It occurred to me that if the "farther faster" hypothesis were true, these children could provide an idealized exemplar of artistic development. Studying exemplars might be more revealing than studying normative development because single individuals would show a fuller range of artistic activity.

It was in this spirit that I first undertook my research into artistic development. I let people know I was interested in studying children with artistic talent and soon received reports about children who were "terrific" artists. In a short time I had a small sample of talented artists, all born within a year of each other (reflecting my cohort's children). When I contrasted these children's drawings and artwork with that of their age-mates a perplexing issue arose. As I had expected, the developmental milestones associated with cognitive changes were clearly evident in their drawings, but almost from the beginning their drawings looked distinct from those of their age-mates. Shortly after the ancestral stage represented by "tadpole man," the drawings of talented children seemed to take off, evolving quickly into highly differentiated and complex depictions. The older the children got, the more divergent their artwork became. Figure 1.1a and b shows similarities in the simple clear forms of the animals drawn by a 5-year-old talented and a 7-year-old less talented child, even though a 2-year age gap favors the younger talented child. Within a few years, however, the drawings of talented and less talented children no longer resemble each other even when less talented children are 4 or 5 years older than talented. In Figure 1.2a a less talented 13-year-old girl uses occlusion to indicate depth and in Figure 1.2b a less talented 14-year-old boy shows he

Figure 1.1a. A 5-year-old talented boy.

Figure 1.1b. A 7-year-old less talented boy.

understands perspective by carefully constructing the jet and runway in linear perspective. In comparison, drawings by two younger talented children are strikingly different in the complexity of their content and in the fluid treatment of figures. Even though in Figure 1.3a a talented 9-year-old girl used an oblique projective system instead of the more advanced perspective system to represent the pig stye and fence, she is able freely to rotate the orientations of

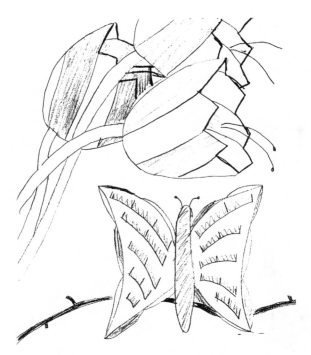

Figure 1.2a. A less talented 13-year-old girl.

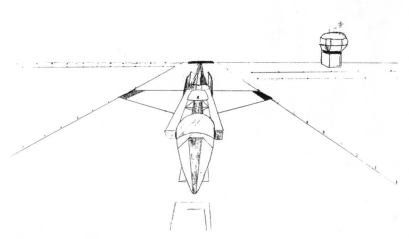

Figure 1.2b. A less talented 14-year-old boy.

The Representation of Form and Space

Figure 1.3a. A 9-year-old talented girl.

Figure 1.3b. A 9-year-old talented boy.

human and animal figures. In Figure 1.3b a talented 9-year-old boy has drawn a dynamic clash of dinosaurs. His flexibility in rendering figure orientations is quite striking.

The conclusion that observable differences between talented and less talented child artists are a matter of developmental rate is not entirely convincing. For one thing, the older less talented children never did seem to "catch up." For another, as the drawings in Figure 1.3 suggest, the level of detail and the complexity of themes attempted by some young talented artists were never matched by those of older less talented children. Did these differences simply reflect individual interests and imagination, or, as Cézanne suggested, did they reflect differences in how children learn to "see" the world? Moreover, were talented and less talented children relying on the same underlying mental processes when drawing?

This book is an attempt to ponder these questions by studying artistic development in both talented and less talented youngsters. My aim is to explore the potential contributions of different mental processes, including cognition and perception, to artistic development. The book is divided into two unequal parts. In the first and larger part the focus is on children's abilities to construct forms and coordinate spatial relationships among elements in their drawings. In the second part children's ability to compose visually balanced artwork is examined. Throughout, I use the term *talented* rather than *gifted* because *gifted* has the connotation of high IQ, which is not necessarily related to artistic talent (Winner, 1996). Despite the separation of children into two talent groups, I use the term *less talented* for the other children to acknowledge a continuum of talent rather than a dichotomy. The study methods combine approaches common in developmental psychology with those of a naturalist: a retrospective and prospective longitudinal design and a cross-sectional design that trace the development of spontaneous or free drawings a child creates naturally. The decision to study spontaneous drawings allows a richer and more complex phenomenon to be studied than would be possible from experimental studies based on life model drawings, but it also limits the conclusions that can be made. Nevertheless many such experimental studies already exist and these are used to elaborate the study results. New techniques for analyzing children's drawings had to be developed because few existed that were not based on drawing from life models.

THE ROLE OF FIGURATIVE AND OPERATIVE PROCESSES IN TALENT: A WORKING HYPOTHESIS

Two groups of hypotheses need to be distinguished. The first focuses on developmental rate and can be labeled the "farther faster" hypotheses. These claim that talented children are more accelerated in their depiction of object properties and spatial relationships because they are either gifted intellectually (Harris, 1963; Winner, 1996) or gifted in spatial intelligence (Gardner, 1983). In either case advanced conceptual analysis explains talent and accounts for the precocious developmental rate that distinguishes talented children's drawings. The second group of hypotheses focuses on figurative processes. Figurative processes are not by themselves inherently conceptual, even though conceptual development influences figurative content and how children operate on it. As a group, these hypotheses can be labeled the "seeing, remembering, and doing" hypotheses. Attention plays a key role in the figurative group of hypotheses because artistic talent only develops when children actively focus their attention on their perceptions, visual memories, or drawing production.

One figurative hypothesis is suggested by Cézanne's letter. Talent in the visual arts arises because visual information is better and more selectively encoded by talented children. Central to this hypothesis is the idea that talented children learn to see the world less in terms of categories and concepts and more in terms of forms, apparent shapes, and visual surface features. A second hypothesis emphasizes the ability of talented children to rely on detailed visual memories (Winner, 1996). Superior visual memory allows them to "call up" or reconstruct explicit visual images that serve as referents for drawing. A third hypothesis considers the process of regulating drawing production, proposing that talented children attend more directly to the act of drawing itself. Selective attention to the act of drawing imposes a perceptual-motor regulation on it that, with successive repetitions, leads to the discovery of lines that convey an intended subject and elimination of those that fail. In this case, skilled motor procedures are built on the basis of attention to and perceptual-motor regulation of the act of drawing. These three figurative hypotheses need not be mutually exclusive; individual differences in children's profiles of figurative abilities can lead to successful performance in the visual arts. Multiple developmental trajectories may also be involved in exceptional talent. In describing spatial intelligence, Gardner (1983) includes perception, visual memory, and the transforming operations inherent in spatial cognition. He notes that any individual with skills in several of these areas is likely to be successful in the visual arts.

In this book I develop the thesis that talented and less talented children quickly diverge in their artistic development because the mental processes that underlie their artistic behavior are quite distinct. I propose two contrasting developmental trajectories. Young children rarely draw from live models. Instead they rely on internal schemas that represent sensory-motor formulas derived largely from information encoded in memory. In very young children this information is represented by an abstracted prototype. Thus the human form "stands" upright topped by the head, whereas animal forms are "bent over" and topped by the back. Most children will continue to use these conceptually derived drawing schemas until middle childhood, when improvements in their ability to analyze and reason about what they see push them to improve their drawings. By this time, however, the gap between what they can draw and what they wish to draw is quite large. Children who develop artistic talent begin by being more attentive to their perceptions and artistic productions. Because they are sensitive to visual discrepancies between what they see and the generalized prototypical forms they draw, they quickly turn to more detailed and specific instances or episodes encoded in memory (episodic memory) to regulate their drawings. These kinds of memories are generally not accessible until children are 4 or 5 years old (Nelson,1992) and may be more vivid and visual in talented children. Training of the artistic eye to see visual surfaces rather than categories, then, springs naturally from biases and proclivities that in many cases may be inborn (Winner & Martino, 1993). What differentiate these two groups of children are *not* their intellectual or operative abilities but their figurative abilities; the heightened perceptual and/or visual memory abilities of talented children function to direct their attention toward the visual arts.

Figurative thought relates to the mental *reproduction* of objects, events, and relationships experienced in the world, not to their transformation (Piaget, 1977). It includes perception, imitation, and the constructed visual image. Piaget assumed that like operations, these derived from sensorimotor activities. But unlike the transforming sensorimotor activities from which operations evolve, figurative thought is based on imitation, which reproduces events and relationships in the world. According to Piaget, figurative thought dominates the thinking of young children. The errors young children make in the classic conservation of liquids task result from this bias. Young children take as evidence the visual appearance of the levels of liquid in two dissimilar containers rather than the operation that produced their equality.

Operative thought acts on objects, events, and relationships experienced in the world to modify or transform them (Piaget, 1977). Counting is a good example. In order to count things, a child must first classify objects as belonging to the class of "countables" or the class of things not to be counted. Second the child must order the objects so that each one receives a unique tag and belongs to a cardinal set. Operative thought includes logical, mathematical, spatial, and causal reasoning. Operative thought has a long developmental course that begins in infancy with the use of sensorimotor actions to transform objects, progresses in middle childhood to interiorized reversible actions, and culminates in adolescents with symbolic manipulation and transformation of objects. Figurative thought develops more quickly. Children 5 years and younger appear to perform as well as adults on tasks of perception and visual imagery when the tasks do not depend on operative development (Kellman, 1988; Kosslyn, 1980; Piaget, 1969).

Mapping three dimensions onto a two-dimensional drawing surface relies on conceptual knowledge (Case, Okamoto, Griffin, McKeough, Bleiker, Henderson & Stephenson, 1996; Piaget & Inhelder, 1956/67). Children must understand the relationships they are trying to depict. If talented children are *more accelerated in their conceptual understanding* of spatial relationships, we would expect to see evidence of this accelerated development in their drawings. For example, perspective drawings should appear in advance of when most children, independently of their abilities to draw, would demonstrate this understanding. On the other hand, if talented children excel in the figurative realm and not in the operative or conceptual realm, they should show some of the same limitations when trying to depict complex spatial relationships common to children of their stage in development. Their rate of progress will be limited by their rate of development in the operative or conceptual domain. Consequently, the development of projective systems and the coordination of a single viewpoint in their drawings will not be developmentally accelerated when contrasted with the norms for these conceptual tasks.

If talented children are *more attentive to perception and to the act of drawing itself,* we might expect an early appearance and differentiation of recognizable forms and a precocious compositional sense. By using their eyes to regulate "what looks good" these children should be able both to capture forms as two-dimensional shapes and to create visually balanced drawings. Less talented children, on the other hand, because they are not selectively attending to their perceptions, or to the act of drawing, will rely on conceptual approaches. Their early drawings will be conceptual equivalents rather than visual equivalents. They may be able to compose a picture by using conceptual approaches, such as part–whole operations and compensation relations (reversibility operations), but at much older ages than if they were using figurative approaches: ages that are consistent with cognitive stages of development for the corresponding operations. If talented children are *using specific and detailed visual representations* to generate and regulate their drawings, then forms should rapidly differentiate with a greater number developing to depict the same object. Specifically, we might expect drawings with varied figural orientations and rotations, drawings that bear more than a passing resemblance to stances, postures, and relationships that real people assume, and the relative absence of stereotypes (canonical views) and formula-driven drawings.

CONCEPTION, PERCEPTION, AND PRODUCTION IN CHILDREN'S DRAWINGS

Before describing the studies presented in this book, it is instructive to review existing approaches to the artistic process in children. I chose three that have had a major impact on research to present. The first emphasizes conceptual development, regarding drawings as consistent with children's ability to reconstruct or internally represent objects and their spatial relationships. The second emphasizes perception, focusing on the development of young children's perceptual abilities and capacity to analyze objects and spatial relationships visually. The third emphasizes the production of a drawing. It holds that development in drawing is based on a child's ability to solve the multitude of problems inherent in graphic production. This includes technical problems imposed by organizing three-dimensional information into two-dimensional representations, and those associated with overcoming strong internal biases. Frequently researchers pit these approaches against each other with strategies that aim to test which approach best explains the competencies and anomalies seen in children's drawings. Results are often complex, favoring different approaches under different experimental conditions. This suggests that all three have an important contribution to an understanding of children's drawings.

Conceptual Development: Object Knowledge and Spatial Cognition

The first approach to children's drawings stresses conceptual development. Two assumptions lay its foundations: One is that stage of cognitive development determines a child's semiotic abilities (Piaget & Inhelder, 1956/67); the second is that strategies that guide perceptual analysis are strongly influenced by cognitive development (Piaget, 1969; Vurpillot, 1976). Two streams in this literature are relevant. On the one hand, some argue that drawings are an index of a child's knowledge about object properties and mirror their underlying conceptual models. On the other hand, others see drawings as accurate reflections of children's geometric knowledge and level of spatial reasoning. Even though most researchers acknowledge a lag between children's spatial reasoning and related drawing performance, some still use drawings to index important developmental shifts in spatial concepts. One rationale in favor of this practice is that since performance cannot occur in advance of understanding, at worst a drawing underestimates a child's reasoning ability. In addition, for certain populations, such as talented drawers, drawings might serve as good indicators of developmental changes in spatial reasoning (Milbrath, 1987).

The construct of intellectual realism has been central to issues of object knowledge. Luquet (1935) first described intellectual realism as a developmental stage in children's drawing dominated by what a child *knew* about objects rather than what a child *saw*. So, for example, when young children view an apple stuck through with a hat pin, they draw the invisible part of the pin (Clark, 1897). This tendency, to draw object parts that cannot be seen, is explained as an internal bias that obliges the child to include known or understood relationships. Clear and unambiguous properties that define an object are also likely to be shown. For example, cups are always drawn with handles because they are an important functional feature of cups; people are drawn symmetrically in front views, and animals, who are ambiguously defined in front view, are drawn in profile (Freeman & Janikoun, 1972, Ives and Rovett, 1979; Palmer, Rosch & Chase, 1981). Naive drawers of all ages prefer contours or outlines for depicting solids such as cubes, cylinders, and even irregularly contoured solids that give maximum information about the object's real shape. They are the same contours used by perception for object recognition (Deregowski, Parker & Dziurawiec, 1996).

According to these models, young children are principally concerned with including features they know are critical to defining an object (by function or shape) or known relationships among objects (also see chapter 4). This model fits well with the observation that young children seldom actually look at what they are drawing, but prefer to work from an internal model of an object. Drawings by children age 7 or 8 years suggest that they begin to look more closely at visual models and notice visual appearances. This transition marks the stage dubbed "visual realism" (Luquet, 1935; Piaget & Inhelder, 1956/67) to indicate that drawings are relatively view-specific. Now only object parts and spatial relationships among objects that are seen when looking at a model are included in a drawing. Visual occlusions are indicated as children struggle with ways of indicating perspective.

Changes in children's understanding of spatial relationships are particularly dramatic during the first 12 years of life. Piaget and Inhelder (1956/67) in their studies of spatial reasoning and projective geometry began with the assumption that a drawing is not a simple copy of perception but a reconstruction based on the child's understanding of the spatial relationships among objects. They used drawings as *one* source of information about children's level of reasoning. According to Piaget and Inhelder, young children's first coherent compositions reflect a simple addition of parts, organized topologically. Only proximities, order, and continuity of elements are effectively mapped onto a drawing. This procedure guarantees that the whole will include the sum of all its constituent parts, but it does not map the composition or its projected spatial relationships as a whole. In drawings of people, for example, a human face may include eyes, nose, and mouth in close proximity within a circle, but the ordering of these parts may be reversed. In a perspective drawing, on the other hand, a child must keep in mind the whole drawing, while focused on each of its parts. Not only must this whole be kept in mind, but the coordination among the parts must take place with respect to three dimensions, not just the two dimensions inherent in the format of the paper. Topologically related objects must be grouped according to a single viewpoint.

Perspective drawing requires coordinating left–right, above–below, and before–behind relationships across the whole drawing. In Piaget and Inhelder's account, the coordination of before–behind relationships shown by overlapped elements links the drawing to a projected view whereas maintaining a single vantage point throughout the drawing links it to a perspective view. The construction of a single line of sight depends on a child discovering her or his own point of view. This discovery, in turn, presupposes an understanding that the child's own point of view is only one among many possible that could be taken. At first, the discovery leads to local coordination of parts so that different parts of a drawing are organized along different points of view (multiple view drawings). Compositions become more coherent as children become increasingly aware of their own point of view.

According to Piaget and Inhelder, the discovery of a single point of view also entails an understanding of the compensating relationship of size and distance such that what an object loses in size it will gain in distance. The simple addition of parts in two dimensions has to give way to multiplication of relationships in three dimensions. This allows the parts to change apparent shape with rotation (farther × shorter) and the whole to undergo changes with perspective (each increase in distance means a proportional decrease in size). As a child progresses toward this understanding, she or he represents the relationship of size and distance more precisely. The relationship of size to distance is expressed as a true proportion rather than qualitatively as simply increased distance × smaller size. The limiting case, in which a line eventually vanishes to a point in the distance, marks the completion of this understanding. This evolution is more than a simple refinement because a new conceptual tool, the unit of measurement, is introduced. Use of a metric allows quantification of size and distance and a more exact expression of perspective, relative size, and proportion (Piaget & Inhelder, 1956/ 67; Piaget, Inhelder, & Szeminska, 1960). After the age of 11 or 12, at the onset of formal operations, children are able to express an understanding of perspective that includes proportional reduction in size with distance.

Data presented by Willats (1977), Saenger (1981), and Jahoda (1981) illustrate a developmental sequence for the depiction of spatial relationships in drawings that points to a clear developmental trajectory toward projective relationships (see chapter 5). This sequence is consistent with the one demonstrated by Piaget and Inhelder for the evolution of spatial reasoning. Case et al. (1996) have also demonstrated a similar drawing sequence in which children move from drawings that reflect only salient features of familiar objects to those that locate objects in two- and then three-dimensional space. Lange-Keuttner and Reith (1995) and Reith and Lui (1995) suggest further that as a child becomes a formal operational thinker, horizontal and vertical coordinates can be used as a reference system that is mentally "projected onto" the visual image to allow a more exact measurement of projected shapes. Similarly, producing and understanding graphic representations such as maps depend on a child's stage of conceptual development (Downs, 1981; Feldman, 1980; Snyder & Feldman, 1984).

In summary, the use of drawings to index conceptual knowledge, especially knowledge related to spatial properties of objects and scenes, has an extended history in developmental psychology. Research on drawing suggests that conceptual knowledge dominates the drawings of young children. Two explanations are offered. One is that young children's impulse to depict what they know about objects interferes with their ability to be visual realists. The second is that complex spatial relationship must be understood before they can be drawn. Constructing a drawing with a single viewpoint emerges from a protracted developmental process in which a child first becomes aware that her or his viewpoint is one of many that could be taken and later is able to construct these alternative views.

Caution is also indicated in interpreting children's performance (e.g., Rosser, 1981). The information demands of a task should be taken into account. A number of neo-Piagetian theorists have stressed the importance of task analysis when assessing children's competence related to a given task, noting that a child's working memory and attentional capacity strongly influence performance (Case, 1992). A task analysis approach is only successful, however, when it rests on a theoretical model that leads to specific predictions. Otherwise, a single task can generate a plethora of such analyses (e.g., the balance beam task) without the ability to defend one or the other.

A careful task analysis is also necessary to consider which competencies a child is using to solve the task. For example, Flavell (1990) in his research on perceptual perspective taking in young children has used highly simplified tasks. Children can respond on the basis of activating a simple categorization to name the perspective of an observer (upside down/right side up; cat/dog) correctly without resorting to any inferential processes (Higgins, 1981). It is also worth keeping in mind that children can effect a given level of performance using a variety of different competencies. Genevans refer to this phenomenon as vertical decalage (Reid, 1978). In cases of disability, children may function at lower stages of development in their disabled domain than in other areas. Or normal children may successfully approach certain tasks using lower levels of reasoning than their stage of development.

Perception and Children's Drawings

The second approach emphasizes the role of perception in artistic processes. In recent years most researchers who have attempted to explain children's drawings by emphasizing visual analysis and perception have relied on the theories of James Gibson or David Marr (but see Golomb, 1992; Lange-Keuttner & Reith, 1995). These perceptually based theories have also been used to explain why younger children's drawings are intellectually realistic or object-centered. *Object-centered* drawings feature conceptual knowledge about the attributes of an object, independently of what is actually seen by the child from a specific vantage point. For example, a child knows that cups have handles so even if the child is looking at a specific model in which the handle of the cup is hidden, she or he draws the handle. In contrast, *view-specific* drawings feature only those aspects of the model that are actually visible from the vantage of the drawer; thus the invisible handle is left out of the drawing.

Gibson's Picture Theory. Gibson (1954), in an early theory of picture perception, proposed a point projection theory of picture perception: A picture was successful to the degree that there was a one-to-one correspondence between the sheaf of light rays to a given point in the real scene and its pictured reproduction. Prevalent since the 18th century, this theory depended on a view consistent with what was known about physical optics: that the pattern of light entering the eye as bits of color and brightness was the only information processed by the visual system. Seeing objects and surfaces resulted from interpreting these sensations of color and brightness. Therefore, a picture that reproduced the same bits of color and brightness would excite the same visual sensations and lead to perceiving the same images in the picture as in the original scene. As Gibson acknowledged, however, for the deception to be complete, the observer's head would have to be kept still and one eye would have to be positioned at the station point on the picture plane.

Radical revisions in his theory led Gibson to new propositions regarding picture perception. In his revised view, Gibson (1966; 1978) recognized that perception was an information processing system that operated on information picked up from the optic array rather than on luminous energy that provided stimulation to visual receptors. The structure of the visual world is analyzed in terms of forms, not points of light, and the boundaries between rays of light corresponding to corners, edges, and surfaces are discerned by their relations, not by the photons in the emitted light. So, for example, depth information is contained in the reciprocal relationships of color and illumination in the layout of surfaces and space, not in the visual cues associated with binocular parallax or convergence. Optical motion produced by movement of an individual within the world provides the critical information utilized by the visual system. Gibson emphasized the ambulatory and transactional nature of visual information pickup. Perception, he stated, is primarily aimed at detecting invariance. What remains invariant under transformations of the whole optic array during locomotion or movement specifies the invariants of the layout in the environment. For example, perspective transformations are those that preserve more invariant properties than nonperspective transformations. Thus, rectilinearity, which specifies the rigidity of an object, is preserved in a perspective transformation rather than simply the topological properties of the array. The rule of invariance formed the basis for Gibson's ecological optics in which perceptual laws are specified by the relationship of a moving and behaving organism to its environment.

One important implication is that perspective in painting is not a convention but a system derived from these rules or science of optics (Gibson, 1971). That is, pictures do have an intrinsic relationship to what they depict. The paradox, however, is that when you walk around an object or rotate it, you do not see a single fixed perspective but a family of perspectives: a family of perspectives that lays bare the invariant information in the object. Thus, ordinarily the whole object is "seen," not the surface of the object. "It is an object in the phenomenal world, not a form in the phenomenal visual field" (Gibson, 1971, p. 31). A picture is successful to the extent that it contains the same kind of information available in the ambient optic arrays of everyday environments. Therefore, congruence between a picture and a real scene results from similarities in perception, not visual sensations; although visual sensations accompany perception they are incidental to it. A good picture must provide the eye with the same invariants so that rather than seeing the front surface of objects the viewer also apprehends the sides and back.

Gibson's construct of perceptual invariants offers a natural basis, rooted in perception, for explaining why young children draw object-centered rather than viewer-centered drawings. According to Gibson (1971) young children have noticed the "set of invariant distinctive features of objects" but not yet noticed their view-specific appearances. Like early cave artists, he argues, children become aware of visual appearances through learning and drawing. Eventually they can attend to either the formless invariants available in visible things or the projected forms derived from visual sensations. Pratt (1985) concurs that children, like naive depicters, are unable to inhibit their everyday perceptions of objects. With training children and naive adults can become more aware of lower-order perceptions that are normally dominated by a top-down processing of invariant object features. Accordingly, Pratt and colleagues were able to improve cube drawings of seven-year-old children by calling attention to the relationship of the lines used in the drawing to their analogues in the model (Phillips, Hobbs & Pratt, 1978).

Gibson's views were further clarified when Sedgwick (1980) suggested that pictorial invariants are structures in the static array of a picture that would remain invariant as ambient and ambulatory features in the optic array of a real scene. However, as Costall (1985) points out, ambiguities can arise such as when optical continuity is signaled by the depiction of "false attachments" resulting from fortuitous alignments of projected edges in the real scene (e.g., a fence meets the eaves of a low roof). In this case optical continuity in the picture incorrectly specifies continuity in the scene. Socially mediated aspects of picture perception (Gibson, 1979) and picture production (Costall, 1985) become important in sustaining the correspondence between real and depicted world. Even though Gibson insisted that what a picture communicates is based on laws of ecological optics rather than artistic convention, it can be argued that different pictorial systems exist and which one is adopted may be a matter of convention (Costall, 1985; Hagen, 1985). The existence of different pictorial systems, however, does not undermine the fundamental logic of Gibson's argument. If we accept Gibson's normative distinction between good and bad pictures, pictures that use a system based on the rules of ecological optics are "better" pictures (Costall, 1985).

On the basis of Gibson's theory, Pratt (1985) proposed that view-specific information is lost in encoding because perception is conservative, tending to abstract hierarchically only information that is useful when we move and act in our visual world. Object-centered information provides us with the kind of information we need to navigate our environment. Such hierarchical structuring determines what is subsequently seen. When an object is familiar, a well-established memory schema becomes associated with and directs perceptual pickup of information. Therefore, depictions of familiar objects, rather than reflecting view-specific properties, are more likely to reflect ambulatory and transactional invariants. Pratt's research suggests that training in art is directed at transcending this conservative but efficient method of information pickup by providing exercises that overcome traditional ways of seeing. Training manuals direct looking activity toward analysis of regularities in structure and appearance (e.g., Edwards, 1979; Nicolaides, 1969). For example, Edwards (1979) includes an exercise in which the viewer is to look at a scene as if it were a puzzle by focusing attention on the shared edges and contours of objects embedded in the scene. This is designed to assist the artist in seeing the scene as a unified whole instead of as individual objects: in other words, to seeing the scene as a series of visual surfaces rather than phenomenal objects. Prescribed "looking" strategies ultimately result in task-specific schemas that facilitate information pickup and lead to more accurate or realistic drawings.

Marr's Perception Theory. Although Gibson extended the study of perception beyond the realm of philosophy into a more computational model of perception, he underestimated the complexity of information processing in vision (Marr, 1982). Marr (1982) provided an explicitly computational model that attempted to show how different levels of the visual system represent visual input. He was influenced not only by neurological and computer models of vision but also by results reported in clinical neurology. Warrington (cited in Marr, 1982), for example, had reported the abilities and limitations seen in patients with either left or right brain lesions in the parietal cortex. Patients with lesions on the left side could clearly recognize the shape of an object from any view but were unable to name it or tell anything about its use. Patients with lesions on the right side knew the name and use of an object but could only recognize it by its shape if its view was the conventional one for the object. These reports suggested to Marr that information about the shape of an object and conceptual knowledge about the object were stored and represented independently. Moreover, consistent with neurophysiological findings, Marr proposed that the visual system automatically builds a description of shapes and their spatial arrangement from smaller and more elementary units, known as visual primitives. Visual primitives, such as light intensities, edge segments, or discontinuities, are available from the visual image and are independent of acquired knowledge.

Marr (1982) and Marr and Nishihara (1978) identified four sequential levels of visual processing, each of which receives as visual input and processes different visual primitives and each of which yields a different representational output. At the earliest levels, the visual primitives processed refer to a shape's local surface properties but are insufficient for shape recognition because they depend heavily on the viewer's vantage point; thus they are view-specific. It is only at the highest processing level that object-centered information, which defines an object independently of its context, and visual characteristics are coordinated to represent shapes in their spatial context independently of viewpoint. Marr and Nishihara (1978) argue that an object-centered coordinate system is necessary for shape recognition (i.e., perceptual shape constancy). Thus a visual processor must transform local viewer-centered point primitives to an organized three-dimensional (3-D) object-centered representation that includes depth, volume, and spatial context.

The constructed 3-D model representation includes volume and surface primitives organized as modules in a hierarchy. The visual processor first identifies a shape by its natural axes on the basis of the shape's global elongation, symmetry, or axis of motion. Additional axes of a shape's component parts are then successively identified. Each of these is tagged in relation to the others at the lower level in a two-dimensional image. This tag is preserved in the higher level 3-D model of component parts. To reconstruct the shape as a 3-D model, component parts must be further identified by a series of relational specifications that indicate how components relate to each other and to the viewer's coordinate system. At this juncture that transformation from a viewer-centered to an object-centered coordinate system takes place giving access to both viewer- and object-centered coordinates and allowing processing to go in either direction. If an important axis of a shape is obscured or foreshortened an object can still be identified because component 3-D models are indexed in relation to the larger description or 3-D model of the whole object. The whole, therefore, can be accessed from the parts. Because the internal shape representation used for recognition is based on a shape's *natural axes*, canonical views have a privileged status and allow easiest recognition of objects. An important strength of modular organization is that representations can be broken down into constituent parts, recombined, and used flexibly.

Marr (1982) argues that artists use representational primitives to convey the most elementary units of information available from visual analysis. For example, in Picasso's *Rites of Spring* three silhouettes are shown. In order to interpret this picture the viewer makes the assumption that visual primitives such as the contours of the outline approximate real features of the viewed surfaces. In effect, one-dimensional picture primitives, that is, the continuous contour lines, are mapped back into two-dimensional scene primitives, to generate continuity, boundary, and orientation of surfaces (Willats, 1992).

Willats (1987; 1992) uses Marr's analysis to derive an information processing model for how children translate internally represented shapes onto the picture surface. From his point of view young children are limited with respect to the marks they are able to use. In order to distinguish between the round shapes of the head or body of a person and the elongated shapes of the arms and legs, a child uses a circle or region extended in all directions for the head with body and a line extended in only one direction for the arms or legs. Willats argues that these are natural symbols for representing "lumps" and "sticks," the scene primitives given by perception. The child starts with a rule in which picture primitives (i.e., an enclosed region) and scene primitives (i.e., the head with body of a figure) belong to the same dimensional order.

Picture primitives must come to stand for their dimensional equivalents before a child can draw later developing transformational systems such as projection. Initially, for example, children use an enclosed region to denote a whole cube with the enclosing lines standing for the cube's surfaces. If the cube is to be drawn in perspective, the enclosed region must denote only the exposed face of the cube and the line must stand for an edge, not a surface. Thus, there is a developmental progression toward using picture primitives to denote progressively lower-order dimensional scene equivalents. Drawings that were centered on an object's coordinates become transformed to those centered on the viewer's coordinate system. Willats (1985) claims this sequence has a natural basis because it corresponds to Marr's account of the processing sequence of the visual system and results in drawings that come progressively closer to the unanalyzed retinal image.

In summary, Gibson's newer theory of perception suggested a perceptual solution as to why young children's drawings are object-centered rather than viewer-centered. According to Gibson, perception is aimed at detecting aspects of the optic array that remain invariant under movement-induced transformations. As we move around our environment, rather than seeing a single fixed perspective, we see a family of perspectives from which we read the optic invariants of an array. Objects, therefore, are perceived as wholes including front surfaces, sides, and backs rather than as visual surfaces. Children's drawings reflect this aspect of perception and it is only with training and practice that children learn to overcome this natural tendency to express the invariant features that distinguish objects.

Marr proposed a more complete computational model of visual perception that attempted to explain how such top-down visual processing occurs. He argued that perception was built up in layers through a series of transformations from local viewer-centered visual primitives that specify the properties of visual surfaces, to organized 3-D object-centered representations that include depth, volume, and spatial context. According to Marr, the organization of these representations is modular such that parts index the whole and the whole can be disassembled into its parts for flexible reassembly into new wholes. Because shapes are defined internally by their *natural axes*, the most efficiently accessed view is a canonical view. Therefore, these views have a privileged status within the visual system.

Willats has used Marr's theory of visual processing to suggest an explanation for a sequence in drawing development. This sequence starts with symbolic equivalents that stand for whole objects, that is, the top level of visual processing. Gradually, the child differentiates the various lower levels processed by the visual system so that a shape that initially stood for the whole comes to stand for an object's surface and the lines that at first merely bounded the object come to stand for the object's edges. The developmental progression involves differentiating the symbolic equivalents used in a picture to denote progressively lower-order visual equivalents.

Production Strategies and Response Biases in the Organization of Drawings

The third approach emphasizes the difficulties young children have planning and executing a drawing; three dimensions must be translated into two and a coherent whole must be organized. Freeman (1980) is one of the strongest advocates of this approach. He makes a sharp distinction between performance and competence that has been echoed by others in the field of child development (Flavell & Wohlwill, 1969). Freeman argues that drawing tasks frequently fail to capture a child's ability to represent relationships internally and point more directly toward inadequacies in planning and execution strategies. For instance, many classic hallmarks of children's drawings such as synthetic incapacity, intellectual realism, and mixed viewpoints are better explained as childish strategies for organizing a drawing than as failures in perceptual analysis or conceptual understanding of spatial relationships.

Synthetic incapacity, or the inability to unite parts in a drawing to make a whole, is an example of a construct that merges a number of different production errors as if a single conceptual process limited the drawing. In reality two kinds of errors dominate these types of drawings: errors of relative position, in which, for example, figure parts are juxtaposed but incorrectly ordered, and errors of overinclusion, in which, for example, two eyes might be drawn on a profile. Freeman has extensively studied errors of relative position using young children's tadpole drawings. *Tadpole drawings* resemble a tadpole because the torso is missing and limbs are attached directly to the head of the figure. His studies showed that this phenomenon is the product of two processes: on the one hand, *the body proportion effect*, in which children tend to attach arms to the larger of two circles, whether or not it is designated as the head or the trunk; on the other hand, *the serial position effect*, in which children take their cue from the larger circle and anchor legs as an end point on either the head or trunk depending on their relative size.

This approach links errors of overinclusion, some aspects of intellectual realism, and mixed viewpoints to another difficulty, young children's *inability to inhibit* their internal generic representations of things in the world. This phenomenon is dubbed *canonical bias.* Drawing errors such as intellectual realism are explained by the tendency to draw directly from an internal generic representation of the object rather than from the visual model. Notice this interpretation of intellectual realism differs from one that centers on a child's desire to communicate her or his knowledge or one that emphasizes the natural biases of the visual system. In this case, it is the child's use of an internal model and failure to use the visual model.

Such characterizations suggest that conceptual factors do influence children's drawing strategies and execution biases. Davis (1985), however, has demonstrated that if an investigator manipulates the task demand, young children will respond with drawings that are either object-centered (canonical bias) or view-specific depending on the context. One key ingredient of the view-specific drawings appears to be the need to present strong visual contrasts in a drawing. When children are asked to draw a model of two cups, one with a hidden handle and the other without, they respond with a view-specific production presumably to distinguish the two cups. Conversely, most children include the handles in their drawings (canonical bias) when both cups are presented identically with the handles hidden. Curiously, when glass cups are presented so that the handles can be seen through the cups, children draw the handles, but not as they are seen behind the glass cups but to the side (canonical view). One explanation is that children use a drawing strategy that reserves the inside boundary of a cup to indicate the inside of the cup. This was the interpretation Taylor and Bacharach (1982) gave drawings children produced when asked to depict a flower decal that was pasted on an opaque cup. Children drew the decal inside the boundaries of the cup when it was pasted on the inside of the model but failed to depict the decal altogether when it was pasted on the outside of the cup. When Davis (1985) paired one glass cup in the canonical orientation with a glass cup turned so the handle was behind, the same children who had drawn canonical drawings when the glass cups were both turned with handles behind now drew them as seen. In this contrast situation children were perfectly willing to abandon the cue conflict that might arise from using the "inside" of the cup to show the behind relationship.

Several investigators have demonstrated that children's decisions are sensitive to the drawing context and cannot be interpreted without careful analysis of the context (Barret & Light, 1976; Cox, 1985; Davis, 1985; Light, 1985). Cox (1985) showed that changing the demands of the task, either by giving the task more meaning (i.e., embedding it in a story of cops and robbers) or by calling attention to the visual distinctiveness of its view, resulted in more view-specific drawings. Even 4-year-olds overcame their natural tendency to draw objects segregated and horizontally aligned to produce drawings that partially occluded one object placed behind another.

Light (1985) has suggested that when objects are very familiar to a child, the child looks at a model only long enough to classify the object and then produces a drawing that is representative of the type (generic). Young children are particularly likely to produce these kinds of drawings if their attention is not specifically focused on the visual properties of a model. In addition, Light has emphasized that young children are not aware of the drawing strategies they use or of those they could use to solve a graphic problem. A young child's typical performance, therefore, may not indicate all the strategies in her repertoire. When tasks are designed that focus a child's attention on view-centered properties of a model, young children can spontaneously use graphic strategies that clearly differentiate the view presented in a model.

Mixed viewpoint drawings are less well studied than errors of overinclusion or intellectual realism. Freeman (1985) asserts that these are also cases of canonical bias in that different objects have a preferred or canonical orientation for representation. A cube, for example, is both most likely to be preferred and to be drawn in oblique projection (Mitchelmore, 1985; Saenger, 1981). Combining a number of different objects in a single scene, each with its preferred canonical view, results in drawings of mixed viewpoint. Piaget and Inhelder (1956/67) referred to these drawings as containing a medley of viewpoints but ascribed this characteristic to a different cause than Freeman, the inability of young children to differentiate and coordinate a single viewpoint.

Although there is only weak evidence supporting any single interpretation of mixed viewpoint drawings, Duthie (1985) has demonstrated that different kinds of forms do lend themselves to depiction with different drawing systems. In a series of elegant studies, Duthie found that adolescents did not choose a consistent projective system as the best drawing of a given form but changed their choices depending on the form. When they were asked to choose the best picture of a tower with a spire, that is, of two combined forms each with a different "ideal image," most adolescents chose a drawing in "adjusted perspective" that formed a compromise between the two ideals. But when they were asked to draw the tower and spire, a wide variety of compromises appeared and few children used the adjusted perspective compromise. Even in copying a drawing of a single form, such as a cube in isometric projection with letters written on it, adolescents had difficulty maintaining a unitary drawing system. Most adolescents attempted to conserve the right angles of the letters, apparently seeing them as detached from the cube, while the cube was copied as projected. Duthie argued that children try to find a method by which individual forms can be related to each other in a credible manner rather than selecting a single consistent drawing system for depth representation. Multiple view drawings result from the production difficulties in reconciling these different forms. On the basis of her studies with children and adults, Hagen (1985) agrees, stressing that the amateur artist simply attempts to draw what is visually possible in terms of the geometry of a broadly construed natural perspective (i.e., orthogonal, affine, or perspective projections). In contrast, Hagen asserts, the skilled artist has learned the canons of the artistic culture that favor a particular natural perspective.

The most detailed account of how a drawing is produced is provided by Van Sommers's (1984) studies of temporal sequence in drawing production. He observed a logic in drawing performance such "that stroke making and sequence have a basis in mechanical and economic forces" (p. 60). Subject matter with its variety of shapes strongly influences the starting point and stroke sequence of a drawing but other design factors such as similarities or repetitions and proximities can also guide sequencing decisions. Another factor that alters execution strategy is the meaning given to a representation. Van Sommers found that meaning imparts a segmentation to the structure of subject matter and this influences the order in which parts are laid down. Anchoring of one element to another (e.g., a roof to a house) is one of the most ubiquitous constraints in the drawing process in that although it is possible to draw separate elements that are later united, drawings are almost never produced this way.

Van Sommers's studies also point to the potent role of perceptual analysis in drawing performance and the way it interacts with the drawing process. He found that drawing sequences were consistent with perceptual strategies for organizing the structure of a design (i.e., a swastika or a knot). But the structure of these designs could also be perceptually organized by alternative strategies. In less skilled drawers certain of these strategies were more successful and others invariably led to drawing errors. His work neatly demonstrates the kinds of production difficulties that influence drawing and strongly suggests that early choices in compiling a drawing can overdetermine the final result.

In summary, researchers who emphasize production difficulties claim that young children are more competent than their drawing performance indicates. They interpret the classic errors in young children's drawing as inadequacies in planning and execution strategies rather than as indicators of conceptual immaturities or failures in perceptual analysis. Freeman concludes from his studies that young children have difficulty organizing a drawing because certain mental biases guide drawing production, including canonical bias, which according to Freeman results from the child's inability to inhibit internal generic representations. This appears to be particularly true when children are asked to draw familiar objects in nontraditional orientations. A number of like-minded researchers have demonstrated that this bias can be overcome when drawing context is manipulated. Then even young children produce visually realistic drawings. In addition, young children may not know when to use the drawing strategies that they do have. When children are made to focus on certain aspects of a model, they can use strategies that clearly differentiate the views of the presented model. Research on production sequence suggests further that certain mechanical and economic forces influence the logic of drawing production. Drawing strategies are also influenced by how an artist interprets and perceptually analyzes a model. A key point made by all is that production decisions made early in the drawing determine the direction a drawing takes.

THE ROLE OF VISUAL EXPLORATION, MEMORY, AND REPRESENTATION IN DRAWING

Literature reviewed so far indicates that children are often a good deal more competent than their spontaneous behavior indicates. It also indicates that although a number of mental processes are potentially available, young children only use a few when drawing. The literature suggested that children's drawings are influenced by both conceptual and figurative mental processes. In this section some of the figurative processes involved in drawing activity are examined further. These include (1) visual exploration and sensitivity to visual details; (2) visual memory; and (3) the mental representation.

The Role of Visual Attention in Encoding the Visual Environment

Visual Exploration. One important element in drawing activity is the encoding process, that is, the degree to which young children focus their attention on specific aspects of their environment and take explicit account of how things look. Studies of children's visual exploration generally find that before the age of 6 years, children do not explore their visual environment sufficiently to compare parts of a configuration to the whole or to make judgments about equivalency of stimuli (Vurpillot, 1976). Visual activity of younger children is slower, less accurate, and more poorly organized than that of older children. Children younger than 6 have difficulty organizing their looking strategies in relation to a specific task. Instead they explore areas of a stimulus that have the greatest attraction value or focus their attention on only those stimuli that arouse their interest. But when motivated by interest, children as young as 3 years are capable of the visual displacements necessary for adequate visual exploration.

Vurpillot (1976) reported that differences of form are first to be considered by young children in making similarity or difference judgments whereas relational properties, such as size or relative spatial locations, are last. Between the ages of 5 and 6, children were able to match parts in one stimulus to parts in another before making a similarity judgment. This implied they were using an adult strategy requiring exhaustive exploration of stimulus parts. But they were unable to take into account the spatial relationships of the parts; they treated them as additive rather than in relation to the whole, inspecting each part for its similarity to other parts but not for its relative location. In Vurpillot's view what was missing was a cognitive strategy that guided exploratory behavior. Moreover until children were between 5 and 6 years of age, training in visual exploration was ineffective, supporting her position that cognitive level was driving exploration strategy.

Vurpillot's studies imply that children younger than 5 or 6 years old are unable to encode more than global attributes of objects. Indeed, young children's conceptual representations appear to function from holistic models and only under certain conditions are more specific features of stimuli accessible (e.g., size, orientation) (Kemler, 1983). Smith's (1989) studies of perceptual classification indicate that part of the difficulty is attentional focus. It is her view that the mental representations constructed from perception are more differentiated (competent) than a child's response (performance) indicates. In her studies, 2- and 3-year-olds only attended to general similarities of stimuli because they both failed to focus their attention and lacked true identity relations (see Inhelder & Piaget, 1964). But when they were asked to generalize nonsense names to new and novel objects, the 3-year-olds showed they had attended to at least one component dimension by using a consistent rule for naming. Children ages 4 and 5 years selectively attended to some specific dimensions but still lacked strategies for establishing true identity relations. Eight-year-olds performed much like adults on these simple perceptual classifications tasks, attending to all relevant dimensions and demonstrating true identity relations.

On the basis of these studies, Smith concluded that even very young children represent more than holistic aspects of objects. As children grow older, they are increasingly able to focus their attention on several dimensional attributes of stimuli. One implication is that the dimensional structure of a stimulus is included in the representations of young children (see also Callahan, 1993) but that accessing more than its global structure is difficult. This is because young children cannot selectively focus their attention on the component dimensional attributes encoded in their representations. Older children and adults, on the other hand, can more easily access component dimensions of represented stimuli because they can shift their focus of attention to relevant dimensions of the representation.

These studies also imply that conceptual understanding plays an important role in strategies for accessing represented information. Research by Pillow and Flavell (1986) confirms this interpretation. They found that 3-year-olds perceived projective-size distance and projective-shape orientation relationships. But although this information was potentially available to them, they showed no understanding of these relationships. In contrast, 4-year-olds demonstrated categorical but not quantitative understanding of these relationships.

Looking and Drawing. There is ample evidence that visual exploration plays an important role in the quality of a drawing. In drawing tasks, time spent looking at a model has been shown to shift with age. Parallel developmental changes occur in the quality of a drawing (Pecheux & Stamback, 1969, cited in Vurpillot, 1976). Up to the age of 7 years children seem content to use the drawing schemas they already have to reproduce a model globally. After that age, children become more exacting and begin checking the model more frequently by to-and-fro eye movements between their drawing and the model (Vurpillot, 1976). Both frequency and total duration of visual exploration are associated with accuracy of drawing.

Other researchers report that manipulations that facilitate careful visual analysis of models result in drawings that are closer approximations of them. For example, the drawings of 5- or 6-year-old children improve when they are given training that promotes greater flexibility in accessing perceptual structures based on a model (Callahan, 1993) or training that relates parts in the model to parts as they are drawn (Phillips et al., 1978). Similarly children's drawings come closer to the model when their attention is directed toward differences in stimuli (Cox, 1981) or they are required to draw an unfamiliar model that cannot be easily assimilated to representations already in memory (Reith, 1988). Van Sommers (1984) reported that the "good" adult drawers in his studies made a better perceptual analysis, organizing a presented pattern into reproducible segments, rather than simply using better drawing strategies. Although "good" drawers did use better strategies for drawing difficult graphic models, they also drew successfully with some of the same production approaches that led "bad" or less successful drawers into serious production difficulties.

Studies comparing art and nonart students find that art students spend more time visually exploring a model before drawing it. Pratt (1985) found that art students had more looking activity and more accurate representations when asked to copy line drawings of familiar objects (a cube) than a group of psychology students. These differences disappeared when random line drawings were used as a model. But when looking time was increased in another experiment the accuracy of the psychology students improved when they copied the random line patterns. When drawings made from memory were contrasted with those from the models, drawings of familiar objects (e.g., cube) were indistinguishable but those of random lines were much poorer from memory. Accuracy for familiar objects was always superior in the drawings of the art students, but whether they drew a familiar model from memory or looked directly at the model their accuracy was the same.

Differences in accuracy of memory for familiar objects as contrasted with random configurations indicate that information pickup is facilitated by well-established memory schemas. Pratt suggested looking time operates to improve accuracy by creating task-specific memory schemas that direct perceptual activity. In the case of the art students, multiple looks were used to modify existing structures so that perceptual activity could be more specific to the task at hand. In the art students well-established memory schemas did not inhibit looking time but rather stimulated it. This is in contrast to results reported for children and general samples (e.g., Reith, 1988). Pratt points out that artist's manuals prescribe the use of knowledge-based looking strategies that are specific to a task. They indicate perceptual activity should be directed toward noting regularities of structure and appearances of objects.

Taken together the aforementioned studies suggest some conclusions that are relevant to a model of drawing. Both the amount of visual exploration and its organization play a role in graphic competence. More detailed memory schemas can serve to organize looking strategies toward an efficient analysis of information. In artists, memory schemas for familiar objects appear to do just that and looking is facilitated. In less skilled drawers and normative samples of children, memory schemas for familiar objects appear to inhibit looking.

The Role of Memory in Drawing

The theory that there is a one-to-one relationship between the mental representation of a scene and what is seen was discarded quite some time ago. In its place is a constructivist account that emphasizes the active mental work of reconstructing knowledge about objects and their relationships. Memory as well as spatial and conceptual knowledge play leading roles in the construction process. Memory can add, omit, or distort features of a scene. Likewise spatial and conceptual knowledge can reconfigure the scene to be consistent with the cognitive level at which spatial relationships and other concepts are understood (Liben, 1974; but see Liben, 1975; Furth, Ross & Youniss, 1974).

Recent research on memory points to evidence for two encoding systems (Squire, 1987; Squire, Knowlton & Musen, 1993). An explicit declarative system functions relative to knowledge that is intentionally acquired and intentionally retrieved as either semantic or episodic knowledge. An automatic procedural or implicit system functions in relation to sets of motor, perceptual, or cognitive procedures that are acquired in the absence of conscious awareness. Procedural memory includes skills, priming effects, and simple conditioned habits and is often characterized as memory of "how things go" rather than "what things are." It is almost certain that implicit memory plays a significant role in drawing even if it is only responsible for the perceptual-motor procedures children and adults use to draw. Evidence of its relation to drawing comes from observations that within seconds after having drawn an object, children and adults are virtually unable to report how they proceeded. Yet there is remarkable consistency from drawing to drawing for the same objects (Stacy & Ross, 1975; Van Sommers, 1984).

It is likely that young children use prototype or global structural information retrieved from implicit memory to develop and regulate their drawing procedures and seldom use semantic or episodic memory from explicit memory, even when these are potentially available. Implicit memory functions ontogenetically very early, whereas explicit or declarative memory develops gradually as the associated areas of the neocortex mature and become integrated with temporal and diencephalic long-term memory structures (Sullivan, Rovee-Collier & Tynes, 1979). Implicit memory has been implicated in abstracting and encoding prototype and global structural information (Cooper, 1991), especially in the modality of visual perception (Milner, Corkin & Teuber, 1968; Schacter, Chiu & Ochsner, 1993). Young children, therefore, can generate perceptual-motor representations from the implicit memory system without explicit knowledge of what things look like or of the procedures they use to draw them. Older children and adults can access declarative memory more easily but may not necessarily use it in drawing, preferring to use habitual motor procedures or routines unless challenged.

Artistically talented children may have more efficient access to declarative or episodic memory and use it when they draw. A number of researchers report superiority in visual imagination (Hermelin & O'Conner, 1986; O'Conner & Hermelin, 1983) and visual memory (Rosenblatt & Winner, 1988) in artistically talented children. A study of talented and less talented children at the Cleveland Museum Art School exemplifies these differences (Munro, Lark-Horovitz & Barnhart, 1942). Noting that talented students appeared to have exceptional visual memory, researchers presented all students with a ceramic polar bear rotating on a base. After viewing the bear for a few minutes, the children were asked to draw it from memory. At specified intervals for up to 3 years later they were again asked to draw the bear from memory. Less talented children drew a bear that was more or less "bearish" according to their ability, "refreshing their memory by the concept 'bear', trying to reason out its characteristics, even adding natural surrounding . . . [yet] unable to maintain their rigid but deteriorating 'bear' memory" (Lark-Horovitz, Lewis & Lucca, 1973, p. 135). In contrast, the talented children were able to retain "their first impression to a remarkable degree, reproducing details . . . its texture and the slightly curving direction of the body. . . . The gifted child . . . recalls clearly, with great completeness, *a detailed visual image*" (p. 135).

In this book a few remarkable drawings made when talented children were under the age of 5 years also suggest the early use of specific rather than global visual representations. Figure 1.4 shows two spontaneous drawings by Kate at age 4. The male figure is a generalized human form typical of her human figures at this age but the female figure is strikingly different. The naturalistic gesture and rear view pose of the figure appear to capture a specific moment. A second example comes from Hondo, at age 4. Figure 1.5a shows a water scene with the generalized human forms and "prototype" shark typical of his age. Contrast this with the remarkably specific shark, shown in Figure 1.5b and drawn spontaneously at the same age. It was inspired by a recent viewing of *Jaws*. These drawings suggest that the children used a specific or episodic memory, whereas contrasting drawings indicate they used general

Figure 1.4. A 4-year-old talented girl.

descriptions or prototypes stored in implicit memory. Once declarative memory becomes developmentally available, talented children may switch to using specific (episodic) memories to guide their drawings and build a more differentiated set of drawing schemas. These early examples indicate the approximate age at which episodic memory was first utilized by these children. When interviewed between the ages of 8 and 11, most of the talented children studied in depth reported using visualization of specific poses or body parts as a reference for their drawings.

Another important aspect of memory is working memory, or the information-processing capacity available to the child to operate on memory. The developmental limits imposed by working memory are defined as the attentional capacity of a child (Case, 1992). Working memory grows as children get older. Growth is best de-

Figure 1.5a. A 4-year-old talented boy.

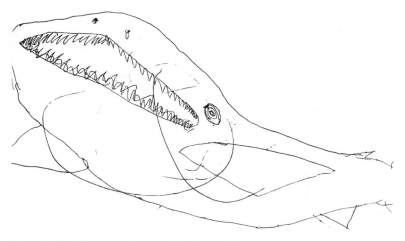

Figure 1.5b. The same 4-year-old talented boy.

scribed as the ability to hold in mind and attend to different schemes stored in memory. It has been shown to constrain a child's cognitive capacity on a variety of tasks (Case, 1992; Pascual Leone, 1988; 1995). Using a neo-Piagetian model, a few researchers have investigated how working memory influences children's drawing ability. Morra, Moizo, and Scopesi (1988) studied its influence on children's free and constrained drawings. Free drawings were elicited by asking children to invent their own drawing whereas constrained drawings were evoked by giving the children a list of items to include in the drawing. In the constrained condition children were asked to make a number of drawings, each one designed to increase the demand on working memory. Morra et al. reasoned that when children were asked to produce free drawings, the demands on working memory would be minimal or lower than their true potential. In contrast, when children were asked to draw constrained drawings, the load on working memory would be increased. They predicted working memory capacity would be linearly related to children's success (scores) on the increasingly demanding constrained drawings. On the whole, the results confirmed their predictions. Dennis (1992) found similar results when she presented children with five drawing tasks that increased in number of spatial relationships to be included. Even when age was partialed out, a child's success (score) with a given drawing was predicted by her or his working memory capacity assessed independently by standard tests of working memory.

The Mental Representation

Development. Issues of what the mental representation "looks like" are far from solved. Those who favor the construction of a mental image over propositional representations to access certain kinds of information have proposed that young children predominantly use visual images to access information in memory (Kosslyn, 1980). As children mature and gain experience such information is encoded propositionally. What matures in this view is not the structure of the visual representation but related capacities. Studies by Kosslyn and his colleagues on the properties of mental images find that children aged 5, 8, and 14 show some adultlike processing capacity for mental images. They are all equivalent in ability to maintain an image but younger children are poorer at scanning, rotating, and generating images (Kosslyn, Margolis, Barrett, Goldknopf & Daly,

1990). Surprisingly, primary differences were between the two younger age groups and the 14-year-olds and adults, not between the 5- and 8-year-olds as predicted by Piagetian theory (Piaget & Inhelder, 1971). Other researchers find that only children of 8 years or older are capable of image rotation (Childs & Polich, 1979; Dean, Duhe & Green, 1983; Kail, Pelegrino & Carter, 1980), suggesting as Piaget and Inhelder (1971) did that conceptual development strongly influences the quality of the image.

The Mental Representation and Drawing. Karmiloff-Smith's (1990) research indicates that the perceptual-motor procedures used in drawing can be sources of endogenous representational change. Knowledge previously represented as an efficiently functioning procedure becomes explicitly available through a process of representational redescription at higher levels of abstraction. Karmiloff-Smith traced this process in drawing by asking young children to draw familiar themes such as a man, house, or animal and then to draw "a man (house etc.) that doesn't exist." This forced the children to operate "in some way on their internal representation." She then studied the types of modifications introduced. Younger children aged 4 to 6 were only able to change the shape of elements or delete elements whereas older children aged 8 to 10 also showed insertion of new elements, position and orientation changes, and cross-category insertions (e.g., animal parts inserted in drawing of man).

Of greatest interest was the effect these alterations had on the child's drawing procedure. Deletions made by younger children were always at the end of a drawing, indicating that the sequence of the drawing procedure was uninterrupted. The redescription available to the younger children, therefore, was constrained by the sequential order of the drawing procedure; this, according to Karmiloff-Smith, is the first level of redescription, where knowledge is specified as a sequentially fixed list. Older children, on the other hand, showed greater flexibility. They could delete at any point in the drawing and were also able to add extra parts at any point in the procedure. Karmiloff-Smith points out that although the sequential constraint restricts flexibility, it also facilitates development by preserving the sequential nature of the representations in domains where sequence is important, like language and drawing. As further redescription takes place later in development, the sequential constraint is relaxed and the representation specifies a structure that can be flexibly ordered and manipulated.

It is likely that perceptual-motor procedures are part of the implicit memory system and that, as children get older, these procedures become refined by practice and interaction with categorical knowledge stored in declarative memory. But most children probably continue to rely more heavily on implicitly derived perceptual-motor procedures when drawing. There is evidence that perceptual processing can be dissociated into two components occurring in different hemispheres. Categorical spatial relationships (i.e., left/right; top/bottom, etc.) are associated with the left hemisphere, whereas specific coordinate spatial relationships (i.e., 2 mm and at a 45-degree angle from a referent) are associated with the right hemisphere (Koenig, Reiss & Kosslyn, 1990; but see also Bailystock and Olson, 1987). In most children, who are typically left hemisphere dominant, categorical spatial knowledge may play the greater role in generating representations for drawings than specific coordinate spatial knowledge. Thus spatial relationships depicted in drawings by most older children still bear the stamp of drawing formulas or perceptual-motor procedures that are habitual and routinized even though practice and interaction with developing conceptual knowledge may have lent them an air of increasing sophistication. In right hemisphere dominance, which has often been associated with artistic talent (see Winner & Martino, 1993; Winner, 1996), specific visual information may be more readily accessible and therefore easier to utilize in generating representations as referents for drawing.

If as Smith (1989) suggests the mental images of young children can include structural properties of stimuli, then under conditions that favor the encoding and retrieval of these properties, children may perform quite well. But children may not rely on the types of representations that encode specific dimensional attributes of stimuli when drawing. This is both because selective attention during retrieval is difficult and because explicit attention to structural aspects of the visual world does not normally occur during encoding. That is, young children do not normally selectively attend to their visual world in ways that favor detailed encoding of its dimensional structure in explicit memory. Instead they rely on prototype representations implicitly abstracted (learned) from experience and interactions with the world to generate perceptual-motor procedures for drawing. As development unfolds these perceptual-motor procedures interact with and are influenced by conceptual knowledge. The initial holistic drawings characteristic of the early "symbolic" stage of drawing give way to drawings enriched by conceptual knowledge and characteristic of the stage of "intellectual realism." Eventually in the stage of "visual realism" visual exploration improves, guided by conceptual development, and an increasing number of object features and range of spatial relationships can be realized in a drawing.

SUMMARY AND PREDICTIONS

In this chapter, I began with the thesis that artistically talented and less talented children employ different mental abilities when drawing. Two groups of hypotheses related to talent were contrasted; one concerned conceptual development and the other figurative thought. I presented three major theoretical approaches to the problem of artistic development, one emphasizing conceptual development, another perception, and the third planning and producing a drawing, as their central themes. All three approaches have made significant contributions to understanding artistic development. A rapprochement among these approaches can be effected in explaining individual differences. One inference from the additional literature reviewed on the role of visual exploration, memory, and mental representation in drawing is that talented children may make optimal use of these figurative processes. Figurative thought is distinct from slower developing operational reasoning that determines the construction of conceptual knowledge.

It is proposed that a bootstrapping procedure that integrates figurative processes with operational thought throughout development is critical in the development of artistic talent. Talented children's drawings reflect responsiveness in both figurative and conceptual domains. When they are very young, less talented children rely on some of the same figurative processes but conceptual development appears quickly to dominate. The drawings of less talented children reflect categorical properties rather than visual properties of the topic. As these children get older, planning and production difficulties begin to constrain what they can do in a drawing because their repertoire of drawing procedures is limited. It is likely that these same constraints hold for the mentally constructed visual images of less talented children. Some research indicates that the absence of a detailed visual representation further constrains information pickup by the visual system. Thus a developmental sequence that conspires to maintain these children's biases toward conceptual rather than visual descriptions is set in motion. In the subsequent chapters, we will trace the development of talented and less talented children and study the paths individual talented children actually follow before judging the adequacy of this proposed model.

Certainly direct experimental tests of claims about the different contributions of figurative and operative processes to drawing activity of talented and less talented children are possible (although identifying a highly talented sample with certainty at a very young age might be a challenge). Most accounts of the development of drawing are based on experiments using life models. When these experiments are well designed they have the obvious advantage of producing strong evidence. But such accounts neglect one of the most fundamental aspects of drawing as a cognitive behavior. Children, especially younger children, rarely draw from life models. Instead they draw spontaneously from internal representations constructed in memory, representations that are presumably based on visual exploration and information pickup from the environment as well as on conceptual knowledge. Before future experiments can be designed to look at these important features in relation to talent, a careful naturalistic study of drawing should be made. This book attempts to do that by observational study of talented and less talented children's spontaneous artwork. The importance of the studies presented here is not that they provide a direct and definitive test of the proposed model but that they present much needed observations on the phenomenon of artistic development in talented children as contrasted with less talented children. In addition, the book presents a model that goes some distance in unifying the different theoretical approaches to children's drawing.

What kinds of predictions do the operative and figurative hypotheses suggest about the spontaneous drawings of talented and less talented children? First, the dimensions of observation against which our two groups of hypotheses can be assessed must be established. The dimensions are labeled in brief form in Table 1.1. The first is the elements with which a drawing is constructed, lines and shapes (chapter 3). The second is the poses these forms assume

TABLE 1.1
PREDICTIONS FOR OPERATIVE AND FIGURATIVE HYPOTHESES[a]

Dimensions of Observation	Farther Faster Operative	Seeing, Remembering, and Doing Figurative
Elements: Line and Shape	T < LT in age of use	T uses differently than LT
Figure Rotations: Canonical	T ≈ LT in use	T < LT in use
Natural	T ≈ LT in use	T > LT in use
Spatial Milestones	T earlier than Norms LT ≤ Norms	T ≈ Norms LT ≤ Norms
Overall Drawing Development	T rate faster than LT rate	T different from LT
Sophistication of Compositions	T ≈ Developmental Stage LT ≈ Developmental Stage	T < Developmental Stage LT ≈ Developmental Stage

[a]T = talented, LT = less talented.

(chapter 4). The third is the spatial milestones depicted in a drawing (chapter 5). The fourth is the overall rate of drawing development (chapter 6) and the fifth is the ability to compose artwork (chapter 9).

Table 1.1 lists a different set of predictions for each group of hypotheses. If the "farther faster" hypotheses hold, most outcomes will have to do with rate of development. These hypotheses assume that the same skills are developing in both groups of children but development will be precocious in talented children. Talented children, therefore, might be expected to use lines and shapes earlier than less talented children but all children will use them in the same way. Likewise talented children will begin to rotate figures at an earlier age than less talented children. But once they catch up, less talented children will show the same use of different figure orientations. Since operational thought and/or spatial reasoning is developing at an accelerated rate, spatial milestones such as occlusion and perspective should appear early in the drawings of talented children when compared to norms established for these milestones. Their appearance in less talented children should roughly approximate or lag behind the norms. When the separate indices of drawing development are combined as a whole, talented children will show a faster but parallel trajectory of development. If compositional strategies are determined by a child's stage of development, their sophistication should approximate a child's developmental level. Therefore, the rate of development of more advanced strategies will be faster in talented than less talented children but what develops will be the same.

The second set of hypotheses, "seeing, remembering, and doing," leads to a different set of predictions. The heightened figurative abilities of talented children are assumed to result in distinctly different developmental trajectories for the two talent groups. Lines and shapes, the building blocks of drawing, will be put to different uses by talented children from the very beginning of artistic development. Talented children will also make much greater use of natural poses that involve three-quarter rotations and much less use of canonical or conceptually derived poses. Since the appearance of spatial milestones in a drawing is still assumed to be dependent on the development of spatial operations, spatial milestones in the drawings of talented children should approximate the norms for the development of spatial concepts. This should also be true for less talented children, although it must be acknowledged that these children may have greater difficulty mapping the rules of projective geometry onto a drawing. In looking across all the indices studied in overall drawing development, this set of hypotheses would predict a different trajectory for development; that is, what is developing in talented children is always different because it is much more strongly guided by figurative processes. This leads to the final predictions about development of composition strategies. If talented children are able to use figurative processes to compose their drawings, we would expect them to use sophisticated strategies quite early. If comparisons are made between the spatial milestones in a drawing and its composition, this outcome can be distinguished from the outcome predicted by developmental rate. The figurative hypotheses would predict that composition strategies used by talented children will be well in advance of spatial milestones reflected in their drawings. Less talented children, because they are visually less responsive, will employ conceptual approaches (e.g., part–whole relations) to composition that will depend on their stage of development.

The predictions shown in Table 1.1 are meant to provide a framework for reading and thinking about the studies presented in this book. But the studies themselves do not have the experimental rigor that would be necessary definitively to establish one set of hypotheses over the other. Instead, the table should be used as a guide against which outcomes presented in the chapters can be compared. Some readers may be disappointed in this approach, but it is important to emphasize that very few studies, if any, have followed the development of a group of talented children over a 10-year period. Some controlled experiments related to the development of composition are presented, but it was not possible to identify enough talented children in the composition samples (based on teacher selection) for meaningful analysis. Instead, these studies focus on establishing the normative course of development for composition and identifying and tracking over time a group of children who did show unusually sophisticated strategies, strategies that appeared to fall outside the normative picture of development.

2

SAMPLES AND METHODS FOR THE SPONTANEOUS DRAWINGS STUDIES

IDENTIFYING TALENT

How does one go about finding a sample of children with exceptional artistic talent? What criteria should be applied? In other studies of gifted child artists, some going back to the 1900s, these children were not easy to identify especially at young ages (Goodenough, 1926; Haas cited in Golomb, 1992; Kerschensteiner, 1905) and a number of researchers came to the conclusion that exceptional artistic talent in young children is rare (Feldman & Goldsmith, 1986; Lark-Horowitz, Lewis & Luca, 1973). Seldom have there been reports of very young children identified for their artistic skill. A notable exception was Nadia, reported by Selfe (1977; 1983). Nadia, an autistic child, spent hours looking through her favorite picture books. When Nadia's disability was diagnosed at age 6, her mother gave the evaluating psychologist several amazing drawings that were stimulated by the pictures in Nadia's favorite books. Although identical in many details to the pictures in the books, the figures had been rotated and rendered in views that would be challenging even for adults, views that required foreshortening.

In a study of children ages 11 to 15 taking classes at the Cleveland Museum, 8% of the 11-year-olds and 33% of the 15-year-olds were identified as gifted, but no younger children were (Lark-Horowitz et al., 1973). Researchers at the museum looked for the early appearance of specific milestones in the children's drawings. A talented child's technical skill was revealed by the early depiction of representational forms and success with motion. Talented children also surpassed average children in organizing and composing their pictures, excelling in grouping objects to communicate their interrelationship and in obtaining an aesthetically pleasing product. They were more original with and better able to exploit a variety of artistic media and attempted more challenging and provocative subjects. In addition, other characteristics were unique to talented children. One was their ability to select from visual experience elements that were more successfully adaptable to pictures. A second was their visual memory, which appeared to preserve, over long periods of time and in great detail, visual images of objects. Finally, talented children were marked by their commitment and desire to learn. Whereas most children preferred to be left alone when engaged and were content to repeat their drawing schemas, talented children sought out instruction both from other people and by looking at and analyzing pictures. They showed a strong interest in changing and enriching their drawing schemas.

Three indices of exceptional talent are suggested in the literature (see Milbrath, 1995): The first is the ability to draw recognizable forms at an early age. Typically, young children recognized as talented begin drawing representationally a full 1 year to 2 years before other children. Although this has had long-standing currency as a way of identifying talented children (Winner & Martino, 1993), Lark-Horowitz, Lewis, and Luca (1973, p. 129) caution, "Accelerated development in representation may mean no more than precocity and facility and may have little significance from the point of view of mature artistic achievement. . . . Nevertheless, accelerated development is one of the most pervading and significant characteristics of the talented child." Susanne Langer (1953) also observed that most children identified early for their technical mastery never become acclaimed professional adult artists. Although she equated talent with technical mastery, she distinguished it from genius, which includes "the power of conception." The latter is unlikely to be found in the work of a child, but "grows and deepens from work to work . . . long after technical mastery has reached its height" (p. 409).

A second index is the degree of originality or creativity shown in a child's artwork. This is equally if not more important to later artistic success than precocity in representational drawing. Lark-Horowitz et al. describe one aspect of creativity as imaginative ability, which the talented child has "to an extraordinary degree" (p.

130). They point out that "the shaping of fantasy depends on the richness of visual concepts stored in his mind, and on the extent to which he can manipulate these to express his ideas" (p. 130). Getzels and Csikszentmihalyi (1976) relate creativity to *problem finding,* which correlates better with later artistic success than successful problem solving. In their study, young artists still in art school were asked to compose and draw a still life from a collection of objects. Students who engaged in a prolonged process of problem finding, measured by manipulating more objects and delaying closure prior to deciding on an arrangement, were judged more successful 7 years later and were more likely to have received recognition for their art 20 years later (Csikszentmihalyi & Robinson, 1986).

A final index is the motivation or the commitment a child shows to her or his talent domain. This helps shape how skilled and artistically developed a child becomes and determines whether or not a child perseveres despite obstacles. In a study of talented teenagers in five talent domains, including the visual arts, Csikszentmihalyi, Rathunde, and Whalen (1993) found that the best measures of commitment to a talent area were an adolescent's own reported commitment and the highest-level course taken in a talent area. These measures especially indexed engagement and the report of flow experiences during engagement. Flow experiences are defined operationally as those in which persons' concentration is so intense, their attention so undivided and wrapped up in what they are doing, that they are unaware of things of which they would normally be aware. The relationship between flow experiences and commitment is not trivial. At its core are profound enjoyment and the exhilaration of creating, making it highly likely that an individual will continue to be engaged by the activity and develop her or his talent.

One problem with establishing *specific* criteria for identifying talented children to study is the potential circularity between criteria and results. For example, identifying children as artistically gifted because their drawings have motion would perforce lead to the result that talented children's drawings have motion and less talented children's do not. Ideally selection criteria and dimensions of study should be independent. So although specific selection criteria could be rigorously applied, doing so might end in circularity. One solution is to use global criteria. Ideally, global criteria might surface by asking art teachers to nominate exceptional artists from their classes without providing a definition of exceptional talent (Csikszentmihalyi et al., 1993). But classroom teachers and even parents might also be expected to recognize exceptional talent simply because they attempt to match what a child does artistically with implicitly understood norms gained from experience with children and with current societal standards for what is valued in art. There are limitations to this approach. Since the criteria for identification remain unspecified, it is possible that only one salient dimension such as early representational ability will be used for identification.

SAMPLING AND DESIGN FOR STUDIES

Two separate studies of children's drawings are presented here: one, a cross-sectional study of talented and less talented children whose ages spanned 4 to 14 years and two, a retrospective and prospective study of the drawings of eight talented children over the same 10-year period, from ages 4 to 14.

Cross-Sectional Study

Like other resource teachers in the elementary grades, art teachers are a vanishing breed in our public schools. There are still privately run art schools, however, and publicly funded children's art programs at some museums. Most public high schools offer courses in art and even some junior high schools have maintained their art programs. In addition, some urban communities have magnet schools for the arts even at the elementary level. Local art contests for children also provide additional motivation for drawing and can be used as a resource for obtaining drawings from children with a broad range of talent ability. Drawings from a total of 188 children were obtained for the cross-sectional sample from all these sources. Not all these children were in the final study sample.

The children came from three adjacent cities in a large urban area. The cities encompass a broad range of cultures and include people of all races. The recruitment settings were a public junior high school (grades 6–8) with an excellent academic program, an arts magnet elementary school, a private art school catering to young children, and a museum art program for children of all ages. Children's drawings collected from a local art contest for children ages 10 and under were included to fill out the normative sample. Age, race, and gender of each child were obtained but not socio-economic background. The final sample composition included 57%

Caucasian, 12% African-American, 11% Asian, 1% Latino, 11% of mixed origins (e.g., African-American and Caucasian, Asian and Caucasian) and 6% unidentified. Children were sampled in each of six age blocks: ages 3 to 4, 5 to 6, 7 to 8, 9 to 10, 11 to 12, and 13 to 14.

Across the four school settings, art teachers identified 15 children as especially artistically talented; 12 of these were boys and 3 were girls. This was 8% of the total number of children in the original sample. Art teachers were asked to pick out children who they thought had exceptional artistic talent from the list of participating students in their classes. No attempt to impose criteria was made. When teachers were later interviewed about the criteria they used for identifying talent they all stated that their judgment had been based on seeing the children perform at a consistently high level across a variety of art projects and media and not on a single project or with a single medium such as drawing or painting. The projects included design exercises, figure drawing, still life drawing in preparation for watercolors, color studies, multicultural projects (masks or murals), and composition studies. The media included drawing; painting with watercolors, tempera or acrylic; collage; sculpture; and mask making.

The teacher who taught in a private art school setting, primarily for young children, said that she had chosen children who excelled in spatial thinking, defined as the way in which a child used the three-dimensional pictorial space. She gave depth and detail in their artwork, better proportions, rendering of forms, and use of color and line as important in her decision. She also stated that these children showed a greater interest in and ability to understand and interpret drawing technique. After saying that his criteria were on an intuitive level, the teacher who taught in the arts magnet public school program (kindergarten through fifth grade) gave a list of five he used in identifying talented children: a child's creativity; a child's ability to be expressive of feelings in the artwork; how much a child challenged herself or himself; how resourceful a child was in selecting, using, and interpreting materials; and a child's overall performance across the range of art projects and media with which the class worked. The teacher who taught in the public middle school art program (sixth to eighth grade) also said that her criteria were intuitive but that she had selected children who consistently stood out across the assigned and graded projects in her classes.

Although she had less information about sixth-grade children, she was able to see their work across color studies, composition exercises (e.g., collages), and pencil drawing. Seventh- and eighth-grade children had been in her classes longer and she was able to observe them over several classes and across more media (i.e., painting with watercolors, tempera and acrylics; mask building; and still life drawing). The teachers' responses strongly suggested that no single criterion had been used for their selections. Their selections were based on knowing a child's performance across time and different artistic media. The criteria also appeared to differ across teachers, perhaps because of differences in the ages of the children with whom they worked. Nevertheless, taken together as a group, the criteria appear to incorporate all the indices discussed at the beginning of the chapter: early ability to render forms, originality or creativity, and motivation or commitment.

Because there are fewer settings with art teachers for younger children, it was more difficult to obtain young talented children. Therefore, children identified by public school classroom teachers and in some cases by parents were used to fill out the talented sample. This increased the sample to 22 with 16 boys and 6 girls. In order to increase the sample further for more reliable statistical contrasts, drawings from the 8 children in the talented longitudinal sample (see next section) were added. Only drawings from one of the six age blocks for a child were added. The age block was chosen to fill out the most incomplete cells of data; for example, the ages 7 to 8 years contained 4 boys and no girls. Two of the 4 talented girls in the longitudinal study were randomly selected and their drawings from years 7 and 8 were placed in that cell. The final sample used for data analysis included drawings from 30 talented children; 20 were boys and 10 were girls (see Table 2.1).

From the remaining larger sample of children not identified as talented, 75 children were randomly selected in order to have the six age blocks balanced for gender of artist. Only 10 of these children were from the art contest and they were evenly distributed across the age blocks to fill out incomplete cells. The drawings from art contestants showed ability that suggested most were within the normal range for their age. When there was a question, the child's drawing was not used. This resulted in a less talented sample distributed approximately equally by gender across the six age blocks; there were 38 boys and 37 girls. Table 2.1 shows the number of boys and girls sampled by age block and talent group. The greatest gender disparity occurred in the 9 to 10 age range, where there were 8 boys and 6 girls. All parents and children gave informed consent for the use of their drawings. In the schools a negative permission slip was sent home by the art teacher. Parents of children in the art contest were called on the telephone by the researcher to obtain consent.

Children were asked to submit at least two dated drawings made within the last 3 months. These were to be spontaneous drawings made from the child's imagination and not copied from pictures or drawn from live models. I suggested that drawings of figures and scenes were best and stipulated that design drawings were not wanted. At least one usable drawing was obtained from each consenting child and in some cases three or four were obtained from the same period. If a child submitted more than one drawing, all of them were used under the assumption that sampling more drawings allows a child to display her or his range of skill level more fully (Fisher, Bullock, Rotenberg & Raya 1993). Drawings obtained from children in the art contest were those they had submitted for the contest. The theme of the contest was to draw a gingerbread house, a theme that lent itself well to analyses of spatial relationships and perspective.

Longitudinal Study

Children for the longitudinal study were recruited separately from the cross-sectional study through nominations from teachers and parents. Somewhat surprisingly, none of these children was in an art program at the time of recruitment and few had taken any formal art classes in the years prior to recruitment. One girl had taken a class at age 5 and another at ages 6 and 7. This may have been because the children were still in elementary school at the time of recruitment. But also it may have been the type of relationship these children had established with their art. Their art was a form of highly personalized expression in which they were deeply invested, spending many hours a day after school either alone or with siblings or cousins drawing. One boy, when he reached high school, expanded his early drawing relationship with his brother to include one or two close friends, creating a drawing-based action game for the small group (Milbrath, 1995). Taking formal instruction at an art school might have been experienced as intrusive, at least when

TABLE 2.1

CROSS-SECTIONAL SAMPLES BY GENDER AND AGE BLOCK

Age Block	3 to 4 Years	5 to 6 Years	7 to 8 Years	9 to 10 Years	11 to 12 Years	13 to 14 Years	Total
Less Talented							
Girls	6	6	6	6	7	6	37
Boys	6	5	7	8	6	6	38
Total	12	11	13	14	13	12	75
Talented							
Girls	1	1	3	2	1	2	10
Boys	3	3	2	4	4	4	20
Total	4	4	5	6	5	6	30

these children were young. After recruitment, however, three children took a summer drawing class and one child went on to an arts magnet public high school.

Long-term prospective studies involve a risk. A child who appears highly talented at a very young age may never realize her potential in later years. Children in the longitudinal study, therefore, were identified between ages 8 to 10, not at young ages. This allowed both a prospective and a retrospective approach to the study. There were between 4 and 6 years of prospective study and an equal number of years of retrospective study. Five of the children were 10, two were 9, and one was 8 when recruited. Half were boys and half were girls.

Besides nomination, participation in the study required that a child's parents had saved some portion of her or his artwork since at least age 5 and agreed to continue to save and date drawings over the remaining period of study. Although dating of retrospective drawings was not always done at the time of drawing, a rough chronology tied to the child's age had been kept by all parents. Therefore, drawings were dated by year rather than by exact date for this sample.

The Children. Seven of the 8 children were born within 2 years of each other. The eighth child was approximately 7 years younger than the other children. Three of the 8 children had an IQ in the range considered eligible for gifted academic programs, between 135 and 150. No other IQ data were available but all the other children, except one, were high achievers in high school and graduated with distinction. The 7 older children are now in their late twenties. Four of them have graduated from college, one with a fine arts degree, two with degrees in psychology, and a third with a degree in mathematics. Those who studied psychology also studied art during their college years. Two of the college graduates went to graduate school; one young man completed a graduate degree in business; the other young man is completing a degree in statistics. The other 3 children had some college education; one girl was in art school for 2 years before dropping out for life experience and a boy is returning to college after a tour of duty in the army. The youngest subject is in her early 20s and currently in art school.

Only two of the young artists are currently pursuing art as a career but almost all of them expressed an interest in continuing to do their art and some of them in being able to combine their art with a career. The young man who graduated with a degree in business has used his graphic skills designing web pages for a large computer company. Another young man would like to pursue a career in fashion and one of the young women has thought of advertising as a field where she could use her art skills creatively. The major reason given by these young adults for why they were not pursuing a career in the arts was economic. Few of them are willing to take the economic risks that they see as part of the life of an artist. The young man who is pursuing a career as an artist since graduating from college with a degree in art has been struggling to find a place and time to paint because he must work a day job to survive. The young woman who is still in art school is committed to a career in the arts but has not decided in which direction she will go. She still loves drawing but also printmaking and sculpture.

The Families. The socioeconomic background of the families was middle class. In almost all cases, both parents were college-educated and six parents had education beyond a bachelor's degree. All children were Caucasian. Some of the parents were themselves skilled in the visual arts. The parent of one boy is a recognized artist. One girl's father was a working artist and her mother an elementary school art teacher while she was growing up. A third girl has a father who works in the art-related fields of film and exhibit construction for museums. The other parents work in fields outside the arts, such as classroom teaching, college level teaching, technical writing, and administration. About half the families reported that one parent drew with their child when the children were very young. One father who drew with his daughter placed a pen in her hand when she was around 11 months. Another father seated his son on his lap at age 2 and drew with him. Almost all the parents reported that their child had started drawing by age 2. At the time of recruitment, five of the eight children were primarily living with only one of their biological parents. Only two of the children had siblings living with them and five had no other siblings at the time of the study.

Parent and Child Interviews and Collecting the Drawings. Parent(s) and child were invited to participate in the study and told that this was a study of the development of drawing in talented children.

Once parent and child agreed to participation, they were interviewed. The interview focused on reviewing a child's drawings and taking a history of significant artistic milestones in the child's life. To review the drawings the parent and I first arranged them chronologically, and then individual drawings were discussed with the child. From this parent collection, a subset of drawings was selected for study based on obtaining a distribution that was representative of the types of drawings produced at each age. An approximately equal number of drawings was selected for each year. Once chosen, the drawings were borrowed for a 2-week period for photocopying and photographing. Each photocopy was given an identification number and only photocopied drawings were retained for the study.

After the initial interview, I returned approximately every 6 months until a child was age 14 to review recent drawings and select some for documentation. The same selection criteria and procedures were applied prospectively as used retrospectively but because more drawings were available per year, more were documented. On each visit children were interviewed about recent drawings and their artistic progress. On the average, parents and children had saved a total of 472 (median = 430) drawings per child or an average of 54 per year (median = 46). Almost one-third of these were chosen for documentation or an average of 17 drawings per year (median = 16) for each child. Not all documented drawings were scored. Drawings were randomly selected for scoring from the documented drawings to include an approximately equal number from each year. This was about 4 drawings per year for each child or a total of 347 drawings across the 10 years of study.

Scoring the Drawings

Drawings for both studies were scored by me and Ana Caminos, an artist with a college degree in fine arts. Ana was trained by me to use the scoring procedure. Each drawing was identified by a number that had been assigned when the drawing was documented. Ana was blind as to the age and identity of a child but because I had spent many hours looking at the drawings with the child and parent, I was usually able to identify an individual child's drawing by style. Reliabilities were calculated for both studies. We scored approximately 25% of the longitudinal study drawings (90 drawings) and 10% of the cross-sectional drawings (30 drawings) for reliability. We scored many more of the longitudinal study drawings

TABLE 2.2

RELIABILITIES FOR CATEGORIES SCORED IN SPONTANEOUS DRAWINGS

Categories	Talented Longitudinal Sample		Cross-Sectional Sample	
	Cohen's Kappa	% Agree	Cohen's Kappa	% Agree
Line Analysis[a]				
Line Orientation	.70	82	.70	78
Active to Passive Line	.58	77	.82	92
Symmetry/Asymmetry	.62[b]	76	.76	88
Circles/Ovals	.58	72	.49	71
Triangles/Triangle Type	.61	95	.80	90
Plane Analysis				
Ground Line	.75	92	.86	95
Ground Plane	.72	87	.71	81
Pictorial Devices	.81	87	.89	93
Rotations	.90	96	.66	81
Points of View	.89	96	.73	90
Drawings Systems	.82	93	.88	96
Perspective Indicators	.67	79	.88	90
Other Measures				
Number of Elements	$r=.92$		$r=.96$	
Perspective Measurements	$r=.98$		NA	
Figure Proportions	$r=.97$		$r=.99$	
Horizon Line	$r=.91$		$r=.93$	

[a] Line analysis reliabilities include absence, low, and high levels.
[b] For absence and high code only.

for reliability because they were generally of much greater complexity than the cross-sectional study drawings. Table 2.2 presents the reliabilities for the two studies. Reliabilities were stable across the two studies.

Coding Drawings for Spatial Representations. Scoring a drawing for the way a child handles spatial relationships has typically been approached in a piecemeal fashion. Investigators have tended to focus on one or two aspects of a drawing at a time. Goodnow and Friedman (1972), for example, rated the orientation of a figure axis relative to the eye–nose–mouth axis of the figure. Piaget and Inhelder (1956/67) focused on size diminution in children's perspective representations of railroad ties. Willats (1977) developed a procedure with broader scope looking at both pictorial devices for representing the position and relationship of objects in depth, and drawing systems for representing planes projected in depth. Willats's procedure has been one of the more influential and parts of it have been adopted by a number of investigators (e.g., Crook, 1985; Jahoda, 1981; Saenger, 1981). Researchers at the Cleveland Museum of Art also developed a comprehensive scoring procedure but criteria were not always clearly operationalized and reliabilities are not reported (Lark-Horowitz et al., 1973).

A comprehensive procedure was needed for spontaneous drawings that could include the full range of what children do at different ages and with highly varied themes. For example, 4-year-olds are often satisfied drawing a single figure. At 6, more complex themes, often intended as narratives, are drawn, such as cars or trains speeding over mountains or, as one 6-year-old titled his drawing, "Man falls overboard and is eaten by shark in New York; a true story." Showing human or animal figures projected in depth presents a different set of problems than those posed by the parallel planes of buildings or roads projected in depth. A system that scored the full range of solutions to drawing spatial relationships of both organic and geometric forms needed to be devised. Existing procedures were not ignored but freely borrowed and new ones were also devised. The end result was a scoring system that included scoring of lines, planes, and figures. Although it was time consuming to use, the rich results were well worth the labor.

The scoring system was based on dimensions that Piaget (Piaget & Inhelder, 1956/67; Piaget et al., 1960) and Arnheim (1974) thought were important in representing spatial relationships. I also drew on the notebooks of Paul Klee (1978) for some categories of line analysis. In brief, a categorical scoring system was devised that included ratings of the following dimensions:

- *Line orientation* relative to the eye–nose–mouth axis of a figure (Goodnow & Friedman, 1972), or if a picture axis was present, to the picture plane.
- *Types of shapes* such as circles, ovals, and triangles.
- *Line use* to denote a plane or enclose a plane; *active line* stands as the representation by itself, *active plane* stands as the representation by itself, *active line* and *active plane* each carry representational value.
- *Assessment of the picture plane* for the appearance of ground lines,

ground planes, and number of points of view represented in the drawing.

- *Figure rotations* as front, profile, three-quarter, and back views.
- *Types of pictorial devices*, means used to suggest relative positioning including horizontal segregation, vertical segregation, and overlap (Willats, 1977).
- *Types of drawing systems*, nonprojective, projective, and perspective systems (Willats, 1977).
- *Perspective indicators*, including foreshortening, modeling, and shading or shadow.

Several numerical measures were taken as well:

- *Drawing system* judgments were validated by a measure of the angle of convergence for lines representing parallel planes projected in depth (Willats, 1977).
- *Figure proportions* were assessed by calculating a ratio of different parts of the body such as the head in relation to the trunk.

Selfe (1983) and others (Thomas & Silk, 1990; Thomas & Tsalimi, 1988) working with figure completion tasks have advocated using ratios of area as the most satisfactory measure, but the large variation in conditions of measurement using spontaneous drawings made this unfeasible. Instead, the vertical height of each body part was used in this study (Nash & Harris, 1970; Allik & Laak, 1985).

These categories and measurements were operationalized into a scoring manual that can be obtained from the author (Milbrath, 1982). Ana and I trained using the manual prior to achieving reliability and used it as a reference when we scored the drawings.

Statistical Models. In general the categorical data from this study were analyzed using loglinear analyses (Kennedy, 1992). This type of analysis provides an overall likelihood ratio for the entire analysis and individual values for the adjusted residuals of cells in the analysis. Adjusted residuals are an acceptable approximation to z-scores for individual cell goodness of fit (Haberman, 1978) and can be used to evaluate the observed values in individual cells against the expected values. When loglinear analyses were used, the categories within a dimension of analysis (e.g., drawing systems) had to be mutually exclusive. Therefore, individual categories were re-scored with a computer algorithm that arranged the data in an ordered hierarchy. The orders were based on expectations grounded in the literature and on observations of the developmental sequence for the categories within a dimension. The computer assigned the score of the highest category in the drawing. The complete details of the loglinear analyses performed on the data and the computer algorithms are presented in Appendix 2.1.

3

FROM LINE TO
REPRESENTATION

For the present . . . let us content ourselves
with the most primitive of elements, the line.
At the dawn of civilization, when writing and
drawing were the same thing, it was the basic
element. And as a rule our children begin with
it; one day they discover the phenomenon of
the mobile point, with what enthusiasm it is
hard for us grown-ups to imagine. At first the
pencil moves with extreme freedom, wherever
it pleases. But once he begins to look at these
first works, the child discovers that there are
laws which govern his random efforts. Children who continue to take pleasure in the cha-
otic are, of course, no artists; other children
will soon progress towards a certain order.
Criticism sets in. The chaos of the first play-
drawing gives way to the beginning of order.
The free motion of the line is subordinated to
anticipation of a final effect; cautiously the
child begins to work with a very few lines.

(Paul Klee, 1978, p. 103)

Somewhere between the ages of 1 and 3 children discover that a
pencil, pen, or magic marker makes wonderful marks on paper,
walls, and even their own bodies. These first scribbles are products
of motor patterns (Golomb, 1992; Piaget & Inhelder, 1956) and
give most young children great pleasure. In observing his own children, Mathews (cited in Golomb, 1992) noted three specific behav-

iors that were precursors to later marking directed at surfaces. During the second year of life he observed a downward vertical arc of the arm, a horizontal sweep, and a push–pull action. About a year later these behaviors, which had first been continuous, could be broken up and controlled; by combining a pull action with a horizontal sweep, the children were able to achieve their first circular scribbles.

In the next phase, Mathews observed that his children accompanied their marking movements with sounds, such as the engine of an airplane, and a brief narrative describing the action. They appeared motivated to draw by their desire to create a narrative. Such drawings mark a transition between motor exercise and the production of intentionally representational shapes. Golomb observed that when she asked children about their narrated scribbles they could identify parts of the drawings and locate the top and bottom of the picture. She points out that these early action representations are not truly symbolic because the drawings themselves cannot stand independently of the narratives or the actions that represent the narrated events (Golomb, 1992). Symbolism begins when children start to assimilate the shapes and lines they are able to create to their narratives. Like symbolic play, this early activity is largely assimilative but in most children it lags 1 or 2 years behind play.

Luquet (1935) described a different transitional process, one that puts more emphasis on perceptual activity and on the process of accommodation. Children start with basic schemas derived from the first shapes they master and then alter them in the service of a more faithful representation. In this instance, picture making appears to motivate drawing, as a child creates increasingly realistic representations to stand for objects in the world. For Luquet the transition to intentional representation is signaled when children notice and accentuate a resemblance between their drawing and a subject in the real world. For example, a circle with an angle might be seen as a bird because of a fortuitous similarity between the sharp angle of a bird's beak and the angle in the scribble. If the child adds "legs" to the underside of the circle it becomes more birdlike. After many repetitions of this fortuitously derived "bird" or bird schema, Luquet saw children spontaneously produce a "new" drawing, which looked very much like the bird drawing but several essential features were modified to transform the "bird" into a "kitty." In this way children successively modify their drawing schemas to produce a greater and greater number of different representational types.

It is often assumed that a child's early marks and scribbles are a form of necessary practice that teaches the child to control the primary elements of two-dimensional form and informs her about the potential representational status of *picture primitives,* such as points, lines, and circles. Kellogg (1979) gave such a singular status to scribbling and viewed it as a necessary precursor to symbolic drawing. She identified several early phases in which children progress from drawing a basic set of scribbles, to drawing basic shapes, and then to more complex patterns that combine shapes and lines in the form of mandalalike diagrams. A review of studies involving nonliterate cultures, however, where drawing with pencil and paper was unknown until the researchers arrived suggests otherwise. These studies found that adults could progress from scribbling to the use of closed planes to stand for a human figure in a single sitting without the benefit of extended practice (Harris, 1971, reviewed in Golomb, 1992).

More compelling are studies that demonstrate that congenitally blind children and adults employ picture primitives in the service of representing a figure or object much as sighted people do but without previous experimentation with scribbling (Kennedy, 1993; Millar, 1975). A series of studies carried out by Golomb (1992) also indicates that children who are still in the scribbling stage can be provoked to draw coherent human figures when parts are dictated in an organized sequence. Children were able to figure out not only where a dictated body part went but what lines and shapes to use to denote the part. Golomb concludes that a step-wise progression from marks to scribbles to shapes is not necessary for the appearance of representational drawing. In this sense drawing may be quite distinct from other semiotic activities such as language, in which early babbling constitutes an important sensory-motor exercise in the progression toward language.

But if practice with isolated lines, circles, and angles is not essential, then how do children come to use these elements in their drawings? Willats (1985; 1992) has proposed that children learn a denotation rule system, by which *picture primitives* – that is points, lines, and regions – come to stand for *scene primitives,* the vertices, edges, surfaces and bodies of objects and scenes. For example, initially a child might use a region such as an enclosed plane to stand for the single face of a cube. Later in the child's development, the same region might stand for all the faces of the cube with the bounding line of the enclosed plane denoting the surface rather than the edge of the cube. This suggests an early rule in which picture primitives and scene primitives belong to a different dimensional order; the line that extends in only one direction is used for the solid surface of a cube that extends in three dimensions. Willats points out that this developmental trajectory leads to a dead end: "A child who can only use regions to denote faces but not lines to denote edges, cannot progress to any system of oblique projection. The idea of an oblique direction across the picture standing for directions in the third dimension is associated with lines, not regions, so that the development of a denotation system in which lines stand for edges must precede the acquisition of the later transformational systems" (Willats, 1981, p. 30). Gradually a child comes to use picture primitives to stand for their dimensional equivalents; that is, a region serves as the exposed face of a cube, while a line serves as an edge and line junctions serve as vertices. In other words, the denotation relationships between picture and scene primitives must be intradimensional. The child's developmental task, therefore, is to discover the rules by which these primary elements or picture primitives can come to denote features of objects in the real world. In this chapter we trace developmentally how children use line and shape in their artwork and whether or not there are differences in the denotation rules talented and less talented children adopt.

THE ELEMENTS OF DRAWING

Line

Line is the essential element in any work of art. The types of lines children employ in their drawings have been only roughly documented and mostly with respect to age of appearance, not how they are used. For example, investigators have noted a primacy of vertical over horizontal lines in line orientation and copying tasks; vertical lines are usually copied more accurately (Berman, 1976; Freeman, 1980; Graham, Berman & Ernhart, 1960). Oblique lines appear hardest for children to master (Berman & Golab, 1975; Olson, 1970). The rectangular frame of a sheet of paper and the more distal cues in the environment provide strong vertical and horizontal cues that likely bias against reproducing oblique lines. But even when proximal cues are eliminated by using a circular frame, young children still have difficulty reproducing an oblique model.

One suggestion is that the child's own body acts as a strong vertical referent (Berman, Cunningham & Harkulich, 1974). In addition, crossing the midline of the body presents a difficult motor task for young children. Olson (1970) favors a conceptual explanation. He argues that young children lack a system for representing parts in relation to the whole. A diagonal must start in one corner and finish in another. This requires integrating the starting and ending points in relation to the whole. In his studies, the pattern of errors children made suggested that they had difficulty integrating these two points. Children became centered on the point of their activity and failed to keep where they were going or the end point in mind. Olson equated the motor difficulty of producing different types of lines by using a response board made to resemble a checkerboard. A child only had to place a series of checkers in the proper squares to reproduce the presented model line so putting a checker on any square should be motorically equivalent regardless of the direction of the line (e.g., vertical or oblique). He also ruled out potential inequalities in perceptual analyses of patterns by demonstrating that children who could not reproduce a diagonal on the checkerboard could still visually match a diagonal pattern to a model.

Sensitivity to parallel alignment of lines is evident in children as young as 4 (Bryant, 1969; Mitchelmore, 1985) and young children have no difficulty using parallel alignment cues when asked to make constructions (Freeman, Chen & Hambly, 1984; Naeli & Harris, 1976; Piaget & Inhelder 1956). But drawing one line parallel to another line has rarely been studied. Mitchelmore (1985) found that 7-year-old Jamaican children who had hardly ever used a pencil made few errors in this task. The fewest errors were made for horizontal parallels, followed by vertical parallels and finally by oblique parallels.

Shapes

The circle stands as the first truly representational shape because it is a natural product of motor activity and practice and because it has a perceptually favored status based on its symmetry and simplicity (Golomb, 1992). As a closed shape, a circle has inherent representational meaning, conveying roundness, solidity, and harmony. Golomb suggests that its representational status need not be explicitly taught because such closed shapes are a fundamental carrier of meaning. Willats (1981) emphasizes its utility; as a bounded region it is able to convey both the surface and the volume of an object. Kennedy (1993) found that even subjects blind from birth used closed shapes to denote volume. The priority of the circle over other closed shapes is supported by data that show it is the first closed shape that children can copy, roughly a full year before a square (Graham et al., 1960; Piaget & Inhelder, 1956).

Studies of children's ability to copy forms show that the first distinctions children are able to make are closed versus open forms. Piaget and Inhelder (1956) argue that these are the significant topological features of simple forms. They suggest that to begin with children ignore Euclidean relationships such as angles. Therefore, circles are drawn as copies of all closed forms including circles, squares, and triangles, and lines are used for open forms such as crosses. Starting at about the age of 4, children in their studies were able to distinguish curved shapes from straight-sided ones but initially roughly the same representation was used for triangles and squares. The square and triangle were distinctly drawn about the same time the children were able to use oblique lines to separate their drawings of an x model from the cross model. Between 6 and 7 all the models presented, even complex ones, were correctly copied. In studies by Graham, Berman, and Ernhart (1960) children's ability to copy angles preceded their ability to copy squares and squares preceded their ability to copy triangles. Last to appear was the ability to copy a diamond shape, although some of the angles copied earlier had oblique lines.

Conclusions

Many of the studies mentioned were largely concerned with the difficulty or ease children have in copying. They suggest that children's first spontaneous marks will be circular or curved line scribbles in which closed shapes appear only accidentally. The first true shape should be the circle, and shapes distinguished by their Euclidean properties should appear later. Spontaneous drawings from younger children, therefore, might feature circles over other closed shapes and children might begin by using circular shapes in modular fashion as building blocks (e.g., picture primitives) for more complex forms such as people.

Since vertical and horizontal lines are easiest for young children to copy, younger children may show greater preference for using these lines in their early symbolic drawings and only later use oblique and contoured lines. When a referent is given, constructing parallel alignments is easy for young children but the ease or difficulty of drawing two lines parallel has not been well studied. Parallel lines can be used to denote edges of geometric objects so their developmental course has added significance. On the basis of Willats's (1981) research we might expect that once they appear, parallel lines will first be used to denote the surfaces of geometrical objects and only later their edges (Willats, 1981). Although the age of an artist is important, themes will also influence the type of lines that children use. Drawings of organic shapes will favor the use of contour lines; drawings of geometrical shapes will favor the use of parallel lines.

LINE, SHAPE, AND PLANE IN THE SPONTANEOUS DRAWINGS STUDIES

Both Willats and Klee put great emphasis on a child's discovery of the denotation rules associated with graphic representation if she or he is to become an artist. By studying how children use line and shape to construct a plane we can make inferences about when these rules begin to appear. Do talented children discover these rules sooner than less talented children and do some less talented children fail to discover them? Data to explore these questions came from judgments made about what types of lines and shapes dominated the production of a drawing. For example, when children move beyond scribbling to drawing with controlled lines, when do they first use vertical, horizontal, oblique, parallel, or contour lines and triangles, angles, or circles as elements in constructing a drawing? What are the most frequently used lines and shapes in the drawings of children of different ages? And how much are children guided by symmetry in constructing a drawing? For example, in the case of a house, are windows and doors arranged symmetrically? Some research suggests that younger children overregularize their copies of shapes toward symmetry (Graham et al., 1960).

Critical to deciding whether or not a child has mastered a given denotational rule is how a child uses line. Willats (1985) developed a very detailed way to code drawings for the denotation rules children use. His method, however, was too detailed and time-consuming for a study of this size. Instead a quicker way to code drawings for line use was devised with the following logic: If lines are used by themselves to stand for three-dimensional volumes then they are the active elements in creating a drawing. If lines are used to enclose planes then the planes become denotationally active. A plane is most active when it is filled in solidly, for example, with color, because the line is subordinated (passive) to the plane leaving only the plane to stand for the object. But when a plane is left open or unfilled in a drawing, both the line and the enclosed plane remain active and can clearly assume different denotational roles. These characterizations of line and plane were adapted from Klee (1978) who designated a *line active* when it did not enclose a plane, a *plane active* when the line enclosed a plane and the plane was colored or filled in, and both *line and plane active* when a line enclosed a plane but the plane was left unfilled (Milbrath, 1982). At what point do children begin to represent objects with planes and how do they first treat the planes they construct? When do line and plane take on their distinct denotational roles?

Analysis of Line

First Appearance of Controlled Line. The first aspect of line use studied was the simple presence or absence of controlled lines in a drawing. Table 3.1 shows at what age a given type of line was first present in the drawings of talented and less talented children. Talented children were using all four types of single lines and the three types of parallel lines at younger ages than less talented children. The disparity between the same levels of use was approximately 2 years. In the cross-sectional sample, half to all of the talented children were using the four types of single lines by age 3 whereas similar levels of use by the less talented children did not occur until age 5 or 6. Three-quarters of the talented children were showing some use of parallel lines by the age of 4, whereas less talented children did not show similar levels of use until age 6.

In the talented longitudinal sample there were four children for whom there were drawings prior to 3 years of age. Nevertheless, consistent use of all controlled lines did not occur until age 3. This is quite consistent with results for the talented cross-sectional sam-

TABLE 3.1
PERCENTAGE FIRST APPEARANCE OF LINE[a]

	Two Years	Three Years			Four Years		
	Talented-L (n = 4)	Talented-L (n = 6)	Talented-C (n = 2)	Less Talented-C (n = 3)	Talented-L (n = 6)	Talented-C (n = 4)	Less Talented-C (n = 9)
Single Lines							
Vertical	0	83	50	33	67	75	33
Horizontal	50	100	50	33	83	75	22
Oblique	25	100	100	33	100	75	33
Contour	100	83	100	0	100	75	44
Parallel Lines							
Vertical	0	83	50	0	83	75	22
Horizontal	0	67	50	0	83	75	22
Oblique	0	67	50	0	67	75	0

	Five Years			Six Years			Seven Years		
	Talented-L (n = 8)	Talented-C (n = 2)	Less Talented-C (n = 9)	Talented-L (n = 8)	Talented-C (n = 3)	Less Talented-C (n = 9)	Talented-L (n = 8)	Talented-C (n = 4)	Less Talented-C (n = 9)
Single Lines									
Vertical	50	50	56	63	100	56	75	75	44
Horizontal	88	50	68	88	100	68	100	50	56
Oblique	100	100	78	100	100	78	100	100	78
Contour	100	100	100	100	100	100	100	100	89
Parallel Lines									
Vertical	88	50	78	100	100	78	100	75	89
Horizontal	88	0	78	88	100	78	88	75	67
Oblique	100	100	78	88	67	78	88	75	67

[a]Talented-L = Longitudinal Talented Sample, Talented-C = Cross-Sectional Talented Sample, Less Talented-C = Cross-Sectional Less Talented Sample.

ple. It should be noted, however, that since the talented longitudinal sample was used to fill out deficient age groups in the talented cross-sectional sample, one of the two 3-year-olds in the two groups is the same subject.

Frequently Used Lines. The second aspect studied was to observe which lines dominated a drawing or were used frequently in constructing a drawing. Initially each category of frequent line use was studied separately to examine differences over the three age blocks, ages 3 to 6, 7 to 10, and 11 to 14. When the individual categories of line use were examined by age in the cross-sectional sample, frequent use of vertical lines in the drawings declined with age whereas frequent use of contour lines increased. All three types of parallel lines showed a similar developmental course. They increased over the first two age blocks and peaked in drawings of children between ages 7 and 10 and then declined in older children's drawings. The percentages of line types by age are shown in Table 3.2.

Several significant differences between talented and less talented children in the cross-sectional sample were found. These are also shown in Table 3.2. Talented children were more likely to construct their drawings with contour lines than less talented children. Talented children were also more likely to construct their drawings by placing lines in parallel. Twice as many of the talented children's drawings were dominated by parallel vertical and parallel horizontal lines as those of the less talented children's drawings.

The many drawings sampled for the talented children studied longitudinally allowed stable proportion values to be computed at each age block for each category of frequent line use. These were analyzed with separate repeated measures analysis of variance. Significant increases with age were found for mean proportion of drawings with contour lines and oblique and horizontal parallel lines; contour and oblique parallel lines increased between ages 3 to 6 and 7 to 10, and horizontal parallels increased between ages 3–6 and 11–14. These results are presented in Appendix 3.1. They are very consistent with the developmental findings shown for the cross-sectional sample.

Line Scale. The types of frequently used lines were also considered together in the same analysis using loglinear analysis. In this case,

TABLE 3.2
CROSS-SECTIONAL SAMPLE: PERCENTAGE OF
CHILDREN FREQUENTLY USING EACH LINE TYPE

Age in Years	Frequent Line Type	Less Talented	Talented	Total Sample
		$n = 23$	$n = 8$	$n = 31$
3 to 6	Vertical	13	25	16
	Horizontal	9	25	13
	Oblique	26	13	23
	Contour	56	75	61
	Vertical Parallel	22	38	32
	Horizontal Parallel	22	50	29
	Oblique Parallel	4	0	3
		$n = 27$	$n = 11$	$n = 38$
7 to 10	Vertical	0	9	3
	Horizontal	7	9	8
	Oblique	11	27	18
	Contour	82	100	87
	Vertical Parallel	59	92	68
	Horizontal Parallel	37	91	53
	Oblique Parallel	26	45	32
		$n = 25$	$n = 11$	$n = 36$
11 to 14	Vertical	0	0	0
	Horizontal	4	9	6
	Oblique	20	45	28
	Contour	92	100	94
	Vertical Parallel	36	73	47
	Horizontal Parallel	36	55	42
	Oblique Parallel	24	45	31
				Chi Square
		$n = 75$	$n = 30$	$n = 105$
All Ages	Vertical	4	10	1.43
	Horizontal	7	13	1.21
	Oblique	19	33	2.61
	Contour	77	93	3.70*
	Vertical Parallel	40	70	7.72**
	Horizontal Parallel	32	67	10.58**
	Oblique Parallel	19	33	2.61

*$p \leq .05.$ ** $p \leq .01.$

the line categories were scored in the ordered hierarchy described in Appendix 2.1. This allowed an exploration of the children's highest level of competence in relation to talent and age. On the basis of the developmental findings for the individual categories, the scored categories in scaled order were scribbles or uncontrolled lines, single straight lines, parallel lines, and contour lines. A child's drawing only received the score for the highest frequently used line type in the drawing.

Although clear group differences had been found for the individual line categories, when drawings were scored for the highest scaled line frequently used, the two cross-sectional talent groups did not differ significantly. But when development across the three age blocks was studied in the entire sample, clear changes in three of the ordered line categories were apparent. This analysis is shown in Appendix 3.2. As would be expected, many of the youngest children between ages 3 and 6 scribbled or could not control the lines they drew, whereas the 7- to 14-year-olds rarely if ever drew uncontrolled lines or scribbles. The pattern for single lines did not change with age but frequent use of parallel lines did. Younger children ages 3 to 6 rarely used parallel lines whereas older children ages 7 to 10 made the greatest use of parallel lines. Contour lines increased in use between the ages of 7 and 14; younger children showed significantly less than expected use and older children showed significantly greater than expected use.

These results confirm the data for the first appearance of controlled lines by suggesting that many young children between the ages of 3 and 6 still have trouble controlling the lines they draw. Some children these ages, however, are also using controlled lines and beginning to construct lines in parallel. In the drawings of most children ages 7 to 10, parallel lines dominated. Parallel lines hold a special place in drawing because once they can be used to construct geometric objects, a child is in a position to discover their denotational significance as geometric edges. In the same way, the proper use of contour lines, to outline the shape of organic forms, can also lead to the discovery of line as an edge. In this sample, the oldest children made the greatest use of contour lines.

When data from the less talented children's drawings were analyzed alone for changes with age, the observed pattern was similar to that of the entire group; frequent scribbling was common in the drawings of younger children, parallel lines dominated the drawings

TABLE 3.3
PERCENTAGE OF CHILDREN FREQUENTLY USING
SCALED LINE TYPE

Age in Years	3 to 6	7 to 10	11 to 14	Mean Percentage
Cross-Sectional Less Talented	$(n = 23)$	$(n = 27)$	$(n = 25)$	$(N = 75)$
Scribble	39	4	0	14.33
Single Line	13	4	4	7
Parallel	26	67	48	47
Contour	22	26	48	32
Cross-Sectional Talented	$(n = 8)$	$(n = 11)$	$(n = 11)$	$(N = 30)$
Scribble	13	0	0	4.33
Single Line	25	0	13	12.67
Parallel	33	100	55	62.67
Contour	25	0	27	17.33
Longitudinal Talented	$(n = 28)^a$	$(n = 32)$	$(n = 30)$	$(N = 90)$
Scribble	0	0	0	0
Single Line	14	0	3	5.67
Parallel	61	63	67	63.67
Contour	25	38	30	31

$^a n$ = One drawing per year per child but not all children have drawings for every year.

of children ages 7 to 10, and contour lines were most likely in drawings of older children. Unfortunately too few talented children were available in the cross-sectional sample to compare the talent groups over the three age blocks. Nevertheless, reference to Table 3.3, which shows the percentages of talented and less talented children at each age block for each of the scaled line categories, indicates that talented children made the most consistent use of parallel lines. This concurs with the results for the individual unscaled categories.

The talented children studied longitudinally started drawing recognizable representations several years before less talented subjects sampled in the cross-sectional study. Therefore, in most cases the scribbling phase had already passed before the study began. In one case, drawings were available for age 1, and although some scribbles were observed in that year, the child was drawing recognizable representations by the second year. Therefore there were few if any drawings that scored as scribbles by age 3. This is in contrast to the drawings of a few of the youngest talented children in the cross-sectional sample, who were still scribbling at that age.

When development across the three age blocks was analyzed using the hierarchically ordered line categories, little change with age was found in the drawings of this talented sample. Table 3.3 shows the percentages for each category by age. Visual inspection suggests that when these children were between ages 3 and 6, single, parallel, and contour lines dominated their drawings whereas when they were between ages 7 and 10 parallels and contours were more frequent. But frequent use of parallels and contours was always most characteristic of these talented children; their use began early and was consistent throughout the study period.

Comparison of the three groups in Table 3.3 suggests that when the talented cross-sectional children were between the ages of 3 and 6 their use of line was similar to that of the less talented children, but between ages 7 and 10 talented children were exclusive in their use of parallel lines. In contrast, the types of lines frequently used by the talented longitudinal children did not change significantly with age. Overall, however, the most striking aspect was that irrespective of age, parallel lines dominated the drawings of talented children whereas the drawings of less talented children of different ages showed greater variety of line use.

Analysis of Shape

Young children will use a circle to represent a face or the sun and a triangle to depict the roof of a house. When such shapes are used unmodified and whole, they can be thought of as modular elements that a child uses symbolically with little attempt at visual realism. The frequent use of whole shapes such as circles and triangles in a drawing did not statistically distinguish talent groups or ages of children in the cross-sectional sample. Nevertheless, the percentages of children by age did suggest that circles were drawn more frequently by the youngest children (29%, 16%, and 8%, respectively), and triangles and angles somewhat more by children ages 7 to 10 (36%, 42%, and 36%, respectively). On the whole, triangles and angles were used more than circles (38% versus 17%). Over the whole study, 66% of the drawings were composed with frequent use of modular shapes, but across the three age blocks the percentage of such drawings decreased (74%, 74%, 53%, respectively).

Talented children studied longitudinally did show significant changes with age in their use of circles as modular elements in a drawing (Appendix 3.3). As the children got older their use of circles declined dramatically. Use of triangles and angles increased slightly but not significantly with age. The use of both circles and triangles and angles was highest when the children were 7 to 10 years of age. Whereas in the drawings from the cross-sectional sample the most dominant modular form had been the triangle, in the drawings of these children it was the circle. This may reflect differences in complexity of themes drawn by the children. About 62% of the drawings were drawn with dominant modular elements. When divided by age blocks these types of drawings declined as children got older (89%, 56%, 43%, respectively). So although these talented children relied heavily on the circle when they were young, they shifted to increasingly less modular forms of representation as they got older. This was not unique to their talent, however, because the cross-sectional sample also showed this shift away from modularity but at a slower rate. Later chapters will emphasize figural distortions that are part of rotation and foreshortening and that work in opposition to use of modular shapes such as the circle.

Analysis of the Shift from Active Line to Plane

When children first begin to draw they start with a line or as Paul Klee put it, "a mobile point." Klee characterized a line as active when it is used by itself to represent elements in a picture. When a line is used to enclose a plane, and the bounded region is filled in, the plane becomes active and the line becomes passive or inactive; what Klee (1978) meant by this was visually active for the viewer. When the line is active, single lines are used graphically to convey meaning. When the plane is active, the plane carries meaning. Activation of a plane can be enhanced by filling it in because this imparts volume and solidity to the depicted plane. Line and plane can also be given equal visual weight by leaving the enclosed plane unfilled. In that case, both line and plane are active and both can be used graphically to convey meaning.

Observation of this natural shift, from lines that stand for objects by themselves to planes that take on this denotation role, provides data on how children of different ages use line and plane. This transitional phase from active lines accompanied by narratives or labeled after the fact because they "look" like something, to an early symbolic phase in which recognizable representations emerge from intentionally enclosing planes and juxtaposing their shapes can be studied in the drawings of young children. Most young children do not start depicting human forms with stick figures (i.e., active line) but by using enclosed planes in combination with active lines. The first human forms are usually "tadpole" drawings, a large circle with legs attached (Golomb, 1992). In this case, the enclosed shape is used to denote the face and perhaps the body as well (see chapter 4). Later several such shapes are placed in relation to each other to construct a more complete human figure. In Willats's (1985; 1992) terms tadpole drawings use picture primitives of different dimensional orders (i.e., line and plane) as if they belong to the same dimensional order; that is, both the line and the plane are used to represent the three-dimensional volume of the human figure.

Older children abandon the practice of using single lines to represent volume and use bounded regions or planes to convey three-dimensional forms. Further study of how children construct an enclosed plane might suggest what they intend when they enclose a plane. For example, is the enclosing line simply bounding a region or is it meant to stand for the surface or the edge of the enclosed plane? When the line is totally subordinated to the plane it cannot stand for anything independently of the plane. In this case it simply describes the boundaries of the enclosed region. In order to be perceived clearly as a surface or an edge, the line must be distinct from the region it encloses. When children begin to use both line and plane to carry meaning, they are in a position to experiment with the unique potential each has to denote different aspects of objects. On the other hand, when a child is thinking of the enclosed plane as a solid volume, making the plane active and the line inactive by coloring or filling the plane in enhances the solidity and volume of the enclosed region; leaving the enclosed space open or unfilled can lead to uncertainty.

Cross-Sectional Sample

The drawings were rescored so that each drawing received a mutually exclusive category score (Appendix 2.1), which was then used in loglinear analyses. The original categories were assigned for frequent use, not simple presence or absence. For example, a tadpole-type drawing would receive a score of active line for the use of line alone to denote the legs and/or arms and active plane or active line/

plane for the enclosed plane depending on whether it was filled in or not. Therefore, the assigned scores described the dominant denotation features of a drawing. The rescored categories included all possible combinations of the three original categories, active line, active plane, and active line/plane.

Talent significantly influenced the degree to which line or plane was active in the children's spontaneous drawings (Appendix 3.4). The strongest differences were in children's use of active line/plane; more than twice the percentage of drawings by talented children contained active line/plane as those by less talented children. In addition, talented children never used line by itself to represent three-dimensional volumes whereas younger less talented children did. The group percentages by category are presented at the bottom of Table 3.4. The total absence of purely active line in the drawings of talented children suggests that a shift to planar representations may have predated the study period. By the time these children were 3 years of age, they were already using enclosed shapes to depict people, animals, and objects. In addition, the fact that talented children did not use active line even in combination with other categories suggests that they passed very quickly, if at all, through a phase in which all picture primitives were used as part of the same dimensional order (see the qualitative illustrated section). Their preference for leaving enclosed shapes unfilled suggests further that talented children may not have needed to activate the plane by itself in order to have it stand for an object's volume. They may have intended the enclosed plane to denote the surface of the object rather than its solidity. The discovery of the denotation rules that clearly assign the line to stand for an edge and the plane to stand for a surface may have occurred at a young age. This proposal is explored more directly in the qualitative illustrations section later in the chapter.

When changes in the way the whole sample of children used line and plane were studied by age, age had a significant influence (Appendix 3.5). Between the ages of 3–6 and 7–10 years, children's use of active line in combination with planes declined, whereas their use of active plane increased. When less talented children were analyzed alone, this pattern was repeated in many of its essentials. The percentages of children in each talent group by age for the categories of line and plane activity are shown in Table 3.4. In drawings of less talented children, active plane increased between the ages of 3–6 and 7–10 and active line combined with active plane decreased. Although not significant, the use of purely active line dropped after the ages of 3–6 years. These developments with age may indicate a transition between drawings in which one- and two-dimensional picture primitives were used equivalently to denote three-dimensional scene primitives to those in which two-dimensional picture primitives took on the primary denotation role. This suggests that younger children adopted a drawing rule in which both line and plane were part of the same dimensional order. Older children between the ages of 7 and 10 appeared to use a rule that employed a filled region to denote a solid object.

Talented children did not appear to use the same denotation rules used by the less talented children. Even though there were too few subjects to statistically analyze changes in age for this group alone, the percentages for the two groups can be compared in Table 3.4. Like the less talented children, the talented children increasingly drew active planes between the ages of 3–6 and 7–10. But they primarily used active line/plane at all ages and almost never used active line by itself or in combination with an enclosed plane. Remarkably, even the youngest talented children studied appeared not to use line by itself to denote extensions in two- or three-dimensional space. Instead their early drawings were dominated by unfilled enclosed planes, suggesting that even the youngest talented youngsters studied had a different intention with respect to representing regions and volumes than the less talented children. The uses to which talented children put line and plane will be examined more carefully in the qualitative illustrations section.

Longitudinal Sample. Surprisingly the use of active lines and planes did not change significantly with age in this group. As in the cross-sectionally sampled talented children, there were no drawings characterized by use of active line to represent figures or objects. These children also did not use active line alone or in combination with either active line/plane or active plane as dominant forms in their drawings. Instead, as was found for the cross-sectional talented sample, these talented children primarily drew enclosed unfilled planes in which line and plane were both visually active irrespective of age (74%, 82%, and 66%, respectively). Purely active planes were used slightly more when these children were younger (22%,

TABLE 3.4
PERCENTAGE OF CHILDREN IN CROSS-SECTIONAL
SAMPLE FREQUENTLY USING ACTIVE LINE, ACTIVE
PLANE

Age in Years	Active Line or Plane	Less Talented	Talented	Total Sample
3 to 6		$n = 23$	$n = 8$	$n = 31$
	Active Line	9	0	7
	Active Plane	9*	13	10*
	Active Line/Plane (AL/P)	22	75	35
	Active Line & Active Plane	22**	0	16**
	Active Line & AL/P	17	0	13
	Active Plane & AL/P	17	0	16
	All Three Combined	4	0	3
7 to 10		$n = 27$	$n = 11$	$n=38$
	Active Line	4	0	3
	Active Plane	44*	27	39**
	Active Line/Plane	26	55	34
	Active Line & Active Plane	0	0	0
	Active Line & AL/P	0*	0	0*
	Active Plane & AL/P	22	0	21
	All Three Combined	4	0	3
11 to 14		$n = 25$	$n = 11$	$n = 36$
	Active Line	0	0	0
	Active Plane	24	18	22
	Active Line/Plane	28	63	39
	Active Line & Active Plane	0	0	0
	Active Line & AL/P	16	0	4
	Active Plane & AL/P	32	0	25
	All Three Combined	0	9	3
All Ages		$n = 75$	$n = 30$	Total Sample
	Active Line	4	0	3
	Active Plane	27	20	25
	Active Line/Plane	25	63**	36
	Active Line & Active Plane	7	0	5
	Active Line & AL/P	11	0	8
	Active Plane & AL/P	24	13	21
	All Three Combined	3	3	3

*$p \leq .05.$ **$p \leq .01.$

13%, and 14%, respectively). Active plane and active line/plane as combined forms were very infrequent.

The dominance of active line/plane throughout the development of talented children suggests that talented children quickly learn a denotation rule that appropriately assigns the respective dimensions for lines and planes: a rule that abandons the passive use of lines as boundaries of a solidly filled in plane and assigns a distinct denotation meaning to lines and planes. One interpretation is that these children quickly catch on to the idea that a line can function as an edge and that the enclosed plane can denote a surface rather than a solid volume. In fact, as demonstrated later in the qualitative illustrations section, when these children did activate the plane by filling it in, it was often because they added texture to an animal's skin or decoration to clothing, techniques that emphasize surface features rather than solidity or volume (e.g., Figures 3.1 and 3.5b).

QUALITATIVE ILLUSTRATIONS OF SIMILARITIES AND DIFFERENCES IN DRAWINGS OF TALENTED AND LESS TALENTED CHILDREN

The talented group of children studied longitudinally began their artistic careers like most toddlers. Somewhere between the ages of 1 and 3 they seized a pencil, pen, or magic marker and discovered the wonder of marking a piece of paper with dots, lines, and squiggles. Most children spend the first few years of their artistic life enjoying scribbling and rarely if ever attempt to copy pictures adults draw for them. But this was not always the case in this talented group. One talented girl did make a clearly precocious attempt to copy an adult drawing. Prior to the development of any clear representational schemata (schemas), Claire at 2 years 9 months copied a female figure her father had drawn. In Figure 3.2a her drawing appears to the right of her father's model(s). With remarkable accuracy Claire captures the closed character of her father's figure, the simple enclosure of the arm within the figure, and the separation of the hair from the face. She has conserved the simple topological relationships contained in the model. This suggests an astonishingly early ability to analyze the model visually.

During the second or third year most of the talented children began the transition to intentional representation. Four children had

Figure 3.1. Joel, talented boy age 14, example of active plane by filling in to texture surface.

drawings saved from age 2. All were able to draw either a recognizable face circle or a *tadpole* figure using a circle to stand for the head and/or body with arms or legs attached. Six children had drawings from age 3. Four of them drew tadpole figures and two of the four also drew *transitional* figures, with a circle for the face and open lines to indicate the body. A fifth child drew *conventional* figures, with a separate enclosed plane for the body. In each case the transition to distinct forms occurred approximately 1 to 2 years earlier than for less talented children.

At 3 years 3 months (age 3; 3) Claire began to draw a face schema using an elongated oval (Figure 3.2b). Initially this face schema served as both a human face and a dog's face. The dog's face was made distinct by the addition of large drooping ears and a round black nose. At this point, it is likely that the enclosed planes are meant to stand for the whole figure, even though the planes are left unfilled. It is hard to interpret what Claire intended to represent with the single lines that trail from both figures; perhaps they are legs. Six months later, this generic schema had evolved into two distinct schemata, one for a dog (Figure 3.3a) and one for a girl (Figure 3.3b), but each schema still strongly recalled the other. The

Figure 3.2a. Claire age 2; 9, copy of father's figure.

Figure 3.2b. Claire age 3; 3, multipurpose tadpole figure.

82 *The Representation of Form and Space*

Figure 3.3a. Claire age 3; 9, differentiated dog schema.

Figure 3.3b. Claire age 3; 9, differentiated girl schema.

Figure 3.3c. Claire age 4, fairies and bird.

dog schema is distinguished by the absence of arms, a more clearly differentiated torso, and the inclusion of ears. Enclosed planes instead of lines are used to depict the dog's legs. In the girl schema, which is transitional between a tadpole and a conventional figure, hair takes the place of ears and the body or dress is filled in by parallel lines inside the lower part of the figure. In this case, the indicated plane remains unclosed and active lines are used to represent arms and legs. By age 4, Claire has developed a more detailed and conventional person schema; two fairies are shown in Figure 3.3c. The early use of modular circular shapes to construct the figure is evident. But Claire also uses modular circular elements to fill in the figure. These appear to function decoratively but they may

Figure 3.4a. Kate age 2, tadpole figure.

also add solidity to the figures. The body of the bird above one of the fairies is not filled in, however, suggesting that filling in to impart solidity is unnecessary. This is consistent with the statistical results for talented children that emphasize their early and consistent use of unfilled planes.

Kate, another talented girl, began with the same circular generic face schema as Claire. Figure 3.4a, drawn at age 2, shows the tadpole figure with the trailing single line used to represent arms, legs, or body. At age 3; 1, Kate juxtaposed circles to construct a series of figures (Figure 3.4b). As did Claire, she always correctly ordered face parts. Another drawing from the same age indicates that Kate was capable of more complex depictions. In Figure 3.4c, she carefully aligns several tadpole-type figures on an implied baseline, again constructing the figures from modular elements, in this case triangle and square shapes. Active lines are used to depict hair, which is equivalent dimensionally to a line, but they are also used for the legs and feet, which are not dimensional equivalents. Although these figures are advanced they still are similar to drawings

Figure 3.4b. Kate age 3; 1, figures drawn with circles.

Figure 3.4c. Kate age 3, figures drawn with geometrical shapes.

The Representation of Form and Space

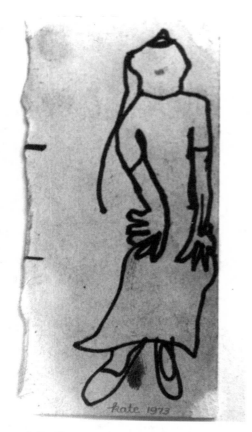

Figure 3.5a. Kate age 4, gesture drawing.

of less talented children in that active lines are used in combination with planes to construct tadpole figures. On the other hand, Figure 3.5a, drawn at early age 4, is qualitatively distinct. Kate is already capable of freeing herself from the canonical symmetrical figure schema most children develop at this age. Beyond the appeal of its well-differentiated form, its gesture is highly expressive and suggests the portrayal of a specific and vivid episode (compare with Figure 1.4). Shapes are no longer used as modular elements in constructing the figure. Instead a clear contour line is employed to outline the figure in such an expressive manner that the figure is in motion.

By age 4; 5 Kate had made remarkable progress in figure drawing. She quickly abandoned a modular approach to figure drawing in which a shape stood for a whole volume and began to use line to denote the contours of a form and the enclosed plane its volume or surface. In Figure 3.5b the continuous outline of the figure and the clear separation of body parts indicate this change in the status of line. Whereas in Figure 3.4c the line enclosing a plane serves to define a shape or bound a region, here it functions to convey the contoured edges of the figure and figure parts. Modular shapes are relegated to decorative elements that enhance surface features and perhaps the solidity of the figure but do not obscure the contour line. The clothing is filled in with parallel contour lines, filled and unfilled circles, and diamonds. This form of decorative filling in suggests that Kate was thinking of the enclosed plane as a surface (e.g., dress fabric), not a solid. The spatial relationships depicted in this drawing are also very advanced; the female figure partially occludes the male figure. For most children, even for other talented children studied, this was not achieved until after age 5 or 6.

Hondo, an exceptionally talented boy, shows the beginning of differentiated representational forms by age 3 (Figure 3.6a). He uses unfilled shapes in a modular fashion to depict the body of a bird and a person but draws a more differentiated outline to represent a reindeer. Active lines are used to indicate the elongated regions of body parts, such as neck, beak, wings, and legs of the bird. Later in the same year, Hondo draws a soldier of the queen's household guard and outlines the hat and legs (Figure 3.6b). The shapes are unfilled and some, such as the head and body, appear modular. Active lines are used to denote the arms of the figure, indicating that Hondo still employs a drawing rule that assigns line and plane to the same dimensional order.

Not all talented children began drawing conventional human figures by using shapes as modular elements. Peregrine used outline at a surprisingly young age. Figure 3.7a shows a self-portrait done at age 2; 3 for her mother's birthday. Active lines are only used to denote hair, their dimensional equivalent, and enclosed planes are left unfilled. Figure 3.7b, drawn later that year, shows her ability to use contour lines to outline clearly a well-differentiated human form. Again the planes used to construct the human figures are left unfilled and active lines are only used to represent the hair. Two remarkable drawings from the following year at age 4 show that Peregrine has already abandoned her earlier symmetrical treatment of the human figure. Although some filling in of enclosed planes occurs in Figure 3.8a, the parallel lines used on the skirt function

NOVEMBER 1973

Figure 3.5b. Kate age 4; 5, elaborated people schemas.

to suggest the surface texture of feathers; lines on the harp may indicate the contours of its rounded volume. In Figure 3.8b a few spare lines are used to suggest hair or elements of the clothing but the outlines of the two figures are left unfilled and the contour edges of the figures are clearly indicated by the outline. It seems certain that by this age, Peregrine is already using a denotation rule that assigns line and plane to different dimensional orders: Lines are used to outline the edges of contoured figure parts or to show regions that extend in one dimension, like harp strings or hair; planes are left largely unfilled or decorated to indicate texture.

Drawings from less talented children in the cross-sectional sample show that although these children start representational human forms later than the talented children, there are some initial similarities. Both groups of children typically start with a face circle or

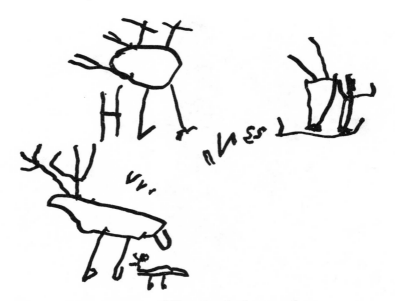

Figure 3.6a. Hondo age 3, differentiated schemas.

Figure 3.6b. Hondo age 4, the queen's household guard.

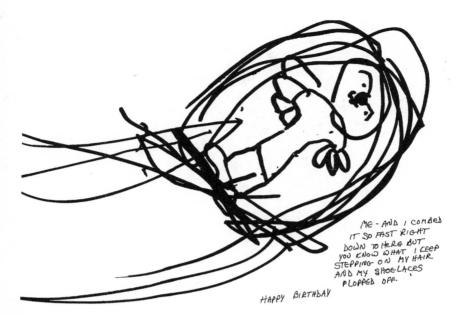

ME - AND I COMBED
IT SO FAST RIGHT
DOWN TO HERE BUT
YOU KNOW WHAT I KEEP
STEPPING ON MY HAIR
AND MY SHOELACES
PLOPPED OFF.

HAPPY BIRTHDAY

Figure 3.7a. Peregrine age 2; 3, self-portrait.

Figure 3.7b. Peregrine age 2, mother and baby.

Figure 3.8a. Peregrine age 4, girl with harp.

Figure 3.8b. Peregrine age 4, fairy-tale figures.

92   *The Representation of Form and Space*

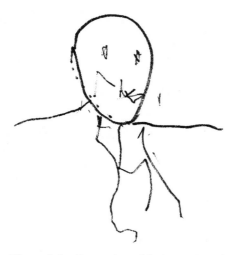

Figure 3.9a. Less talented boy age 3, tadpole.

Figure 3.9b. Less talented boy age 4, tadpole.

tadpole figure but the less talented drawers always make more use of active lines to refer to body parts such as limbs. As they get older a different denotation rule appears to underlie their use of enclosed planes. Drawings in Figure 3.9a and b from children age 3; 6 and 4 show two tadpole human forms made with an unfilled circle to indicate the head and/or head and body and active lines to indicate the arms and legs. A *transitional* human figure appears in Figure 3.9c. Here the 4-year-old girl draws a filled tube for the body that suggests the solidity of the form. A *conventional* human figure by a girl age 4; 6 is shown in Figure 3.10a. She juxtaposes a circle and triangle for the body and uses active

Figure 3.9c. Less talented girl age 4, differentiated girl schema.

Figure 3.10a. Less talented girl age 4; 6, little girl.

lines to indicate arms, legs, and hair. The body and feet shapes have been filled in, and the impression that they are solid regions is strong.

Older less talented children abandon the use of active line except to denote hair. Line is used to outline a figure but not necessarily to define a figure's contours. Clothes and body parts may be solidly colored in. In Figure 3.10b, a 6-year-old filled in the entire figure. In some instances the filled areas, such as the waistband and cuffs,

Figure 3.10b. Less talented girl age 6, little girl.

appear decorative but otherwise the filling in appears to give solidity to the figure. The outline of the dress and hands is still visible but the outline of the head and legs is lost in the filled plane. Such lack of concern for keeping line and plane distinct suggests that they may not serve different denotation purposes and that the chief intent of the outline is to bound the solid filled in region. In Figure 3.10c, by a girl age 7; 6, the outline is no longer visible and has become part of the solidly filled in region. The form is aesthetically very pleasing but highly symbolic. Where the line is visible to define the legs, it clearly functions to bound the region rather than as a contoured edge. It is also worth noting that all figures show the human figure in its preferred frontal and symmetrical orientation.

CONCLUSIONS

The general impression given by the quantitative analysis of the way line and shape are used in a drawing is that although in some aspects of development talented and less talented children are similar, in many aspects they are quite distinct. The most frequent use of single straight lines in a drawing occurs in younger children and contour lines are increasingly used by older children. Talented chil-

Figure 3.10c. Less talented girl age 7; 6, little girl.

dren, however, are able to construct lines of different orientations and lines parallel to each other several years sooner than less talented children and at ages in which scribbling still dominates the drawings of less talented children. The use of shapes such as circles or triangles as modular elements in a drawing appears to decline in both talent groups with age, although the decline is more marked in talented children. All children also favored the circle at younger ages and triangular and angular shapes at slightly older ages. If we take stock in relation to the guides provided in Table 1.1, such differences appear to reflect rate of development and, therefore, can only support a "farther faster" hypothesis.

But several other aspects of how lines were used to construct drawings were more consistent with the "seeing, remembering, and doing" hypotheses. For one thing, the use of parallel lines was altogether higher throughout development in the talented children. More important, however, were the differences in how talented and less talented children mapped a scene onto a drawing. When they were younger, less talented children used predominantly single lines to denote three-dimensional objects and figures. To use Willats's (1981) language, these children were using a denotation rule that assigns the use of one-dimensional picture primitives to denote two-dimensional regions and three-dimensional volumes. In contrast, talented children of the same age rarely if ever used single lines in this way and were already constructing two-dimensional planes in which line and plane remained equally active visually. Older less talented children also drew enclosed planes, but in large part these planes were filled in, visually subordinating the line and leaving only the plane active. In this case an impression of a solid volume was enhanced.

Most striking was the fact that talented children, rather than showing characteristic developmental trends, used line to enclose planes from the earliest point of study and throughout the study period. But rather than solidly filling in an enclosed plane to reify its solidity as less talented children did, they rarely filled in the planes they constructed. This suggested that the line did not function as part of the region symbolized by the plane, but was assuming a distinct denotation role. Talented children quickly learned a rule that assigns line and plane distinct denotation functions. The qualitative observations amplified these quantitative findings. By age 4, talented children were already using line to outline the contours of a figure, suggesting strongly that the line stood for the contoured edges. In most cases they left planes unfilled so that line and plane were visually equal. When planes were filled it was usually to decorate clothing, or when they were older to shade or give skin texture; what was enhanced by this type of filling in was the impression of a visual surface. The denotation rule used by the talented children, therefore, appeared to be quite different from the one used by the less talented children. Quite early these children began to think of line as distinct from the plane it enclosed and to use picture primitives to stand for scene primitives that were their dimensional equivalents. In chapter 5, further reflections on these differences in children's denotation rules are considered when the development of drawing systems is studied in the two talent groups.

4

THE HUMAN FIGURE

> One must beware of formula, *good for every-thing*, that will serve to interpret the other arts as well as reality, and that instead of creating will only produce a style, or rather a styliza-tion.
>
> (Georges Braque, 1917, quoted in Chipp, 1968, p. 260)

THE HUMAN FIGURE EMERGES

Development studies of human figure drawings are all unanimous in citing "tadpole man" as one of the first consistently recognizable representations of the human figure. At the end of the last chapter, some examples were presented in drawings by talented children. Tadpole drawings received this designation because of the "fusion of head with trunk" yielding an undifferentiated circular shape with dangling tail or legs. When arms are present they are generally attached to the middle of the circle. These drawings are the symbolic successor of more primitive circular depictions of the human figure (Golomb, 1992). But tadpole figures can also be thought of as generic or undifferentiated animate forms that could represent human or animal figures (Golomb, 1992). A lively debate surrounds their interpretation that rivals the attempts to decipher what toddlers mean with single-word utterances: Determining how tadpoles are to be understood is much like deciding whether the single words of the toddler stand for a whole sentence or simply name an object. Are tadpole drawings failed attempts to draw an internally represented model that is more differentiated (Luquet, 1935)? Are they simply products of planning difficulties imposed by the demands of the task (Freeman, 1980)? Or are they an abstraction that represents the child's best solution to the problem of translating three dimensions into two while preserving a structural correspondence to the depicted object (Arnheim, 1969; Golomb, 1992)? A brief summary of the research this enigmatic form has engendered follows.

Tadpole Man

Some of the most important studies in this area have been undertaken by Freeman and his colleagues. In the first of these Freeman (1975) demonstrated that children who spontaneously draw tadpole figures are sensitive to the body proportions of predrawn figures. They consistently attach arms to the larger of two segmented circles even when facial features cue the larger segment as standing for the head. In a second study (Freeman & Hargreaves, 1977) the effect children's natural drawing sequence has on their interpretation of predrawn figures was controlled, ensuring that they noticed and classified all figure segments and could accurately mark the smaller of two. This study established the persistence of the "body proportion" effect. Despite the direction to make a nose or a navel on the head or tummy segments before placing the arms, tadpole drawers still put arms on the larger of the two segments even though they correctly placed noses on the upper circle and navels on the lower. It appeared that misclassification of body parts or poor motor control was not an adequate explanation for this phenomenon.

Nor did it appear that tadpole drawers were obeying an understood rule that arms should be placed on the trunk. Further analysis of spontaneously drawn tadpole figures and children's placements on predrawn figures indicated that arms were drawn lower on a larger head segment than on a larger trunk segment (Freeman, 1980). This suggested that *where* on the larger segment arms are positioned is controlled by whether or not children think they are placing arms on the head or on the trunk. Freeman concluded that although a child's designation of a segment as head or trunk determines fine positioning of arms, gross positioning, or *which* segment should receive the arms, is governed by proportional relationships of the entire figure.

For Freeman this highlights the relationship between a drawing and the process of producing the drawing. He argues against a hypothesis that interprets tadpole man as symbolic of both the head and trunk of a figure and favors the hypothesis that the tadpole truly represents a trunkless figure. He proposes that serial ordering, in which the first and last items in a series are best remembered or end-anchored, might apply to drawing and explain the phenomenon. Freeman notes that most observations of drawing order confirm the head as the starting point and the legs as the end point. Children omit trunk and arms because they occupy intermediate positions in the drawing series. Planning difficulties can also lead to omissions. Often children spontaneously start with heads that are scaled too large for the paper, leaving little room for the rest of the figure. It is conceivable that trunks may get short shrift in this process and be omitted altogether, whereas legs, as end anchors, will be more reliably drawn.

Other researchers interpret the tadpole figure as an undifferentiated head and trunk. A study by Cox and Parkin (1986) called into question the assumption that tadpole drawers have a complete and segmented mental representation of the figure that is overshadowed by planning and production problems during the drawing process. They could not induce tadpole-type drawers to produce conventional figures even when they simplified the task by asking them to copy a figure, complete a jigsaw figure puzzle, or draw figure parts as they were dictated. Golomb (1992) rose to the challenge of confronting the serial order and planning hypotheses directly with a series of studies that attempted to establish the tadpole as a global undifferentiated representation that intentionally stands for the whole figure. In one study of drawing sequence, she noted that although children invariably started with the head and worked down to the legs they did not always end with the legs. Instead, facial features, hair, arms, and clothing were often added after the legs. Figure completion, therefore, rarely terminated with legs. Similar sequences were also observed by Trautner (1996), who made another important discovery: Order of drawn parts was independent of a child's age.

In another study Golomb asked children to draw a human figure, name the figure parts, and dictate the figure parts to be drawn by the experimenter. She found a good deal of variability between the order of naming and the order of dictating with many more parts given in the naming task. The number of parts produced in the dictating task stood halfway between the naming and the more highly constrained graphic task of drawing the figure. In a third study, she asked children to start their drawings with a part of the figure they normally did not begin with in order to disentangle spatial and temporal ordering of parts. Each child produced four drawings, one in their habitual way and one each starting with the legs, arms, or tummy. When children started in a novel place, half of the 3-year-olds improved their drawings by including parts previously omitted and the rest drew at the level of their habitual drawings. This suggested that retrieval of figure parts was not dependent on a linear top-to-bottom serial order.

In a final series of studies, Golomb stressed the role of graphic context in differentiating figures. Children were asked to draw a "person with a flower" or "teacher reading a story to the children." Many children were able to improve their drawings to meet the task, producing more differentiated figures with arms to pick the flowers or hold the book. Golomb concludes that when the request is for a general picture, the representation instantiated is the habitual global undifferentiated form; when the request is more specific, the usual graphic sequence is disrupted and attention is directed toward parts less frequently depicted. She emphasizes children's tendency toward simplicity and economy in their spontaneous drawings; they will portray only what are essential features of a figure in its context.

These highly enlightening studies by Freeman and Golomb indicate that processes underlying children's early graphic forms are quite complex. They underscore the importance of considering performance as well as competence issues when evaluating children's drawings. It is clear that although the production process poses a considerable challenge to young children, they are capable of more than they typically demonstrate in a particular drawing. It was Luquet's (1935) opinion that there was more than one type of tadpole figure, suggesting that both a hypothesis of production constraints and one of representational constraints may apply, depending on a child's intentions. Van Sommers (1984) also noted a great deal of variation, most often toward simplification, when children were asked to repeat a drawing. It is probably fair to say that planning and production difficulties notwithstanding, the tadpole figure evolves as a simple and undifferentiated graphic schema that is derived from the earlier circular schema.

Conventional Figures

Conventional human figures with heads and trunks reliably appear in the drawings of children aged 5. Drawings of animals that were once simple modifications of tadpole forms also become more readily interpretable as dogs, cats, and horses. Questions arise about the relationship of conventional human and animal figures to the earlier tadpole forms. Although conventional figures appear ontogenetically later, their relationship to the earlier forms has not been clearly established. For example, in longitudinal observations of six children during the transitions from tadpole to conventional figure drawings, Cox and Parkin (1986) could not find clear evidence that conventional human figures had been adapted from tadpole forms. Even though tadpole figures reliably appeared before conventional figures, two of the six children never went through the tadpole stage. The four who did either drew tadpoles for a very short time (days) or drew both transitional forms (no distinct body parts but arms or body features placed apart from the head) and conventional forms simultaneously over several months. In addition to the damning evidence of developmental sequence, there was no obvious adaptation of later forms from earlier ones; that is, a conventional trunk did not emerge from tadpole legs but was drawn as a round complete contour. This points to the coexistence of two distinct drawing schemas that may vary in use depending on how the child defines the drawing task. Cox and Parkin suggest that tadpole drawings reflect either incomplete mental representations or poorly integrated analysis of more complete representations. On the other hand, the coexistence of conventional and tadpole drawings signals competence or the ability to utilize a more complete mental representation successfully but an inconsistent stance with respect to performance.

Evidence of a more generative sequence was found by Silk and Thomas (1986) when they examined contemporaneous drawings of a man and a dog made by 360 children. They concluded that animal drawings were adaptations of the schema for drawing a human figure because none of the drawings of the human figures contained dog features whereas a number of the dog drawings contained human features (16% of features in 3- to 4-year-olds' drawings and 8% of features in 5- to 6-year-olds' drawings). Furthermore, some of the children rejected their first dog attempts as being too human

("It's turned out to be a man!" p. 406). My qualitative observations in chapter 3 of Claire's adaptation of her circular "face" schema to a dog and the subsequent appearance of two distinct but related dog and girl schemas also suggest derivation from an earlier tadpole figure.

The sensitivity to figure proportions shown by Freeman in younger tadpole drawers persists in children who draw conventional figures. Generally the head is made smaller than the trunk. But some investigators have commented on young children's overestimations of the head in relation to the trunk or to the rest of the figure (Arnheim, 1974; Eng, 1957; Freeman, 1980; Goodnow, 1977, Nash & Harris, 1970; Selfe, 1983). A number of explanations have surfaced. Some emphasize the symbolic importance of the head and face in young children (Di Leo, 1970; Koppitz, 1968; Nash & Harris, 1970); others note that the head must be made large enough to include facial features (Freeman, 1980; Henderson & Thomas cited in Thomas & Silk, 1990; Silk & Thomas, 1988). Freeman (1980) stresses the planning and production sequence, pointing out that the head is almost invariably drawn first and therefore can occupy more space. Depending on the placement of the head on the paper, a child may have relatively less room for the remaining parts of the figure.

Young children show consistent relationships between head and body across free drawings and completion and selection tasks that point to a simple relational rule: Larger heads go with larger bodies (Allik & Laak, 1985). When Selfe (1983) asked children to complete a headless figure, rather than an overestimation of the head relative to the trunk, an underestimation resulted. This effect can be accounted for, however, by the kind of neck used in the incomplete figure task. When a narrow-necked body (such as employed by Selfe) is used the head is underestimated but when a wide-necked or no-necked body is used the head is drawn relatively larger (Thomas & Tsalimi, 1988). Surprisingly, Thomas and Tsalimi (1988) found that with a no-neck body, children between 5 and 8 years drew heads that were approximately in visually correct proportion and that in free drawings children of 3 to 4 years of age showed the least tendency to overestimate the head relative to the trunk.

A second experiment by Thomas and Tsalimi (1988) underscored failures in planning as one chief reason for exaggerating head size in relation to the trunk. Noting that most children drew the head first in free drawings, they manipulated the drawing order of body parts by asking children between the ages 5 and 8 to start with the trunk or the head. When children started with the trunk, the trunk to head ratios were very close to the visual standard; when they started with the head, the head was overestimated. Furthermore, when the drawings were inspected as to whether sufficient space had been left for remaining figure parts, all trunk first drawings had sufficient space but many of the head first drawings did not, confirming the role of planning failures in figure proportions. The head, in fact, has been found to be less consistent in size relative to the trunk across drawings, suggesting that children have difficulty choosing an appropriate scale for their drawings (Allik & Laak, 1985). Planning failures can easily ensue when heads are drawn "too big" for the drawing frame/paper. When predrawn headless figures are used, head size becomes more consistent (Allik & Laak, 1985).

Canonical Representations and Object-Centered Drawings

At the same time as more differentiated drawing schema for figures are evolving children are also developing formulas for drawing them. Originally the construct was called *stereotype* by Gridley (1938), who defined it as a drawing formula developed for a specific topic. Luquet (1935) referred to it as type constancy. It is a drawing schema that assures a minimal standard of likeness across repetitions of a topic and as such refers to a mental model. But stereotypes also encode solutions to production difficulties that a child encounters in rendering certain topics and, in a less creative light, prevent the child from encountering new ones (Luquet, 1935). Once these formulas are worked out to a child's satisfaction, they may continue into adulthood relatively unchanged. For example, between the ages of 8 to 10, I was afflicted with the gender-specific mania for horses. This passion was shared by my younger sister and together we spent hours drawing horses. The horse schema I developed during those few years of diligent practice is today the best drawing of a horse that I can make and the one I most reliably reproduce when my children ask me to draw. At the same time, it is clear that my internal mental representation of a horse far outstrips this simplified drawing schema.

Why do children develop drawing formulas? And at what point

in development do these semiotic equivalents depart from mental representations? When, if ever, are they good approximations of each other? Luquet (1935) defined a stage beginning after the fifth year, called *intellectual realism*, in which a child, having solved some of the fundamental difficulties inherent in organizing a drawing, becomes concerned with depicting what she or he knows about a subject. Some of the most interesting and striking drawing errors are seen during this stage. For example, at this stage children often insist on drawing x-ray treatments of trees in order to show the roots or the contents of a shark's belly to show the prey it has devoured. The child strives to portray the complexity of what she or he can internally represent.

Elements invisible from the child's view of a drawing model are also included if they are integral to defining the subject of the drawing. The handle of a cup, although not seen by the child, will still be included because it defines its "cupness." Likewise in drawing the human figure from memory, the parts that clearly define it as a person are included. These result in somewhat predictable forms that can be interpreted as generic exemplars of a subject class (Freeman, 1972). For Luquet (1935) generic exemplars are tied closely to the child's "internal model." This model is not synonymous with conceptual knowledge but is more accurately "a schema of criterial details" (Freeman, 1972, p. 136) that is an active reconstruction from perceptual experience containing only the essential defining elements – related ideas are shared by many contemporary cognitive theorists (i.e., use of prototype by Cantor & Mischel, 1979, or use of schema by Fiske, 1982). Hochberg (1978) uses the term *canonical forms* to refer to views that best display an object's characteristics, and Freeman (1980) uses *canonical representations* to refer to drawings that result from these generic, internally represented exemplars.

Two observations are closely allied in demonstrating children's preference for using canonical representations. The first has to do with the use of characteristic orientations for different subject matter and contexts. Human figures are almost always shown in front views by young children, and animals are portrayed in side view. In fact, portraying animals in side views is ubiquitous across a variety of cultures and artistic periods (Deregowski, Parker & Dziurawiec, 1996). Ives and Rovet (1979) studied drawings from children age 3 through high school age as well as adults. They noted that although reliable orientations were not produced until a child was 6 years old, all ages had biases toward rendering certain types of subject matter in distinct orientations. Humans and owls were almost always shown in front views, and horses, boats, and cars were shown in side views. However, if children and adults were asked to depict the subject matter in motion, the bias switched to side views for all types of drawings by age 7. Often only part of the human figures and owls were turned, giving a mixed view. There was some decline in the tendency to use these standard orientations in the high school children and adults, perhaps reflecting increased graphic competence. A subsequent experiment demonstrated that these biases were persistent, even when drawers were asked to draw from models that opposed the standard orientation (Ives, 1980). More recently Pinto and Bombi (1996) demonstrated a similar contextual bias for figure drawing. When children ages 4 to 11 were asked to draw a person and a person walking almost all drew a canonical view for the person but 61% drew a profile view for the person walking. The number of children who drew profile views for the person walking increased reliably with age. None of the children younger than age 6 drew a profile, whereas between 75% and 88% of those between 7 and 11 years drew profiles. In a second study, however, 25% of the children age 5 were induced to draw profiles when they had to draw two friends fighting.

The second observation has to do with young children's apparent reluctance to copy a visual model faithfully when features that are not visible from a child's viewpoint are those that unambiguously define structural relationships in the model or define the object itself. First studied by Clarke (1897), this phenomenon has perhaps engendered more research than any other aspect of children's drawings. Clarke presented children with an apple stuck through by a hat pin and found that they ignored the visual appearance in favor of depicting the pin inside the apple. Since then Clarke's observations have been replicated using atypical exemplars of a number of familiar objects (Barrett & Light, 1976; Freeman & Janikoun, 1972).

Drawings that ignore the specific view available to a viewer in favor of unambiguously defining the object have been called *object-centered* to distinguish them from those that are *view-specific*. Light (1985) allies object-centered drawings with intellectual realism but differentiates them from canonical representations because the latter are true generic representations of familiar objects whereas the former also demonstrate knowledge related to novel objects. Freeman distinguishes between the two types of drawings as well but on the basis of performance factors. Object-centered drawings such as Clarke's example result from one type of performance difficulty, the failure to eliminate a line that should be hidden (hidden line elimination); canonical drawings reflect another, the inability to inhibit the underlying habitual generic mental representation (Freeman, 1980).

The fact that children often do not reliably draw a model accurately until age 9 or 10 (Light & Simmons, 1983) suggests an inherent bias toward repeating internal models and knowledge-centered schemas that is not easily overcome even by looking closely at drawing models. Nevertheless, children between the ages 5 and 7 can be influenced to draw either object-centered or view-specific drawings depending on which properties of an array are called to their attention. Reith (1988) noted that children use different strategies in drawing novel or familiar models. In his study of children ages 4 to 9, familiar models elicited more schematic and less visually realistic drawings than novel models. When the model was unfamiliar and children lacked an internal model from which to draw, visual exploration of the model was important in producing more realistic drawings. But his research also demonstrated that internal models of familiar objects can serve as useful guides in planning a drawing when children are asked to depict very complex models.

Allowing children to inspect a model or name the model or emphasizing the function of model parts increases object-centered drawings (Bremmer & Moore, 1984; Krascum, Tregenza & Whitehead, 1996), whereas simultaneously providing children with two contrasting models that draw their attention to specific features of a view increases view-specific drawings. In the classic cup experiment by Freeman and Janikoun (1972) young children ignored the model's orientation and consistently drew the cup with the hidden handle depicted. But if conditions of this experiment are modified so that the visual differences presented in a model are emphasized, view-specific drawings are facilitated. Thus, Davis (1985) found that if a second cup was added, oriented in the canonical position with respect to the original model with occluded handle, object-centered drawings of the original cup were significantly reduced. In this condition children drew the first cup with an occluded handle, the way it was really oriented, and the second cup in the viewed canonical position. Davis used other manipulations to contrast visual differences between paired models that influenced how children drew the models. Replicating the experiment with two glass cups allowed a child to show the first glass cup in its true orientation and the handle as it was seen through the glass; pairing an opaque cup with a sugar bowl promoted an increase in canonical drawings of the cup because the cup had to be distinguished from the handleless sugar bowl. Davis argued that strong visual contrasts call the child's attention to visual differences and pull for view-specific drawings whereas reducing that contrast favors knowledge-based drawings in which the structural description of an object dominates.

Cox has also emphasized that when children's attention is directed to a visual model they make a more careful visual analysis. Cox (1985) was able to improve view-specific drawings by asking children to draw a robber hiding from the police behind a wall. This focused the children's attention on context and they had to draw to communicate that context. In another variant of the contrast paradigm, Crook (1985) changed the context of Clarke's classic experiment by adding two other conditions: In one condition, a single hat pin was broken into two segments that were pushed through the apple until they almost touched, leaving a small gap. In the second, a single pin that changed colors at the halfway point was used. Although the two pin condition decreased the percentage of transparency responses by two-thirds, the single pin with a color change reduced the transparencies altogether. Crook also argued that contexts that draw attention to view-specific aspects of an array produce more accurate drawings. But unlike Cox he did not propose that improvements were a result of stimulating a more careful visual analysis of the array. Instead he emphasized that changes in context require a transformation of the internal representation from which a child draws. In most cases, argued Crook, children's drawings are dominated by their structural description of a scene; often, as has already been suggested, this is congruent with a "best view" or canonical view.

Performance and Competence

A number of influences on young children's drawing performance were demonstrated by the studies reviewed. Freeman emphasized the role planning and production of a drawing have in young children's depictions. Other observers of process in children's drawing have pointed to the early emergence of drawing formulas or stereotypes that might, on the one hand, incorporate successful solutions to production problems a child has had to overcome and, on the other, be representative of generic knowledge a child uses to define a drawing topic. For some drawing topics, particularly of familiar things, this results in canonical depictions that portray the drawing subject in its "best" or most easily recognized view. In other cases, the portrayal may reflect the criterial knowledge a child uses to define an object or relationships among objects. In this case the resultant drawing is said to be object-centered. Under certain conditions, children's normal bias to produce these types of drawings is overcome and they construct view-specific drawings that indicate greater competence. Giving them unfamiliar visual models or models in which strong visual contrasts or contexts demand they produce a different type of drawing elicits more view-specific drawings. A key element appears to be getting the child to pay closer visual attention to the model, although changing the internal representation may be just as crucial. What is clear is that young children's performance in this area usually underestimates their competence.

This makes it probable that when a child draws spontaneously, frequently repeated subjects taken from memory will be based on generic object knowledge and a child's internal mental representations will combine with well-rehearsed drawing formulas to produce the drawing. It is likely that to overcome this strong bias to produce canonical and/or object-centered drawings, a child would have to make a more exacting visual analysis of objects in the world, an analysis that could transform a generic internal drawing model into a view-specific drawing model. In addition, a child would have to use these more specific memory representations as guides during the development of drawing schemas. Studying the spontaneous drawings of individual children, therefore, is unlikely to reveal how competent a child really is. It may tell us a great deal about the approach and processes a child uses when she does draw.

Since our interest is in the processes talented and less talented children use when drawing, studying how children treat drawings that are highly susceptible to such biases should be revealing. The human figure is arguably one drawing subject for which the canonical bias is strong. Accordingly, this chapter examines how spontaneous drawings of the human figure change with age in talented and less talented children. It begins by looking at the development of figure proportion in drawings of the human figure. It then looks at how children begin to modify figure orientations to index departures from the canonical orientation for human figures. One question is, Do children modify their drawing schema of the human figure as normative developmental changes in mental representations, visual exploration and analysis, and view-specific understanding occur, or is the canonical bias sufficiently strong that canonical orientations persist well beyond normative changes in underlying competence?

There are limits to my approach. One is that the substantial literature on normative development is used to infer that a competence is or is not available to children. Although there are those who would disagree with this approach, it seems reasonable to assume that when a preponderance of normative evidence exists, norms can serve as adequate benchmarks in assessing specific competences of children (e.g., Gesell & Armatruda, 1941; Uzgiris & Hunt, 1975) who appear to function within the normal range of intelligence or even groups of individuals (e.g., Greenfield, 1966). Second, use of spontaneous drawings does not control the child's intention with the result that talented children are more likely to draw complex scenes that require figures to be in motion. As reviewed, research demonstrates that when a drawing schema is disturbed by intention, canonical forms are often abandoned. The purpose, however, of building a theoretical model of skill differences is not necessarily compromised, since talented children may choose more challenging contexts for their drawings precisely because they are more likely to be successful in producing the corresponding drawing. If children have continually modified their drawing schemas to accord with changes in underlying competences, they will "know" and be able to make use of "how a drawing goes." Less talented children are likely to fall back on simpler contexts because although they may know as much about objects such as the human figure, they know less about "how a drawing goes"; that is, drawing procedures may have been modified by developmental changes in generic object knowledge but not by exacting visual analysis or changes in understanding of view-specific information.

DEVELOPMENT OF FIGURE PROPORTIONS

Figure Proportions in the Spontaneous Drawings Study

Classical Greek artists developed a set of proportional relationships between the parts of the body that lent elegance, grace, and dignity to the human figure. The head was made slightly smaller in relation to the total figure than in nature. Using the head as the unit of measurement, classical proportions establish the figure at 8 heads tall, whereas in nature it is approximately 7.5 heads. Of course children cannot be expected to adopt the classical Greek standard without specific instruction. Nature, however, can act as an approximate guide, through the child's continuous experiences of looking at people, drawing, and looking at their drawings. The proportions children used in their drawings, therefore, were contrasted with measurements taken from nature. Average ratios were calculated to serve as standards based on making the same kind of measurements used for drawings (see Milbrath, 1982) on three photographs of people. Male and female proportions differ slightly so only the averages for males were used as a standard. The proportional relationships based on the classical (Sheppard, 1991) and the natural standard appear in Table 4.1.

Not all children in the study submitted human figure drawings suitable for measurement. At the very least, it had to be possible to measure the head and total figure. A number of the figures, especially those by the younger children, lacked arms or were clothed with dresses, making it impossible to determine the torso and leg measurements, so fewer drawings were available for these measurements. Measurements of "tadpole man" were not included because of the ambiguity about whether or not the "head" counts as a head or a body. The following questions were of interest: How closely do the figure proportions children adopt approximate natural proportions? Average ratios taken from the male photographs were used as population parameters in a series of z statistics to test the significance of deviations from nature's standard. Do the figure proportions children use change with age and are talented children better at estimating natural figure proportions? Analyses of variance were used to answer these last two questions.

Cross-Sectional Sample. Forty-five children had drawings with human figures that could be reliably measured: 19 of the 30 children in the talented group and 26 of the 75 children in the less talented group. The greater number from talented children may reflect some sampling bias because 13% of the drawings from less talented children age 10 and under were obtained from the gingerbread house art contest so human figures were less frequent in these drawings. Table 4.1 presents the ratios for the total sample and for each group by age as contrasted with nature's standard. In the total sample the size of the head in relation to the figure ($F_{2,39} = 9.67$, $p < .01$) and to the trunk ($F_{2,35} = 4.81$, $p < .05$) decreased significantly with age, closely approximating nature's proportions by ages 11 to 14. Other relationships evolved in the opposite direction. Younger children drew the trunk, arms, and legs too small in relation to the body, and older children increased their size relative to the total figure.

Contrasting each talent group with nature's standards showed that talented children began drawing proportional relationships close to those seen in nature at younger ages than less talented children. Legs were drawn in approximate natural proportions between ages 4 to 6; arms approximated natural proportions by the ages 7 to 10. Less talented children had more trouble obtaining natural proportions for the limbs and deviated significantly from nature's proportions at all ages. Presumably if figures had been obtained from less talented children older than age 14, proportions would have eventually approximated those found in nature, since most changes with age were in the proper direction. When the two talent groups were compared with each other significant differences were found in the head to body ($F_{1,39} = 5.18$, $p = .028$), arm to body ($F_{1,36} = 4.30$, $p = .045$), and leg to body ($F_{1,34} = 7.08$, $p = .01$) ratios. Less talented children were more prone to overestimating the size of the head and underestimating the size of the arms and legs relative to the body whereas talented children more closely approximated natural proportions.

Longitudinal Talented Sample. A total of 86 drawings produced by seven children had figures suitable for measurement. One child specialized in dinosaurs and cartoons and produced only two human-

TABLE 4.1
HUMAN FIGURE PROPORTIONS

	Cross-Sectional Sample			Longitudinal Sample	Standard Proportions	
	Total Sample	Less Talented	Talented	Talented	Natural[a]	Greek
Head to Trunk Ratio						
3–6 years	0.8707	1.0683**	0.673**	0.6549**	0.3364	0.3636
7–10 years	0.6613	0.739**	0.5393**	0.4645		
11–14 years	0.4084	0.4545	0.3545	0.3939		
Head to Body Ratio						
3–6 years	0.308	0.357**	0.2508**	0.2255**	0.1403	0.125
7–10 years	0.2184	0.2349**	0.1923*	0.1711		
11–14 years	0.1605	0.1787	0.1364	0.1544		
Trunk to Body Ratio						
3–6 years	0.3085	0.2654**	0.3601*	0.3707*	0.4195	0.3438
7–10 years	0.3761	0.3829	0.3655*	0.3747*		
11–14 years	0.3979	0.3947	0.4016	0.3971		
Arm to Body Ratio						
3–6 years	0.2935	0.2894**	0.2992*	0.3402**	0.425	0.4375
7–10 years	0.3891	0.3252**	0.5064	0.3509**		
11–14 years	0.4061	0.3773*	0.4522	0.398		
Leg to Body Ratio						
3–6 years	0.3557	0.2845**	0.4626	0.3584**	0.4619	0.5
7–10 years	0.3993	0.3813**	0.4275	0.4541		
11–14 years	0.4041	0.3775**	0.4306	0.4396		

[a] Natural proportion based on adult male.
* Significance of z score deviations $p \leq .05$. ** $p \leq .01$.

like figures during the study period, so he was not included. A child's proportion scores were averaged over each age block for analysis. The total number of observations, therefore, was 21 for the three age blocks. When the proportional values for each age block were compared with natural proportions most differences were consistent with those observed for the talented cross-sectional sample (Table 4.1). In some instances these children's proportions approximated the standard sooner than the cross-sectional sample, for example, the head to trunk and head to body ratios. In other instances, they were a little slower, for example, the limb to figure ratios. Generally, however, in both samples the limb to figure ratios were the most variable. In part this was because they were more difficult to measure if rotated or posed in action. In the drawings from the talented sample this was usually the case. Developmental changes were the same as those observed for the cross-sectional sample. Head to torso ($F_{2,14} = 6.29$, $p = .009$) and head to figure ($F_{2,14} =; 6.77$, $p = .009$) ratios decreased significantly and leg to figure ratio increased significantly ($F_{2,14} = 7.64$, $p = .006$) over the three age blocks.

Summary. Developmental changes in figure proportions showed the same general trend in both talent groups. As children got older, their figure proportions increasingly approximated proportions found in nature. The rate of development in the two talent groups, however, was different. Figure proportions in the drawings of talented children were close to nature's standards 2 to 3 years earlier than those in drawings of less talented children. Even the oldest less talented children observed failed to achieve natural proportions for limbs. Presumably if drawings from older less talented adolescents had been sampled these proportions would eventually have reached those found in nature because those for the other figure relationships did. This suggests that only the rate of development is affected by talent for figure drawing proportions.

A child's general visual experience with natural proportions is likely a key aspect in development of natural figure drawing proportions. As a child's visual analytic abilities mature, the figure proportions in her drawings improve. The results suggest that this aspect of the human form is accessible to both talented and less talented children at ages that correspond to the marked improvements in looking strategies that appear with cognitive development (e.g., Vurpillot, 1976). But because talented children both are more attuned to their visual world and draw more, they are likely to make a better visual analysis of their drawings. Therefore, their drawings more immediately reflect the development of cognitive capabilities to direct perceptual analysis of visual stimuli.

It can also be speculated that the general accessibility of proportionality in all children results because it is a dimension available from the general structural descriptions of part–whole relationship encoded in implicit memory. Research by Schacter and Cooper (reviewed in Cooper, 1991; also see Schacter, 1990) indicates that global structural information about objects is encoded in implicit memory whereas specific features, meaning, and function of objects are coded in explicit memory. In this respect proportionality might be similar to general structural characteristics of the human figure such as shape; both improve or become more differentiated with age. Presumably improvement results from a better visual analysis based on more systematic part–whole comparisons that appear with cognitive development. Cognition appears to play an enabling role in both talent groups, but talented children are able to make more immediate use of it whereas less talented children lag behind. This absence of reliable differences in the developmental trajectory of proportionality for the two types of drawers stands in marked contrast to the manner in which the two groups attempt and achieve rotations of the human figure as they mature.

DEVELOPMENT OF FIGURE ROTATION IN THE SPONTANEOUS DRAWINGS STUDIES

Description of Changes with Age in Human Figure Orientation

More of the drawings had human figures suitable for studying figure orientation than figure proportions. In the cross-sectional sample 66 of the 105 children's drawings had a human figure; 39 were from less talented children and 27 were from talented children. Because so many drawings were sampled from the longitudinally studied talented children, drawings with human figures were obtained from every child for most study years. Rather than exclude the child who primarily drew dinosaurs and cartoons from this part of the study, the humanlike figures in his cartoons and fantasy drawings were scored for figure rotations.

In brief, human figures were scored for the following orientations: front (180 degrees), profile (90 and 270 degrees), three-quarter (45, 135, 225, 315 degrees), back (360 degrees), or mixed views (see Milbrath, 1982). Mixed views included front and profile mix, pure profile mixtures, front and three-quarter mix, profile and three-quarter mix, and pure three-quarter mixes. Each figure in a drawing received a category score so it was possible for a drawing to receive more than one score. Bearing this in mind, changes with age in front views, profile views, and three-quarter views of people are shown for all three samples in Table 4.2. Back views were very rare in all samples but did occur in drawing of talented children (Figure 4.1a & b and see Figure 1.4). They are not included in the tables and analyses.

Cross-Sectional Sample. By following the changes summarized in 2-year intervals in Table 4.2, it can be seen that front views declined in both the talented and less talented children after the age of 10. A greater percentage of the youngest talented children ages 3 and 4 were drawing human figures. It might be tempting to assume that less talented children were using another form of figure orientation, but this was not the case. There were just fewer human figures in the early drawings of these children. In part this reflects the sampling bias for younger children discussed in the previous section. But the relative infrequency of human figures was also found in drawings of older less talented children even though some of them were beginning to draw more complex rotations. Only a small percentage of less talented children at any age drew profiles or profile mixes or three-quarter mixes and pure three-quarter rotations.

Table 4.2 indicates another aspect of difference in drawing from the two talent groups. Talented children often drew more than one human figure with each in a different orientation. All talented 3- to 4-year-olds drew a figure in front view but half also drew a figure in mixed profile view. Likewise, all talented 9- to 10-year-olds drew one figure in profile but two-thirds also drew a figure in front view and one-third drew one or several varieties of three-quarter view. In other words, many children in this group were producing more than one type of figure orientation in a drawing. This was not the case for less talented children. A few older less talented children's drawings did have more than one type of figure orientation. But a simple count indicates it was only 24% of the figure drawings and

TABLE 4.2
PERCENTAGE OF CHILDREN DRAWING HUMAN FIGURE ORIENTATIONS

	Ages 3–4	Ages 5–6	Ages 7–8	Ages 9–10	Ages 11–12	Ages 13–14
Cross-Sectional Less Talented	(n = 12)	(n = 11)	(n = 13)	(n = 14)	(n = 13)	(n = 12)
Front View	41.7	36.4	38.4	50	23	25
Profile	8.3	18.2	15.4	14.3	15.4	8.3
Profile Mix	0	9.1	7.7	14.3	15.4	0
Three-Quarter Profile/Front Mixes	0	0	0	14.3	7.7	8.3
Three-Quarter	0	0	0	0	0	16.7
Pure Three-Quarter Mixes	0	0	0	0	0	0
Cross-Sectional Talented	(n = 4)	(n = 4)	(n = 5)	(n = 6)	(n = 5)	(n = 6)
Front View	100	50	60	66.7	20	33.3
Profile	0	25	20	100	20	16.7
Profile Mix	50	0	60	0	20	0
Three-Quarter Profile/Front Mixes	0	0	20	33	20	50
Three-Quarter	0	0	0	33	20	50
Pure Three-Quarter Mixes	0	0	0	0	0	0
Longitudinal Talented	(n = 6)	(n = 8)	(n = 8)	(n = 8)	(n = 8)	(n = 7)
Front View	100	100	87.5	75	75	100
Profile	66.7	62.5	87.5	87.5	75	50
Profile Mix	50	75	37.5	37.5	0	0
Three-Quarter Profile/Front Mixes	16.7	50	75	87.5	100	87.5
Three-Quarter	0	25	62.5	75	75	100
Pure Three-Quarter Mixes	0	0	25	37.5	62.5	42.9

Figure 4.1a. Katy E. age 5, talented child, early back view.

Figure 4.1b. Claire age 11, talented child studied longitudinally, back views.

of these over half (56%) were drawings of front and profile views. In contrast 80% of the talented children's drawings had more than one type of figure orientation and only one-third of those were drawings of front and profile views exclusively. It is worth remembering, however, that this observation is based on a limited sample of drawings from any given child, most often only one. Therefore, a child's performance on a particular drawing cannot accurately index all that she or he is capable of doing.

Figure 4.2a. Tyler L. age 4; 8, talented child, mixed front and profile view.

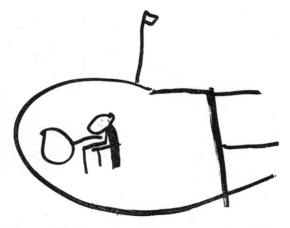

Figure 4.2b. Less talented boy age 4, early profile.

A greater percentage of younger talented children than less talented children were able to draw profiles (Table 4.2). These early profiles were also qualitatively different. The talented children ages 3 to 4 drew profile mixtures (see Figure 4.2a), combining a profile with a front view, whereas the one less talented child who was able to do so drew a uniform profile (Figure 4.2b). It is my view that profile front mixed views mark an important step in the eventual

Figure 4.3a. Katy E. age 5, talented child profile view.

accomplishment of three-quarter rotations. This idea is treated at greater length in the single case studies of talented children at the end of the chapter. At age 5 to 6, talented children began to draw uniform profiles (Figure 4.3a) and by age 7 to 8 parts of the figure were drawn in three-quarter rotation (Figure 4.3b). Profiles or profile mixtures increased with age in the talented group until by age 9 to 10 all of the children were drawing people in profile. Some of the 9- and 10-year-old talented children also drew pure three-quarter views and by early adolescence, talented children began to show a preference for representing the human figure in three-quarter and mixed three-quarter views (Figure 4.4a & b). In contrast, most of the less talented children drew the human figure in front view at all ages and very few drew other types of rotations. In general, most of these children appeared unable or unwilling to produce any other but the canonical orientation of the human figure. At ages 5 to 6 and older, a few less talented children did draw profiles and profile mixtures (Figure 4.5a & b) and some older children began to draw parts of the figure in mixed three-quarter rotations (Figures 4.6, 4.7a & b). Only two of the oldest less talented children drew a figure in uniform three-quarter view.

The changes in figure orientation found with age for these children can be compared with those reported by a group of researchers

Figure 4.3b. Gabriel S. age 7; 5, talented child, mixed three-quarter with front and profile, mixed profile, and profile views.

working at the Cleveland Museum of Art. They studied 1,015 children ages 6 through 15 who participated in the Saturday art classes offered at the museum (Lark-Horowitz et al., 1973). Only a small percentage of the children younger than age 10 were considered exceptionally talented. Their findings are very comparable to those for this study. They found that in their total sample, profiles were not attempted until after age 6 and thereafter increased steadily, replacing front views by age 10. Front views, however, became the preferred view again after age 10 as children began to discard their stereotyped schematic drawings and attempted to draw figures true to appearance. In this study, front views were very frequent up until age 10 and thereafter were replaced by mixed profile or three-quarter views in the talented sample. Mixed front and profile views

Figure 4.4a. Victor N. age 13, talented child, mixed three-quarter view with front view.

Figure 4.4b. Bryan P. age 13, talented child, three-quarter face view.

Figure 4.5a. Less talented boy age 5, mixed front and profile views.

Figure 4.5b. Less talented child age 6; 3, profile view.

of the type seen in this study were observed in the drawings of children in their study between ages 6 to 8 and pure three-quarter views were not seen until age 9, but were always rare and limited to a small number of children. This time course agrees well with the data presented here.

Longitudinal Talented Sample. The drawings of these talented children are more instructive in tracing the development of figure orientation and give a more detailed picture of talented children's use of figure rotation. This is because there were many more drawings per year from each child so a much broader range of figure orien-

Figure 4.6. Less talented girl age 9, mixed three-quarter with front and mixed front and profile.

tations was available for study. Table 4.2 indicates that every talented child in this sample was also capable of a variety of different types of figure orientations. One striking difference is that front views remained consistently well represented in these children's drawings at all ages with only a slight decline between ages 7 and 12. The appearance of portraiture during adolescence accounted for many of the front views by older children (Figure 4.8).

Profiles and profile mixtures appeared very early in drawings by these children and at a startlingly high rate: Well over half the children ages 3 to 4 drew profiles. Profile mixtures peaked during ages 5 to 6, giving way to uniform profile views and to three-quarter front or profile mixtures by age 7 (Figure 4.9). Some children began three-quarter rotations of figure parts as early as age 5 or 6 but more typically pure three-quarter rotations and mixed views appeared by ages 7 to 8. Between ages 11 and 12, all of these children drew at least one human figure in three-quarter mixture with profiles or front views and by ages 13 to 14, all drew a full three-quarter view (Figure 4.10 a & b). The fact that profile mixtures give way to full profiles and that front and profile three-quarter

Figure 4.7a. Less talented boy age 12, mixed three-quarter with front.

Figure 4.7b. Less talented girl age 14, mixed three-quarter with front and profile.

Figure 4.8. Kate age 14, talented child studied longitudinally, portrait.

mixtures precede but are eventually overshadowed by full three-quarter views argues for the importance of these types of mixed views in the development of more uniform treatments of the figure. For example, they represent trial and error experimentation with figure orientation that eventually leads to development of drawing procedures that allow for greater consistency in producing profile and three-quarter orientations of the human figure. Pure three-quarter mixtures are ontogenetically the last type of figure rotation to appear.

Canonical Views of Human and Animal Figures

Animal and human figures are both well represented in the spontaneous drawings of children in both the cross-sectional and longitudinal samples. The discussion of the development of rotations of the human figure demonstrates that both talented samples were capable of a great deal of flexibility in human figure orientation at quite young ages. Front views as the canonical presentation of the

Figure 4.9. Claire age 7, talented child studied longitudinally, figure parts in three-quarter with profile and front views (dancing girl).

human figure were prevalent in all children of any age, but few of the less talented children of any age spontaneously attempted any other type of human figure orientation. Data gathered on rotations of animals tell a similar story. For most animals the canonical orientation is a profile. Although talented children in both samples drew animals in profile they also were able to draw them in front and three-quarter rotations. Less talented children rarely if ever drew animals in any other but the canonical orientation. In Table 4.3 the percentage of children by age drawing animals in the different rotations is shown.

Talented children were less likely to draw animals in canonical orientations. They were able to vary the orientations of animals, adapting them to the more complex and detailed scenes they chose as subjects for their drawings. Although analysis of the repetition

Figure 4.10a. Hondo age 12, talented child studied longitudinally, three-quarter views.

Figure 4.10b. Peregrine age 11, talented child studied longitudinally, three-quarter views.

The Representation of Form and Space

TABLE 4.3
PERCENTAGE OF CHILDREN DRAWING ANIMAL FIGURE BY ORIENTATION

	Ages 3–4	Ages 5–6	Ages 7–8	Ages 9–10	Ages 11–12	Ages 13–14
Cross-Sectional Less Talented	($n = 12$)	($n = 11$)	($n = 13$)	($n = 14$)	($n = 13$)	($n = 12$)
Profile	8.3	27	39	36	15	0
Front Views	1	9.1	0	0	15	0
Three-Quarter	0	0	0	7	0	0
Cross-Sectional Talented	($n = 4$)	($n = 4$)	($n = 5$)	($n = 6$)	($n = 5$)	($n = 6$)
Profile	25	50	60	50	20	0
Front Views	25	0	40	17	0	0
Three-Quarter	0	0	0	33	0	17
Longitudinal Talented	($n = 6$)	($n = 8$)	($n = 8$)	($n = 8$)	($n = 8$)	($n = 7$)
Profile	67	63	75	63	63	14
Front Views	17	38	38	25	25	14
Three-Quarter	0	13	13	50	63	43

in stereotyped schemas of figures is not possible for the cross-sectional sample, one can speculate that less talented children are prone to repeat a well-rehearsed canonical figure schema over many drawings. Drawings from the longitudinal talented sample, however, indicate that figures do not get schematized as stereotypes, not even with respect to orientation. Figures are drawn in a wide array of orientations by the same child and in the same drawing. This will be demonstrated in the case studies at the end of this chapter.

Statistical Analysis of Human Figure Rotation

Loglinear analyses were used to study the effects of age and talent on children's ability to rotate the human figure (see Appendixes 4.1–4.3). Based on the developmental chronology just described, the original data were rescored into a four level rotation scale from the simplest to the more advanced rotations and each drawing was given only one score to indicate the highest-level rotation in the drawing (see Appendix 2.1). Briefly, the four levels in order were (1) front views, (2) profile front view mixes and profiles, (3) three-quarter front or profile view mixes, and (4) pure three-quarter views.

Cross-Sectional Sample. Since a total of only 66 figure drawings were available, age and talent were analyzed separately. Reference to Table 4.4 shows that when the highest level rotation achieved by a child in a drawing is considered, talented children produced significantly more mixed three-quarter views and less talented children produced significantly more front views. The age of a child also strongly influenced the level of rotation achieved in a drawing. Children between the ages of 3 and 6 primarily drew the human figure in front view whereas those between the ages of 11 and 14 were more likely to draw three-quarter rotations but less likely to draw profile and profile front mixes. Although changes with age in three-quarter profile or front view mixes were not significant, reference to Table 4.4 indicates that only one talented child between ages 3 and 6 accomplished this rotation whereas approximately 30% of all older children drew them.

Table 4.4 suggests that age may have had a different influence on the development of rotation in talented and less talented children. Although there were too few children in this analysis to ex-

TABLE 4.4
PERCENTAGE OF CHILDREN IN CROSS-SECTIONAL SAMPLE AT
HIGHEST LEVEL ROTATION

Age in Years		Less Talented	Talented	Total Sample
		(n = 11)	(n = 7)	(n = 18)
3 to 6	Front	54	50	56*
	Profile + Profile Mix	46	25	39
	Three-Quarter Front/Profile Mix	0	14	5
	Pure Three-Quarter	0	0	0
		(n = 14)	(n = 10)	(n = 24)
7 to 10	Front	36	10	25
	Profile + Profile Mix	50	40	46
	Three-Quarter Front/Profile Mix	14	30	21
	Pure Three-Quarter	0	20	8
		(n = 14)	(n = 10)	(n = 24)
11 to 14	Front	43	0	25
	Profile + Profile Mix	21	10	17*
	Three-Quarter Front/Profile Mix	14	50	29
	Pure Three-Quarter	21	40	29**
		(n = 39)	(n = 27)	(n = 66)
All Ages	Front	44*	19	33
	Profile + Profile Mix	38	26	33
	Three-Quarter Front/Profile Mix	10	33*	20
	Pure Three-Quarter	8	22	14

*$p \leq .05.$ **$p \leq .01.$

plore the interaction between talent ability and age, the effects of age could be analyzed in the less talented group independently. Remarkably, when this was done, the influence of age was no longer significant. Reference to Table 4.4 indicates why this is the case. Eighty-two percent of the less talented children used either front or profile figure orientations regardless of age. Even 64% of the less talented children ages 11 to 14 were drawing front and profile views. This supports a conclusion that changes with age found in the whole cross-sectional sample are largely the result of developments in talented children. Inspection of percentages in Table 4.4 for talented children indicates that they are consistent with this conclusion.

Summary. Less talented children at all ages were primarily drawing human and animal figures in their canonical orientations but some children, even young children, also drew the human figure in profile. In Figure 4.2b, an example of an early profile from a less talented child shows a figure piloting a rocket. This demonstrates young children are capable of simple variations in figure orientation in order to convey a particular topic (Golomb, 1992). Nevertheless, such modifications were relatively simple when contrasted with those made by talented children of comparable ages. For example, the profile shown in Figure 4.2b and the mixed profile shown in Figure 4.5a by less talented children only involve a simple displacement of arm positions. Figure 4.5b by a less talented child shows more complex modifications including partially modifying the head and torso contour, displacing the nose, hiding one arm, and putting the other in the middle of the torso. True distortions of the figure contours and modification of internal parts of the figure such as appear in Figure 4.3a, however, were not evident until less talented children were older. These observations are consistent with those by Pinto and Bombi (1996). They studied the types of modifications children of different ages used to achieve a profile. In their study children of 4 and 5 years were unable to draw a profile. Children ages 6 and 7 did draw profiles but used very simple modifications, for example, displacing parts of the face such as the nose while conserving the front view form. Children ages 8 and 9 began to modify the contour of the figure but only the oldest children studied, ages 10 and 11, used combinations of hiding figure parts and modifying figure contour and internal parts.

When talent groups were contrasted, talented children showed greater use of three-quarter mixed views and less talented children showed greater use of front views. In fact, more advanced figure rotations did not develop appreciably in less talented children. A few older less talented children varied figure orientations, but most continued to draw front views or at best profiles. The permanence of these simpler figure orientations was supported by the absence of reliable age-related changes in figure rotation for these children. These children did not appear to be catching up to talented children as they got older. In contrast, analysis of the entire cross-sectional sample indicated pure three-quarter views increased in drawings of older children and profile or profile mixes decreased. Table 4.4 shows that talented children were responsible for these age-related changes. Overall, the developmental trajectory indicated for talented children was an increase in the variety of figure rotations as children matured. Older talented children were able to abandon canonical orientations and distort the figure to portray more natural figure poses. Visual reference to the presented drawings suggests further that less talented children were most concerned with conveying structural information about the human figure. They made few modifications that distorted the figure. The kinds of modifications made by even very young talented children showed no such concern. Instead they appeared to convey specific visual views of the human figure.

Longitudinal Sample. The longitudinal sample allows a better exploration of the variety of figure rotations in talented children. Although the children studied were few in number, the many drawings collected afford ample opportunity to observe the range in their ability to rotate figures. In order to capitalize on the many drawings available, the data were divided as described in Appendix 2.1. This resulted in 78 instead of 90 data points because two subjects were missing human figures for 1 year and a third subject rarely if ever drew human figures.

The age-related changes indicated for the cross-sectional talented sample were confirmed by this sample. Age had a strong influence on the types of rotations these talented children drew (Appendix 4.3). When they were between ages 3 and 6, they were primarily drawing front (33%) or profile and profile mixed views (50%). After age 7, they began to include three-quarter mixes and three-quarter views in more of their drawings. Sixty-one percent of the drawings from ages 7 to 10 and 81% from ages 11 to 14 included at least one figure drawn in pure three-quarter view. Although these talented children appeared to show a more rapid rate of development than the talented cross-sectional sample, the end points are very similar with approximately 90% of older talented children drawing three-quarter rotations.

Scaling the rotations of the children's figure drawings obscures the fact that the longitudinal talented children did continue to use rotation types attained at earlier ages throughout the study period. The percentage of children at each 2-year interval who used the different types of figure rotations is presented in Table 4.2. Although the major shift from profile to three-quarter views suggested by the loglinear analysis is still evident, the dominance of front views over other types of views and the continued use of profiles even in adolescence are hidden when the data are scaled. Front and profile views continue to play a major role in the drawings of these children. Another noteworthy feature mentioned already is the early peak in mixed front and profile views at 5 to 6 years of age and their subsequent decline. This is of interest because these drawings may represent an important transition between front or profile views and three-quarter rotated views. This transition is examined in the case studies of the development of figure rotation.

CASE STUDIES OF THE DEVELOPMENT OF ROTATION IN TALENTED CHILDREN

In studying the evolution of figure drawing, it became apparent that there were at least two developmental lines for arriving at rotated views in talented children. In the more typical case, exemplified by Kate, mixed front and profile views preceded any attempts at three-quarter rotations. By the time Kate was 6 years old she had already mastered front views and uniform profiles. In Figure 4.11, Kate began mixing front and profile views in this view of a dancer drawn at age 6. The dancer is primarily drawn in front view but one leg is in profile. Kate is not attempting to rotate the figure but merely intends to suggest a dance step. Notice, however, that she appears completely comfortable distorting the oval of the face in order to portray the dancer lifting her face upward. The following year, in Figure 4.12a, Kate draws a highly imaginative and artistic composition in which a rotated look for the protagonist seems the objective. This is one of Kate's early attempts to rotate the figure and the result is a figure that resembles a three-quarter rotated view. Closer inspection of a detail of the figure (Figure 4.12b), however, reveals that the view is three-quarter in appearance only: a semblance created by amalgamating a front and a profile view. The detail of the young artist (painting a portrait of an artist) shows that the rotated look is obtained by coupling a front torso view with a profile view of the legs. The following year Kate shows consistent mastery of rotation and complete familiarity with the necessary distortions of the human figure needed to portray a three-quarter figure rotation. Figure 4.13, a detailed drawing of a woman playing the harpsichord as a French courtier looks on, dem-

Figure 4.11. Kate age 6, talented child studied longitudinally, front profile mixed view.

Figure 4.12a. Kate age 7, talented child studied longitudinally, front profile mixed view to give three-quarter rotated appearance.

Figure 4.12b. Detail of figure.

onstrates the sensitivity and skill this talented child has with her subject matter and her rapid progress in three-quarter rotations.

Nor was this method of arriving at rotation unique to Kate. Examples from Claire (Figure 4.14a) and Daniel (Figure 4.15a) at slightly older ages show a similar practice. Both figures, but particularly the one drawn by Claire, give the viewer a sensation that the figure is turned in a three-quarter pose without disturbing its basic structure. Distortions in the figure that accompany true rotations, although possible in theory by age 7 or 8 (discussed later), can compromise the communication of basic figure structure. It is possible that, like their less talented peers who rarely if ever distort the human figure in the service of rotation, these children are still strongly influenced by their structural knowledge of the human fig-

Figure 4.13. Kate age 8, talented child studied longitudinally, three-quarter and back views.

ure and therefore find it difficult to violate a canonical portrayal of that knowledge. In that sense, their spontaneous drawings are still object-centered. Difficulties in producing these types of figures associated with planning a drawing or generating appropriate drawing procedures are much less likely to be influencing these children because they already have excellent control over line and form.

By age 10 Claire is able to outline clearly the distortions related to the portrayal of a figure partially rotated in three-quarter view (Figure 4.14b). Daniel accomplished the three-quarter rotation at a slightly older age. In Figure 4.15b, drawn at age 12, Daniel depicts one figure primarily in three-quarter rotation and begins to experiment with portraying dynamic actions. Drawings from the following year show that he has begun to practice the human figure in different action stances and orientations.

The second method of arriving at rotated views takes its lead from the child's internal model. Most children, especially younger children, do not draw from live models. They approach drawing from their imagination and rely on their ability to imagine what objects look like in static, moving, and rotated states. In this case, the imagined or internal model includes both conceptual knowledge and the visualized image. For the most part, talented children studied longitudinally reported that they did use internal visualizations

Figure 4.14a. Claire age 9, talented child studied longitudinally, front profile mixed view to give three-quarter rotated appearance.

Figure 4.15a. Daniel age 10, talented child studied longitudinally, front pro-file mixed view to give three-quarter rotated appearance.

Figure 4.14b. Claire age 10, three-quarter view.

Figure 4.15b. Daniel age 12, three-quarter view and mixed views.

of objects when drawing but the degree of reliance on such mental images varied. Kate reported that she drew from a "picture" in her mind, sometimes making changes but usually directly copying her visualized image. Hondo reported using a detailed mental image when drawing, particularly if the view was a difficult one. Claire said she pictured certain parts of a drawing in her mind but usually not the whole thing. But since these children were first interviewed around age 10 or 11, when their graphic vocabulary was already well developed, it is difficult to know how much they had relied on concrete visual images during their earlier years.

One case was much clearer; Joel at age 11 reported drawing from both live models and pictures but most drawings were from images in his own mind. In his case the transition from front or profile views to three-quarter views was less laborious and more sudden than the sequence described previously. Prior to the age of 7, Joel produced many drawings of the variety seen in Figure 4.16a showing stiffly posed animal family groups. Close to 50 such drawings were saved by Joel's family and shown to the author. After age 7, there was an abrupt shift in the character of Joel's drawings. Figure 4.16b shows this new variation. The theme, an animal family, has not changed but now the figures are animated and in motion. Rotation is evident in the position of the mother dinosaur's angry face, the father dinosaur's torso and legs, and the difficult view of the father's curved tail. In addition a background and foreground that are differentiated by a ground line and by other details appear.

How can this transition be accomplished so abruptly? One possibility is that Joel relied primarily on a visualized mental image for his drawings, an image that is perhaps reconstructed from visual memories of other dinosaur portrayals, including in this instance cartoons (see Milbrath, 1995). When Joel was young these images may have been static, like the drawing in Figure 4.16a. But as Joel's ability to think and reason developed from earlier preoperational to concrete operational thought, so would his ability to manipulate and move these images. This development in cognition appears to be directly reflected in the change in his drawings between ages 6 and 7 (Figure 4.16b).

Language use between ages 1½ and 2 years is usually taken as evidence that a child has internalized a mental representation of the world (Bretherton, 1984; Piaget, 1951). According to Piaget (Piaget & Inhelder, 1971), the early internalized representation is limited

Figure 4.16a. Joel age 6, talented child studied longitudinally, profile views. Figure 4.16a appeared first in *The Development of Artistically Gifted Children,* edited by C. Golomb, 1995, Hillsdale, N.J.: Lawrence Erlbaum Assoc. Reprinted with permission.

to a highly schematized static representation until a child reaches concrete reasoning at 7 or 8 years of age. For example, even a simple object such as a pencil can only be drawn either upright or on its side at its full extent, that is, in the states showing the beginning and end of its rotation. However, when a child advances to concrete operational thought, around 7 or 8, she or he gains the ability to imagine objects in motion and the transformations of ap-

Figure 4.16b. Joel age 7, three-quarter mixed views. Figure 4.16b appeared first in *The Development of Artistically Gifted Children*, edited by C. Golomb, 1995, Hillsdale, N.J.: Lawrence Erlbaum Assoc. Reprinted with permission.

parent views that accompany rotation of figures and objects become possible. The critical mental processes necessary for dynamic representation of movement and rotation include the ability to think about displacements (movement) and transformations (rotation) by linking static states in succession (Piaget & Inhelder, 1971). This mental process has its analogy in Winsor McKay's historical first animation, "Gertie the Dinosaur," which was made by temporally linking together many drawings, each representing a slightly different static state of the figures.

Crucial in this process are the ability to place images in a given order of succession and to anticipate and make deductions about relationships as they undergo transformations. Alterations in apparent shape that accompany rotations of objects may present a problem similar to conservation for children. In order to recognize that transformed quantities are the same as the original quantities (conservation of quantity), a child must be able to deduce from her or his experiences with environmental constancy across transformations the compensations that allow objects to remain stable across their transformed states. The important age-related advances

Figure 4.17a. Joel age 10, talented child studied longitudinally, three-quarter view.

suggested by Piaget for constructing three-quarter rotations and poses consistent with dynamic motion are transitivity and conservation. Joel's skill in conserving form through successive rotations is strikingly apparent in a series of parrots drawn when he was 11 (Figure 4.17a, b & c).

It is important to note, however, that there are rare examples of difficult rotated views in drawings by very young autistic children, such as Nadia (Selfe, 1977; 1983; 1995). By the age of 5 Nadia was able to draw foreshortened and rotated figures. These were not images preserved eidetically in memory because although many drawings were from images Nadia had seen in books, the orientations and poses of the figures were altered and more complex than the originals. Nadia may have been able to reconstruct the whole figure in orientations never actually seen from parts encoded in visual memory. Therefore, although conceptual development may play a strong enabling role in the appearance of rotation in normally developing children, in cases of intellectual impairment rotation of objects may be accomplished through processes other than the construction of transitive relationships and conservation.

Figure 4.17b. Joel age 10, profile views with some figure parts in three-quarter.

Figure 4.17c. Joel age 10, a variety of figure orientations.

The use of figurative thought may provide another avenue for its development, an avenue that is inaccessible in children whose brain is developing normally. Recent research by Gazzaniga on split brain individuals suggests specialization of right and left hemispheres in humans. He describes (reported in Blakeslee, 1996) an individual who had the connection between the right and left hemispheres surgically cut for treatment of seizures. The patient was able to write a word presented to her right hemisphere without comprehending it and to read and comprehend a word presented to the left hemisphere without being able to write it. This suggests that when the two hemispheres are dissociated and work independently direct graphic translation of what is "seen" but not understood is possible. In other words, aspects of figurative and conceptual thought can function with complete dissociation. In chapter 5, the drawings of another autistic savant are presented and the role of figurative processes is discussed at more length.

5

THE EVOLUTION OF A SINGLE VIEWPOINT

As a painter I am becoming more clear-sighted in front of nature, but . . . with me the realization of my sensations is always very difficult. I cannot attain the intensity that is unfolded before my senses. . . . Here on the edge of the river, the motifs are plentiful. . . . I think I could be occupied for months without changing my place, simply bending a little more to the right or left.

(Cézanne, letter to his son, quoted in Chipp, 1968:22)

The last chapter reviewed literature showing that although young children can be coaxed to use view-specific information when they draw from live models, they typically rely on internal models that encode structural descriptions of familiar objects. When they draw topics spontaneously from memory this is even more likely to be true. Spontaneous drawings of the human figure are particularly apt examples. We saw from the analyses of such drawings that irrespective of age, normative drawers largely drew human and animal figures in canonical orientation. In contrast, talented children rendered human and animal figures with greater flexibility and began their experimentation with rotation at very young ages. The drawings suggested that the children were not drawing from a rigid structural description of the human figure but from internal models that contained view-specific information acquired through visual exploration and study of the human figure in motion and undergoing rotational transformations. Limitations, however, were also noted even in these exceptional children. Relatively few attempts at three-quarter rotated views appeared prior to age 7. In essence, even these highly talented children lacked the cognitive maturity to utilize the transformation information potentially available from visual exploration. This is consistent with literature that demonstrates that young children have difficulty in methodically exploring their visual environment (e.g., Vurpillot, 1976). Improvements in looking strategies appear tied to more fundamental developmental changes in cognition.

This chapter revisits the theme of object-centered versus view-specific drawings but shifts attention from intrafigural relationships to those between figures and objects in a drawing. The aim is to track the development of three-dimensional depictions, starting with the construction of the picture plane and culminating in the construction of drawings with a single point of view. Two questions are asked: When and in what sequence do children organize their drawings from a viewer's perspective? And how do children of different levels of talent organize their drawings with respect to the viewer? Although it is acknowledged that linear perspective as an end point in artistic development may be an artifact of 20th-century artistic preferences (Hagen, 1985), examination of children's abilities to *understand* a single viewpoint, even if they can't draw it, supports a conclusion of protracted development for its construction. Observations in the literature suggest that the ages at which children shift from an object-centered to a viewer-centered perspective roughly approximate the ages at which important developmental shifts occur in children's spatial reasoning. It seems reasonable to suppose that cognitive changes in children's understanding of spatial relationships are basic to the construction of view-specific drawings.

This brings us to the second focus, the differences between talented and less talented children. Will all children be able to use their spatial knowledge when drawing? If we assume the ability to use perspective information in drawings is conceptually driven, we would expect children to arrive at single-viewpoint drawings after a protracted period of development. Accordingly, we would predict that children who are least impeded by difficulties of planning and producing a drawing would be most able to reflect their developing spatial concepts directly in a drawing. If, as the "farther faster" hypothesis suggests, these children are accelerated in their conceptual understanding, they may draw single viewpoint perspective correspondingly earlier than the norms for reasoning about perspective transformations. If conceptual development is not accelerated in this group of children, the development of perspective drawing could parallel normative changes in spatial reasoning. But what about children who are less skilled with line and form? They could encounter considerable obstacles when planning and producing perspective drawings and some children may give up and return to simpler and more manageable drawing topics. Nevertheless, these children should be able to demonstrate some of the same milestones in perspective development.

TOWARD REALISM IN REPRESENTING SPACE

Scholars of children's art generally agree that children try for realism (Arnheim, 1974; Freeman, 1980; Gardner, 1980; Golomb, 1992; Goodnow, 1977; Luquet, 1935). But realism does not necessarily mean visual realism. At the age of 6 or 7, children are intellectual realists, so concerned with including features that define objects that they often ignore apparent visual relationships in favor of their intellectual knowledge. Their drawings more often describe rather than identify a depicted object by a specific view. As a research puzzle this has frequently translated into the question of why children depict hidden parts of an object or array. In chapter 4 the distinction between object-centered and view-specific drawings was introduced from the point of view of drawings that favor canonical structural descriptions of objects. This literature is now reviewed with an emphasis on the spatial relationships between objects and the depiction of hidden parts of an array.

Drawing Occlusion

As we saw from the review in chapter 4, when the attentional focus of a child was manipulated, for example, by enhancing the contrast between the visual views of two otherwise like objects, children as young as 5 years could produce drawings that contained view-specific information by showing occlusions. But even when a child's attentional focus is not manipulated, young children demonstrate they are attending to some view-specific aspects of a model. In one study, 5- and 6-year-olds were presented with a model of two different colored toy pigs in four different orientations but always in the same relation to each other (Light & Humphrey, 1981). Two conditions were lateral views and these were always correctly drawn. In the other two conditions one pig partially occluded the other. Although the children were unable to draw these views, their drawings reflected some view-specific information. The pigs were generally drawn side by side, but over 80% of the children preserved the correct order of colors with the red pig on the left or "in front of" the green pig. In a more complex version of this experiment, Ingram (1985) found similar results. Children ages 3 to 8 were presented with two blocks joined by a shaft as either a vertical stacked "pile" or a horizontal "file" with one block occluding the other. Even though occlusion in drawings of the file condition was unreliable until age 7, younger children accurately depicted the order of the blocks with the closer block drawn at the bottom of the page and the rear block at the top. When hair and facial features were added to the smaller of the two blocks to make a doll, the 3- and 4-year-olds drew the doll in canonical upright orientation regardless of the presented view. Five-year-olds persisted in canonical drawings for the file condition but correctly reversed the canonical orientation of the doll to correspond with the view in the pile condition by drawing the smaller block on the bottom and the larger block on the top. Ingram concluded two codes were available to the younger children and become integrated between 5 to 7 years of age. One is a symbolic code that favors intellectual realism; the other is a view-specific code that favors encoding spatial relationships. In younger children symbolic encoding overrides spatial encoding but once the two codes are integrated, children begin to include view-specific information.

Ingram's explanation of young children's drawings makes the assumption that a child executes a drawing consistent with her or his internal representation of an object (see also Crook, 1985, reviewed in chapter 4). But this ignores the problems young children have planning and producing the drawing itself. According to Freeman (1980), young children have difficulty with partial occlusions because they have problems planning how the intersection of lines should go when part of an object is missing from the drawing. Freeman calls this *hidden line elimination* (HLE). Although such a hypothesis may help explain some types of errors children make, it cannot be the source of all occlusion errors. An ingenious experiment by Light and MacIntosh (1980) indicates a more complex cause for some types of view-specific failures. Children ages 6 and 7 were presented with a toy house put either behind or inside a glass beaker. When the house was behind the beaker, children drew the two objects segregated. When the house was inside the beaker they drew a realistic representation. Since the visibility of the house in either condition made HLE unnecessary, the authors concluded that HLE could not be the source of the object-centered drawings produced in the "behind" condition. In fact, many of the object-centered drawings produced included some view-specific information. Almost two-thirds were drawn with the house above the beaker, representing the near–far spatial relationship between the two objects as the top and bottom of the page. Light and MacIntosh (see also Taylor & Bacharach, 1982) argued that this task was confusing for young children because they were guided by a drawing rule that interfered with accurate depiction of spatial relations, a rule that reserves the space inside drawn objects to denote the inside of the object. This rule competes with the view of the array that demands the two objects be shown as transparently overlapped. Young children, therefore, resorted to segregation to portray the overlap but had no difficulty drawing the transparent overlap to indicate one object inside the other. It is also worth considering that if young children are guided by this rule in all situations they would likely not depict an occluded object as a transparency because the object is not inside but behind the occluding object. In fact, only a small percentage of young children use a transparency to depict the structural relationship of occlusion between objects. Most children use segregation.

Taken together the studies on occlusion suggest that even younger children between the ages of 5 and 7 can and do include array-specific information in their drawings. Although no single explanation convincingly unifies all examples of object-centered drawings as instances of the same phenomenon, the extensive research makes clear that young children are a good deal more capable than their performance often indicates. Young children's object-centered drawings, therefore, may be less a function of their competence than strong cognitive preferences that influence their performance. We have already observed in chapter 4 that talented children between the ages of 5 and 7 appear a good deal more competent than normative drawers in presenting specific poses of the human figure that depart from canonical orientations.

Nevertheless, research using viewing aids calls attention to conceptual problems younger children have with drawing occlusions. While acknowledging that young children are less adept at graphic techniques associated with drawing occlusion, Radkey and Enns (1987) argue that the development of cognitive understanding in perspective taking is fundamental to developmental changes in drawing occlusion. They observe that the novelty of the Renaissance discovery of central perspective was not improvement in graphic technique but the realization and application of a specific vantage point in a drawing. This discovery became accessible by the development of viewing devices such as the camera obscura and da Vinci window. These devices allowed an artist to view a scene through an aperture that guaranteed a specific and consistent viewpoint that could be easily traced to a transparent vertical surface interposed between artist and scene. By employing only the aperture device (and not the vertical drawing surface), Radkey and Enns found that 6-year-olds were able to draw one ball partially occluding another more accurately, whereas without the device few children could. Five-year-olds, however, were not aided by the viewing device when it came to producing partial occlusions; they drew the balls segregated.

A study by Klaue (1992) argues more strongly for gradual development in children's ability to map these spatial relationships onto pictorial space. In Klaue's study, two balls, one either occluding the other or behind the other on a diagonal, were to be drawn on a horizontal or vertical sheet of paper with the model either present or hidden. The performance of the 5-year-olds was unaffected by either the visibility of the balls or the paper orientation, suggesting that they did not experience a conflict between orientation of the graphic surface and the viewed scene because they ignored the model. Older children of 7 to 9 years matched the spatial array to represented space but were unable to coordinate viewpoint consistently. The 7-year-olds were only sensitive to graphic surface orientation; the 9-year-olds were sensitive to both graphic surface orientation and visibility of the model. Sensitivity to graphic surface orientation was shown when the vertical drawing surface facilitated drawing distances and angles as perceived whereas the horizontal surface facilitated drawing the actual or geometric spatial distances.

Visibility of the model affected the 9-year-olds by improving performance with the horizontal surface but inhibiting viewer-centered drawings with the vertical surface. Children of 11 years of age were able to match their representations to the viewed relationships of the model equally under all conditions, demonstrating stable coordination of a single viewpoint.

These studies indicate a more protracted period of development based on a general understanding of how perceived space translates into pictorial space. They also suggest that the stable construction of occlusion relationships is fundamental to coordinating a single point of view, a conclusion reached as well by Piaget and Inhelder (1956/1967) when they traced the development of spatial knowledge in children. The importance of the construction of spatial knowledge in improving children's understanding of how perceived or actual space is mapped onto pictorial space has also been demonstrated for other types of graphic representations. Liben and Downs (1991) in their studies of how children understand and use maps found that the development of spatial knowledge influenced children's ability to understand how space represented in maps related to actual space. Similarly, Piaget and Inhelder (1956/1967) and Feldman (1980) link spatial and logical development to children's progress in constructing a map that coordinates spatial and numerical correspondences into an appropriately scaled representation.

Drawing in Perspective

One of the more consistent debates in the literature is the degree to which the development in children's drawing can be portrayed as a natural progression toward perspective drawings (Hagen, 1985). A number of taxonomies have arisen to describe drawing development. One of the earliest, and still the most generally cited, is that of Luquet (1935), which culminates at age 8 or 9 in visual realism with perspective as a primary concern. According to this account, children pass through an early stage of fortuitous realism marked by scribbles that come to be interpreted by the child as representing people, animals, or objects. In the following stage of failed realism children have the intention of representing specific subjects but are generally unable to plan a drawing, with the result that natural relationships among parts of a figure are poorly organized. In the next stage of intellectual realism children draw generic prototypes that convey their knowledge about objects. In the final stage of visual realism they demonstrate increasing mastery over specific and realistic views of their drawing subjects.

Despite theoretical differences in interpretation, most observers of children's drawing activity agree with Luquet's general outline of development: That is, although drawing is always a symbolic activity, children's drawings do progress toward more realistic versions of the visual world (Freeman, 1980; Golomb, 1992; Piaget & Inhelder, 1969; but see Krascum et al., 1996, for a different interpretation). A very influential study by Willats (1977) focused in particular on the development toward visually realistic drawings. Willats asked children ages 5 to 17 to draw a real scene from a specific viewpoint and then classified their drawings according to the number of points of overlap and the type of drawing system employed. He found that both the number of points of overlap and the use of more complex types of drawing systems increased with age. Few children used overlap before the age of 10 and the largest developmental gains were made between the ages of 10 and 12.

Use of drawing systems showed a natural progression from systems that failed to portray any depth relationships to projective drawing systems at about the age of 9 with the use of the simplest projective system, orthographic projection. In this type of projection the lines depicting an object are parallel and strike the visual surface at right angles, reflecting the size and shape of the object in the same way its shadow would if it were cast on a wall directly in front of the object (Dubery & Willats, 1972). Vertical oblique projection, in which planes orthogonal to the picture plane are represented as verticals, was used by children between 11 and 12 years of age, and oblique projection, in which orthogonal planes are depicted as obliques, was used by children between 13 and 14 years of age. Perspective drawings, with planes orthogonal to the picture plane depicted as converging on the picture plane, were drawn by children between 13 and 14 years of age but most of these drawings were in naive perspective with orthogonals converging well above the viewer's eye level. Few children managed a true perspective view with a single point of convergence at eye level. Surprisingly, in view of the conclusion reached by many researchers that the ability to construct occlusion is a developmental milestone toward coordinating a single point of view, Willats found that the number of points of overlap and type of drawing system were unrelated.

Even though Willats's results have been replicated (Jahoda 1981; Saenger, 1981), his developmental taxonomy has been critiqued. In Hagen's (1985) opinion linear perspective is peculiar to children imbued with the culture and values of Western art. The implication is that Willats's taxonomy would not hold up cross-culturally. In one attempt at cross-cultural replication (Jahoda, 1981) with schooled and unschooled adults in Ghana, the whole range of drawing systems was observed. But unschooled adults and those with limited schooling almost never employed a system more complex than the vertical oblique class. In contrast, over half of the university students employed oblique projection or naive perspective. Only one individual drew in linear perspective, a man with limited schooling. Jahoda concluded that although the absence of an environment rich in perspective drawings makes it unlikely that the boundary between vertical oblique representations and oblique representations will be crossed, the less complex projective systems appear to develop without explicit cultural exposure or teaching. In addition, Jahoda replicated Willats's results of developmental independence in the use of overlap and drawing systems. If such results are accurate, they challenge the widely held assumption that occlusion is a necessary step in establishing a single viewpoint.

These studies of perspective drawing strongly support a protracted developmental period for the appearance of projective and perspective drawings, a period that is consistent with literature reviewed in chapter 1 relating the development of children's conceptual understanding of a single viewpoint (e.g., Piaget & Inhelder, 1956/1967; Piaget et al., 1960). But it can be argued that some of the difficulty children have with drawing perspective transformations may be unrelated to conceptual competence. Acknowledging this, some researchers have simplified the demands of the task by using viewing aids to explore the relationship between the projective image and conceptual understanding.

Reith, Steffan and Gellieron (1994) compared the drawings children 5, 7, and 9 years old produced when viewing a model through a da Vinci window to drawings made under normal viewing conditions or with the model hidden. They used a tilted bottle, half filled with a colored liquid much like that originally used by Piaget and Inhelder (1956/1967) to study children's construction of an external gravitational system of reference. Age-related changes in drawings were consistent with Piaget and Inhelder's original results when children drew from memory; only 9-year-olds represented the correct relationship. When the model was visible under normal viewing conditions, many of the 7-year-olds also correctly drew the water parallel to an external horizontal axis. But when the model was visible through the da Vinci window, even the 5-year-olds drew it true to visual appearance. The authors concluded that the window focused the young children on the visual projection of the model and allowed them to operate directly on it with sensory-motor activity by tracing it on the glass. It did not require that they understand the relationships that are involved or even understand that lines can be used to denote these relationships.

In another study Reith (1994) explored how well children analyze and utilize the information contained in the projective image. Again he had children view a scene through a da Vinci window. When children were asked to select a paper cut out of the projective image of the scene (two beach balls shown segregated or occluded and a wide rectangle), the scene itself rather than the child's age was more closely related to whether position, shape, or size of the projected image was correctly noted. Nevertheless, young children could differentiate the types of shapes (e.g., a circle versus a crescent for the two beach ball arrays), but quantification of a shape's specific dimensions and spatial position was inconsistent even in older children. Nine-year-olds were correct on only 50% of the trials. This led Reith to conclude that even when children's conceptual development is advanced enough to understand such relationships, children have difficulty utilizing the projective image. Even adolescents and adults are poor at analyzing and utilizing projective information. Nicholls (1993) placed a ladder in a small model room in one of several orientations. The ladder could be seen through a viewing window. Her aim was to study how children use projective principles such as converging lines. Children from 6 to 14 years and young adults were asked to select the perspective of a doll who could be stationed at one of three viewing windows to match a drawing of either parallel or converging lines. The ladder was presented as either parallel or nonparallel to a viewing window. Although the ability to use the drawings as accurate perspective transformations increased with age, older children and adults still had difficulty with presentations that required converging line matches. It appears that even with simplified tasks and sufficient conceptual maturity, individuals do not always understand how to map the projective image onto two-dimensional space. It is also possible that even for adults, the knowledge that ladders have parallel sides was so compelling converging matches were ruled out. Thouless has called this "phenomenal regression to the real object" (Thouless, 1931). Certainly studies with older children have found that exposure to a three-dimensional model of a cube induces them to produce object-centered rather than view-specific drawings (Krascum et al., 1996; Moore, 1987).

Several points should be highlighted before considering the quantitative results from the spontaneous drawings studies. The most obvious is that children's drawing performance and underlying competence can be quite disparate. This may be especially true when studying spontaneous drawings. We have seen that there are a variety of conditions, such as emphasizing visual contrasts or providing meaningful context, that improve visual realism in young children's drawings. We have also seen that the penchant to make drawings based on one's knowledge of objects instead of one's view of objects is quite strong and can possibly override translating projective knowledge to drawings even in adults. Nevertheless, the studies that have traced the development of perspective drawing have found that the age-related ability to use projective drawing systems is consistent with the construction of spatial knowledge. Therefore, although not a sufficient condition for the appearance of perspective drawings, conceptual knowledge of perspective relationships is very probably a necessary prerequisite in normal development. Normal development is emphasized here because in previous chapters the exceptional drawings of a few rare children with autism like Nadia were mentioned. It was suggested that Nadia's remarkable ability may have been a result of her conceptual impairment, an impairment that may have allowed her to operate directly with figurative thought unconstrained by conceptual processes. At the end of this chapter in the case studies section we present drawings from another autistic child gifted in perspective.

TRACING THE DEVELOPMENT OF PERSPECTIVE IN THE SPONTANEOUS DRAWINGS STUDIES

We next consider the quantitative results from observations on the use of occlusion and projective systems in the talented and less talented children. One important focus is developmental differences with age. A second is the difference between the two populations. If conceptual understanding has an important role in children's ability to analyze and use perspective information in their drawings, we might expect a protracted developmental period for the appearance of single viewpoint drawings. On the other hand, spatial concepts may develop early in some young children. In that case we might expect a remarkably early appearance of single viewpoint drawings, particularly in talented children who are both more likely to attend to their perceptions and more skilled at drawing.

The classification of spatial relationships was based in part on the taxonomy published by Willats (1977). As reviewed earlier, Willats attended to two developments in the depiction of spatial relationships: the development of drawing systems used to construct projected views and the relative positioning of objects that when viewed were seen as overlapping. In his study he identified six classes of drawing systems that formed the following developmental sequence: no projection system, orthographic projection, vertical oblique projection, oblique projection, naive perspective, and linear perspective. All of these were also observed in the present studies, but some were so rare in the spontaneous drawings that they are omitted from analysis. Orthographic and vertical oblique projections, frequent in other studies, were rare in this study. Differences can be accounted for by the use of spontaneous drawings not based on life models in this study. Other researchers who replicated Willats's developmental sequence used life models and found that the vertical oblique class was the most well represented (Jahoda, 1981; Saenger, 1981). These two classes may be very acceptable solutions to depicting a real scene but not preferred ways of handling a favorite spontaneous topic (Duthie, 1985).

This study used two approaches; one was simply to classify the drawings on the basis of visual inspection. The second was to measure the angle of convergence in the same manner as Willats. The agreement between classification and measurement was 96%, suggesting that the measurements were a valid procedure to use even though a model was not present. Not all drawings that could be classified could be measured. Only those drawings that represented geometric objects with one "face" parallel to the picture plane and two projected parallel sides could be measured. This included as examples drawings of houses, tables, buildings, or streets. Across all samples there were 102 such drawings but 70% of these were from the longitudinal sample.

Whereas Willats attended to the number of points of overlap between objects drawn from the model, this study simply observed whether figure parts or different objects were overlapped in a drawing.[1] In addition, other types of relative positioning between depicted objects were noted; these included horizontal segregation of elements, transparencies, and vertical segregation to indicate depth. Another aspect scored was whether or not a child had constructed the picture plane and whether the picture plane was constructed with a ground line (two-dimensional) or a ground plane (three-dimensional). Finally, other pictorial devices to indicate perspective were noted. These included the use of foreshortening, modeling, and shading or shadow to suggest a light source. In all, observations of four dimensions related to drawing spatial relationships were made: *establishment of the picture plane, pictorial positioning devices, drawing systems,* and other *perspective indicators.* As in previous chapters models were tested by loglinear analysis, and because cross-sectional sample sizes were often too small to test a full two-factor model, the effects of age and talent group were usually tested separately. The details of how dichotomous scoring of individual categories was transformed for these statistical analyses are in Appendix 2.1. The following presentation traces a logical developmental trajectory by beginning with results for the establishment of a picture plane, followed by those for positioning devices, drawing systems, and finally other perspective indicators.

Establishing the Picture Plane

Children typically establish the picture plane by placing figures and objects in horizontal alignment on the bottom of the page. Often a line is drawn to indicate the ground. Figure 5.1a demonstrates the early appearance of this technique in a drawing by Kate done at age 4. Somewhat later several lines might be used to denote different heights of the ground surface (e.g., Figure 5.1b) and this technique might also be mixed with coloring in between the lines to denote the ground's surface. Golomb (1992) has suggested that initially children use multiple ground lines as a way of accommodating more

---

1. These two types of overlap were combined in further analyses after analyzing for differences in age of onset and finding none.

Figure 5.1a. Kate, talented girl age 4.

Figure 5.1b. Less talented boy age 7.

Figure 5.2. Less talented boy age 11.

figures. In some instances, however, a child may intend these lines to function as indicators of foreground and background from the beginning. Eventually, the line denoting a two-dimensional surface is replaced by techniques that emphasize three-dimensional aspects of the ground: use of color or textured lines to fill in areas of ground coupled with vertical segregation of objects so that what is below denotes near and what is above denotes far, and partial occlusion of far objects by near objects (e.g., Figure 5.2).

Cross-Sectional Sample. All drawings received a score on this dimension; therefore, the sample size was within the range for testing the full model for talent group (talented or less talented) by age (three age blocks) on the picture plane (four levels) with loglinear analysis. The drawings of talented and less talented children did not show differences in the construction of ground line and plane. Age of the child, however, did influence whether or not she or he drew a ground line or plane. The results confirmed the development progression suggested by qualitative observations (Appendix 5.1). Reference to Table 5.2 shows that most of the children between 3 and 6 years failed to establish a picture plane in their drawings but children between the ages of 7 and 10 years used both a ground line and a ground plane to establish the picture plane. By adolescence, when children were between the ages of 11 and 14, the use of lines to indicate the ground was abandoned altogether in favor of using color or shading to suggest the surface of the ground.

Table 5.1 shows the proportion of children scoring on a particular category broken up into six age groupings. The progression suggested by the table confirms the similarity of the developmental sequence in the two talent groups. But it also demonstrates that the talented children were approximately 2 years in advance of the less talented children, a fact obscured by grouping the six age blocks into three. Half the youngest talented children used a ground line and one younger talented child established a picture plane by the fourth year, whereas none of the 3- and 4-year-old less talented children established a picture plane in her or his drawings.

Longitudinal Sample. Analysis of these drawings revealed a somewhat faster developmental sequence (see Appendix 5.2). Age had a significant effect on the development of the picture plane but in this instance children between the ages of 3 and 6 began to use both a ground line and a combined ground line and plane. By the age of 11 and 14 years children primarily structured the picture plane with a ground plane. If reference is made to Table 5.1 the developmental progression can be traced more precisely. Between 3 and 4 years most of the children either failed to establish a picture plane or established one with a ground line, whereas by 5 to 6 years, almost all children used both line and plane simultaneously. The sequence of development for children in the longitudinal sample, therefore, was similar to that of the talented cross-sectional sample, but the rate of development was faster than that of the less talented cross-sectional sample. Before the age of 7 almost all these talented children had at least one drawing in which the plane and line were mixed.

Positioning Devices

Cross-Sectional Sample. Drawings from some of the younger less talented children were not included in these analyses because they contained only single figures and could not be scored for positioning relationships. An initial test of the full model revealed that both talent group and age affected the depiction of spatial relationships by positioning. Analysis of groups alone showed that the primary differences in depicting spatial relationships were in the use of hor-

TABLE 5.1
PERCENTAGE OF CHILDREN USING PICTORIAL DEVICES

	Age					
Pictorial Devices	3–4 Years	5–6 Years	7–8 Years	9–10 Years	11–12 Years	13–14 Years
Less Talented[a]	(n = 12)	(n = 11)	(n = 13)	(n = 14)	(n = 13)	(n = 12)
Ground Line	0	55	77	50	9	8
Ground Plane	0	46	77	71	77	92
Vertical Segregation	0	9	39	43	31	50
Overlap	0	18	31	57	77	100
Mixed Views	17	9	31	50	23	25
No Projection	33	64	77	64	39	8
Oblique Projection	0	0	0	14	15	42
Naive Perspective	0	0	0	0	0	0
Linear Perspective	0	0	0	0	0	8
Foreshortening	0	0	0	7	15	17
Modeling	0	0	0	0	23	50
Shade and Shadow	0	0	0	7	23	17
Cross-Sectional Talented[a]	(n = 4)	(n = 4)	(n = 5)	(n = 6)	(n = 5)	(n = 6)
Ground Line	50	50	60	50	20	17
Ground Plane	25	75	100	100	60	100
Vertical Segregation	50	25	60	100	40	83
Overlap	25	75	100	100	100	100
Mixed Views	50	25	80	83	20	17
No Projection	50	100	100	83	0	0
Oblique Projection	0	0	60	67	20	17

	(n = 6)	(n = 8)	(n = 8)	(n = 8)	(n = 8)	(n = 7)
Naive Perspective	0	0	20	50	20	0
Linear Perspective	0	0	20	0	40	50
Foreshortening	0	25	40	50	40	83
Modeling	0	25	40	83	100	83
Shade and Shadow	0	25	40	67	60	100
Longitudinal Talented[a]						
Ground Line	67	75	63	38	13	0
Ground Plane	17	100	100	100	100	100
Vertical Segregation	50	63	63	88	88	71
Overlap	33	88	100	100	100	100
Mixed Views	33	38	75	38	50	14
No Projection	50	100	75	38	13	0
Oblique Projection	0	38	75	50	88	57
Naive Perspective	0	0	25	38	25	14
Linear Perspective	0	0	25	13	75	71
Foreshortening	0	25	88	88	100	86
Modeling	0	38	100	88	100	100
Shade and Shadow	0	25	63	75	75	100

[a] Percentage of children who had at least one drawing showing response.

izontal segregation and/or transparency and the simultaneous use of vertical segregation and overlap (see Appendix 5.3). Talented children were more likely to use vertical segregation and overlap and˙less likely to use horizontal segregation and transparency, whereas the reverse was true of less talented children. When age was considered it became apparent that the positioning device differences between talented and less talented children also reflected the developmental differences between younger and older children (see Appendix 5.4). Table 5.2 shows the group and total sample percentages for the three age blocks. Younger children used horizontal segregation and transparency whereas the oldest children used overlap alone. Children between the ages of 7 and 10 primarily drew the relative position of objects as a combination of vertical segregation and overlap.

Even though the developmental trajectory in the two talent groups is in the same direction, examination of Table 5.2 indicates that a greater percentage of the talented children ages 3 to 6 used vertical segregation or overlap with transparencies. Fully 82% of the talented children between the ages of 7 and 10 employed vertical segregation with overlap whereas only 24% of the less talented children used these more advanced devices. Although this suggests that developmental shifts may be occurring more slowly in the less talented group, approximately the same percentage in both groups used overlap alone by ages 11 to 14. Still, a quarter of the less talented children 11 to 14 years of age were still using horizontal segregation and transparency, vertical segregation alone, or overlap with transparencies, whereas none of the talented children was.

Longitudinal Sample. Age had a significant effect on the use of different types of positioning devices (see Appendix 5.5). When the children were between the ages of 3 and 6, they primarily employed either horizontal segregation and transparency or vertical segregation and overlap with transparencies. They shifted to the predominant use of vertical segregation with overlap by age 7 to 10 and by age 11 to 14 a little less than a third were using overlap alone but most of the children still mixed vertical segregation with overlap. Reference to the proportion of children using the various positioning devices in Table 5.1 indicates that even as young as 3 or 4 years old, half of the children had begun to use vertical seg-

PERCENTAGE OF CHILDREN IN CROSS-SECTIONAL SAMPLE AT HIGHEST LEVEL ON PICTURE PLANE AND POSITIONING SCALES

Age in Years	Scales for Development of the Picture Plane	Less Talented	Talented	Total Sample
3 to 6		($n = 23/n = 15^a$)	($n = 8$)	($n = 31/n = 23$)
	Ground Absent	61	38	55**
	Ground Line Alone	17	13	16
	Ground Line/Ground Plane	9	38	16
	Ground Plane Alone	13	13	13**
	Horizontal Segregation/Transparency	80	25	61**
	Vertical Segregation/Overlap with Transparency	20	50	30
	Vertical Segregation and Overlap	0	25	9**
	Overlap Alone	0	0	0*
7 to 10		($n = 27/n = 25$)	($n = 11$)	($n = 38/n = 36$)
	Ground Absent	7	0	5**
	Ground Line Alone	19	0	13
	Ground Line/Ground Plane	44	55	47**
	Ground Plane Alone	30	46	34
	Horizontal Segregation/Transparency	32	0	22
	Vertical Segregation/Overlap with Transparency	32	18	28
	Vertical Segregation and Overlap	24	82	42
	Overlap Alone	12	0	8
11 to 14		($n = 25/n = 25$)	($n = 11$)	($n = 36/n = 36$)
	Ground Absent	12	9	11
	Ground Line Alone	4	9	6
	Ground Line/Ground Plane	20	9	17
	Ground Plane Alone	64	73	67**
	Horizontal Segregation/Transparency	8	0	6**
	Vertical Segregation/Overlap with Transparency	16	0	11*
	Vertical Segregation and Overlap	36	64	44
	Overlap Alone	40	36	39**

[a]n for position analysis; significance of cell value, * $p \leq .05$. ** $p \leq .01$.

regation. By 5 and 6 years of age, drawings with both vertical segregation and overlap were common.

These results are consistent with the course of development suggested by the cross-sectional sample, where it appears that the rate of development was more rapid than in the talented than the less talented children. Talented children in both groups showed early use of vertical segregation and overlap to indicate the third dimension of the picture plane. One child in the longitudinal sample who was able to use overlap at age 4 is shown in Figure 5.1a. Kate has drawn most of the animals carefully to show the parts in an unobstructed view, but one overlap occurs between the mouse and the elephant (see also Figure 3.5b).

The literature reviewed previously on the use of positioning devices demonstrates that under favorable conditions children as young as 6 or 7 will use vertical segregation to indicate depth and some can also produce partial occlusion drawings. Although related, those studies are quite distinct from this one in that drawings were elicited from a model under highly specific conditions rather than from the child's imagination. Nevertheless, they are consistent with what we observed in the spontaneous drawings, which showed younger children can draw an object occluded by another as overlapped. But the low frequency of these types of spatial relationships in the less talented children's spontaneous drawings suggests that typically children do not choose to draw them until adolescence. In general, younger children appear less aware of what the visual cues to depth are, and although both talented and less talented children can demonstrate their ability to understand these cues when faced with a model, only the younger talented children appear to recognize the utility of such a pictorial device in making a drawn scene more visually realistic.

Drawing Systems

Cross-Sectional Sample. Since only geometric representational drawings could be judged on this dimension, fewer children were included in this analysis. Talent group and age, therefore, were analyzed independently and both showed a significant influence on drawing systems (Appendixes 5.6 and 5.7). Talented children showed greater use of perspective drawing systems and less talented children showed greater use of elevation and plan drawing systems. Eighty-two percent of the less talented did not use a projective system. Even among the children 11 to 14 years of age, half of the less talented children were not using a projective system to draw geometric representations whereas all of the talented children used a perspective system. When the entire sample was analyzed for the effects of age, the expected developmental progression was found. Table 5.3 shows the percentages of children by age achieving each level of the drawing system scale. Children between the ages of 3 and 6 almost uniformly failed to use a projective system whereas about a quarter of the children between the ages of 7 and 10 used one of the projective systems; in most cases this was one of the oblique projective systems. Two-thirds of the older children used one of the projective systems with over half of these choosing a perspective system.

Because the full model could not be tested, development for the less talented group was examined alone. Age still had a significant effect on the use of drawing systems. The results suggested that the developmental trajectory in this group was in the same direction but more curtailed than in the talented children. All of the younger children used elevation and plan drawing systems whereas many of the older children used oblique projected systems. A comparison of the two talent groups in Table 5.3 indicates that whereas the talented children switch to a projective system between the ages of 7 and 10 and a perspective system by age 11 to 14, less talented children almost uniformly fail to use a projective system until adolescence and very few use a perspective system.

Scaling the data by the highest level achieved in a drawing obscures the development of the different drawing systems. Differences in development for the two talent groups can be examined further by referring to Table 5.1. Talented children ages 7 to 8 began to use oblique projective and perspective systems in some drawings but also continued to use elevation and plan. By early adolescence, the talented children had stopped using elevation and plan altogether, shifting primarily to a linear perspective system. In the less talented children, use of elevation and plan drawing systems also declined around age 11 or 12 but less than half of these older children used a projective system in any of their drawings and only one less talented adolescent drew with a perspective drawing system. This drawing, shown in Figure 1.2b, is a careful construction drawn with a ruler.

What of the relationship between positional devices and drawing

TABLE 5.3
PERCENTAGE OF CHILDREN IN CROSS-SECTIONAL SAMPLE AT HIGHEST LEVEL ON DRAWING SYSTEMS AND PERSPECTIVE INDICATORS SCALES

Age in Years	Scales for Development of Perspective	Less Talented	Talented	Total Sample
3 to 6		($n = 11/n = 23^a$)	($n = 7/n = 8$)	($n = 18/n = 31$)
	No Projection	100	100	100*
	Oblique Projection alone	0	0	0
	Perspective	0	0	0
	No Perspective Indicator	100	87	97*
	One Perspective Indicator	0	0	0
	Two Perspective Indicators	0	0	0
	Three Perspective Indicators	0	13	3
7 to 10		($n = 19/n = 27$)	($n = 10/n = 11$)	($n = 29/n = 38$)
	No Projection	90	40	72
	Oblique Projection alone	10	40	21
	Perspective	0	20	7
	No Perspective Indicator	93	28	74
	One Perspective Indicator	7	18	11
	Two Perspective Indicators	0	27	8
	Three Perspective Indicators	0	27	8
11 to 14		($n = 10/n = 25$)	($n = 4/n = 11$)	($n = 14/n = 36$)
	No Projection	50	0	36
	Oblique Projection alone	40	0	29
	Perspective	10	100	36*
	No Perspective Indicator	56	0	39
	One Perspective Indicator	24	27	25*
	Two Perspective Indicators	16	36	22*
	Three Perspective Indicators	4	36	14

$^a n$ for perspective indicators analysis; differences in age, $^* p \leq .01$.

systems? The studies by Willats (1977) and others indicated that these two types of techniques were developmentally independent. When the association between the two for the cross-sectional sample was analyzed this was found not to be the case. The two types of techniques did show an association: When no projective system was used, children primarily used horizontal segregation and transparency and only rarely vertical segregation or overlap; when oblique projection was used, children seldom used horizontal segregation and transparency; and when a perspective system was used, children favored vertical segregation and overlap. But when the association was explored for the less talented group alone, the significant association disappeared. Since perspective systems were rarely used by these children, the association between advanced positioning devices and perspective systems found for the whole sample can be attributed to the talented children. It should be re-emphasized, however, that the method of measuring positioning devices in the Willats study and this study were quite different. Willats assessed the number of points of overlap drawn relative to those visible in the model, whereas this study only assessed the type.

Longitudinal Sample. Age also influenced the use of drawing systems in these children. The results were similar to those of the cross-sectional talented sample in that these children primarily drew without a projective system when younger and with a perspective system when older. Examination of the percentages in Appendix 5.8 indicates that the children were most likely to use an oblique projective system at age 7 to 10 although some also used this drawing system when they were both younger and older. The longitudinal talented sample can be more directly compared to the cross-sectional talented sample in Table 5.1. The similarity in developmental course for projective drawing systems in the two talented samples is striking. Both samples began to experiment with oblique projection and perspective drawing systems between ages 7 and 8 and both showed a shift toward linear perspective by age 11 or 12. In general talented children show an orderly progression between the ages of 3 and 14 that begins with drawings in which elevation and plan are the primary ways of representing geometry to drawings showing objects and buildings in oblique projection and finally in perspective. This progression replicates the basic developmental findings of Willats and others when a drawing from life is requested. The difference, of course, is that the models for the drawings studied here are taken from the children's imagination and demonstrate their ability to use linear perspective across a range of drawing topics.

The association between positioning devices and drawing systems was significant in this talented sample but surprisingly only because of the association between children's use of positioning devices and the absence of a projective system. Children primarily used horizontal segregation and transparency and seldom used vertical segregation and overlap with nonprojective drawing systems. The importance of positioning for perspective drawings suggested by the cross-sectional analysis was not replicated. This leaves the relationship of positioning devices and drawing systems in talented children unresolved. A future study should specifically target this issue in talented children because it is primarily these children who develop the ability to use projective systems in their drawings spontaneously.

Several points are worth considering when contrasting the results for the development of drawing systems in talented and less talented children. Although rate of development may be a primary difference, a more profound divergence is also potentially indicated. We know that in general the frequency of drawing declines with age in less talented drawers whereas the output of talented children remains high or even increases. It is likely that as less talented children get older, their progress in understanding spatial relationships and in detecting the disparity between what they have drawn and what they see inhibits their drawing performance particularly in the realm of projected geometrical objects; most of the less talented children who drew geometric objects did not use a projection system. In addition, when compared to the talented children, a smaller percentage of the less talented children tackled themes that would have required the use of a projective system (57% compared to 70%). These children may have lacked production strategies to handle geometric themes effectively. Willats (1992) has suggested that critical to producing a projective drawing is the discovery of a denotation rule that allows lines to stand for edges and planes to stand for surfaces of objects. We have already seen from the analysis in chapter 3 that less talented children may have failed or been quite delayed in this discovery whereas the talented children appeared to use such a rule quite early. This early discovery allowed the talented children to experiment with projective drawing systems and develop strategies for drawing geometric themes, even though they were unable to coordinate a single point of view until early adolescence. In the next section observations related to children's experimentation with drawing systems are studied by looking at the development of mixed viewpoint drawings.

Mixed Viewpoint Drawings

When more than one point of view was represented, a drawing was categorized as a mixed viewpoint drawing. Often drawings by younger children were mixtures of nonprojected views or lacked a point of view altogether. A drawing with no projective system might have parts of the drawing in elevation and other parts in plan view. Typical examples of drawings without a projective system but with mixed viewpoints are contained in Figures 5.3a–c. The first of these, by Claire from the longitudinal talented sample when she was 6 years old, depicts a scary Halloween night. Despite several points of overlap and some attempts at projection of small objects in the picture (i.e., the dish and lid of the garbage can) most parts of the drawing, the street level or the window level, are shown as if the viewer were stationed directly in front of the viewed portion. Figure 5.3b, drawn by a less talented 4-year-old, mixes a schematic elevation view of a sailboat with a bird's-eye view of the water. In Figure 5.3c a 4-year-old talented girl from the cross-sectional sample mixes a plan view of the freeway under the Bay bridge with a view of the upper deck in elevation. In Figure 5.4a, Claire, at age 8, attempted to take a specific point of view on the drawing but drew different parts from different views. The cars at the lower right hand side are shown from an aerial view, whereas the viewpoint on the figures crossing the street is from a somewhat lower vantage. Finally, the figures across the street and laundry are depicted as if the viewer were at eye level with them.

Older children mixed projective views, for example, some geometric objects depicted in oblique projection and others in perspective. Figure 5.4b was drawn by Tara when she was age 11. Tara has drawn her dream house in cutaway. Inside, she uses a consistent scale to show figures and furnishings including plants, vases, books, and clothes in the closet. Although the scale is very small, careful inspection of the furniture reveals that different pieces are drawn with different drawing systems. For example, the television

Figure 5.3a. Claire, talented girl age 6.

mounted on the bedroom wall in the upper right is shown in oblique projection, whereas the vanity on the third floor right suggests perspective. Other pieces are shown in orthographic projection such as the stuffed chair (left bottom) or the bed (right bottom) on the first floor. Some mixed viewpoint drawings were not classified because the mixed views did not depict two types of geometric representations. One example by a less talented 13-year-old is shown in Figure 5.5a. The house is drawn in oblique projection but the shells on the beach and the beach are shown from an aerial view.

Table 5.1 shows the proportion of children in the two cross-sectional samples and the longitudinal sample who showed at least one mixed viewpoint drawing. In the talented cross-sectional sample mixed views were most frequent between ages 7 to 10. After

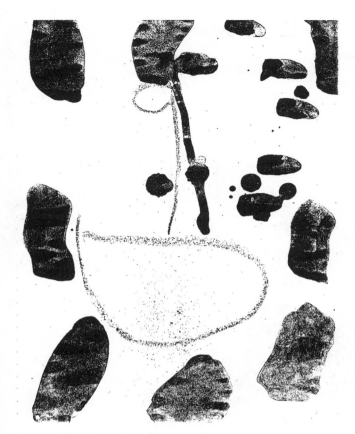

Figure 5.3b. Less talented boy age 4.

age 11 few talented children were drawing mixed viewpoint drawings; this was because they were able to draw from a stable point of view. In the longitudinal talented sample, mixtures were most frequent at ages 7 to 8 and again at age 11 to 12. In the less talented sample mixed view drawings were done most frequently between ages 9 and 10.

The total percentage of mixed drawings was not very different in the three groups. But in the less talented group a smaller percentage of children accounted for the number of drawings (27% of sample drawing mixed drawings; 16% of drawings). The talented cross-sectional children produced the greatest number of mixed viewpoint drawings (21% of the drawings) but these were produced by half the sample. All the talented longitudinal children drew some

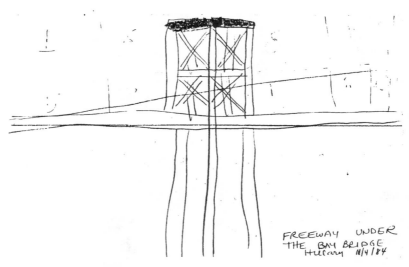

Figure 5.3c. Talented girl age 4.

Figure 5.4a. Claire, talented girl age 8.

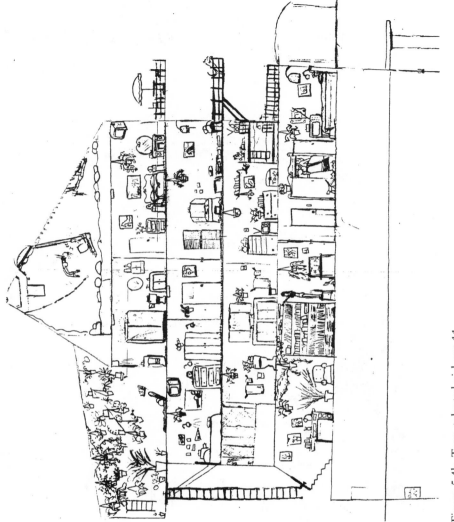

Figure 5.4b. Tara, talented girl age 11.

Figure 5.5a. Less talented girl age 11.

Figure 5.5b. Less talented boy age 12.

The Representation of Form and Space

mixed view drawings, but the total number of drawings was still about the same as that of the other groups (15% of drawings). The sheer volume of drawings sampled from these children ensured that at least one mixed viewpoint drawing from every child would be included but not every child drew mixtures with great frequency (mean per child per age block = 2.3 drawings; range 2 to 17). The development of the talented child with the greatest frequency of mixed viewpoint drawings is described in the later case studies section to illustrate the role these drawings may play in drawing development.

Figure 5.6 shows the percentage of mixed view drawings by type and age for each talent group. For all groups the percentage of unclassified drawings is highest for the youngest children and declines thereafter as mixtures increasingly become the product of children's attempts to draw geometric representations with a viewpoint. Overall the less talented children showed the fewest types of mixed views, sticking primarily to mixtures of elevation and plan in the first two age blocks or no projection and oblique projection mixes. Older less talented children drew oblique mixes.

Both talented groups of children showed a rich variety of mixed viewpoints, especially between the ages of 7 and 10, when mixtures were most frequent. Particularly noteworthy is the appearance of oblique projection and perspective mixtures as well as naive and linear perspective mixtures. By the time these children reached age 11, some of them were already experimenting with drawing systems that are best suited for producing single viewpoint drawings. After age 11, mixed viewpoint drawings began to decline and were replaced by linear perspective drawings in which a single point of view was maintained across the drawing.

A comparison of Figure 5.5b with Figure 5.4b underscores the differences in mixed views drawn by talented and less talented children. In Figure 5.5b a less talented 12-year-old boy draws a scene of a chemistry experiment primarily in elevation but the flask on the center left pedestal and the shadows cast in front of the pedestals are projected. The projected shadows are solidly filled in just the way they could actually appear. Nevertheless, despite his use of projected shadows, evidence of the denotational rule that equates a line with an edge is strikingly absent. The pedestals are represented by rectangles, the tops of which appear to function as surfaces for the chemistry flasks instead of as their dimensional equivalents,

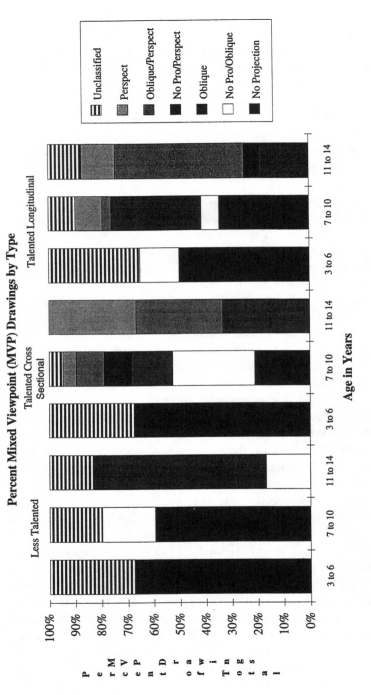

Figure 5.6. Percentage of types of mixed drawings within each age block by sample.

edges. In contrast in Figure 5.4b, Tara has exploited a rich variety of projective drawing systems. Although the scale is small, in each case the lines she uses are clearly meant to stand for the projected edges of the furnishing. Objects placed on the vanity drawn in perspective (third floor right side) lie not on the line but on the unfilled plane that denotes the surface. Where orthographic projection is used, the base of planters appears slightly occluded by the leading edge of the furniture (see dresser top right hand room).

Perspective Indicators

Beyond the application of drawing systems used to depict geometric objects, children used other types of perspective indicators when drawing figures and scenes. These included *foreshortening*; *modeling*, such as thickening the line of the rounded portions of a figure; and *shading* and *shadow* to indicate a light source. Table 5.1 shows the proportion of these categories by age and talent groups. Evident immediately in both talented samples is the very early appearance of these perspective indicators when compared to those of the less talented children. Roughly one-quarter of the talented children in both samples used foreshortening, modeling, or shading and shadow in their drawings by age 6. By age 8 in the longitudinal sample and by age 10 in the cross-sectional sample, almost all the talented children had employed at least one or more of these devices. The slowest indicator to develop and least employed was shading and shadow. On the whole, less talented children rarely used any of the perspective indicators until preadolescence. Even between ages 13 and 14, only half the children attempted modeling figures and far fewer used foreshortening or shadow and shading.

Cross-Sectional Sample. The effects of talent and age on the use of one, two, or three of the perspective indicators combined were analyzed separately (Appendixes 5.9 and 5.10). As suggested by the single category proportions described, the two cross-sectional talent groups showed significant differences in their use of perspective indicators. Less talented children were very unlikely to use any perspective indicators whereas talented children were highly likely to use them, especially in combinations of two or three. Age also influenced the children's use of perspective indicators. Few of the children age 3 to 6 used any of these indicators. In contrast children 11 to 14 years commonly used one or two. The percentage of children in each talent group by age using perspective indicators is reported in Table 5.3. The contrast is striking. Eighty-three percent of the less talented children never used a single perspective indicator, whereas two-thirds of the talented children used at least one or more. Most of the less talented children who used perspective indicators were adolescents and they generally used only one type. In contrast, most talented children used two or three indicators. One talented child was able to use all three at age 6 and almost three-quarters of the talented children ages 7 to 10 used perspective indicators. By adolescence, all of the talented children used one perspective indicator and most used two or three combined.

Longitudinal Sample. Age also had a significant effect on the appearance of perspective indicators in these children (Appendix 5.11). The results support the development progression observed in the cross-sectional sample of talented children. Perspective indicators were largely absent in the drawings of talented children younger than age 6. By age 7 to 10 use of at least one perspective indicator was already frequent (72%) and by age 11 to 14, use of two or three indicators became frequent (50%).

Summary

When the construction of a drawing that serves as a three-dimensional representation was traced developmentally, it was observed that both talented and less talented children constructed a picture plane before they attempted to depict complex spatial relationships between objects. Once this milestone was achieved, talented children very quickly began to utilize positioning devices that separated the background of the picture from the foreground, often combining a vertical spatial mapping of depth (vertical segregation) with occlusion (overlap) to indicate distance in depth. Less talented children were much slower to differentiate these depth relationships, largely sticking to horizontal alignment of elements until age 9 or 10. But although slower to develop, the ability to use occlusion was evident in all the older less talented children. This leads to the conclusion that it is largely the rate of development of the picture plane and positioning devices used to indicate depth that is affected by children's talent.

More marked differences in developmental rate were observed in the emergence of drawing systems effective in representing geometric objects or three-dimensional scenes. Talented children began to use a projective drawing system around age 7 or 8, often experimenting with several different types in the same drawing to achieve more visually realistic views. This experimentation with viewpoint and drawing systems had a rich payoff. Several years later, during their early adolescence, most of these children discovered and applied a true perspective drawing system. Many of the geometric drawings of the oldest talented children were single viewpoint drawings in linear perspective. In contrast, few geometric objects and scenes drawn by less talented children were rendered with a projective drawing system; even most of the older less talented children failed to use a projective drawing system and only one older less talented boy drew a perspective drawing. Nevertheless, with age there was a progressive appearance of projected views even in these children, suggesting that if drawings from children older than age 14 had been sampled there might have been greater use of projective and perspective drawing systems. In Willats's (1977) study of drawing systems oblique projection was frequent between the ages of 13 and 14 but the use of a perspective drawing system was infrequent until 15 to 17 years.

These types of shortcomings in rendering visual realism were also observed in drawings of themes that did not require geometry. Foreshortening and modeling of figures as well as use of shading and shadow were seldom observed in drawings by less talented children and even older less talented children were generally unable to use foreshortening although a few children combined shading and modeling. Talented children began to use these devices quite early. Their drawings showed a clear progression with age from those with one indicator by itself to those with two or three combined in a single drawing. Foreshortening, despite the distortions in the structure of a figure it produces, appeared to be as easy for talented children to use as modeling. Shading and shadow developed more slowly.

The disparities between talented and less talented children in drawing systems and figural perspective indicators intimate that differences in developmental rate may not be the whole story when it comes to perspective drawing. On the basis of earlier analyses of line use (chapter 3), I suspect that talented children were discovering something unique about the denotation of three-dimensional objects at an early age: That is, that rather than being reserved to indicate the boundaries of objects, lines could be used more specifically to stand for their edges. Similarly, the space between an enclosing line could be used to represent a visual surface rather than the solid volume of the whole object. As these children got older, these denotational rules were continually applied to depict developments in their understanding of spatial relationships. By the time the talented children reached adolescence and were able to reason more fully about spatial relationships, they already had drawing strategies that could be effectively combined with their conceptual understanding of perspective. It is certain that the less talented children, like all children, developed a similar conceptual understanding of complex spatial relationships as they got older but for the most part they failed to develop drawing strategies that could translate this knowledge into a drawing. In depicting spatial relationships in depth, few of these children went beyond using positioning devices such as occlusion. Even many of the adolescents appeared not to have discovered fully a denotational system that could effectively translate the geometry of three-dimensional objects and figures to a two-dimensional drawing surface.

In the next section two case illustrations of the development of perspective drawings are presented. In the first case of a talented child a protracted but linear developmental rate suggests a close parallel with normative development in spatial reasoning. The norms for the development of spatial reasoning and how they are reflected in talented children's drawings are discussed in the conclusions to this chapter. In the second case, of an autistic savant, developmental rate is at least 6 years in advance of norms for spatial reasoning. The puzzle presented by this second case is quite instructive, because we must try to understand how a child who presumably would not be able to reason about projected shapes and the effects of a single fixed viewpoint can construct these relationships in her or his drawings.

CASE STUDIES OF THE DEVELOPMENT OF PERSPECTIVE DRAWING

Hondo: An Illustration of the Development of a Single Perspective in a Talented Boy of Normal Development

Hondo is a good example of a highly talented child who drew in perspective early in adolescence. The first crucial development toward perspective drawing was the construction and differentiation of the picture plane. Tracing his development from age 3 shows that Hondo begins intentional representations with alignment of figure parts but fails to orient figures to the axes of the paper consistently (Figure 5.7a). The following year Hondo constructs the two-dimensional picture plane by introducing single and multiple ground lines as horizontal coordinates and aligning figures and machinery vertically with respect to the ground. His progress is rapid and by age 5 he adds oblique lines to represent the third dimension. In Figure 5.7b, an oblique line representing a hill projected into the picture plane invades the picture plane. Hondo reinforces his intent by drawing a truck in partial projection mounting the hill. Although not entirely successful this drawing heralds an early beginning of projected views. Hondo also differentiates the foreground and background in this drawing by vertically segregating the multiple horizontal ground lines. Elements meant to be in the background are lined up on the top ground line and those meant to be in the foreground are lined up on the ground line at the bottom of the picture.

A second crucial development was experimentation with multiple views. Children often arrive empirically at solutions for representing objects in space, trying out first one idea and then another. These solutions leave parts of a drawing uncoordinated with other parts and several contradictory solutions to representing depth might appear in the same drawing. The result is that several points of view are depicted at once with little attempt to give the viewer a single cohesive viewpoint. The importance of these drawings lies both in their capacity to instruct the child through trial and error and in their reflection of the child's increasing awareness of potential points of view that can be taken on a scene. Two phases of experimentation appeared in the drawings of talented children. In the first, children experimented with unprojected views whereas in the second they experimented with projected and perspective views. Prior to the appearance of multiple views, most drawings were in simple elevation. Strictly speaking, elevation represents no particular point of view at all since the upright parts of all objects or figures are represented in two dimensions as if the viewer were at eye level with respect to all parts. Less frequently, children attempted bird's-eye or plan views. In observing these early drawings, it is not surprising that the first multiple view drawings combined elevation and plan view representations.

Figure 5.7a. Hondo, talented boy age 3.

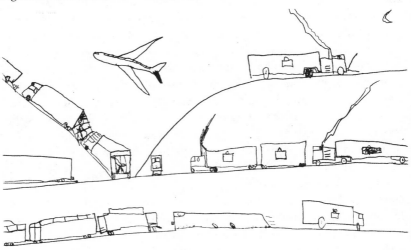

Figure 5.7b. Hondo, talented boy age 5.

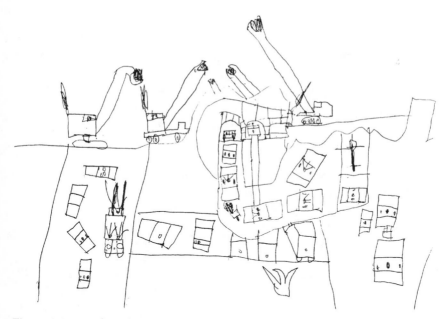

Figure 5.8. Hondo, talented boy age 6.

At age 6, Hondo took as many as five points of view on the complex road scene shown in Figure 5.8. This drawing is interesting because it indicates an early and highly developed sense of the potential points of view in such a scene and at the same time shows a complete disregard for the single point of view of visual realism. This drawing primarily mixes elevation and plan views but some trucks are shown partially projected. Of equal salience is the activity depicted in the drawing. It introduces an alternate way young children can coordinate views in their drawings. If our eyes follow the cars emerging from the tunnel under the cranes (slightly to the upper right of middle), we notice that the view changes as the cars "descend" the curving ramp, until at the "bottom," below the ramp, the cars and trucks appear primarily in plan view, although a few are partially projected. As a whole, this suggests a view children might take if the cars were toys and their eyes followed their hand as it guided a car down the ramp, finally placing it at rest, parked at the bottom. Rather than representing a static point of view, the point of view taken appears to follow a narrated action sequence imparted while drawing. A cohesive view is not provided by the eye but from the coordination of the action depicted in the drawing and the narration of that action. This indicates that some children may use the action of a narrative to coordinate views in a drawing well before they search for visual coherence. Such drawings give a child practice in strategies for producing the same objects from multiple viewpoints. Developmentally later, children practice different projected views in the same drawing and talented children mix projected with perspective views as they move toward a stable visual viewpoint.

A third crucial development was the simultaneous adjustment in relative size that accompanied the progress in differentiating background from foreground. Although it is difficult to quantify, some qualitative observations can be made about drawings of talented children. Initially, distinctions in size appear to indicate relative importance of the characters. Those that play a major role in the picture are usually larger than other elements in the picture. For example, in Figure 5.9 from age 7, Hondo used size inconsistently across the picture. Soldiers along the top ground line, perhaps those most central to the story, are larger than those at the bottom. The size of the airplanes varies in a way that seems unrelated to the rest of the picture, and the house or bunker, hidden behind a hill, is almost as large as the hill. On the lower left is an outsized figure fallen behind a small hill. The figure is meant to be the artist, clearly the most important soldier in the battle!

Figure 5.10, drawn later that year, begins to suggest a qualitative metric that adheres loosely to natural size differences. Fire trucks, in orthographic projection, are manned by fire fighters who are approximately the right size relative to the trucks. Cars appear smaller than the trucks. The main protagonist, Batman, however, is drawn as large as the cars. Batman holds the collapsing road together so that a tow truck can pass while under him is a figure already hurt by rubble. Hondo has also used an interesting artistic device related to size that suggests he intended the whole scene to be seen as if viewed from a distance (corroborated by the artist). A bird, several insects, and plants in the upper left appear relatively large, indicating their presence in the foreground.

As relative size differences begin to indicate qualitative differences in natural size, background elements are drawn smaller than foreground elements. These differences become increasingly quantitative as talented children get older. In Figure 5.11a, the buses are proportionally diminished in size with increasing distance and

Figure 5.9. Hondo, talented boy age 7.

Figure 5.10. Hondo, talented boy age 7.

Figure 5.11a. Hondo, talented boy age 10.

Figure 5.11b. Hondo, talented boy age 12.

Hondo uses converging lines to heighten the linear perspective view. In Figure 5.11b, background size diminution and foreshortening are used simultaneously to establish a realistic metric. In Figure 5.12 towers aligned to indicate a projected view diminish appropriately in size with depicted distance. Diminishing size with distance is even more pronounced in Figure 5.13. Hondo coordinates elements shown projected in depth by combining converging lines with size diminution. He also includes a horizon line approximately one-quarter of the way up the picture plane; the sailboat rides the "true" horizon line, which is largely obscured by the hill. Hondo uses a curious artistic device in this picture as well. A fly shown in

Figure 5.12. Hondo, talented boy age 11.

actual size appears "on" the drawing, as if to suggest a scale for the actual viewing distance.

Alex: An Illustration of Perspective Drawing in a Talented Boy with Atypical Development

Although operational reasoning appears to limit most talented children's artistic performance there are individual cases of exceptional drawing ability for which this conclusion is untenable. Selfe (1983) presented the case of Nadia, who by the age of 5 was able to draw foreshortened and rotated figures in perspective despite obvious limitations in her overall cognitive abilities. This ability to draw in perspective has been noted in other artistically talented children with autism. Drawings by Stephen Wiltshire published by Selfe (1983) show that he already used an oblique projection system in the first year he began drawing, at age 5. By 6½ he had shifted to drawing in linear perspective. As with Nadia, the early stage of intellectually derived drawings, observed in talented but otherwise normal children, appeared to be absent. Recently, I had the good

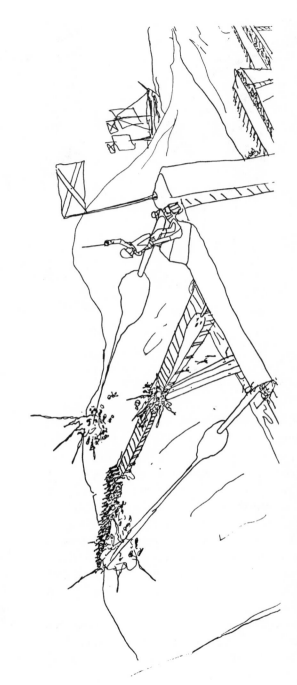

Figure 5.13. Hondo, talented boy age 12.

fortune to collect some drawings from another autistic savant, Alex, seen at my university clinic (Milbrath & Siegel, 1996).

When I obtained the drawings for this study, Alex was 6 and met DSM-IV diagnostic criteria for Autistic Disorder. The results of Alex's performance on the Weschler Pre-school and Primary Scales of Intelligence (WPPSI) help shed light on his savant abilities. Alex obtained a full-scale IQ of 66, indicating mild mental retardation, and an overall mental functioning of 4 years 4 months. But on Geometric Design, the WPPSI performance subtest measuring visual-spatial perception, he achieved the highest possible scaled score. In contrast Alex performed poorly on the Picture Completion test, which requires identifying a missing component of a picture, for example, the leg of an elephant. To achieve success on this test, a child must be able to perceive the whole and realize which of its parts is missing: a part to whole comparison. This suggests that a representation of the whole was not guiding Alex's success on design completion. Instead, each part may have been represented with equal saliency rather than in relation to a whole. One question is whether or not this applies to his drawings, as parts and even different perspectives of the same object share a similar type of quasi-independent representation. In addition to autism and mild mental retardation, Alex had some mild neuromotor impairment, not typical for autism. At the time of diagnosis Alex had an idiosyncratic pencil grasp consisting of fistlike holding of the pencil with his right hand, which is then controlled via pushing and pulling movements by the left hand. This is important in evaluating his drawings, because there was considerable motor cost to their production that is not evident in the final products.

Alex's Drawings. The drawings presented are representative of those Alex drew between ages 3 and 8 and chronicle the lightning progress he made in depicting three-dimensional perspective representations. Alex, like many autistic children, developed a passionate obsession with particular and often unusual themes. These he drew from memory even though the themes themselves were objects he had encountered in real life. Most children's aim in drawing is either to complete a picture that can be admired or to narrate a story as part of play. Alex's drawings indicated that he engaged in neither. They are not organized in the same way a normal child's drawings are. Alex typically superimposed one drawing on top of

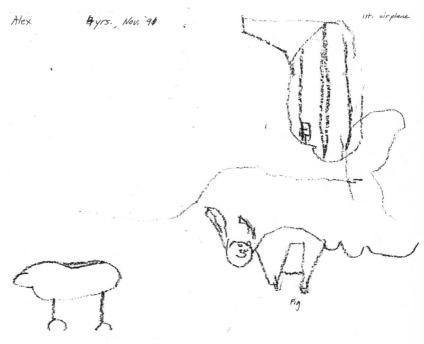

Alex   4 yrs., Nov. '90   1st. airplane

Pig

Figure 5.14a. Alex, autistic savant age 4, airplane. Figure 5.14a appeared first in "Perspective Taking in the Drawings of a Talented Autistic Child," by Milbrath & Siegel in *Visual Arts Research*, 1996, *22(2)*, 56–75. Reprinted with permission.

another and showed the same object from different perspectives, with apparent disregard for the viewer. His father reported that once Alex was finished with a drawing he rarely had any further interest in it; nor did he show it to others. It was the process of drawing itself that appeared most salient for Alex. This changed somewhat with age so that by the time Alex was 8, he was drawing some interrelated scenes. Whether or not Alex views these finished products as pictures worthy in their own right is not clear.

Alex's father assembled Alex's drawings of aircraft drawn between ages 3 to 6. Figure 5.14a shows one of his early airplanes from age 4 when his mental age would have been around 2½. The accuracy of the outline is quite remarkable for a child his age and suggests that Alex is already using lines to represent contoured edges. The following month, Alex adds wings and an engine to the

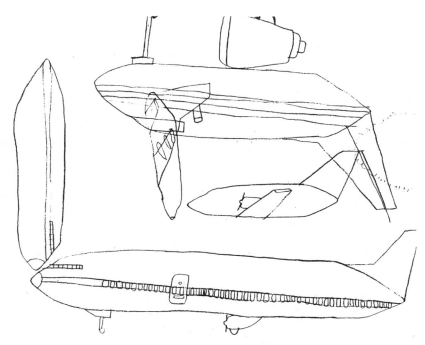

Figure 5.14b. Alex, autistic savant age 4, airplane. Figure 5.14b appeared first in "Perspective Taking in the Drawings of a Talented Autistic Child," by Milbrath & Siegel in *Visual Arts Research*, 1996, 22(2), 56–75. Reprinted with permission.

plane (middle view) and begins experimenting with three-quarter views of the wing (Figure 5.14b). When Alex was 5, he had an airplane ride in his uncle's Cessna. The airplanes in Figure 5.15 were drawn after the trip. The flexibility with which Alex draws the form of the airplane and varies its orientation implies that he is not drawing from a prototype concept of an "airplane" but instead has specific representations in mind. Of special interest is Alex's treatment of the airplane's parts. Even though the overall "gestalt" shape of an airplane usually has a special status as the carrier of primary meaning, Alex has spent considerable effort on the individual parts. The shape of each part is clearly outlined and accurately articulated with the other parts as if all parts have a special status for Alex as adjacent and simultaneous gestalts.

Airplanes were not the only theme Alex drew during his early years. He was also fascinated by the backhoe, houses, street lamps,

Figure 5.15. Alex, autistic savant age 5, "Uncle Chuck's Cessna." Figure 5.15 appeared first in "Perspective Taking in the Drawings of a Talented Autistic Child," by Milbrath & Siegel in *Visual Arts Research*, 1996, 22(2), 56–75. Reprinted with permission.

a factory he visited, and occasionally animals or people. When Alex was 6, a visit to his grandmother's house initiated drawings of houses. Behind her house a housing development was in construction. Alex's father reports that he would climb on a stool and watch the building process with great concentration for hours. About a month later, quite separated in time from viewing, Alex began to draw the houses. When he came for diagnosis at the university clinic, I asked him to draw these houses. The drawings he produced are shown in Figure 5.16. Remarkably, Alex matched the drawing sequence to the building process he observed much as if he was following a visual narrative. In houses 1 and 2, Alex drew the internal framing, but he abandoned these drawings because he did not like using the thick lined magic marker given him. When he was offered a pen, he began drawing house 3. At first it was difficult to recognize it as a house because he began with the angles and rectangles of the roof instead of the outline of the house. First he

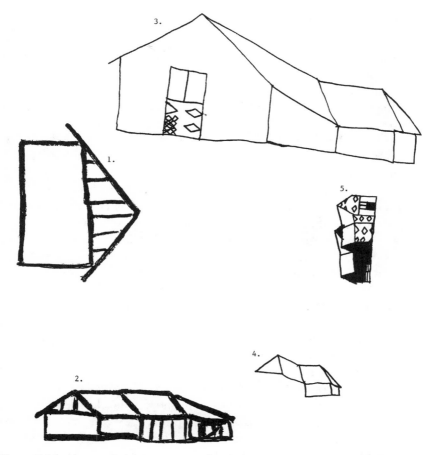

Figure 5.16. Alex, autistic savant age 6, houses. Figure 5.16 appeared first in "Perspective Taking in the Drawings of a Talented Autistic Child," by Milbrath & Siegel in *Visual Arts Research, 1996, 22(2), 56–75.* Reprinted with permission.

completed the rectangle on the left and then attached the parallelogram on the right. He then added the triangle of the roof on the right and the oblique line of the roof to the extreme left and front wall. It was only at that point that Alex drew each of the other four-sided shapes that make up the rest of the house that the outline of the house in perspective was revealed. He then began house 4, but, dissatisfied with the drawing, he moved to house 5. Again he commenced with the rectanglelike shapes of the roof but rather than producing one house, he attached adjacent shapes to produce two, one house occluded by the other. It appeared as if Alex was not bound to a single drawing formula for a house but could easily recombine different parts of the house to create a new view of two overlapping houses. Each house was constructed from smaller units represented as shapes (i.e., parallelograms, squares), albeit in a somewhat rigid sequence, that could be flexibly combined toward an intended representation.

When Alex completed the basic structure of the house, he added the framing and then the diamonds and then started filling in over the framing and insulation, saying, "Somebody put that on." This was meant as the final stucco application to the outside of the house. His father clarified that the diamonds were the trademark that appeared on the insulation of the houses Alex saw being built. At this point Alex returned to drawing 3, adding the door and an inside view of the insulation. It is not uncommon for autistic children, even nontalented autistic children, to include such idiosyncratic geometric features as the insulation trademark that are irrelevant to the identity of objects in their drawings (Lewis & Boucher, 1991).

Recently, Alex's father sent me drawings from Alex's seventh and eighth years. His father reported that at age 8½, Alex's communication skills were more age-appropriate. He was reading but rather than memorizing the physical form of words as his father expected because of his exceptional visual memory, Alex learned by using phonics. Nevertheless, without prompting, Alex will "stare at a sentence for hours, literally, without making a move." To read the word he must be prompted each time. Alex's father also noted that although Alex takes on age-appropriate responsibilities at home, he is still unable to at school, and although he can perform what is required of him at school, he does not unless prompted. Alex is still drawing at a prodigious rate but his father observes that his drawings, particularly of new themes, are simpler, more abstract, conceptual, and stylized.

Several interesting changes can be noted in his drawings. Alex attempts to draw a more complete scene with interrelated parts. For example, in Figure 5.17 he still draws houses and repeats parts of the drawing in an unrelated manner but he also has placed the houses in a context by constructing a ground plane with irregular lines at the bottom of the drawing. The drawing is somewhat confusing because it appears as if he has drawn one set of houses and

Figure 5.17. Alex, autistic savant age 8, houses.

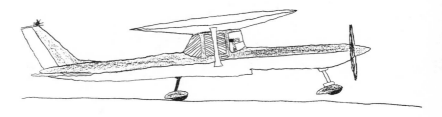

Figure 5.18. Alex, autistic savant age 8, airplane.

Figure 5.19. Alex, autistic savant age 8, "Man Going Up in the Ceiling."

their context on top of another. A clearer example of this development occurs in Figure 5.18, where Alex uses a single ground line even though he has drawn the airplane in perspective and with great detail. His father reports that this airplane is from Alex's imagi-

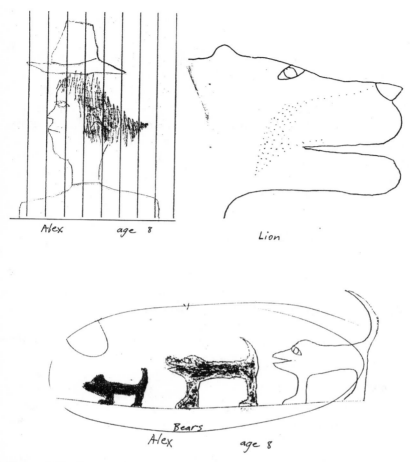

Figure 5.20. Alex, autistic savant age 8, animal and human figures.

nation. He has combined various parts of different airplanes to "invent" an airplane he has never seen. Another imaginal example that includes the interrelationship of elements in a scene is in Figure 5.19. This was based on a dream and shows a "man going up in the ceiling." But although the view is projected, there is no evidence of true perspective. Despite further elaborations of his previous themes such as the airplane and house, Alex made less progress in his drawings of animate subjects. Some examples are shown in Figure 5.20. Most are drawn schematically in canonical orientations but Alex also varies the characteristics of the human profiles he has drawn.

CONCLUSIONS

The development of the depiction of spatial relationships in drawings was traced in this chapter. Initially, we asked the question as to whether or not the emergence of spatial relationships among elements in a drawing and the appearance of single viewpoint drawings were dependent on conceptual development or whether children can arrive at these milestones by using purely figurative processes. If figurative processes could be used alone, then children with exceptional talent might draw in perspective very early. But if conceptual development is necessary then even in children with exceptional talent the development of perspective drawing would follow a similar protracted period of development as its conceptual understanding. The results from the group studies and from the individual case presentations do not point to a simple answer. We see that in normal development even when talent is exceptional, conceptual development appears to limit drawing performance. However, in atypical development when conceptual development is itself limited, figurative processes appear capable of guiding the evolution of perspective drawings. Let us take up these issues point by point.

Conceptual Development

The first point is that children's ability to map three-dimensional spatial relationships onto a two-dimensional drawing surface developed slowly over the 10 years of study. Table 5.4 shows a comparison between the development of a drawing skill and the norms for spatial reasoning in the talented and less talented children. In both talented and less talented children, the construction of a two-dimensional picture plane, the addition of a depth plane, and the use of simple indicators of perspective such as occlusion appeared in the same sequence as normative reasoning about these relationships. In the less talented children the timing of these milestones in drawings was somewhat delayed relative to the norms but in the talented children their appearance paralleled the youngest ages found in normative studies of spatial reasoning measured without reference to drawings. The sequence for the talented children (see Table 5.4) is described in greater detail below.

In the talented samples observations indicated that prior to age 5, most talented children represented figures with correct placement and order of body parts, but few constructed a picture plane. These findings are in close correspondence to the main features of Stage I responses obtained by Piaget in that relationships depicted in both task-related drawings and model constructions simply preserved topological relationships internal to a figure (Piaget & Inhelder 1956/67, chaps. 2 and 14).

Talented children showed significant development in the use of a ground line and ground plane between the ages of 4 and 6, establishing the two-dimensional coordinates of the picture plane. This implies that an external two-dimensional frame of reference was used earlier than predicted from Piaget's water task (Piaget & Inhelder, 1956/67, chap. 13). But other investigators have found that children as young as 3 years old can choose the correct depiction of a chimney in relation to a roof even if they cannot draw the chimney vertically with respect to the ground (Perner, Kohlmann & Wimmer, 1984) and that by age 4 children mentally represent the location of an object in relation to a single axis (Case et al., 1996). The fact that the figure was primarily used before the age of 5 and the paper afterward could suggest that these first reference systems depend on local relational coding instead of an understanding of gravitational coordinates (Bryant, 1974; Ibbotson & Bryant, 1976; Harris, 1977).

Almost immediately after this major accomplishment, talented children began to invade the two-dimensional picture surface by representing depth with complex positioning techniques of vertical segregation and overlap. Between the ages of 5 and 6 they began using simple positioning techniques of overlap and vertical segregation that involved coordinating foreground and background simultaneously. But horizontal segregation, a two-dimensional device, still dominated and drawings were entirely without a projective or perspective system. Even figure rotation, a conceptually simpler indicator of viewpoint than perspective (Huttenlocher & Presson, 1973), was primarily either front view, profile, or a mixture of the two (see chapter 4). These results suggest that an abrupt transition from two-dimensional representations to those with depth occurred almost as soon as the picture plane was established. This transition happened more quickly in these children than in the children studied by Piaget. In coordinating viewpoints, Piaget's Stage IIB children distinguished points of view (picture selection) but attempts at representation resulted in egocentric responses (Pia-

TABLE 5.4
COMPARISON OF SPATIAL MILESTONES ACHIEVED IN DRAWING WITH NORMS[a]

Drawing Skill	Approximate Age of Achievement[a]		Norms for Spatial Milestone
	Talented	Less Talented	
Absence of Picture Plane			**Stage 1 ≤ 4/5 years**
Vertical and horizontal relations within figures are correctly organized.	2 to 3 years	3 to 4 years	Copy topological relationship of a model internal to a figure (Piaget & Inhelder, 1956/1967).
			Children choose correct depictions of a chimney in relation to a roof even if they cannot draw the chimney vertically with respect to the ground (Perner, Kohlmann & Wimmer, 1984).
			Local relationship coding (Bryant, 1974; Ibbotson & Bryant, 1976; Harris, 1977) that coordinates object with respect to a single referent (Case et al., 1996).
Construct two-dimensional picture plane			**Stage IIA ≈ 4 to 6 years**
			Coordinating within a reference system.
			Reconstructing route to school:
Ground line Horizontal segregation	3 to 4 years	5 to 6 years	Children represent relationships along a single dimension (left–right) but such relationships are only organized with respect to smaller local group (Piaget, Inhelder & Szeminska, 1960).
Canonical figure orientations	3 to 4 years	5 to 6 years	Constructing perspective:
No projective system: elevation and plan	3 to 4 years	5 to 6 years	Perspective egocentric-salient features of array reproduced (Piaget & Inhelder, 1956/1967).

	Age	Stage / Description
Construct three-dimensional plane		**Stage IIB ≈ 6 to 7/8 years**
Ground plane		Coordinating within a reference system.
Vertical segregation or overlap	7 to 8 years	Reconstructing route to school:
	5 to 6 years	Children attempt to represent foreground and background but such relationships are only organized with respect to the smaller local group (Piaget, Inhelder & Szeminska, 1960).
		Constructing perspective:
		Children distinguish points of view (picture selection) but attempts at representation result in egocentric responses in Three Mountain Problem (Piaget & Inhelder, 1956/67).
Local Coordination of Viewpoint		**Stage IIIA ≈ 7 to 9 years**
Three-Quarter Figure Rotations	Index not met	Coordinating within a reference system.
	7 to 8 years	Reconstructing route to school:
Foreshortening	Index not met	Children unable to use a stable and coherent reference (Piaget, Inhelder & Szeminska, 1960).
	7 to 8 years	Constructing perspective:
Oblique Projection applied locally	13 years (42%)	Simple changes in shape with changes in perspective of objects.
	7 to 8 years	Children take account of either left–right reversals or before–behind in Three Mountain Problem (Piaget & Inhelder, 1956/1967).
Mixed projective drawings	9 to 10 years	
	7 to 8 years	

TABLE 5.4 (cont.)

| Drawing Skill | Approximate Age of Achievement[a] | | Norms for Spatial Milestone |
	Less Talented	Talented	
Application of Single Perspective to entire drawing			**Stage IIIB ≈ 9 to 11 years**
Naive Perspective	Index not met	9 to 10 years	Coordinating within a reference system. Reconstructing route to school: Children maintain a fixed reference that expresses a coherent order and position of landmarks but lacks accurate expression of the size and distance relations of the model or route (Piaget, Inhelder & Szeminska, 1960).
			Constructing Perspective: Changes in shape and position coordinated into a single perspective (Piaget & Inhelder, 1956/1967).
Quantification of perspective			**Stage IV ≈ 11 to 12 years**
Linear Perspective	Index not met	11 to 13 years	Quantification of distances and proportional reduction in scale with distance obtained when children construct a route or plan of the village (Piaget, Inhelder & Szeminska, 1960).

[a] Positive age index for a group was 50% of the children showing the competence.

get & Inhelder, 1956/67, chaps. 6 and 8). In coordinating view-points with a reference system (Piaget & Inhelder, 1956/67, chap. 14; Piaget et al., 1960, chap. 1) small groups of objects were organized correctly locally but remained unrelated to the whole. Stage IIA children represented relationships along a single dimension (left–right) and IIB children made attempts to represent foreground and background but such relationships were only organized with respect to the smaller local group.

Prior to age 7, the talented children almost uniformly used an elevation and plan drawing system. Mixed viewpoint drawings were mixtures of these unprojected drawing systems. These mixtures indicated children were working locally on parts of the picture, shifting points of view for new parts without relating parts to a coherent whole. Such behavior is classically characteristic of Stage II children across a variety of tasks (Inhelder & Piaget, 1964). In addition, mixed rotations were primarily mixtures of canonical views. *Canonical* in this context means simple two-dimensional representations with salient identifying features. In Piaget's Three Mountain problem, children of this age made egocentric responses (Stage II) that preserved both the features and the organization that identified the array for a child. Even when Stage IIB children attempted to take a doll's point of view their choice was dictated by a dominant feature of the array. Similarities in the features of egocentric and canonical preferences suggest that egocentric responses relate strongly to a child's understanding of the canonical representation of a subject (Freeman, 1980).

What is striking is that despite the large and fluid graphic vocabulary of the talented children, they did not attempt to apply a single specific viewpoint uniformly to the entire picture until quite late, between ages 9 and 10. Simple positioning techniques were used to represent the third dimension before projected views appeared. These kinds of devices do not necessitate coordinating an object along a specific line of site nor do they rely on maintaining a coherent referent for the relationships between objects. Even oblique projected views that appeared between ages 7 and 8 do not necessarily entail the use of a specific line of site to coordinate a coherent view across the entire drawing. Instead an oblique drawing system can be applied locally to one object or a few objects in a picture. Coincident with this period were the highest number of mixed view drawings. These mixtures were primarily mixed projected views, indicating a growing awareness of other potential specific viewpoints but an inability to coordinate a single viewpoint. It was not until naive perspective, the first attempt to coordinate a single point of view, that the three-dimensional coordinates began to be applied uniformly and coherently to the entire drawing.

The progression that is suggested by these findings is that children first altered shapes of objects with changes in view (e.g., foreshortening, three-quarter rotations, and oblique projections) and later attempted to coordinate the entire picture from a single point of view in a specific perspective (naive perspective). These findings are comparable with the simple changes in shape with changes in perspective Piaget obtained at Stage IIIA and alterations in the shape of all objects with coordination into a single perspective at Stage IIIB (Piaget & Inhelder, 1956/67, chaps. 6 and 8). Likewise, in constructing a diagram of a model village or in representing their route to school, Piaget's stage IIIA children were unable to use a stable and coherent reference (Piaget et al., 1960, chap. 1; Piaget & Inhelder, 1956/67, chap. 14). Stage IIIB children, on the other hand, maintained a fixed reference that expressed a coherent order and position of landmarks but lacked accurate expression of the size and distance relations of the model or route.

Drawings in linear perspective were further delayed until talented children reached an age at which projective concepts usually become quantified. In terms of Piaget's stages, it is not until the stage of formal operations that the understanding of the continuous and proportional relations between objects along a line of sight allows a child to construct and appreciate a specific point of view in true perspective. Quantification of distances and proportional reduction in scale with distance were obtained by Piaget (1956/67, chap. 14) when Stage IV children constructed a plan of the village. In this study children began to use a true (linear) perspective system around the age of 11 or 12 but oblique projective systems were still more common. Finally, in the last 2 years of the study, perspective drawing systems (naive and linear) began to replace oblique projective systems.

Figurative Processes

The second point in this discussion has to do with the use of figurative processes to generate perspective drawings. We have seen that despite highly developed figurative thought generally observed in talented children (Munro et al., 1942; Rosenblatt & Winner, 1988), the development of spatial relationships and single viewpoint drawings in the talented children studied here followed a trajectory approximately parallel to the norms for conceptual development. Talented children appear generally unable to utilize figurative process to generate perspective drawings in the absence of conceptual supports. Nevertheless this is not always the case. The case of Alex shows that perspective drawings can emerge in the absence of corresponding conceptual supports.

Alex arrived at perspective drawings between the ages of 4 and 6, well outside the range for normative development of supporting spatial concepts. In addition, Alex tested as mild mentally retarded with the indication that conceptual milestones were delayed between 2 and 4 years. But his performance on the WPPSI subtest for visual-spatial performance was at the highest level, suggesting that like other artistically talented children, Alex has some remarkable figurative abilities. Recall also that Alex's performance on the Picture Completion test was extremely poor. This requires perceiving an object as a functional whole and then identifying a missing part. This mosaic of abilities is further illuminated by a recent study undertaken by Biskup-Meyer and Siegel (1995) of visual-spatial processing in autistic and normal children with the developmental level and mental age of 2 or 4 years. They showed that autistic children solved puzzles by shape or form alone, entirely ignoring the puzzle's content. Nonverbal autistic children completed blank, abstract, or representational puzzles of the same cut and shape difficulty with equal rapidity. In contrast, the normal children completed the representational puzzles, for which semantic labels could aid problem solving, much more rapidly than the other puzzles. Those who were verbal often verbally labeled the dissembled object before assembly.

Alex appeared to produce his house drawings in much the same way, from a series of juxtaposed shapes. He never outlined the house. He assembled the whole bottom-up from its parts. At first the house was indiscernible until enough of its parts were placed in relation to each other to "add up" to the house. Alex appears to have drawn the parts as individual shapes that he put together much as he put the pieces of the WPPSI geometric block puzzles together, not so much guided by the whole as by the pattern of the parts. Most children, even talented children, do not approach drawing in this way. More typically they start with a top-down approach by outlining the whole and then filling in the details. Alex's strong visual bias appears unconstrained by conceptual knowledge of the object or the category to which an object belongs. Instead of seeing the object as a "house" he appears to see it as visual surfaces or the series of shapes it assumes from a given vantage point. Each shape has saliency equal or greater than the shape of the whole. This ability to see the world in terms of visual surfaces is coupled with an exceptional visual memory with which Alex can later recall and even reconfigure new orientations from the remembered parts (Marr, 1982).

But another aspect of Alex's development allows us to observe the influence conceptual development has on figurative thought. Initially Alex showed a marked decalage between his visual-spatial and conceptual abilities. His drawings between ages 4 and 6 seem to suggest that only his figurative abilities affected his drawing performance. But as Alex made progress in his intellectual development his drawings became more conceptual and less visually realistic. Alex's father reported that by age 8 he was making intellectual progress in school and his drawings also showed a corresponding change. Generally, his father stated, the stunning realism of his younger drawings was less common but the conceptual aspects were more advanced (e.g., Figures 5.19 and 5.20). At the same time Alex began to draw scenes but the scenes themselves were not in perspective. In fact, these drawings are more nearly similar to those of talented children who are otherwise normal. It may be that deriving a perspective drawing from the assembly of apparent shapes is not possible for scenes in which the wholes themselves must be interrelated. The ability to reason about spatial relationships may be necessary. Therefore, even though Alex's conceptual development has expanded his imagination and enriched his drawings, it also appears to have dampened his ability to perceive the world in terms of visual surfaces. Instead of drawing and composing shapes, he is beginning to draw concepts and categories.

The Drawing Schema

The final point relates to the influence of conceptual and figurative thought on drawing production. All children develop drawing schemas for depicting repeated themes. Talented children seemed quickly to reflect their current state of knowledge related to space in their drawing schemas by rotating and foreshortening figures and using projective and perspective drawing systems. In contrast less talented children appeared to repeat their drawing schemas rigidly, changing them relatively little with age. This was particularly evident in their figure drawings, where canonical orientations dominated at all ages and foreshortening was rarely used. One question is why less talented children were unable to reflect their progress in spatial reasoning in their drawings. Since most children studied were sampled from art classes it seems unlikely that training in the arts or exposure to drawing techniques provides an answer. Instead the expertise developed by talented children is likely a consequence of how they focused their attention and harnessed their initial figurative abilities toward developing drawing technique.

The amount of drawing practice engaged in by the talented children has already been emphasized in chapter 2. In other domains the knowledge that results from focused practice has been found to be uniquely organized. Chi and her colleagues (Gobbo & Chi, 1986; Chi, 1978) studied the differences between expert and novice performers in a variety of domains. They found, as have others (see Norman, 1983; Simon & Simon, 1978), that the knowledge structures or cognitive schemes of experts are organized so that they are extensively cross-referenced and interconnected, so although the working memory capacity (M capacity) of experts and novices is the same, the organization of memory or the "chunk" structure of experts is different. For example, experts appear to have overlapping chunks so that retrieval of one chunk serves as a cue for another. This raises the interesting possibility that because the expert efficiently structures information, the demands put on working memory are lower for the expert than for the novice on domain-relevant tasks.

Another facet is the hierarchical organization of the domain-relevant knowledge. Within a chunk the information is organized so that retrieval of the "top" or superordinate element allows unpacking of all subordinate elements organized in the hierarchy. Novices encode the same information in two or more chunks and must retrieve each separately. When the expert–novice approach is translated to the domain of drawing, there are obvious parallels in the time talented children spend thinking about, planning, and representing aspects of the domain. But of greatest interest are the potential differences in the organization of drawing schemas in memory. The drawing schemas of talented children may be hierarchically organized and interconnected in overlapping chunks whereas the same information in less talented children may be represented across different individual and unconnected schemas.

The talented child starts by differentiating more schemas because her aim is visual rather than conceptual. Through differentiation and practice these schemas become hierarchically organized and interconnected. What does this mean for any given drawing? If drawing schemas of talented children are organized in a hierarchy, they can be unpacked or decomposed. For example, a drawing schema of the human figure might be organized as an interconnected family of drawing schemas that includes the human figure in many different orientations. Any particular orientation may be further decomposed into smaller component schemas for the parts of a human figure, such as the hand. A drawing schema for the hand itself may be additionally organized hierarchically so as to include another family of hand schemas, each in a different orientation. The hand, therefore, can serve to access a variety of figure poses in which a specific hand schema or related hand schemas are embedded. Experimentation with and practice of these procedures to draw component parts of a larger drawing schema would dictate how many branches and interconnections such organizations would develop. Joel, one of the talented children, describes consciously practicing starting a drawing from different parts of the figure and varying the figure's orientation. He would start a dinosaur drawing, "feet first . . . tail first. It was hard at times, you get thrown off . . . but real important to do that. . . . I was always trying to do things from different orientations." The advantage of developing this type of differentiated schema is that when a child wishes to vary the orientation of a figure or of parts of a figure, the schema to accomplish the variation is readily accessible from any point in a drawing. When a new type of drawing is needed, for example, one that better reflects current spatial knowledge, the schemas for component parts can be broken out and recombined in new ways to meet the situation.

Contrast the difficulties a novice encounters in producing a drawing. The drawing schemas of the novice are to begin with poorly differentiated. There may only be one or two human figure schemas because they are adequate to fulfill an aim of conceptually defining the figure as a person. In addition, rather than having component parts that cross-reference each other, each part is rigidly bound to the single schema. The hand, for example, is not part of a family of interconnected schemas for hands, but of a single human figure schema whose parts are serially linked by the act of production. This means that the drawing can only be started at a single origin point. Much like the novice trying to remember the tune (or words) of an Irish jig, the novice artist must go to the "beginning" to retrieve the parts because they are only known in fixed sequence. The whole cannot be decomposed into parts. When the novice needs a new drawing, motivated by developments in spatial knowledge, there are only one or two schemas at her disposal and since they cannot be easily decomposed and recombined, the novice repeats the schemas she has without solving the problem. The novice lacks the expert's interconnected hierarchical organization of related drawing schemas and so keeps accessing the same schema repeatedly.

In sum, the artistic development of talented but otherwise normal individuals is marked by the continual coordination of figurative thought with conceptual development. The aim of the talented child is always visual realism and both figurative and conceptual processes are harnessed toward that aim. This allows the talented child who remains focused on drawing as a meaningful and rewarding activity to develop drawing schemas that through continued practice become organized hierarchically in memory as a rich store of procedures for drawing figures or objects and their component parts. As a child matures and is motivated to develop new ways to draw themes of interest, she can easily decompose and recombine existing drawing schemas to create new drawings. In contrast, the artistic development in less talented children takes a different track altogether. These children appear initially to operate with a much stronger conceptual bias and a correspondingly weaker figurative bias. Conceptual development overpowers their early artistic development, leading them to evolve a set of drawing schemas that more accurately describe rather than visually depict drawing topics. Because their earliest aim of realism appears to be satisfied by an intellectual rather than a visual realism, they do not vary their drawing schemas nor experiment with visually realistic views. This leads to repetition of the same drawing schemas, which are adequate as descriptions but do not approach topics from a visual perspective. As strategies of visual exploration based on conceptual development and spatial reasoning emerge, the aim of visual realism also takes hold of these children. But the drawing procedures to execute such drawings are unavailable and in frustration many decrease or cease their drawing activity. As drawing practice diminishes, attaining the goal of drawing with visual realism becomes increasingly distant.

These two patterns of development in normal children can be contrasted with the emergence of artistic talent in children who otherwise develop atypically. The autistic savant appears to operate with a strong figurative bias but a conceptual system that is developmentally delayed or severely disabled. In this case the child appears to generate highly realistic drawings directly from visual spatial abilities without the constraints imposed by conceptual development. The three artistic paths are qualitatively distinct, yet they arise from a union of the same basic mental processes, figurative and conceptual thought. In the case of the talented but otherwise normal child the two are coordinated throughout development. In the case of the less talented normal child a strong conceptual bias sets the early direction of artistic development. In the case of the autistic savant a decalage between figurative and conceptual thought allows figurative processes to dominate.

6

PUTTING PICTORIAL
SPACE TOGETHER

In the previous chapters we examined different aspects of artistic development as separate and unrelated to each other. In this chapter these aspects are brought together because artistic development does not proceed as isolated progressions of its individual parts but as a unified whole. When a young child uses line, she uses it to represent real things in the world that have surfaces, shape, and volume. Visually she encounters these things from specific viewpoints that are continually varied as she moves. At the same time she is also constructing a conceptual understanding of things in the world that takes a more abstract and general form. Drawing evokes this tension between specific visual instances and their abstracted conceptual representation. The child tries to find a balance between what she *knows* and what she *sees* by producing a drawing that conserves these abstracted concepts but can still be easily recognized visually. Children's drawings of a cube are particularly good exemplars of this dual purpose. After a certain age, a child knows that a cube has parallel sides and square faces but the cube's apparent perspective when she looks at it rarely presents the sides as parallel or the shape as square. At different ages children come up with different solutions to the cube conflict. Eventually, the preferred solution of older children and adults is an oblique projection that preserves both the conceptual features, parallel sides and square shape, and aspects of the visual perspective, edges and surfaces projected in depth (Cox, 1986; Deregowski & Strang, 1986).

It is this tension between conceptual and visual knowledge that strikes at the heart of the qualitative differences between developmental trajectories of highly talented and less talented children proposed by my model of talent development. For all young children, drawing is a highly pleasurable activity that shares elements in common with sensory motor play. Piaget (Piaget & Inhelder, 1956/67) pointed out, however, that play is primarily assimilative because children bend the environment to their design whereas drawing is largely accommodative because children continually modify simpler graphic equivalents toward greater visual likeness. Despite this general observation, most young children appear to focus less on visual elements of their drawings than on conceptual elements. They establish symbolic equivalence with real things in the world primarily by conceptual identity and only globally by visual similarity. For example, the human figure is typically drawn by children of all ages in front view because this view presents a clear structural description that easily shows all the parts that define a person. Less talented children in this study were no exception. Despite their age, most of these children drew the human figure in its canonical orientation. More to the point was the extreme rarity of dynamic and visually realistic poses for figure orientations, the kind that mark specific visual viewpoints. Most figures were drawn static or frozen with few visual details.

In contrast to most children, talented children aim primarily for visual equivalence. They pay close attention to visual similarities from an early age. In following their artistic progress, we observed that two-dimensional depictions of form were visually accurate and detailed when the children were quite young. Many of these talented children drew recognizable representations between their second and third years and by age 4 some were depicting scenes with complex spatial relationships of figures and objects. But translating the third dimension to its two-dimensional equivalent proved more difficult and emerged over a protracted period of development that spanned the childhood years. The addition of three-dimensional features to their drawings appeared linked in age with the normative chronology for spatial reasoning and suggested that conceptual development had a significant impact on their drawing ability. It appeared as if talented children still had to understand a spatial relationship conceptually before they could master it artistically. Nevertheless, the ability of talented children to reflect in their drawings the progress they made in conceptual understanding immediately, indicated a fluid interaction between conceptual and visual knowledge during their artistic development.

The talent differences in children's drawing goals were first made apparent when the way they used line and plane was studied. From the beginning of their development, talented children treated line and plane elements quite differently than less talented children. The way young talented children used line and plane suggested they had begun to work out a denotation system that was more truly dimensionally equivalent to what they saw when they looked at things in the world: A line functioned as an edge and the intervening plane as a surface. For example, young talented children rarely used line alone to stand for objects as less talented children did. They constructed planes but clearly differentiated between the line and enclosed plane by leaving the plane unfilled. This allowed line and plane to serve different denotation roles. Older less talented children also constructed planes but they usually colored them in so that the line and plane merged and the line was no longer visible. In these instances, the line was subordinated to the plane and no longer functioned except as a boundary for the contained region.

The quality of the developmental differences in talented and less talented children is consistent with the model proposed in chapter 1, which emphasizes differences in developmental pathways rather than developmental rate. Qualitative differences of the type described, however, are accompanied by differences in developmental rate. A child who begins drawing by constructing and applying a set of drawing rules that maps visual rather than conceptual features of objects will more quickly discover how to draw complex spatial relationships. In this chapter I approach the issue of developmental rate by examining it in the talent groups as a whole and in individual children. In order to explain the approach I have taken, a discussion of the process of developmental change is presented first.

DEVELOPMENTAL CHANGE

Equilibration

According to Piaget (1985), competence and skills in cognitive realms are thought to develop through a series of equilibrations, disequilibrations, and reequilibrations of developing structures. Equilibration can be likened to the homeostatic process that operates to stabilize biological states but because at each point of equilibration a new state is achieved along a fixed progression, the process is best described as homeorhetic. Since equilibrated structures are continually constructed, Piaget introduced the term *optimizing equilibrations* to express the idea that at each new equilibrated state there is improvement. Improvement takes two forms: First, it can occur in the content of the equilibrated system so that a child is able to extend the system to a wider set of referents. For example, in constructing the spatial perspective of another person at a different location than the self, the transformations applied to left–right coordinates are progressively extended to before–behind. But this new ability will be restricted to a given context unless it is abstracted or detached from the context and the specific operations involved in the context and reconstructed on a higher conceptual level. In effect, the compensations in perspective made for displacement of the viewer in two dimensions and now extended to the third dimension must go beyond using the self as the referent and become integrated with the idea of an external fixed referent point. In that case we arrive at the second improvement, which includes completion of intensional as well as extensional differentiation and allows differentiated subschemes to be integrated with the original scheme. In the example, this includes being able to compare the self's view with all potential displacements and place these within a system of fixed external referents. This allows the newly differentiated scheme of before–behind relations to become integrated through reciprocal assimilation with the previously elaborated left–right scheme from any perspective within a 360-degree circle from the self. There are limits in the accommodation potential of schemes, however, that depend on the plasticity and resistance of those schemes. Piaget sets those limits in accord with the number of subschemes or subsystems already differentiated. The greater the number, the greater the chance of reciprocal assimilation between a novel subscheme and others in the system.

When external objects offer resistance they become an obstacle to assimilation and states of disequilibration arise. The child encounters disequilibrating forces in the environment when she comes up against situations that she cannot understand with the knowledge structures she has already developed. In the case of drawing, this occurs when a child tries to draw something she has never drawn before or tries to draw something she has drawn but in a new way, such as a human figure engaged in an action. But most disequilibration is internally generated by discrepancies or contradictions within the child as she begins to understand her world in new ways. As knowledge structures become well consolidated, the child tries to apply them to every new situation. Rather than producing success, however, overapplication inevitably uncovers new problems that serve as disequilibrating forces. In the case of drawing, this type of disequilibration might be generated when a child's level of visual analysis progresses beyond her ability to draw or beyond her ability to understand and reconstruct in representation (e.g., spatial relationships). In this case a new need arises that is unfulfilled because both actions and schemes to carry out the actions are missing. Drawing techniques that formerly yielded visually satisfying results are no longer adequate and the child will have to create new ways of drawing even highly familiar topics. Chapter 1 reviewed studies showing that around 7 years of age children's perceptual ability to systematically analyze what they see improves dramatically. It is around this age that children's approach to drawing changes as well (Gardner, 1980). They become technically more competent as they search for techniques to make things more visually realistic but the cost is a decline in prolificness and in the spontaneity and individualized style that make the drawings of younger children so delightful.

Disequilibrating states in and of themselves are not the source of progress. They are the trigger that motivates a child's search for new forms to overcome obstacles to assimilation. It is the new forms that function to reequilibrate the system. Progress results from this process of reequilibration, which from the child's point of view is a search for coherence. For example, a very young child is satisfied with the topographic mapping of a drawn scene because it coheres with what she understands. But as she gets older she begins to be aware that some objects in the world are in the foreground and others are behind. Arriving at graphic means to suggest these relationships in a drawing, however, will not be a simple matter of trying different drawing strategies. First she will have to map a system of external coordinates onto the picture plane, a development that presumably depends on a scheme for the system of external coordinates. The coherence obtained by a new development, however, is relative because at each new point of equilibration new problems and possibilities leading to potential constructions based on the preceding level of understanding can arise. Potentially this developmental process is always open-ended. Certainly artistic development both at the level of an individual and at the societal level is an excellent exemplar of a potentially open-ended progression. In this particular example, knowledge of the system of external co-ordinates raises a new problem for the child, of the referent point within this system from which the depicted scene is to be viewed.

Regulations

According to Piaget (1985), equilibration and reequilibration are accomplished by regulatory processes in which each successive action (physical or mental) is either modified toward success or reinforced if successful. These regulatory processes are constructive and conservative at the same time. They are constructive because they retroactively add corrective actions or schemes to the trajectory of actions that can then engender new knowledge. They are conservative because they conserve and stabilize states, sequences, schemes, or subsystems associated with success. During constructions, trial and error play an important role by eliminating failures and retaining successes. At this level of corrections after the fact, coordination comes about gradually through retroactive modifications and proactive anticipations. At some point retroactive corrections become unnecessary because, first, they are transferred to and reconstructed on the plane of representation and, second, they become part of the regulating system itself. A simple example is provided by the classic conservation of liquid task. At first young children operate with figurative schemes and are "fooled" by what they see. But disequilibration results when pouring the liquid back into the original container demonstrates the equivalency of the two contrasting containers. For a time children operate by this kind of corrective feedback, resorting to reversing the actions physically in order to establish the identity of the liquid. But once this kind of reversible action becomes internally represented it can become integrated into a system of operations that "perfectly" regulates the child's reasoning about the liquid.

Regulation applies both to transactions with external objects and to those involving internal coordinations between schemas (schemata) or schemes. These latter reciprocal assimilations and accommodations among schemas and schemes are characterized by multiple regulations and complex relationships between subsystems. In the case of direct transactions with objects, physical properties, for example, shape, must be isolated and abstracted (empirical abstraction) from objects. In the case of internal coordinations among schemes, properties introduced and conferred on objects by completed structures, like order or classification, must be deduced or abstracted (pseudoempirical abstractions) before regulations can be effective. Thus the developmental completion of operatory structures within subsystems necessarily precedes their integration into a regulated total system. In drawing this amounts to the integration through reciprocal assimilation and accommodation of a child's figurative and conceptual schemes with each other and with her or his drawing techniques, a success that only comes about with a good deal of trial and error in drawing practice.

Two types of direct regulatory processes are identified by Piaget. In the first, regulations are automatic or quasi-automatic. For example, in perceptual constancies such as size constancy, perceptual mechanisms compensate for the decrease in apparent or projective size of distant objects. Likewise in simple sensory-motor actions like grasping, displacements of the hand are corrected toward the trajectory of an object. But generally these types of regulations do not lead to conscious awareness. A second type, active regulations, do lead to conscious awareness because they involve representation or conceptualization of actions and as a result they are likely to engender new knowledge. These are initiated when new means to a goal are sought or choices among means must be made. For example, as a child decides between using vertical segregation or occlusion to express depth relationships, it may strike the child that although the former is adequate the latter is more similar to her or his typical visual experience. Eventually active regulations as part of a subsystem or total system are subordinated to higher-order regulators, proceeding from active regulations to regulations on regulations up to autoregulations. The highest level, autoregulations, makes self-organization of systems possible.

By their very nature, these regulations are largely compensatory. Compensations are actions that oppose, neutralize, or cancel out obstacles to a goal. Whereas compensations associated with actions are likely to correct the actions themselves, compensations associated with regulations on regulations internally oppose obstacles, discrepancies, and contradictions until finally, with the completion of inverse operations, compensations become part of an autoregulatory function in conceptual domains. In our example of conservation of liquid, autoregulation occurs in the form of a mental calculation that assesses in a compensatory fashion the height and width of one container against the height and width of the other.

Compensations give both negative and positive feedback. In the case of negative feedback, regulatory compensations can operate either to negate a contradictory result or to differentiate and restructure schemes so that they can accommodate obstacles. For example, many perceptible characteristics of objects are omitted from conscious perception because assimilatory schemes compensate for the disturbance they pose by deleting them. Thus topological schemes lead younger children to analyze visible relationships among objects inadequately whereas the imposition of incomplete Euclidian assimilatory schemes suppresses the analysis or perception of visible projective relationships. A table is "seen" as a rectangle no matter where the young viewer is stationed because her knowledge of its Euclidian shape (scheme) prevents her from seeing its projective shape. On the other hand, the effects of positive feedback are subtler. Positive feedback acts to affirm and strengthen successful actions. But more important in an energetics sense, positive feedback compensates for the deficit that would result from failure and so enhances or strengthens the value of a goal.

Developmental Implications

One implication of Piaget's theory is that development proceeds through periods of structural instability (disequilibration) and structural consolidation (equilibration) (Feldman, 1980). If as Piaget proposes, progress is a product of disequilibrations and subsequent reequilibrations, then one prediction would be that the speed of development would be reflected in the number of these phasic components. At each point in development one might also expect to see novelties or newly emergent skills that mark the frontier of a child's progress. In one case, a novelty might herald a change in underlying schemes. In that case its appearance would not be isolated and once in use it would thereafter be part of a child's drawing practice. It would be part of a larger complex of changes that all result from the development of the same scheme. In a second case, a novelty could act as a source of disequilibration, representing a new potential or the opening of a new possibility. In that case, the novelty might at first appear isolated and only become integrated into the core of a child's drawing practice at a later time.

Finally, the theory prescribes that beyond the differentiation and integration of schemes within a system, integration among different systems occurs as well. We would expect, therefore, that along the path of artistic development, perceptual, sensory-motor, and conceptual schemes related to drawing would be continually differentiated and integrated within and between these systems. The degree of differentiation within each system would determine the limits of assimilation and accommodation possible between systems. The greater the differentiation or number of schemes within a system the greater its potential for assimilating schemes differentiated within a reciprocal system.

A Stage Mixture Approach to Development

One approach to examining how individual aspects of drawing interrelate and change over development is suggested by studies that have categorized children's modal level of performance and variability in performance at a given point in time (Feldman, 1980; Turiel, 1969; Snyder & Feldman, 1984). *Modal level* can be defined as a child's most commonly used organizational level and serves as a single index of her or his developmental stage. *Variability* can be defined as the degree of variation around that single index. It serves as a measure of stage or level variation but more to the point it provides an index of disequilibrium or readiness for developmental change (Feldman, 1980). In the domains of moral judgment (Turiel, 1969) and map making (Snyder & Feldman, 1984), researchers have found that when children are ready to move to the next level of competence, performance becomes much more variable; that is, transitions into the next developmental level are preceded by a greater mixture in level than at other points in development. This heterogeneity in level includes performance at higher stages of development as well as at stage-appropriate or modal levels. It signals a point of marked acceleration in development.

These reports suggest an interesting corollary that echoes the predictions based on Piaget's equilibration theory. Children who have accelerated rates of development should show greater level mixture throughout development than children of normal developmental rate. Since the developmental pathways of talented and less talented children are known to differ in rate (Golomb, 1992; Winner, 1996), it might be expected that talented children should also show a good deal more level mixture during their development. At the same time, it is worth reemphasizing the hypothesis that differences between talented and less talented are also qualitative; that is, what they are doing is different. The number of schemes, subsystems, and systems that are continually coordinated and hierarchically integrated is likely to differ because the differentiation of schemes related to drawing is much greater in talented children. Such differences in degree of differentiation and integration are at the root of the qualitative divergence.

In studies of stage or level mixture, certain key indices are used to assign a child's responses to a modal level but variability is also taken into account by assigning values to all the other levels present. Turiel (1969), for example, noted that children's reasoning about moral issues frequently contained statements that were less and more advanced than the stage that typified their reasoning. Snyder and Feldman (1984) observed a similar phenomenon in children's mapmaking skills. Furthermore, in both these domains greater level mixture was associated with developmental advances whereas responses restricted to modal levels appeared to represent periods of slowed development or consolidation.

The approach in these domains suggested a method for arriving at a modal level and level mixture determination for drawings. In the spontaneous drawing study multiple drawings from approximately the same point in time were obtained from many of the children. Indices in a single drawing could be combined to judge the modal level of a given drawing whereas discrepancies in modal levels across drawings from the same point in time could be used to assess level mixture. In order to classify drawings at a particular level, an algorithm based on the developmental milestones described in the literature for spatial reasoning as well as on the milestones that appeared to describe the major progressive shifts with age for each of the separately studied spatial dimensions of drawing was developed. This algorithm is presented in Table 6.1. To determine its level, a drawing was given a score for each of the four dimensions shown in the table. The final level for a single drawing was obtained by averaging these four scores. A description of how each separately studied dimension was scored appears in Appendix 2.1.

TABLE 6.1
DEFINITIONS FOR DEVELOPMENTAL LEVEL OF THE
REPRESENTATION OF FORM AND SPACE IN A
DRAWING

Ground
Level 0: No development of the ground.
Level 1: Development of the ground by use of a ground line.
Level 2: Development of the ground by use of both a ground line and a plane.
Level 3: Development of the ground by use of a ground plane only.

Position
Level 0: The absence of any relational positioning.
Level 1: The use of transparencies or horizontal positioning.
Level 2: The use of vertical positioning with transparencies instead of overlap.
Level 3: The use of vertical positioning without transparencies or the use of overlap with transparencies.
Level 4: The use of overlap without transparencies.

Rotation and Figural Perspective Indicators
Level 1: The use of front views for people and side views for animals.
Level 2: The use of side views for people or front views for animals and the inclusion of mixed front and profile views.
Level 3: The use of three-quarter rotations or back views, mixed front or profile views with three-quarter views, and at least one perspective indicator.
Level 4: The use of three-quarter rotations or back views, mixed three-quarter views, and at least two perspective indicators. A score of 5 is given for this level.
Level 5: The use of three-quarter rotations or back views, mixed three-quarter views, and all three-perspective indicators. A score of 7.5 is given for this level.

Projection
Level 1: The use of elevation and the absence of any attempt at projection.
Level 2: The use of plan or elevation and plan in combination; and if projection is attempted, the use of orthographic projection.
Level 3: The use of oblique projection or naive perspective in combination with elevation or plan.
Level 4: The use of oblique projection or naive perspective only. A score of 5 is given for this level.
Level 5: The use of linear perspective only. A score of 7.5 is given for this level.

DEVELOPMENTAL RATE IN THE
SPONTANEOUS DRAWINGS STUDIES

The level of a single drawing was defined by averaging across the four-dimensional indices. The modal level and level mixture for a child at a given age were determined across the number of drawings obtained for a child at that age. In the cross-sectional samples, not every child had submitted multiple drawings. A minimum criterion of three submitted drawings was used to select children from those samples. In the less talented sample 24 of the 75 children met the criterion (14 children had three and 10 had four). In the cross-sectional talented sample 26 of the 30 children met the criterion (all but 2 had four). The greater percentage of drawings for this sample could in part be a function of recruitment differences (see chapter 2), but of the original 16 talented children from the same school settings as most of the less talented children, 63% had submitted three or more drawings. It is likely, therefore, that the higher number of drawings obtained from the talented children reflected greater prolificness. In the longitudinal talented sample all children met the selection criterion. The level was determined for all drawings of each selected child and then three drawings were chosen for these analyses from a given 1- or 2-year period so that the distribution of their levels was proportionately representative for the 1- or 2-year period.

Cross-Sectional Less Talented Sample

Figure 6.1 shows the results of the level assignments for drawings from less talented children using all the drawings across the six 2-year age periods of study.[1] Several developmental features stand out. First, Level 1 and Level 2 characterize the children's modal level between the ages of 5 and 12. Second, only the 13- to 14-year-olds attained a higher modal level, and, third, level mixture was most marked across older adolescents, implying that some children had advanced whereas others remained at levels they may have achieved at younger ages. Although using a composite across chil-

---

1. The results looked very similar whether average level per child or level of every drawing was graphed. Thus even though each child did not have an equal contribution of drawings (three versus four) the results were relatively unaffected. Drawings were chosen for graphing rather than children to allow an opportunity for an individual child's level mixture to appear.

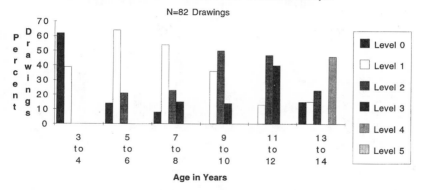

Figure 6.1. Results of the level assignment for cross-sectional less talented sample.

dren of different ages to describe development is not entirely satisfying, the obtained progression indicates a slow and gradual evolution that appears to stabilize between the ages of 9 and 10 and perhaps even stagnate for many children. For other children development appears to continue and by adolescence some children's drawings are two levels above the group mode. The greater level mixture in the final age period might signify that individual differences in drawing ability increased as children got older. If children older than 14 years of age had been included it is likely that greater level mixtures would have been observed as a few children attained higher levels of development while others failed to progress. This is not necessarily surprising because the conceptual stage of older children should allow those who are interested and motivated to draw both to analyze and to solve graphic spatial problems that younger children avoid or fail to solve. Nevertheless, none of the 13- and 14-year-old children received a Level 5 score.

Cross-Sectional Talented Sample

Figure 6.2 shows the same developmental sequence composited for talented children. It indicates that development of talented children does progress both faster and farther in the same period of time. Most drawings of talented children ages 3 and 4 are already at Level 1 and 2. Most drawings of 5- and 6-year-olds are at Level 1, but a few are considerably above the mode. By age 7 to 8 most children's drawings were at Level 3 and by age 11 to 12 many children could

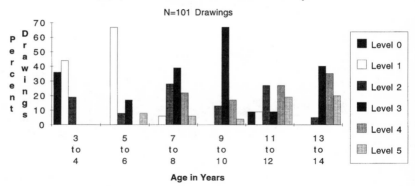

Figure 6.2. Results of the level assignment for cross-sectional talented sample.

perform at Level 4 and 5. At the final measurement point of age 13 to 14, 55% of the drawings were at Level 4 or 5. This compares with 40% at Level 4 for the less talented children. More salient is the marked degree of level mixture for talented children at any given age period. Talented children were much less modal than less talented children and many performed above the group modal levels. This indicates that at any given modal level, talented children can already produce some drawings at higher levels of development. Although it is this "instability" that has been associated with rate of development in the literature, it also buttresses the argument for qualitative developmental differences. That is, at any given point of development these children are able to show a greater range of drawing competence.

Comparing Talented and Less Talented Development

The greater competence of talented children was reflected in the comparison of group modes. As a group talented children (mean = 2.3) were on the average almost one modal level above less talented children (mean = 1.6; $t = 2.10$, $df = 48$, $p = .04$). Both groups, however, showed a strong correlation between mode and age (less talented, $r = .78$, $p < .01$; talented, $r = .70$, $p < .01$).

The degree of level mixture for each child was calculated as the sum of the differences between the level of a single drawing and the developmental mode for a given child divided by the total num-

The Representation of Form and Space

ber of drawings for the child (see Feldman, 1980; Turiel, 1969). For this calculation the direction of differences is ignored. Correlations of level mixture and age or modal level were made for each group. Level mixture was not associated with age in either group but it was associated with mode in the less talented children (less talented, $r = .43$, $p < .05$; talented, $r = .07$ NS). Less talented children at higher modal levels performed with more level mixture than children at lower modal levels. The means for level mixture are compared at each modal level in Table 6.2a. Reflecting the correlation there is a gradual linear increase in level mixture with modal level for less talented children. Talented children show a nonlinear or bimodal relationship that peaks at modes 2 and 4. These two patterns are distinct and further support qualitative differences in the development of the two talent groups.[2] In less talented children, performance becomes more variable with increasing age as some children progress and other do not. In talented children, performance is variable at two points in development, suggesting these reflect critical periods of growth.

Snyder and Feldman (1984) concluded that the degree of level mixture above modal levels or positive level mixture was more indicative of developmental progress than total level mixture. They noted that prior to making a developmental advance in mapmaking children showed more level mixture above their modal level than below. Although such a proposition cannot receive a fair test when subjects at each age period are different individuals, we might still expect that talented children, who are progressing more rapidly than less talented children, would show greater amounts of positive bias. On the average talented children did show more than twice the level of positive bias as less talented children (talented = .41, less talented = .18, $t = 2.62$, $df = 48$, $p < .01$). Table 6.2b shows the distribution of total level mixture and positive and negative bias over the six age periods in the study for the talent groups. Positive bias is highest in talented children ages 5 and 6. In chapter 5, it was observed that an abrupt shift from two-dimensional to three-dimensional depiction occurs in talented children at this age. Negative bias was twice as high in less talented children as in talented (less talented = −.26; talented = −.13) but these differences were

---

2. It is recognized that the conclusions based on these correlations are speculative because very few less talented children scored at the upper modal levels.

TABLE 6.2a
MEAN LEVEL MIXTURES

Mode	0	1	2	3	4	5
Cross-Sectional Less Talented	0.33	0.33	0.43	0.44	1.25	None
Cross-Sectional Talented	0.38	0.57	0.62	0.39	0.65	None
Longitudinal Talented	0.83	0.53	0.71	0.57	0.56	0.54

TABLE 6.2b
MEAN POSITIVE BIAS

Age	3 to 4	5 to 6	7 to 8	9 to 10	11 to 12	13 to 14
Cross-Sectional Less Talented	0.25	0.25	0.16	0.12	0.15	0.17
Cross-Sectional Talented	0.31	0.75	0.42	0.25	0.40	0.45
Longitudinal Talented	0.22	0.23	0.44	0.33	0.22	0.31

MEAN NEGATIVE BIAS

Age	3 to 4	5 to 6	7 to 8	9 to 10	11 to 12	13 to 14
Cross-Sectional Less Talented	0.13	0.15	0.25	0.08	0.13	0.83
Cross-Sectional Talented	0	0	0.30	0.13	0.11	0.15
Longitudinal Talented	0.39	0.31	0.13	0.25	0.23	0.48

not significant. Negative bias is highest in talented children at age 7 to 8 and and in less talented children at age 13 to 14 (Table 6.2b).

Correlations of bias and total level mixture produced much the same picture. Significant correlations between bias and total level were only found for negative bias in the less talented children ($r = .85$, $p < .01$) and positive bias in the talented children ($r = .79$, $p < .01$). These correlations indicated that increases in total level mixture were negatively biased in less talented children whereas they were positively biased in the talented children. Because these samples are based on a developmental composite of different children at each age period, it is difficult to draw firm conclusions about individual trajectories of talented or less talented children. But the developmental implications of level mixture for the trajectories of individual talented children can be explored in the longitudinal talented sample.

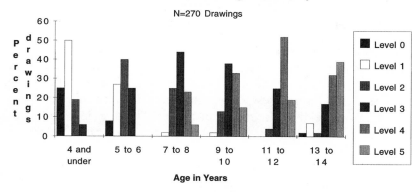

Figure 6.3. Results of the level assignment for longitudinal talented sample.

Longitudinal Talented Sample

Figure 6.3 shows the degree of level mixture across the six age periods. From inspection it is apparent that these children are moving very rapidly through the levels of drawing development. Some modal stabilization at Level 3 occurs between ages 7 and 10 but otherwise each new age period brings a developmental advance. As was found for the cross-sectional talented children, mode and age were strongly correlated ($r = .78, p < .01$) but total mixture and age or mode were not. Instead, as Figure 6.3 suggests, mixture was high throughout the period of study. Comparisons of degree of positive and negative bias showed that in this sample the two were about equal (mean positive bias = .31, mean negative bias = .29). The correlations for total mixture with positive ($r = .52, p < .01$) and negative ($r = .48, p < .01$) bias were consistent with the means. This was unlike the results obtained for the cross-sectional talented children. Perhaps more surprising, in light of other studies, was the negative association found for positive bias and mode ($r = -.38, p < .01$) and positive association for negative bias and mode ($r = .27, p < .07$). The following interpretation is suggested by the distributions shown in Table 6.2a: At lower modal levels these children could only progress (positive bias); at upper modal levels they reached a ceiling so mixture is perforce below their upper limit (negative bias). At the upper levels, this ceiling reflects limitations in measuring artistic development.

INDIVIDUAL TRAJECTORIES FOR TALENTED CHILDREN

The level mixture analysis of the group data suggests that at any given point in development, talented children demonstrated a wide range of graphic competence. It might be supposed that this range was only manifest in a few drawings where advanced solutions were needed to solve difficult graphic problems. The drawings and analyses in the preceding chapters, however, demonstrate that this is not the case. Beginning at an early age and thereafter, talented children appeared deliberately to challenge themselves by attempting themes, spatial configurations, and figure poses that required advanced graphic solutions. It is likely that these kinds of thematic challenges were a major developmental impetus for these children continually to invent new graphic techniques. In other words, they provided a strong source of disequilibration that engendered a search for new graphic means. Two cases were apparent. In the first and more typical case, this search appeared to be mounted on the back of existing cognitive competencies that allowed for progressive transitions that seemed almost coincident with underlying cognitive developments. In the second case, truly novel graphic inventions that were likely in advance of cognitive structural supports appeared. These latter cases would also engender disequilibration, but rather than searching among potential means already supported by existing cognitive structures, the means themselves needed to be invented. The need to invent new means provided the disequilibration. Both of these potentially disequilibrating events are discussed more fully in relation to individual children's development.

Progressive Disequilibrations and Reequilibrations

When children search for new graphic means among those that are potential constructions given their level of development, the means will be assimilated quickly into their graphic abilities. Thus, although the search for effective ways to draw difficult themes is itself disequilibrating, the reequilibration process occurs in a relatively short period. This is because the new means are differentiated by modest accommodations of existing means to the drawing task at hand. If the child keeps on posing new and more difficult challenges, greater numbers of means will become differentiated. As the number of means increases, the chances of reciprocal assimilations between the new drawing techniques (schemas) are enhanced and so are the chances of integrating these with the original schemes from which they were generated. According to Piaget, it is just this kind of circumstance that leads to developmental progress. It is not only that the child generalizes the application of the new means to different drawing content, but the child also modifies her internal scheme relative to the conceptual underpinnings of the task. In other words, the child begins to understand why, not just how. In this case, we might expect that once the child begins to use a new technique, it will almost always be applied in subsequent situations that call for it. Feldman (1980) referred to such changes as occurring "ever after."

If age is a benchmark, much of the development in graphic ability of the talented children studied over time appeared to occur in the context of existing cognitive supports. The "ever after" quality, however, was more relative. In some cases it truly did appear that once the child discovered a new and more effective way to depict a given spatial relationship she always used it whereas in other cases the transition was incomplete and more gradual. Some notable examples of the "ever after" type can be seen in the use of projection and perspective techniques.

Abrupt Achievement. Almost all the children discovered geometric projection around the age of 8 and thereafter used a projective device when they drew geometric topics. Hondo, whose development in perspective was traced in chapter 5, discovered linear perspective at age 10 and thereafter used it to draw geometric projections. Figure 6.4 charts his progress by modal and mixture levels in his drawings. Like other talented children, Hondo advanced swiftly in his early years. At age 10, as Hondo begins to concentrate on geometric perspective (see Figure 5.11a), his performance becomes unstable and he draws one and two levels above his modal level, Level 3. Thereafter, Hondo's modal level moves steadily upward, stabilizing at Level 4 by the end of the study. The drawings at Level 5 reflect Hondo's success with perspective.

Hondo was unlikely to achieve Level 5 drawings through the use of figural perspective indicators because he rarely applied modeling, foreshortening, and shading or shadow (see Table 6.1) to the same drawing. One obstacle to using all three perspective indicators was the scale of Hondo's figures. Typically he drew them extremely

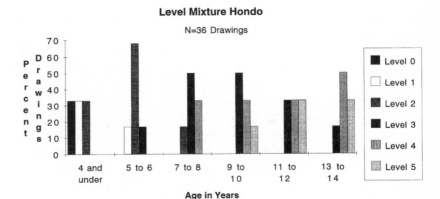

Figure 6.4. Level assignment for Hondo's drawings.

small, often as part of a larger panoramic scene. Foreshortening and shading become very difficult to render at that scale. Nevertheless, once Hondo discovered modeling and foreshortening he immediately integrated these skills into his drawing practice. The integration of these skills with other improvements in his drawing technique is shown in a series of drawing of bees done at ages 9, 10, and 12 and shown in Figures 6.5 and 6.6a and b.

Joel shunned geometric themes. As a young adult, he remarked that he understood early on that there were size differences with distance, but he never liked drawing buildings. So instead of using geometric perspective he liked to use "the cues to perspective, the tricks." Among Joel's favorite "tricks" were perspective indicators such as shadow, shading, and foreshortening. He began using perspective indicators at age 7, first one, then two, and finally all three in a single drawing. Although the following year he appeared largely to practice modeling, by age 9 and thereafter many drawings included all three perspective indicators in a single drawing.

Figure 6.7 shows Joel's development. The shift from modal Level 0 to modal Level 3 in the first two age periods reflects the appearance of many new elements in his drawings. The first drawing, sampled from his seventh year (Figure 4.16b), shows the beginning of Joel's consistent use of three-quarter rotations, vertical segregation, and overlap. In addition a completely new element appears, as Joel foreshortens the snout and tail of papa dinosaur. This drawing, like most of Joel's drawings between the ages 7 and 8, is scored at Level 3. But he is already showing some Level 5 competence at age 7. In the

Figure 6.5. Hondo age 9, interior of bee's nest.

Figure 6.6a. Hondo age 10, bees.

Figure 6.6b. Hondo age 12, bees.

The Representation of Form and Space

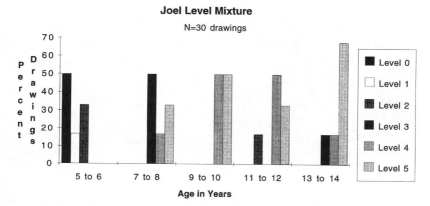

Figure 6.7. Level assignment for Joel's drawings.

Figure 6.8. Joel age 7, "Little Foot." Figure 6.8 appeared first in *The Development of Artistically Gifted Children*, edited by C. Golomb, 1995, Hillsdale, N.J.: Lawrence Erlbaum Assoc. Reprinted with permission.

second drawing from his seventh year, Joel uses two figural perspective indicators, foreshortening and shading. In the third drawing from that year Joel adds modeling (Figure 6.8). In the drawings sampled from the next year Joel practices modeling to the exclusion of other perspective indicators.

Figure 6.9. Joel age 9, "Wading parasaurolophus." Figure 6.9 appeared first in *The Development of Artistically Gifted Children,* edited by C. Golomb, 1995, Hillsdale, N.J.: Lawrence Erlbaum Assoc. Reprinted with permission.

Joel's 9th and 10th years appear to reflect a period of consolidation for his advancements in rendering figure rotations and figure perspective. All of his drawings contain some figures in three-quarter rotations and use of perspective indicators. In half of these, most from his 10th year, all three indicators are used to suggest depth and a light source. Figure 6.9 is typical of this period, although drawn early in his ninth year. Modeling is extreme and some shading is used to suggest light on the surface of the water. The alligator's head is rendered in three-quarter rotation. The head of a dinosaur who hides in the trees on the right is slightly rotated and extremely foreshortened. In the next 2 years, Joel performs most consistently at Level 4, frequently using modeling and shading to suggest figure perspective but also combining these with figure foreshortening. One particularly elegant example that also shows Joel's concern for detail can be seen in Figure 6.10. Joel uses line and space not only to suggest roundness and light source but also to build texture for the skin of the pteranodon. Joel uses an aerial

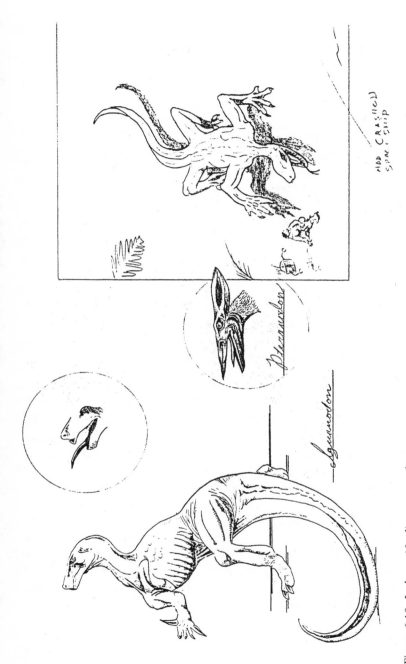

Figure 6.10. Joel age 12, dinosaur studies.

Figure 6.11. Joel age 13, archeopteryx and pteranodon.

view and marks the light source by including a shadow under the giant lizard.

In the final age period of the study, Joel's drawings become stable at Level 5. In one example from this period, done at age 13 and shown in Figure 6.11, Joel skillfully uses size diminution and shading to indicate distance. It carries forward the prehistoric theme, a pervasive theme for Joel throughout the study period (see Milbrath, 1995). One drawing from the previous age period and one from the final do not always match Joel's usual performance levels. These two drawings contained no ground and fewer perspective indicators but it is apparent that they were not meant as complete drawings but sketches. Therefore, they cannot be taken as regressions.

Gradual Achievement. Many of the other changes in graphic skill occurred more gradually. Once a technique was discovered, although not always used it became increasingly a part of the child's

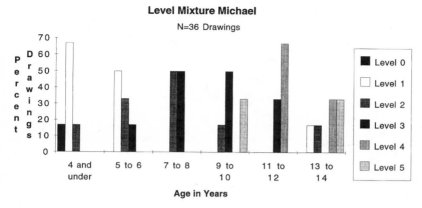

Figure 6.12. Level assignment for Michael's drawings.

drawing practice. This more gradual development may mirror the accommodation and assimilation process involved in developmental change. Some examples can be found in the development of geometric perspective, perspective indicators, and three-quarter rotations.

Figure 6.12 shows Michael's development. Like Joel's, Michael's early progress is largely pulled forward by positive bias but once he nears the ceiling, more drawings appear below his modal level. Michael discovered perspective indicators at age 8 but used them inconsistently until age 9. Primarily, these were either foreshortening or modeling but occasionally he was able to coordinate the two as in Figure 6.13a. Most drawings from age 8 are at Level 3, whereas drawings from age 7 are at Level 2. In his 9th and 10th years, Michael's drawing level fluctuates between Levels 2 and 5 with most drawings at Level 3. Two drawings reach Level 5; they are shown in Figures 6.13b and 6.14. In the first, a humorous portrait of father–son relations, Michael has coordinated figure foreshortening, modeling, and shading. In the second, Michael has added geometric perspective and attempted to coordinate a single point of view. Neither achievement always appears thereafter. In most geometric representations Michael does attempt linear perspective but occasionally he also uses oblique projection.

In figure drawing Michael is more likely to use only one or two perspective indicators. But occasionally, as in Figure 6.15, a beautifully done sleeping figure from age 12, he coordinates shading with foreshortening and modeling of the figure. In the final study

Figure 6.13a. Michael age 8, coordination of foreshortening and modeling.

FATHER AND SON

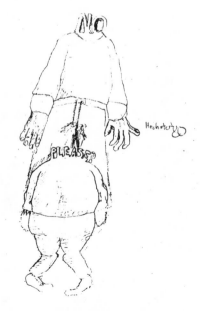

Figure 6.13b. Michael age 10, "Father and Son."

The Representation of Form and Space

Figure 6.14. Michael age 10, geometric perspective.

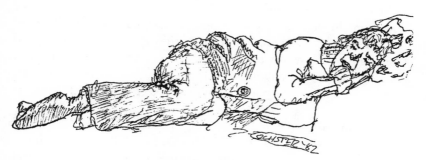

Figure 6.15. Michael age 12, "Feigned Sleep."

years, Michael's drawings suggest that in the future he will progress from Level 4 to Level 5. The drawings that revert to Level 1 and 2 are portraits with no attempt to structure the picture plane. Therefore, despite the sophistication of the drawings they did not receive a high score on the spatial dimensions.

Figure 6.16 shows Kate's progress over the study years. Kate reached modal Level 5 between the ages of 13 and 14 and showed very rapid early development. Her attainment of figure rotation and use of perspective indicators, however, were gradual. It took her 2 years to achieve true rotation and to coordinate combinations of figure perspective indicators. She first used one or another indicator singly and later used combinations of two or three. Midway through her sixth year Kate made her first attempt at three-quarter figure rotation. But most figure rotation attempts during the next 2 years were accomplished by amalgamating front and profile views (see chapter 4, Figure 4.12a & b). Consistent use of three-quarter figure rotations began during her eighth year, when Kate's modal performance jumped a level and she performed consistently at Level 4.

Several other new skills also appeared. Kate began to use figural perspective indicators and three-dimensional projection of geometric objects. In Figure 4.13 she used two perspective indicators, foreshortening and modeling, and oblique projection in rendering the piano. In Figure 6.17 drawn at age 9, both figures are modeled and in three-quarter rotations and Juliet's parapet is drawn in oblique projection. In Figure 1.3a from age 9, Kate has successfully foreshortened the pigs breaking through the fence and also applied some foreshortening to the human figure. She uses variations in thickness of line and curvature to model the figures. The geometric objects, fenceposts and pig trough, are projected obliquely into the picture plane.

Kate remains stable at Level 4 through her 10th year. This stability appears to reflect a consolidation of her skills in figure drawing, as three-quarter rotations and use of foreshortening and modeling become increasingly characteristic of her drawings. In the following year Kate's performance begins to fluctuate. Some drawings are below her modal level but one-third are above. The primary advance was the coordination of all three figure perspective indicators. In Figure 6.18 Kate pokes fun at the absorbed reader and perhaps also at the subjects of conventional life drawing. Although

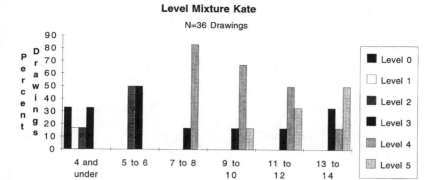

Level Mixture Kate

N=36 Drawings

Figure 6.16. Level assignment for Kate's drawings.

Figure 6.17. Kate age 9, "Romeo and Juliet."

Figure 6.18. Kate age 12, still life.

she still uses oblique projection for the table, the figure and other objects receive a sophisticated treatment. Positive bias clearly characterizes this age period prior to her shift to Level 5 competence at age 13. Some level regressions are apparent at age 14, when, like Michael, Kate turned her talents toward portraits (see Figure 4.8).

Feldman (1980) predicts that gradual achievements are marked by periods of advancement mixed with periods of regression around modal levels as progress alternates with consolidation of level skills. Daniel's record, shown in Figure 6.19, best reflects this prototype. Although initially positive bias signals his movement through Levels 1 and 2 to Level 4, the consolidation of Level 4 skills is suggested at ages 9 and 10 by negative bias. In the next age period, at 11 and 12 years, nonmodal drawings are again purely positive, signaling the transition to Level 5 at ages 13 and 14.

Daniel discovered modeling and foreshortening around age 8 but at first limited their use to parts of a figure. In Figure 6.20a, Daniel takes one of his first stabs at satirical social commentary, a theme that he expanded upon as he got older. Here the face, hands, and

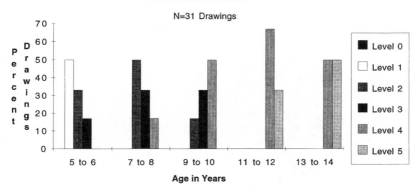

Figure 6.19. Level assignment for Daniel's drawings.

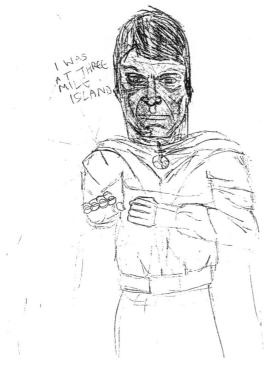

Figure 6.20a. Daniel age 8, social commentary.

Figure 6.20b. Daniel age 9, self-portrait.

parts of the arms are modeled and one arm and hand are extremely foreshortened. Over the next 2 years, at ages 9 and 10, Daniel continued to consolidate his figure drawing skills in a series of satirical drawings. He achieved three-quarter figure rotations gradually through a process of successive approximations (see chapter 4) and produced his first truly rotated figure at age 9; throughout that year, he worked to integrate rotation with foreshortening, modeling, and on occasion shading. In a realistic self-portrait, Figure 6.20b, Daniel used a slight three-quarter orientation, foreshortening, modeling, and shading of the figure to present a serious side of himself.

During the next age period, at 11 and 12, Daniel began to concentrate on drawing strong and powerful superheroes. This interest shaped his figure drawing and motivated him to experiment with more dynamically posed and rotated figures. A particularly active example is shown in Figure 4.15b, from age 12. The superhero in

Figure 6.21. Daniel age 13, "Go Buckeyes."

this case is Daniel, who is avenging himself against one of his teachers. During his 12th year, Daniel switched from oblique projections to linear perspective and thereafter in his drawings of geometric objects he tried for true perspective. In some cases he penciled in the projection lines whereas others were done in a looser style as in Figure 6.21. In this drawing, made when Daniel was age 13, figure rotation, foreshortening, modeling, and shading are coordinated and integrated with geometric perspective.

Disequilibrations Brought About by Novelties

Feldman (1980) made an analysis of novelties in the mapmaking abilities of children and concluded that these isolated appearances of advanced innovations acted to pull development forward. Earlier it was suggested that they do so because they are a source of disequilibration. However, unlike the processes just described, the perturbations or disturbances generated by these isolated innovations are not easily assimilated into a child's drawing schemas and their associated schemes. They are in effect too far in advance of existing structures to be assimilated. Nevertheless, although the child may

Figure 6.22a. Michael age 5, "Batman and Robin."

be unable to repeat the novel techniques for some time, it is proposed that the novelties are likely to trigger a chain of more modest accommodations and assimilations that lead to their eventual reappearance as differentiated and integrated schemas and schemes with the "ever after" quality.

The graphic techniques most likely to make an early and transient appearance were ground plane and partial occlusion. For example, Michael and Claire (Figures 6.22a & 6.23) used an implied ground plane once at age 5 but did not use it again until several years later. Both of these techniques indicate the third dimension of the picture plane, a representational development that likely was not yet understood when the children first used the related drawing technique. I must acknowledge that the ability to sustain speculations about whether or not cognitive developments that support the representation of the third dimension were hastened by these early novelties is limited. Nevertheless, in these cases, visual inspection

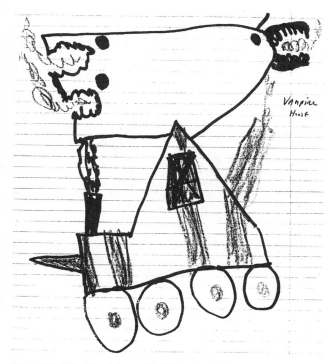

Figure 6.22b. Daniel age 5, "Vampire House."

may promote the early appearance of novel techniques: visual inspection of how things look in the world but also of what the child herself or himself was producing. One example comes from Daniel. Partial occlusion was used in isolation by him at age 5 and did not reappear until several years later. In Figure 6.22b, the occlusions that are part of the Vampire House appear to result from a planning failure that necessitated an on-the-spot novelty for its visual resolution. Surprisingly, Daniel did not resort to transparency. Since this would have been the more expedient solution, his choice suggests he was paying attention to visual aspects of his environment and his drawing. But the fact that his solution resulted in a visual contradiction (roof in front of the vampire and smoke behind) also indicates he did not really understand the spatial relationships he was attempting to draw.

Peregrine's development, shown in Figure 6.24, contains a number of such novelties. Innovations begin to appear during Pere-

Figure 6.23. Claire age 5, baby in crib.

grine's fourth year. In Figure 3.8a the ground is structured by the placement of the girl's foot on an implied line. The girl's arms also partially occlude her own body and the frame of the harp she holds. In addition, Peregrine has mixed three figure orientations. The girl's body is shown in front view and her legs in profile but her face is turned to suggest a three-quarter view. This view, however, does not include the usual types of distortions that three-quarter views necessitate. Instead Peregrine uses a circle and places the features within the circle at a three-quarter orientation. Three-quarter views do not appear again until Peregrine is 7.

Level 3 characterizes her drawings at age 6. The earlier innovations of implied plane and partial occlusion seen at age 4 reappear

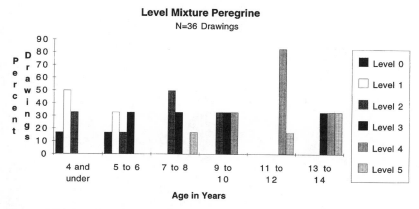

Figure 6.24. Level assignment for Peregrine's drawings.

at age 6 and lead to the new modal level. In one drawing from age 6 and shown in Figure 6.25a, Peregrine suggests figure modeling and vertical oblique projection as well. Nevertheless, not all these skills are integrated into her drawings. During the next age period her modal level fixes at Level 2 instead of Level 3. In the Level 2 drawings, Peregrine continues to use partial occlusion, figure modeling, and even true figure rotations, but she still does not explicitly structure the ground and sometimes figures are more or less hanging in midair. Partial occlusions, rotations, and modeling, however, are consistent from this time forward. In a lovely drawing (Figure 6.25b) done near the end of her eighth year, Peregrine demonstrates her ability to coordinate these skills; the drawing is scored at Level 5. She successfully implies the ground plane and geometric perspective by the placement of the legs of the bed. It is rare for Peregrine to include geometric objects in her drawings. A previous drawing from that year that did showed geometric objects in elevation and oblique projection. This appearance of linear perspective remains a novelty. In subsequent drawings of geometric objects she uses oblique projection and it is not until the end of her 11th year that she appears to switch permanently to linear perspective.

In all cases the mental competencies necessary to support the novel techniques illustrated in these drawings were likely absent or rudimentary when the technique was first used. How then did these children discover them? One answer is provided by the analysis of Daniel's drawing. These children sought out graphic techniques to solve the specific problems that resulted from the challenging

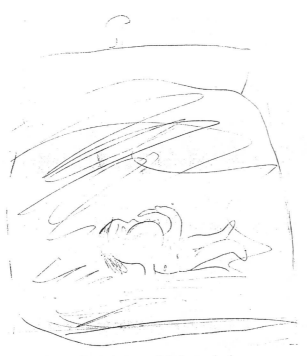

Figure 6.25a. Peregrine age 6, baby on bed.

themes they attempted to draw. Another answer was suggested in chapter 1: Young talented children may have been able to recollect episodic visual memories that gave them momentary access to internal visual representations of a scene, gesture, or pose (see Figures 1.4 and 1.5b). The assimilation of these techniques into a child's drawing practice, however, still took several years of further development as supporting mental schemes differentiated. But once assimilated these techniques were used repeatedly and consistently ever after.

A final comment should be made on why these children are motivated to challenge themselves graphically. No doubt there are strong reasons having to do with their individual personalities. But in line with previous discussions of figurative and operative developmental processes, we might also suppose that because they are able to make more effective use of figurative processes, their visual inspection of the world and things in the world provokes this desire. To put it more simply, because they see largely with their eyes

Figure 6.25b. Peregrine age 8, mother and newborn on bed.

rather than with their mind, they gain a more developed sense of what can be represented graphically. In a similar manner, their visual monitoring of what it is they are producing is likely to be more astute so that as Joel (Milbrath, 1995) said about his development of foreshortening, they see that it looks wrong long before they know why. This also emphasizes a point that will be revisited in the final chapter of this book. The differentiation and integration of drawing schemas and associated mental schemes promoted by the graphic challenges these children pose for themselves involve schemas and schemes that are figurative, sensory-motor, and conceptual. The power of the talented developmental trajectory comes from the continual coordination of these three developing systems during periods that may be critical in the development of graphic ability: that is, when they are still children and have a greater potential for semiotic development. It is the reason that differences in their artistic development are qualitative as well as quantitative. Although this point has not been proposed for the visual arts, it is clear that in learning a second language or a musical instrument, the adult learner is at a significant disadvantage when compared to the child. Furthermore, learners who begin as children in these domains often greatly exceed the potential of those who begin as adults. This is particularly the case in music, where classical training must start quite young for the proper development of soloists and symphony players.

PART II

COMPOSITION

7

COMPOSING THE PICTURE

Academic training in beauty is a sham. We
have been deceived. . . . The beauties of the
Parthenon, Venuses, Nymphs, Narcissuses are
so many lies. Art is not the application of a
canon of beauty but what the instinct and the
brain can conceive beyond any canon.

(Pablo Picasso, 1935, quoted in Chipp,
1978, p. 266)

The first part of this book traced the development of representation
in the artwork of talented and less talented children. It demonstrated
that for most children, even highly talented children, there is an orderly developmental sequence in the construction of pictorial space.
Highly talented and less talented children appeared dependent on the
appearance of certain cognitive competencies to construct complex
and realistic spatial relationships. But there was also evidence that
highly talented children relied heavily on other mental processes besides operational reasoning when drawing. Even very young talented
children applied a sophisticated denotation rule for lines and planes.
Several years later they showed a remarkable flexibility with figure
rotation. These abilities implied a sensitive visual analysis of the
world and capacity to use specific and vivid visual memories. Piaget
and Inhelder (1969) referred to perceptual analysis and visual memory as figurative thought. It was suggested that talented children expand their graphic skills by continually coordinating figurative
thought with their emerging cognitive abilities whereas less talented
children rely more heavily on conceptual reasoning.

In chapter 1 a framework for evaluating two competing groups of hypotheses related to artistic talent was presented (see Table 1.1). One group, the *farther faster* hypotheses, proposes that talent arises from differences in rate of intellectual development. The second group, the *seeing, remembering, doing* hypotheses, proposes that talent springs from differences in figurative abilities. An examination of how children handle the composition of their drawings presents another opportunity to assess these two hypotheses. Adult artists are able to integrate both perceptual and conceptual considerations when composing a piece of art (Cupchik, 1992). Young children, however, are unlikely to be capable of such artistic sophistication (Parsons, 1987). Instead, the theme or action they wish to depict often dictates their approach to composition (Golomb, 1992). But young children could potentially use another compositional strategy. They could use their eyes to decide "what looks good, where" as they execute a drawing. Research early in this century by Gestalt psychologists demonstrated that "what looks good" is often determined by a need for perceptual closure and stability. Closure and stability result when a composition is balanced. The tendency of the human mind to complete open figures and to regroup patterns toward stability develops as part of the perceptual system that in many respects is complete within the first several years of life. If talented children selectively attend to their perceptions, we might expect them to use their eyes when they compose a drawing long before they use their mind.

In this case composing a drawing becomes a two-dimensional problem dissociated from the graphic problems raised by constructing and representing three-dimensional spatial relationships. Arnheim (1988) noted that the added use of the depth plane in composition arose historically quite late. Earlier artists composed paintings and drawings within the two-dimensional frontal plane of the picture. Arnheim suggested that it would be quite natural for children to use only the frontal plane because the depth plane is constructed so late in their artistic development. One consequence of treating composition as a two-dimensional problem that can be solved by figurative thought instead of operational thought is that even young children could be quite good at visually balancing a picture. Nevertheless, children might not approach composition in this manner and could instead tackle balance by using conceptual approaches such as part–whole operations and compensation relations (reversibility operations). In that case, compositionally balanced pictures would only begin to appear with operational forms of reasoning around 7 or 8 years of age. Therefore, before we can evaluate the composition strategies of talented children, we need to know what is normative. One initial question then is, How do children of different ages approach composition?

These issues are the main focus of the second part of this book. This chapter begins by reviewing some important principles of composition and research related to the development of an understanding of these principles in children.

PRINCIPLES OF COMPOSITION

In answering the question of whether or not an artist is compelled to balance a composition, Arnheim (1988) made an important and useful point. An unbalanced composition will *look* accidental and transitory with a tendency for elements to change shape as if their action is frozen while still seeking a state of rest. Such an interrupted movement *stimulates* the viewer to attempt a reshaping of the composition in order to stabilize the structure. Therefore, if the intended meaning of the artist's piece is to be conveyed and a definitive artistic statement made, the composition will have to be balanced. In one sense it need not matter whether an artist proceeds consciously or unconsciously, because there are general features of the perceptual system that allow the artist's eye to tell when visual balance has been achieved. Many of these features were first analyzed and described by Gestalt psychologists who at times collaborated with the artists themselves in their discoveries (Katz, 1935). When these principles are reapplied to the artistic processes, a set of rules that can guide artistic creation and also explain the experience of the viewer emerges.

Gestalt Principles

Many aspects inherent in balanced compositions are easily identified as "field effects" resulting from the operation of primary organization principles of perception. These were first recognized and studied by Gestalt psychologists (Koffka, 1963), whose early research suggested that visual weight might in large part be determined by a number of relational laws built into the visual system. Gestaltists argued that certain relational preferences develop as part of the perceptual system. Particularly clear examples are provided by the "eye's" insistence on visually grouping adjacent or similar elements, by the perceptual privilege or weight the "eye" ascribes to regular forms over irregular forms, and the tendency to complete open figures and regroup patterns toward stability. Most likely artists have always implicitly understood and utilized these principles to create visually balanced compositions.

Recent studies of infant perception indicate that Gestalt principles of similarity, good continuation, and good form exert only weak effects on the perception of infants before 1 year of age, although somewhat stronger effects have been found with familiar test objects (Spelke, Breinlinger, Jacobson & Phillips, 1993). According to Spelke, the chief limitation is the young infant's inability to recognize objects. For example, it is difficult for the infant to recognize unfamiliar stationary objects that overlap or touch as distinct because a model of the object has not yet been constructed. If object recognition is essential for the operation of Gestalt relations, a number of years may be needed before these principles are functional. Nevertheless, there is some evidence that children as young as 2 years of age organize scenes into homogeneous units based on Gestalt grouping principles.

Such findings are consistent with Piaget's (1969) conclusions that sensory-motor development during the first 2 years of life is crucial to the emergence of primary perceptual processes (classically termed innate). The effects of these processes are determined by the relations among elements in a subject's field of fixation (e.g., Muller–Lyer illusion) and are related to the field effects studied by Gestalt psychologists. But Piaget's studies also indicate a more protracted course of development for secondary perceptual processes (classically termed acquired). These processes operate across spatial and temporal intervals and include perceptual activities such as visual exploration, spatiotemporal transposition, and reference to perceptual coordinates. "Good form" is another example because, according to Piaget, it is dependent on having strong assimilatory schemas for the forms themselves. His studies showed that 5-year-olds were much less likely than 9-year-olds or adults to perceive "good forms" embedded in an illusion or to complete incomplete good forms with virtual lines. Piaget argued that not all perceptual processes are the simple summation of field effects as Gestalt psychologists proposed. Instead conceptual factors such as the recognition of an object and the schemas and schemes associated with the object strongly influence what we see.

There is a tension between the Gestalt position and a conceptual approach. Predictions for what capacities young children can utilize to view or compose the two-dimensional picture plane would differ. Gestalt theory might predict that young children would be aware of the relative weights among elements in a picture and would therefore be able to judge from perception whether or not a picture looks visually balanced. A conceptual approach, such as Piaget's, might allow that the relative weights for some dimensions (e.g., size) could exert a strong influence on young children's perception of a picture but that other dimensions such as "good form" develop more slowly. Perceiving visual balance would depend on which dimensions are salient for a child in a picture and on the child's developmental level.

The production of a visually balanced picture could also be treated as either a task for perception (figurative) or operational reasoning. If a child set out with a plan prior to producing a drawing, the task might be strongly influenced by the child's ability to reason about part–whole and compensation relations. We know, however, from observation and prior studies that young children rarely plan a drawing in this way. Instead they work primarily in piecemeal fashion, putting down forms or groups of forms in isolation (Barnhart, 1942). But if young children monitored these placements, they could use perception to determine the interrelations among elements.

Principles of Visual Balance

The Hidden Structure. Arnheim (1974) observed that an organizing framework for the visual artist and viewer is imposed by the boundaries of a piece In the case of a rectangular picture, the organizing framework is "a hidden structure" consisting of a central vertical and horizontal axis and two diagonal axes that cross in the center of the picture plane. A work achieves its greatest stability when elements are located along the major structural axes. Further, because this organizing structure provides a scaffold for the piece, it can also support more weight than other locations in the picture so the elements located there can be "heavier." However, when elements are placed off the central axes of the picture plane, they are *perceived* as heavier because they interrupt the stability created by strengthening the major axes. Therefore, elements used for compositional balance can be "lighter" when their location deviates from the hidden organizational structure.

Static and Dynamic Balance. In its simplest form, a balanced composition rigidly adheres to the hidden structure, resulting in an internal static equilibrium that creates no tension. A more complex and dynamic form of balance can be achieved by asymmetrically counterbalancing compositional dimensions around the structural skeleton to create a cohesive tension within the frame. In teaching composition at the Bauhaus, Paul Klee (1978) defined a composition as *static* if it appeared at rest or in "conditional" or "becalmed motion." A *dynamic* composition was in "unconditional motion," "under its own motion," or "simply moving." Klee aligned static compositions with the vertical, horizontal, and "compensating" diagonal axes of the picture plane. The greatest stability is achieved by using the vertical axis. Static variations result from vertical and horizontal deviations off the central vertical and horizontal axial positions. Dynamic compositions achieve stability by "harmonization of free mobility" through movements and countermovements; its deviations ignore the forces generated by gravity and employ shifts of center and localities dependent on the center. Klee equated static compositions with classical styles in art and dynamic compositions with the romantic period. He envisioned and indeed often achieved an intermediate style in which the sudden disruption of the vertical expressed pathos or a "touch of the dynamic" was given to provide a "peaceful synthesis" to a static, well-balanced, and often quite symmetrical composition.

Symmetrical and Asymmetrical Balance. A composition is described further by the degree to which its balance is achieved through use of *symmetry* or *asymmetry*. Symmetrical balancing results when elements of like properties are counterbalanced around a central axis, creating two mirror images. Elements can be balanced with respect to location, size, shape, tonality or density, color, and the direction of movement of elements. The strongest symmetrical forms use the vertical axis. Although use of symmetry often produces a static composition, it can also yield a dynamic tension if the primary organizing axes are the diagonals rather than the vertical and horizontal axes. Analogously, although asymmetrical balancing techniques often produce dynamic compositions, rigid use of horizontals and verticals can render these compositions static. An asymmetrically balanced composition relies on the use of nonidentical pictorial properties to counterbalance the picture. In its simplest form, this might involve equalizing the masses organized around a central axis by distributing the mass across a different number of elements (i.e., two smaller and one larger). This simple type has also been called complex symmetry (Golomb, 1992) because balance remains a function of one compositional property, e.g., mass. But balance can also be achieved by counterbalancing across quite different compositional properties. For example, a *dark mass* (tonality) shifted slightly off center can be held in balance by a much "lighter" element placed *in the periphery* (location) of the picture. In this case location is used to hold a heavier mass in balance.

Anisotropy of Visual Space. A dynamic center that attracts the eye is always present in any work of art. Sometimes the artist makes it explicit but often it is induced perceptually by the forces within the piece. Our kinesthetic experience of space is anisotropic, as we attempt to overcome the force exerted by gravity. Going up a hill requires more energy than going down. Spatial unevenness is experienced visually in a picture when elements at a greater distance from the central "gravitational pull" of a piece are perceived as carrying more weight. Like our kinesthetic experience, visual anisotropy is felt most strongly on the vertical axis. Elements in the upper part of the frame, which in a physical analogy would have to have more force to maintain their distance from the pull of gravity, are endowed with more visual weight than those in the lower. We tend to overestimate their visual weight. Therefore to balance elements in the top and bottom halves of a frame, elements of less visual weight are put on top.

Unlike kinesthetic anisotropy, spatial anisotropy also applies along the horizontal axis of a picture. There is a visual bias along the horizontal axis, which although not as compelling as the top–bottom inequality, gives initial subjective importance to elements on the left but greater visual weight to those on the right. This effect results from our spontaneous left to right reading of a picture. It may be caused by compensatory attentional mechanisms in the brain that initially overcome the dominance of the right visual field (left brain dominance) by orienting to the left visual field or it might result simply from our training in reading (Arnheim, 1974). The effect, however, is not strong enough to destroy the stability imposed by symmetry. The positions where the diagonals meet the corners of the bounded picture also carry more weight, but in this case it is the influence of the corners themselves as centers of visual attention that intensifies the weight of elements located in their proximity. Finally, the diagonal crossing from the lower left to upper right invites the eye to ascend while the opposing diagonal is traced as descending.

Directional biases are unlikely to result from natural asymmetries in gaze patterns. Studies indicate that the eyes roam irregularly around a picture, exploring the same picture with unique gaze patterns on two different occasions (Molnar, 1992). Molnar (1992) distinguished two phases of visual exploration; in the first phase, exploration is peripheral and influenced by the physical forces of pictorial stimuli (field effects); in the second phase, subjective psychological forces determine what the eye takes as its center of interest. These latter forces can be quite unpredictable, yielding centers that would not normally dominate physically. For example, Arnheim (1988) notes that in Breugel the Elder's *Landscape with the Fall of Icarus,* the tiny figure of a shepherd placed in the center of the picture is overpowered visually by a large and colorful plowman in the foreground. Nevertheless, the shepherd is eventually discovered because his upward gaze is the only response to the "cosmic tragedy taking place."

In contrast, forces imposed by the physical aspects of the picture have a probabilistic determination. Ergodicity, a Markovian property that implies statistical homogeneity, describes the pattern of peripheral exploration associated with well-balanced compositions (Molnar, 1992). Ergodic processes are those that reach a final equilibrium after a definable period. In the case of eye gaze, this indicates that after an initial period of random exploration, the eyes settle on "a determined average path and continue to follow this path (with some deviations) during the entire time that the picture is viewed." Molnar describes other Markovian patterns associated with "bad" compositions; in one, a decomposable process, exploration is limited to a single part of the picture; in another, a periodic process, the eyes oscillate between two distinct elements in the picture. An indication of how well a picture is composed is calculated by the number of steps needed to reach an equilibrated state and the form that state takes. In Molnar's study of exploration patterns of Manet's *Olympia*, an ergodic state that involved five meaningful areas of the painting was reached in fewer than 25 gaze interactions with the picture.

Elements of Composition

Weight. It should be evident that the picture plane can be interpreted metaphorically as a balance beam with its fulcrum as the central point of visual balance and weight and distance from the fulcrum as the elements of visual balance (Arnheim, 1974). Elements with pictorial weight correspond metaphorically to those with physical weight, attracting other elements in the picture, like the pull of gravity. Greater visual weight is given to larger size, to brighter colors, and to more interesting content. Forms with greater complexity (defined by amount of information) or with regular or compact shape or oriented along the vertical axis are perceived as heavier than forms of less complexity or irregular or diffuse shape. Isolated forms carry more weight than embedded forms and enclosed regions are seen as heavier than their surround. Cool or dark colors like blue recede; hot and bright colors like red expand and are therefore seen as heavier. Forms of darker tones like black, however, carry more visual weight than those of lighter tones, like gray or white.

Klee (1978) defines pictorial weight relatively, as the degree of density of one element against another. He notes, "The notion that black is heavier than white applies only while we think of a white surface . . . black is the means of developing energy. The blacker the energy, the greater the impression of weight in comparison to the white surface, another relativity." He goes on to show that if the situation is reversed and the surface is black, darkening the tonal value does little. Instead, white becomes the means of developing energy and the brighter the white the stronger the effect.

Counterbalancing the weight of an element can result from using the same compositional element. One clear example of this type of balancing technique is the symmetrical composition referred to previously, in which both form and color are identical around a central axis. Counterbalancing weight can also be accomplished asymmetrically by using different composition elements. For example, the perception of weight based on the greater size of one element can be balanced by the brighter color of a smaller element.

Location. Similarly to the operation of laws governing physical weights placed on the balance beam, distance from the fulcrum or central point of visual attraction can be used in establishing stability. When the eye is focused on the central point of attraction, pictorial weight of an element increases as its distance from the center increases. Arnheim (1988) attributes this to the force with which we endow this element in order for it to maintain its distance from the "gravitational pull" of the central attractor. But because the center position, where the two diagonal axes intersect, is the heaviest location in the frame, elements placed at increasing distances from that center can also be interpreted as increasingly independent or free of it by virtue of their lightness (Arnheim, 1988). According to Arnheim (1988) these contradictory perceptual interpretations cannot be resolved by uniting the two images, so visual tension is induced as the viewer oscillates between the two opposing images.

Direction. Elements within a work of art also impart a direction to the organized forces. *Direction* refers to the path of movement traced within the work. Klee (1978) distinguishes between two kinds of movement, productive and receptive movement: *Productive movement* is produced within the work itself; it can be accomplished by manipulation of the weight and placement of elements or by the overall shape of the compositional grouping of elements. Elements placed adjacent to each other attract each other by their proximity, influencing the direction of movement within the work. In the case of weight, enlargement and diminution of forms, expansion and contraction of size and shapes, thinning and thickening of tone or color, all create directional movement. Certain shapes, by their very nature, impart a directional force. An angle, a chevron, an arrow, all move in the direction of the angle. A triangle will point away from its broadest base toward its smallest angle. Such shapes can be used as individual elements. For example, Klee's explicit use of arrows in *Separation in the Evening*, *Mixed Weather*, or *Tragedy*. But the shape of the compositional grouping can also impart movement. There are many examples of triangular groupings with the base at the bottom of the picture. El Greco groups the four central figures as a triangle in *Pietà*.

In order to balance movement, countermovement is needed. Thus, for example, the upward movement of the triangle in the composed group of Michelangelo's *Pietà* is counterbalanced by the downward pull of gravity (Arnheim, 1988). In the realm of color, movement of color along the color wheel can be counterbalanced by establishing an oscillation with different parts of the wheel so that in Klee's words a "striving outward" and a "returning home" is created within the piece. The movement imparted by color can also be checked by counterbalancing the size of the area covered by the color. For example, colors of greater weight or density can be used on the smallest surfaces and those of less density on the larger surfaces.

Receptive movement is the movement created by the eye in viewing the picture. Shifting the observer's viewpoint within a picture creates movement and countermovement. This is often accomplished by the subject matter: for example, the inferred motion of a ball placed on the edge of a table or the sidelong glance of the eyes in a portrait. The use of perspective also channels the viewer's gaze to the vanishing point of converging perspective lines. The anisotropy of visual space gives a directional bias to the way a viewer "reads" a picture. The bottom carries more weight than the top but figures tend to rise within a frame toward the top so placement can give a sense of movement toward one point of gravity or the other. The tendency for the viewer's eyes to move naturally from left to right gives movement toward the eye's destination.

STUDIES OF CHILDREN'S ARTISTIC COMPOSITIONS AND AESTHETIC EXPERIENCE

Questions of how children experience a work of art and whether or not they are able to produce visually balanced works have generally attracted less research attention than children's representational skills. Nevertheless some interesting and relevant observations have been made. The bias of developmental psychologists is to expect developmental change in children's aesthetic experiences and their ability to compose well-balanced pictures. Quite predictably they use developmental theory to account for these changes.

Producing Visually Balanced Pictures
Golomb (1992) points out that in order to be able to compose forms on a page, children first differentiate the forms themselves

and second establish some rudiments of interrelating these forms. At the very least, then, an "intuitive understanding of part–whole relations and their mutual regulation" (Golomb, 1992, p. 166) is required. Garfunkel (1980), who studied compositional balance in school-age children, also concluded that the understanding of part–whole relations was necessary to attaining well-balanced compositions. For example, in order to compose a balanced whole, children must be able to relate each part to the larger composition while deciding on its placement, size, or color. This is similar to the problems faced by the child when attempting to construct a coherent spatial referent within a picture (see chapter 5), but it is not as difficult because it does not require the construction of the depth plane.

A child's ability to create visually balanced compositions, particularly more complex forms that use dynamic and asymmetrical balancing techniques, could require reversible operations. For example, it could be argued that establishing an identity of visual weights in different parts of a picture necessitates understanding that greater size can be compensated for by placement of smaller objects at greater distances from the center of a picture. This argument could also be extended to understanding compensatory relationships between size and color or tone, shape and size, and so on. There is a caveat to this argument, however: In order to construct these compensatory relationships, children must first either see or learn to see that certain dimensions (e.g., color, tone, shape) carry visual weight. Although our review of Gestalt principles suggests that young children appreciate the principles of grouping, no studies have specifically set out to study how children understand these properties in relation to artistic composition.

The most recent comprehensive attempt to classify children's drawings according to principles of composition was done by Golomb (1992), who studied close to 1,500 drawings of children 3 to 13 years of age. The children had been asked to draw pictures of six different themes. Although Golomb allowed the drawings themselves to dictate the categories of compositional strategies, her work is strongly influenced by Arnheim's thinking. Two major strategies emerged. The first strategy, used by a majority of younger subjects, was to align elements in gridlike fashion along both the horizontal and vertical axes of the picture. The second was to organize elements around a pictorial center. Even though fewer young subjects used this centering strategy, it was observed in drawings of children of all ages. Golomb noted that whereas the centering approach led to well-balanced pictures often by stimulating symmetry, alignment strategies in general did not appear to promote symmetry or intentionally balanced compositions.

Between ages 7 and 13, children tended to combine the two strategies by aligning figures in groups by size, color, form, or activity, within an overall centric composition. Some of these older children, particularly those with more talent, were able to achieve what Golomb called complex symmetry by organizing elements of equal visual weight around a center. In her sample, however, it was rare to find a drawing in which all elements were well integrated according to principles of compositional balance. At best, the children achieved a local balance for parts of the picture as subunits. They never used dynamic principles of balance that relied on asymmetrical balance by weight, direction, or locations of forms. Golomb found that between ages 9 and 13, compositional competence leveled off; apparently children became preoccupied with other graphic aspects of drawing, such as drawing detail or movement.

When these drawings were analyzed by themes, it became clear that the compositional strategies used were often dictated by theme. The theme of a family, for example, was predominantly organized by alignment strategies as if the family had posed for a photograph. The theme of children playing also pulled for alignment with almost a third of the 7- to 13-year-olds using symmetrical alignments. When this theme was further specified to include only three children playing ball, the strategies became centric and symmetry increased. Symmetrical centric strategies were also used by older children to draw a birthday party theme.

Golomb realized that a child's level of competence in composition could be masked by the pull a specific theme imposes. Accordingly she designed a picture completion study in which children 6 to 13 years were presented with six unfinished pictures and asked to complete them in a "pleasing" manner. The unfinished pictures were all representational but differed in the locations and distributions of forms on the page. Some children failed to realize that additional elements were needed and either colored in areas or embellished and added details to existing elements. At a more advanced level, children realized that new elements should be added but did so without considering their influence on the composition.

At a third level, children were sensitive to spatial and thematic aspects of the picture, but it was only at the most advanced level that the spatial structure of the picture was deliberately taken into account when adding elements and both simple and complex balancing strategies appeared. Use of symmetry increased with age but only the older subjects used more complex balancing strategies.

Two other studies have found that symmetry as a compositional form increases with age. In a study of middle-class schoolchildren's artwork by Garfunkel (1980), children did not produce symmetrically balanced compositions until they were 7 years old. Successful manipulation of a dynamic balancing technique was observed in the drawings of a few of the oldest children aged 11 to 12. Garfunkel, however, did not provide a clear definition for this category. An early but comprehensive study of children ages 6 to 15 enrolled at the Cleveland Museum Art School (Munro et al., 1942) found that children's drawings became increasingly organized as coherent compositions only after the age of 7. But use of symmetry actually declined between the ages of 6 and 10 before increasing again. Organizations with intentional use of balanced asymmetry increased only after age 12 and were used almost exclusively by highly talented children. It is important to note that in the Cleveland sample very few children were identified as highly talented before the age of 11.

A more detailed analysis of 52 children age 5 through 16 in the Cleveland sample (Barnhart, 1942) focused on links among the compositional forms, spatial representational types, and order in which elements were drawn on a page. The analysis suggested that both level of representational skill and drawing order were associated with the compositional form.[1] Thematic differences were eliminated by asking children to draw a picture of children playing out of doors at a park in the snow. Barnhart identified six levels of compositional forms. The first two levels were a disorganized type in which alignments were only suggested and a more organized type

---

1. Barnhart drew his conclusions from a lengthy and excellent qualitative analysis but presented tables amenable to statistical analysis. Computing chi-square statistics from the various tables, I found a significant association between representational type and compositional form and between drawing order and compositional form, confirming his conclusion that representational skill and drawing order influence compositional forms. Representational type, however, was not associated with drawing order, suggesting that these two dimensions were independent.

in which elements were dispersed evenly over the page. At the next level, alignments were drawn along a single or double ground line with most balanced around a central element, but in others, elements were dispersed unevenly along the ground line and lacked order. At the fourth level drawings were organized with elements dispersed as single units in an arrangement over the page. Drawings at the fifth level were of mixed compositional forms in which some elements were dispersed on the page and others were aligned in rows. Some of these appeared organized; in others, the parts appeared unrelated as a whole. At the sixth level, elements were grouped by three organized strategies: a triadic arrangement with elements symmetrically arranged around a center, a diagonal arrangement in which the picture plane could be bisected around a diagonal line, and a rare type in which elements were organized to make a shape such as a circle or triangle.

Barnhart found the same general compositional progression with age suggested by Golomb. Whereas most younger children, between ages 6 and 9, aligned elements in a row in either an organized or a disorganized fashion, older children drew multiplanar compositions organized by a general symmetry or asymmetry along a diagonal axis. Of most interest, however, is the association Barnhart reports among representational type, drawing order, and compositional form. Representational types were classified as either *schematic, transitional*, or *true to visual appearance*. Schematic drawings were almost all composed by using one of the first three levels of compositional form but most had elements aligned in a row along the ground line. Transitional drawings (only 12%) tended to fall within the first four levels, whereas true to appearance drawings (50%) were largely split between the fifth and sixth levels of compositional form. Barnhart concluded that a child's interest in representing a scene in space leads away from alignment strategies and pulls toward finding an organized form.

Drawing order also related to compositional form. Three orders were observed: a spotting procedure in which the child placed individual elements in the "empty spaces" without apparent order, a serial procedure in which the child worked in a serial order across the page from one element to the next, and a constructive procedure in which the child worked from group to group or section to section. Mixed procedures that comprised two of these were also observed. Generally, spotting and serial orders leant themselves to alignment forms whereas constructive procedures, in which the child worked from group to group, tended to result in the more advanced organized forms. The first three levels of compositional form were done with either the spotting procedure, the serial procedure, or a combination of the two. Levels 4 and 5, which suggested a transition between alignment strategies and organized multiplanar forms, were largely produced with a spotting procedure but two well-balanced compositions were produced with a mixed constructive procedure. A description of the drawing order for those two children indicated that they had worked in a balanced fashion, first completing a group on one side of the drawing, then in the center, and then on the other side before returning to different locations to add elements. This is interesting because it suggests that these children were monitoring placements with the intention of achieving a well-balanced composition. At the most advanced compositional form, Level 6, 82% of the children used a constructive procedure.

Summary. These studies almost uniformly indicate that balanced compositions are not produced by young children and that when older children produce them they are often based on symmetry. The studies also suggest that more advanced balancing strategies such as complex symmetry or intentional asymmetry are observed almost exclusively in the drawings of talented children. In fact, compositional balance is used as one criterion for identifying children gifted in the visual arts by Clark (1989). A third point is that thematic content and representational skill strongly influence a child's compositional strategy. Some themes, such as drawing one's family, pull for alignment strategies and others, such as drawing a birthday party, provoke symmetry. If a child is still at a schematic representational level, in which the mapping of real world equivalents onto the picture plane is largely an intellectual discovery and not yet based on visual equivalences, alignment strategies prevail. The dependency between representational skill and compositional forms suggests one reason why compositional balance is observed in the artwork of younger talented children. Talented children reach a higher level of representational skill at younger ages than less talented children. Therefore, if a child has not gone beyond the level of schematic representation, it may be difficult to estimate compositional competence from her drawings. This becomes important when considering how to study children's competence in composition.

Appreciating Visual Balance in the Artwork of Others

Even though most young children appear unaware of compositional elements when producing a drawing, it is possible that they are sensitive to aesthetic considerations when looking at the artwork of others. Empirical research on children's aesthetic sensitivity to art dates back at least 50 years (Taunton, 1982). Most early researchers neglected the responses of very young children but Lark-Horowitz et al. (1973) and several others (see Taunton, 1982) found that children age 6 and younger based their preferences for reproductions of paintings primarily on subject matter and secondarily on color. In a more recent study, Machotka (1966) categorized children's verbatim justifications for their preferences. He asked children ages 6 to 18 to view 15 different reproductions. His analysis separated realism from subject matter, which had often been confounded in earlier studies. Further, he identified a range of more sophisticated criteria used by subjects and noted remarks related to contrast, harmony, style, use of light, and composition. Examples of composition justifications were comments about the organization and balance of a painting.

Despite Machotka's methodological innovations, his results for younger children were remarkably similar to those of earlier studies. At age 6, subject matter and color accounted for 87% of the preference justifications. Realism was not a consistent criterion until after age 7 and increased thereafter up to age 11. Contrast of elements, clarity of painting style, and harmony of elements, although never frequent, were used more consistently as justifications by children aged 9 and older. Children ages 12 to 18 most often cited realism but the emotional quality of a painting was also consistently mentioned. Justifications based on style, use of light, or aspects of composition were rarely given and then only by older children. Machotka used an explicitly cognitive framework to explain these developments by concluding that the appearance of formal operations around age 12 supports the sensitivity to composition and style.

Since the early 1970s, researchers at Harvard's Project Zero have been engaged in a collaborative enterprise with art educators focused on artistic development. Early research by Gardner and his associates attempted to look at the types of aesthetic criteria children were using when judging a work of art (Gardner, Winner & Kircher, 1975; Rosensteil, Morison, Silverman & Gardner, 1978). They interviewed children about their response to reproductions of paintings by well-known artists and found, as others had, that younger children used subject matter and color as their primary aesthetic criteria. After these studies; the group adopted Goodman's (1968) symbolic characteristics "symptomatic" of the aesthetic. For a piece to function as a work of art it should have at least some if not all of four symptoms: syntactic density (organization or relation among elements in the work), semantic density (set of reference classes), repleteness (consistency with which physical elements contribute to meaning), and exemplification (properties a work has and expresses).

In one of the early studies, Carothers and Gardner (1979) examined children's sensitivity to perception and production of repleteness and expressiveness (happy versus sad) by asking them to complete unfinished drawings and select a suitable completion drawing. Generally, first graders neither perceived the aesthetic dimensions nor produced completed pictures that were consistent with repleteness or expressiveness. Fourth graders were perceptually sensitive to the aesthetic qualities and showed some capacity to complete the pictures in a manner consistent with expression and some aspects of repleteness. By sixth grade, many children were able both to perceive the dimensional variations and to complete the drawings in a manner that was aesthetically consistent with all dimensions. A later study examined the interrelation among different aesthetic properties in different domains for children ages 7, 9, and 12 (Winner, Rosenblatt, Windmueller, Davidson & Gardner, 1986). Although children's sensitivity increased with age, the ability to perceive one aesthetic property such as expression or composition did not predict a child's ability to perceive another. There also was no relationship between perceiving an aesthetic property in one domain (i.e., painting) and perceiving it in another (i.e., music). The researchers concluded that sensitivity to aesthetic properties develops property by property and domain by domain.

Other studies using simpler performance tasks have found that although younger children ages 4 to 6 show some sensitivity to artistic style (Walk, Karusaitos, Lebowitz & Falbo, 1971; Winner, Blank, Massey & Gardner, 1983) and expressiveness (Taunton, 1980), they generally cannot explain their choices. But the Project Zero group discovered that when 5-year-olds were asked to label the mood conveyed by abstract paintings or match it to a realistic painting, they performed at levels greater than would occur by chance and many gave appropriate reasons for their choices (e.g., "This one has brighter colors") (Blank, Massey, Gardner & Winner, 1984). The successful children appeared to have considerable sensitivity to expressiveness and many could describe the moods conveyed using terms that were similar to the ones adults used.

On the basis of the overall results from the Project Zero studies, Gardner (1973) concluded that young children function primarily as an audience in relation to the arts, experiencing feelings and making primary distinctions. After the age of 7, children become artists, because they are able to use the symbolic medium of an art form to express their ideas, feelings, and experiences as well as to perceive fundamental aspects of artistic expression in the work of others. It is only after age 12, however, when children enter Piaget's stage of formal operations, that they can function as critics and interpret art.

The most ambitious analysis to date of aesthetic development in children was an outgrowth of the Project Zero research and culminated in a book by Parsons (1987). Parsons used a cognitive developmental approach. He interviewed children and adults about their responses to color reproductions of eight paintings by well-known artists. Subjects were asked to describe and evaluate a painting and to reason about their evaluations generally, and then with respect to emotions, colors, forms, textures, and level of technical skill necessary to execute the painting. The results are richly descriptive.

Parsons constructed a five-stage model of aesthetic development that explicitly drew on Kohlberg's stages of moral development and on neo-Piagetian theories of mind related to taking the perspective of others. As in Kohlberg's model, the stages are not rigidly tied to age, especially higher stages, for which artistic ability and experiences appear necessary. Parsons states that few people are likely to reach these stages without serious schooling in the arts. The stages move from a highly subjective construction of aesthetic experience to one that is more objective and rooted in a dialectic between accepted social evaluations and personal taste. It is instructive to review briefly the major positions represented by each stage.

Stage one is described by young preschoolers' uncritical nature and the intuitive delight they express for all paintings. But as in other studies, Parsons observed that young children took special pleasure in paintings that had strong, bright colors and contained certain favored subject matter. Thus the aesthetic position taken by stage one children is primarily in relation to colors and subject matter. In stage two, characteristic of elementary school children, a more critical tone is taken. A greater objectivity emerges as well, because children infer that what they judge as good can be judged that way by others, even when they don't personally like the painting. A painting is judged good only if it is beautiful and realistically rendered. Beauty is judged by the content of the subject matter. Content that represents a happy experience or things that are nice to look at in nature (e.g., flowers) are judged beautiful. Realism at this stage can refer to schematic or photographic realism, but *it does not* include abstract art, in which subject matter cannot be recognized. Parsons noted that children between age 7 and early adolescence show an increasing interest in realism and concluded that the ability to understand the set of formal requirements, such as overlap or relative size and perspective, imposed by realism is necessary. At the very least this demands concrete operations.

Stage three is marked by a new awareness of paintings as expressive of human experience. Paintings that provoke emotion or an idea are most valued. The criterion for the meaning of a painting resides in this experience and is best captured by looking inward at one's own gut reaction. Although this suggests a new type of subjectivity there is also a simultaneously more objective response. Previous criteria such as subject matter or realism are separated from the experience of a painting so that abstract paintings or those representing ugly events can be appreciated for their expressiveness. In addition, there is a new appreciation for the relationship between artist and viewer. Whereas in the previous stage, children are aware an artist has motives, it is not until this stage that they as viewers speculate about motives and try to connect what is represented with the artist's motives. There is now an artist on one side of the painting who is trying to express a feeling or idea to the viewer who is on the other side.

In stage four, the viewer becomes aware of the subjectivity of the viewer's role in relation to art. Interpretation of art becomes a dialogue in the context of a community of viewers. Whereas in the previous stage, an interpretation was checked against one's own internal response, in this stage it is checked against the facts of the painting, facts that are themselves constructed by a community of viewers. "Expressiveness moves from the private world of the viewer to the public space of the canvas" (Parsons, 1987, p. 110). It is at this stage that formal properties of a painting such as its composition or style are first used as justifications for preferences and the interaction of the artist with the medium is understood as a collaboration that helps to define formal aspects of the painting. In stage two children ignored these formal qualities to concentrate on thematic content. In stage three, although aware of such qualities, they noticed them only as an adjunct to a painting's expressiveness.

Stage five is called the *post-conventional* stage because the viewer is now able to examine his or her own response and no longer accepts the "authority of tradition." The process of examination confronts the viewer with the difficulty of making an objective judgment. Thus, although the viewer still uses the canons of tradition to understand and interpret paintings, she or he is also able to examine these canons critically and take explicit responsibility for her or his judgments. A judgment is validated by reasons that in principle are available to others and not by its agreement with others. The dialogue with the community of viewers that was begun at stage 4 is opened up, allowing for a reinterpretation of the viewer's experience. Thus, for example, the value of a particular painting's style becomes a personal choice that is consistent with a valued artistic direction that both is personal and can be argued as having value for everyone, and not just because it is a good exemplar of a valued style.

It is important to bear in mind that Parsons used a lengthy semistructured interview that concentrated on how children could reason about paintings. Therefore, despite the fact that his results appear somewhat at odds with those of other studies that have tried to establish children's sensitivity to aesthetic properties of paintings, he is really studying a different process. That process can best be summarized as children's and adults' ability to understand and interpret art, a process that clearly relies on their capacity to analyze and elaborate conceptually what they see. It is not surprising then that the full development of these analytical skills is quite protracted and apparently dependent on the maturity of formal operations and serious training in the arts. But also evident from Parsons's results is the young child's ability to engage with art, to discriminate certain aesthetic aspects of a piece, and to begin to make reasoned value judgments about a work. This echoes much of the other literature reviewed in its presentation of the young child as a sensitive consumer of art.

Summary. Recent studies concur with early studies of children's aesthetic responses in demonstrating that young children are most responsive to subject matter and color in a work of art. Young children, however, also respond to other aesthetic properties of a work: for example, those as young as 5 years old can label the expressive quality a painting evokes. Although young children appear to pass through a phase of easy acceptance of any work of art, children become more critical once they enter school and most demand a certain level of realism right through early adolescence. Children's first critical judgments focus primarily on subject matter and whether or not a painting is about a happy experience or portrays something that is beautiful. As children's aesthetic responses develop, they are able to appreciate the expressive qualities of a painting, first on a subjective level and then on the level of what it communicates to a community of viewers. At that point, the formal properties of a work begin to take on meaning. Children become aware that composition and style of a painting influence its expressive quality. But it is only at the most artistically developed levels that postconventional autonomous aesthetic responses appear. These are marked by a sophisticated understanding of a work's aesthetic properties and why these should make a painting more valued. At the same time, a personal choice about a valued artistic direction can supersede those made within tradition.

COMPOSITIONS BY TALENTED CHILDREN

We noted earlier that studies of compositions by young children indicated that they are influenced more by thematic content and less by the design of the two-dimensional picture surface. A child's representational skill and the order in which she draws elements in a picture also appear to influence her compositions. Therefore, systematic analysis of children's drawings as indices of compositional competence have to be made with caution. Children's performance could result more from thematic choices, representational skill level, or drawing sequence than from compositional considerations. For these reasons formal comparative analysis of composition in the spontaneous drawings samples was not undertaken. Instead a series of studies using nonrepresentational materials was designed. These are presented in the next two chapters

Despite this potential confounding of performance factors when assessing compositional competence, there were numerous examples of sophisticated compositional strategies that could be identified in the spontaneous drawings of talented children. These strongly suggested that talented children did take the design of the two-dimensional picture surface into account. It cannot be claimed that children planned such compositions a priori, the way an adult artist might, but rather that during the execution of a drawing talented children were sensitive to compositional properties. Earlier it was proposed that children could be attuned to compositional properties using purely figurative thought if they monitor their drawing activity and are visually responsive to "what looks good" as they place new elements in a picture. The beautifully composed drawings by talented children shown in earlier chapters suggest that they have just such a compositional sensitivity. In this section some of their more exceptional compositions are presented and discussed in relation to the elements of composition laid out in earlier sections.

Examples from the Drawings of Talented Children

Literature reviewed on children's compositional strategies indicated that the first clearly composed pictures done by young children use simple horizontal alignments of elements. Symmetrical placement of elements is more typical of older children, whereas advanced balancing strategies such as complex symmetry or intentional asymmetry have only been observed in drawings by older talented children. The drawings obtained for this study would then appear to be unique because symmetry, complex symmetry, and even asymmetrical balancing were observed in the drawings of very young talented children.

Figure 7.1. Kate age 4, the juggler.

Complex Symmetry. Kate at age 4 predominantly used symmetry of form and colors to balance her drawing of the juggler in Figure 7.1. The juggler stands with hands and feet outstretched symmetrically, braided hair adornments fly symmetrically from his head, and two nearly symmetrical forms spread behind him. But an interesting asymmetry also appears. In his left hand, the juggler holds a tall stack of pineapples, their height perfectly counterbalanced by the greater density of color applied to the otherwise near symmetry of the form behind the juggler on his right. The composition thus achieves its balance not only from symmetrical placement of like forms but also from a balance across two different dimensions, height (size) and color density (weight).

Asymmetrical Balance. A simple but elegant example of asymmetric counterbalancing occurs in Figure 7.2. Claire, at age 8, uses an intense yellow to color the small ball of wool and leaves the much larger form of the cat uncolored and unshaded. The large unfilled space created by the cat is held in balance by the placement of the intense yellow ball of yarn at an equal distance from the center

Figure 7.2. Claire age 8, cat with ball.

vertical axis of the picture. Size and color are therefore used as counterbalances.

Two interesting examples illustrate the use of direction to counterbalance weight and location. In the first example both productive and receptive movement creates visual balance. In Figure 7.3, drawn at age 7, Hondo invokes a chevron shape to organize the drawing (productive movement). Starting at the lower right the cannon directs the viewer's glance with a shot (receptive movement) up the hill to the left toward the eagle. As the shot meets the contour of the hill, directional biases of the eye (up and to the right) (receptive movement) and the outline of the hill converge to guide the viewer's gaze to the soldier, his cat, and the tank grouped on the top right of the picture. The weight of these end elements is held in check by a cannon that shoots off to the left behind the soldier and his cat. A second example of receptive movement is seen in Figure 7.4, a paper cutout piece done by Kate at the age of 6. In this case, the heavier region of concentrated elements on the lower left and the leftward movement of the cat along the fence are counterbalanced by the natural movement of the eye, the central moon, and the greater number of fence posts to the right of center. The cat's movement is also held in check by the color change of its body encompassed by the moon.

Figure 7.3. Hondo age 7, an eagle.

Figure 7.4. Kate age 6, paper cutout.

Figure 7.5. Joel age 11, flying pteranodon and sauropods in water. Figure 7.5 first appeared in *The Development of Artistically Gifted Children*, edited by C. Golomb, 1995, Hillsdale, N.J.: Lawrence Erlbaum Assoc. Reprinted with permission.

In a final example of the use of direction, Figure 7.5 ("Flying Pteranodon and Sauropods in Water"), productive movement is created by the compositional grouping. Joel at age 11 uses the tension created by the oblique position of the bodies and wings of a group of flying pteranodons to produce a dynamic sense of flight. A larger or closer pteranodon on the upper right provides a serene counterpoint to this bevy of activity on the left. The use of such a sophisticated compositional technique to effect movement is reminiscent of techniques used by early masters of religious paintings. One example is the anguished sense of flight achieved by Giotto in his painting *Lamentations* (Arnheim, 1974).

CONCLUSIONS

Most of the literature on children's aesthetic development separates what children do artistically from what they can respond to in a work of art. Development in both arenas is protracted but young children appear more capable of responding aesthetically than of producing a well-balanced drawing or painting. Nevertheless children have the ability to respond critically first with their eyes and developmentally later with their intellect. On that basis, it was suggested that even young children might be capable of creating visually balanced works of art if they used perception rather than cognition as a guide. Developmental studies that have focused on composition strategies, however, suggest that most young children probably do not use perception when they are creating a drawing. Young children pay almost no attention to the overall effects individually placed elements have on the whole when they are composing a drawing. Instead, the theme or subject matter of a drawing is more likely to dictate the type of compositional arrangement they use. It is only when some children reach early adolescence, especially if they are talented, that their approach to drawing begins to demonstrate a compositional sophistication. Complex symmetry and dynamic asymmetry are employed by some adolescents as compositional strategies that achieve visual balance.

The qualitative observations of talented children's drawings studied for this book are at odds with the characterization of the development of sophisticated compositional strategies as protracted. Instead, the many drawings presented throughout the book and especially those used as illustrations in this chapter speak to the compositional sophistication of these talented children. This is not to suggest that the strategies these children used when young were anticipatory and intentionally employed for a given effect. Instead, it is more likely and within the realm of their overall developmental levels that they were basing their creative decisions on perception by using the eye and its inherent sense of weights and good forms to monitor and regulate their drawing activity. If true, this presents another piece of evidence as to the abilities of talented children to employ figurative thought in the drawing process. It also suggests that unlike other children their age who may be more compelled by cognitive factors, these children are responding to subtle aesthetic dimensions based on visual aspects of their artwork. Before such a conclusion can be suggested, however, a more careful study of what children can do without the compositional constraints imposed by thematic content, representational skills, or drawing sequences needs to be made.

8

CONDUCTING THE COMPOSITION STUDY
METHODS AND PROCEDURES

The literature reviewed in the previous chapter revealed that although often sensitive to aesthetic aspects of paintings, young children rarely produce artistic compositions that meet our adult standards of visual balance. Older children do, but primarily by using simple forms of symmetry. Only talented children appear to use dynamic and asymmetrical balancing techniques that characterize the artwork of mature adult artists. A developmental progression that moves from simple alignment of elements to symmetrical placement and later to asymmetrical balancing strategies is suggested. But some serious confounds were brought out by the research. A child's compositional competence could be masked in a drawing by the dictates of a given theme, representational skill level, or sequential order of drawing. Different types of thematic content lend themselves to different organizational strategies. For example, if a child is drawing a picture of her or his family, the family members tend to be aligned horizontally across the page but a birthday party is drawn with a symmetrical organization around the central birthday cake. Likewise, children who are still at a schematic level of representation or those who draw by filling in the available space use simple compositional forms. Studying compositional development might be hindered by the variety of themes in children's drawings or by the children's skill level. When drawings are studied, the compositional forms observed are likely to be confounded with factors extrinsic to the central focus of composition.

It was this logic that led me to search for a way to study composition that would not be tied to a child's drawing ability or to the content of a drawing. Simple abstract shapes that a child could arrange and rearrange to please the eye seemed a good place to start. Accordingly I piloted both a two- and a three-dimensional composition task with elementary school children. The two-dimensional task required children to arrange three flat shapes on a form board. The three-dimensional task used the same shapes but they were made out of blocks of wood. Children were asked to arrange them on a table. It became clear that although children could perform both tasks with ease, the three-dimensional task was much more compelling. The first study of elementary school–aged children, therefore, used two different block sets, one in which only the forms differed and one in which colors and forms differed. Children were asked to make an arrangement with the blocks from which they might draw a still life picture that would be pleasing to them.

An elaboration of this original simplified task led to a second study with older children, who were asked not only to produce a pleasing arrangement of the blocks, but to respond to two- and three-dimensional prepared compositions of the same blocks. Older children were also interviewed about their views on what was important in judging a work of art. Originally, these children were in middle school. Four years later, when the youngest had reached high school, a subset were tested a second time to see whether their approach to composition had changed. In a final study, with a different group of high school children and young adults in college, the two-dimensional compositions were presented by using a paired comparison method. Data from this study was meant to provide a referent for the data obtained in response to two-dimensional compositions in the other studies.

We now turn to the details of the methods used in the composition studies. First, the compositional types that were studied are defined and then the problems that were created to study them are described.

COMPOSITION TASKS AND PROCEDURES
Defining Compositional Types
Elements can be balanced with respect to the following types: (a) location or position of objects; (b) forms as mass, size, or shape of elements; (c) tonality or density, that is, the degree of light or dark of elements; (d) color of elements, such as hot or cold colors; and

(e) direction of movement or vector in a two- or three-dimensional space. Some of these principles were considered in defining three compositional types around which the composition block tasks were constructed. These definitions are based on Arnheim's (1974) framework and Paul Klee's (1978) Bauhaus composition lectures.

- *Symmetrical balance* is counterbalancing elements around a central axis to obtain a mirror image. In drawings counterbalancing might be produced by placing similar or identical forms around a central axis. For example, two trees of similar size might be placed on either side of a centrally placed house.
- *Complex symmetry* does not achieve balance by producing a mirror image but by counterbalancing within a single dimension, such as equalizing mass around a central axis (Golomb, 1992).
- *Asymmetrical balance* relies on the use of two or more dimensions in opposition to counterbalance each other. Balance need not be around a central axis but the piece achieves stability by counterbalancing "weights" across dimensions. For example, a large white/empty square (size) on the right of a drawing can be balanced by a much smaller dense black square on the left (tonality) (see Figure 7.2).
- *Imbalance* results when any of these dimensions or combinations of dimensions is arranged so that the result looks haphazard or unstable and one-sided.

The Composition Tasks

Much developmental literature suggests that children often respond in more competent ways when tasks are simplified (Flavell, 1990). A task is most difficult when a child must both support the task context by herself or himself and produce a novel response. The free composition task represents this end of a task difficulty continuum. At the other end are response selection tasks, in which the child simply selects from a set of available choices. Task context and a set of appropriate possible responses to the task are all given to the child. The picture selection task represents this end. A task that defines the context for response but still requires novel response production can be thought of as midway along this task difficulty continuum. The provoked composition task represented this midpoint.

Free Composition Task. During his years of teaching at the Bauhaus, Klee often used letters of the alphabet and simple shapes as elements in composition exercises. The shapes of the blocks and compositional elements employed in the block tasks were derived from those shown in his notebooks (Klee, 1978). Two three-block sets were designed for use with the elementary and middle school children. One, the blue block set, contained a *T* and two *L*s of a size that exactly duplicated the *T* when properly arranged: A 3½ inch high by 1½ inch wide *T* block with a 3½ inch long top to the *T* and two *L* blocks that were made by cutting an identical *T* block in half. They were all painted blue (see Figures 8.1a & b). The blocks were disposed in this way so that balanced compositions could be obtained by symmetrical or asymmetrical arrangements that either maintained equalities in total size or employed distance to compensate for inequalities of size.

The second, the "gray" block set, was composed of two square blocks (3½ inches cubed), one gray and one white, and a smaller square block (1¾ inch cubed) painted black (see Figures 8.1c & d). The color of the gray block had been made by mixing white and black paint to a color that appeared subjectively to be balanced in color by the white and black blocks together. The mixing of the paint and painting of the blocks were done by a trained artist. Balanced arrangements could be obtained by symmetry (e.g., stacking) or by placement of the small black cube with the large white cube and opposite the large gray cube. This would constitute asymmetrical balancing across two dimensions, size and tonality. Achieving balance with these blocks was, therefore, a more complex problem than achieving balance with the blue block set.

High school children were likely to feel that arranging three blocks was too simple and "boring." In order to challenge this age group and keep the free block task compelling, the set sizes were increased to five. In the case of the blue block set, another *T* and *L* were added whereas two more small black cubes were added to the gray block set. The resultant five-block sets also formed the basis for the provoked composition tasks presented to the middle and high school children. These tasks are described after the discussion of the interviews.

The Interview. After children had completed their first free compositions and before the other composition tasks were presented, children were interviewed about what was important to them in judging a painting or drawing. The interview began with asking them what they thought made a pretty picture and what attracted them to a painting or drawing and made it look good. The criteria

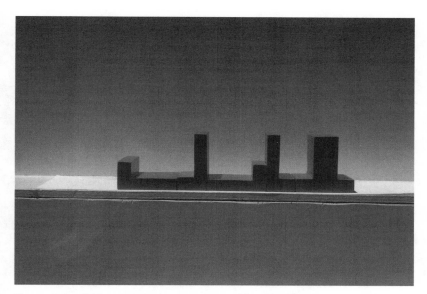

Figure 8.1a. Artist's original composition: blue blocks grouped.

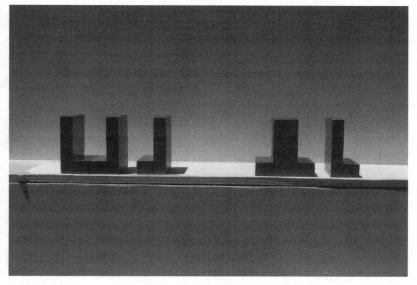

Figure 8.1b. Artist's original composition: blue blocks spaced.

Figure 8.1c. Artist's original composition: gray blocks grouped.

Figure 8.1d. Artist's original composition: gray blocks spaced.

290   *Composition*

a child mentioned were written down. The interviewer also had a list of criteria for discussion and the child was probed about those he or she did not mention. The list included realism versus abstraction, subject matter or theme, use of color, use of perspective, originality, and composition. An attempt to draw out the child on each of these criteria was made.

Provoked Composition Task. The compositions for this task were derived in the following manner. Two artists and an architect were each independently asked to compose visually balanced and pleasing arrangements of the five-block sets. Each composition was sketched by a recording artist. In all cases the artists or architect had achieved visual balance by using either complex forms of symmetry (Golomb, 1992) or asymmetrical balance. The compositions were then reviewed by artists and researcher and several were chosen. Choices were based on which compositions were most amenable to the removal of one block and its replacement into the composition to make either a "symmetrically" balanced composition or a clearly unbalanced composition. Two alternative solutions to each composition, a "symmetrically" balanced and an unbalanced solution, were identified. These are described in the picture selection task that follows. Four problem compositions resulted, two with the "blue" block set and two with the "gray" block set. The compositions as completed by the artists are shown in Figure 8.1. Figure 8.2 shows how they appeared with the removal of one block.

Several additional features of these four problems need to be considered. The problems differed in their use of negative space. Half the problems were tightly grouped, relying primarily on either size or tone and size as visual elements (Figures 8.1a & c), whereas the other two compositions included negative space or distance as additional visual elements (Figures 8.1b & d). Furthermore, only two of the four problems had solutions that could be thought of as truly symmetrical (Figures 8.1b & d), and in the case of one of these, the gray block composition, this was only with respect to the dimensions of size and distance, leaving tone unbalanced. The symmetrical solutions found for the other two compositions were approximate. This particular issue is discussed further under the picture selection task section.

Only the middle and high school children were presented with the prepared compositions. It was thought that they would be too

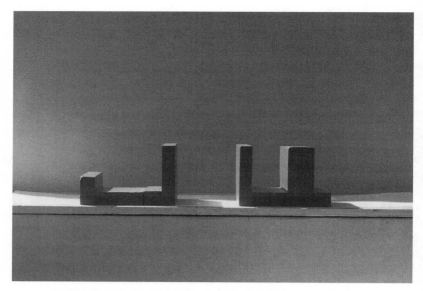

Figure 8.2a. Blue blocks grouped provoked task.

Figure 8.2b. Blue blocks spaced provoked task.

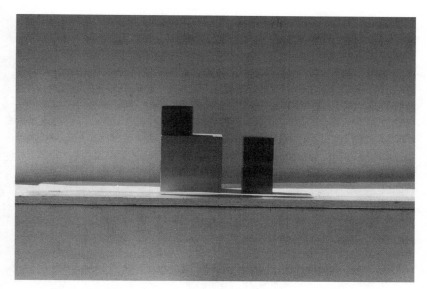

Figure 8.2c. Gray blocks grouped provoked task.

Figure 8.2d. Gray blocks spaced provoked task.

Figure 8.3. Composition stage.

demanding for most of the elementary school children. The compositions were presented after the interview. For presentation, the compositions were mounted on a white rectangular box (34¾ by 10¼ by 8¼ inches) that had a white backboard (34¾ by 13¼ inches) meant to represent the size of the canvas or paper on which such a composition might appear as a two-dimensional picture. Once the rectangular box was placed on a table, its top was approximately at eye level. A picture of this equipment is presented in Figure 8.3. Paper strips with markings for block placement were used as templates for setting up each composition so that all compositions were uniformly presented.

Picture Selection Task. An artist prepared tempera-colored drawings of the four artists' compositions and two alternatives identified as solutions to the placement of the removed block. One alternative represented a symmetrical or near-symmetrical solution and the other represented a visually unbalanced solution. Figure 8.4 shows the drawings of the original blue block compositions and their alternatives. In the first blue block composition, Figure 8.4a, the

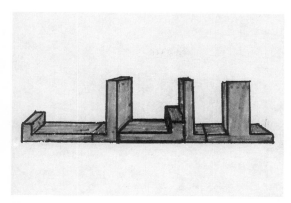

Figure 8.4a. Picture selection alternative blue block grouped task: asymmetrical balance.

Figure 8.4b. Picture selection alternative blue block grouped task: "symmetrical" balance.

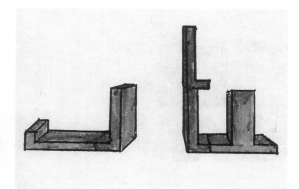

Figure 8.4c. Picture selection alternative blue block grouped task: unbalanced.

Figure 8.4d. Picture selection alternative blue block spaced task: asymmetrical balance.

Figure 8.4e. Picture selection alternative blue block spaced task: symmetrical balance.

Figure 8.4f. Picture selection alternative blue block spaced task: unbalanced.

blocks are contiguous and negative space is not used as part of the composition. Balance is achieved elegantly but simply by the equated dispersal of mass as lengths and heights. In panel b, the near-symmetry solution, negative space marks the central axis. This solution can be considered a complex form of symmetry since mass is equated around the central axis. In panel c, the unbalanced solution, the preponderance of mass on the viewer's right is accented by the increased height and the eye is riveted to one spot of the composition. Figure 8.4d shows the second blue block composition as the artist constructed it. In this case mass and distance or negative space are used to achieve a complex symmetrical balance. Panel e shows the symmetry solution for this composition in which both mass and distance or negative space are exactly equated to form a mirror image around a central vertical axis. In panel f, the unbalanced solution, the exposed flat wall of the stacked block appears in danger of toppling and draws the eye exclusively to the heavy side of the composition.

The gray block compositions are shown in Figure 8.5. The architects' original composition for the contiguously spaced composition beautifully balances mass with tone around a central axis (Figure 8.5a). In the near-symmetry solution, an attempt was made to equate mass by using the negative space in the composition on the viewer's right side (Figure 8.5b). The result, however, leaves an imbalance of tonality and the right side looks "heavy" compared to the left. In the unbalanced solution (Figure 8.5c) the mass and height on the viewer's left gives the composition an unstable look. The fourth composition, shown in Figure 8.5d, again balances mass with tone but employs a more complex use of negative space, since the placement of a small black block fills the right side of the central axis. This draws attention to the open left side and makes the area of negative space more central to the composition. The symmetrical solution in the next panel (Figure 8.5e) perfectly equates mass and distance around the central block but leaves tonality on the left side heavier. This kind of imbalance is exploited further in the final panel (Figure 8.5f), showing the unbalanced solution for this composition.

Conducting the Studies

The Elementary School Study. The elementary school study was conducted in a local elementary school of a small middle- to upper-

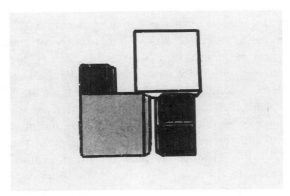

Figure 8.5a. Picture selection alternative for gray block grouped task: asymmetrical balance.

Figure 8.5b. Picture selection alternative for gray block grouped task: "symmetrical" balance.

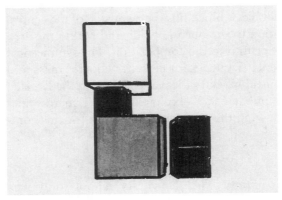

Figure 8.5c. Picture selection alternative for gray block grouped task: unbalanced.

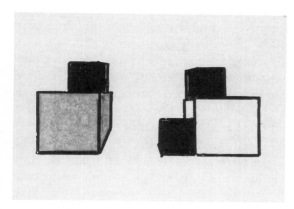

Figure 8.5d. Picture selection alternative for gray block grouped task: asymmetrical balance.

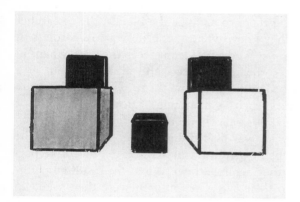

Figure 8.5e. Picture selection alternative for gray block grouped task: symmetrical balance.

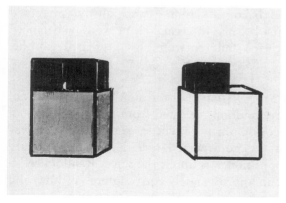

Figure 8.5f. Picture selection alternative for gray block grouped task: unbalanced.

middle-class school district. Two hundred and eighty children were enrolled in the elementary school with approximately 15% Asian, 80% Caucasian, and 5% mixed among other races. Negative participation slips were sent home to all parents in targeted grades; only one parent declined to have her child participate. Ten children were selected from the kindergarten classes (M age = 6 years 2 months), from a second third grade combination class (M age = 8 years 3 month), and 12 from the fifth-grade classes (M age = 11 years 2 months). Children were randomly selected from the class rosters so that an equal number of boys and girls would participate in the study. Each child was seen individually during the schoolday in a small room provided by the school.

Children were presented the block sets on a 36 by 24 inch rectangle or a circle 30 inches in diameter that was placed on a larger table top. Before asking them to arrange the blocks, the researcher asked them whether they knew what a still life was. Regardless of their answer, a still life was always defined for them as when an artist takes flowers or other still objects and arranges them in a specific way in order to draw or paint them. The children were verbally given examples, such as paintings of flowers in a vase or a bowl of fruit, and almost all children were familiar with such paintings. Great emphasis was placed during this discussion on the fact that when artists paint or draw still life objects, they take particular care as to how they arrange them so that the resulting painting will be pleasing to their eye. The children were then asked to arrange the blocks in a three-block set so that if they were to draw or paint them the picture would be pleasing to them. The entire session was videotaped so that a child's composition could be judged later for visual balance. Children were always presented with the blue blocks first because the visual elements to be balanced were simpler. Kindergarten children were only presented the blue blocks.

The Middle and High School Study. For the middle and high school study 76 children were randomly selected from the middle school art classes during the course of a year. The same school district was used, and although it was somewhat larger than the elementary school, the racial composition was about the same. Random selection was done so that an approximately equal number of boys and girls participated at each of the three grade levels. All sixth graders had to take at least one semester of art. Enrollment of seventh and eighth graders was limited to those who selected the art classes. Thirty-six sixth graders (*M* age = 11 years 5 months), 20 seventh graders (*M* age = 12 years 6 months), and 20 eighth graders participated (*M* age = 13 years 6 months). Negative participation slips were sent home to parents and none was returned. Participation was always voluntary and children were seen during the art class in a separate room. Children spent from 20 to 30 minutes on the various composition tasks.

When the sixth-grade children reached high school, 40 of the children in the original study were asked to participate again. All but a handful of those who had originally participated were still in the school district. The children were randomly selected from the original group so that numbers of boys and girls would remain approximately equal. Their picture selection responses from the first time they were tested were also checked to make sure that a representative sample of children who might still show developmental shifts in that task would be included. The sample that resulted included 15 10th graders (*M* age = 15 years 2 months), 13 11th graders (*M* age = 16 years 2 months), and 12 12th graders (*M* age = 17 years 1 month). Each child was again seen individually for about 20 to 30 minutes during the schoolday in a room provided by the high school.

This study was more complex than the elementary school study but it began much the same way. Children were asked whether they knew what a still life was and regardless of their answer, a still life was defined for them in the same way as it had been for the elementary school children. Like the younger children, the middle school children were then asked to arrange the three blue block set so that the picture they might draw or paint from the arrangement would be pleasing to them. The blue blocks were presented first because it was assumed they were simpler to compose. The children composed their arrangements on the top of the white rectangular box with the white backboard. They were asked to imagine that the backboard was like the paper or canvas on which a drawing or painting could be done. The children were seated and the top of the rectangular box appeared to them approximately at eye level. Two free compositions with the blue block set were obtained and afterward each child was asked to discuss what he or she had done before moving on to the general interview about the child's criteria in judging a work of art.

After the children had been interviewed they were presented with one of the two prepared compositions for the blue block set, except that instead of three blocks the set now contained five. The presentation of the two prepared compositions was counterbalanced so that half the children received one of the blue compositions first and the other half received the other composition first. The children were told that they were going to be shown a still life that someone else had made. They were told that the model was not quite complete. It still needed to have one more block placed in it. They were asked to place the block where they thought it would look best, to make the prettiest picture. They were encouraged to take their time and try out several ideas. After placing the block, the child was asked to explain why she or he had made that placement. Several probes were used to try to find out whether a child's placement was arbitrary (could it just as easily have been placed on this other side?) and whether she or he was thinking of the whole composition or only local features of adjacent blocks. Children were then asked to find a second place for the block. Following the discussion of their second placement, children were shown the three alternative completion pictures for the composition and asked to select the one they liked best and the one they liked second best. The reasons for their choices were discussed. The entire procedure was then repeated with the remaining prepared blue block composition.

After completion of the blue block tasks, the gray three-block set was brought out. Children were asked what was different about these blocks. If a child noted only size and not color or tonality differences, the researcher mentioned these differences. Children were then asked to create a model for a still life from these blocks as they had with the blue blocks. Once two free compositions had been elicited from them the two prepared compositions were presented in a counterbalanced manner. Additional probes were used to elicit whether or not a child made a placement by considering the colors of the blocks. Consideration of color could be local, for example, when a placement was made because a child liked black and white contrast; or the consideration could be related to the whole, for example, when a child discussed the effects of equalizing the weight of the gray and black blocks by placing the white block with the two black blocks. After each provoked phase, children were presented with the three alternative completion pictures.

The procedure for the high school study was much the same. Only two changes were made. First, the block sets for the free composition task were increased from three to five. Second, whichever block set, the blue or gray, was used first was counterbalanced across the children so that half received the blue first and half received the gray. Younger children had been given the simpler blue block set first because it was felt this would give them a chance to familiarize themselves with the task before approaching the more challenging gray block task, but with the high school children this seemed an unnecessary precaution.

Paired Comparison Study. This study employed the paired comparison method common to perception studies. The pictures of the 12 (4 × 3) compositions were photographed and made into slides. Each alternative for a given composition was paired with each of the other alternatives. The three resulting pairs for a composition were presented three times to the subjects in the study, making a total of 36 paired comparison presentations (12 × 3). The order of presentation was random. Two slide projectors were used and which alternative appeared projected on the right or left was determined randomly.

Students in two art classes at a local high school were used as subjects. All of the students in class on the day of the study participated. The slides were presented to the students in a class as a group. This was a total of 47 students, approximately half of them male (23). Sixteen students were in 9th grade (*M* age = 14 years 3 months), 8 were in 10th grade (*M* age = 15 years 9 months), 7 were in 11th grade (*M* age = 16 years 5 months), and 16 were in 12th grade (*M* age = 17 years 5 months). Students in the 9th grade had an average of 2½ art classes at the time of the study. Tenth graders averaged 4 art classes and 11th and 12th graders averaged 5. The media of greatest interest to these students included drawing, painting, ceramic, sculpture, film, and photography.

The college sample was taken from an art class at a large midwestern university. The procedure was the same as for the high school students. Twenty-two students participated (M age = 23 years 2 months), 10 male and 12 female. On the average students had 3.5 years of college and 7½ art classes. The media of greatest interest were very similar to those of the high school students.

ANALYZING THE CHILDREN'S COMPOSITIONS

The main thrust of the composition studies was to study development of children's abilities to balance their artwork visually. Even though a working definition of visual balance was accessible from the writings of artists and psychologists, its measurement was difficult. Researchers who had examined children's compositions tended to classify drawings by their organization with the assumption that certain organizations, like symmetry, were visually balanced (Golomb, 1992; Barnhart, 1942). This has an appeal because the definition of visual balance is tightly integrated with the classification taxonomy a priori.

Picture Selection Task

Each alternative composition in this task had already been classified according to working definitions for asymmetrical and symmetrical balance and for imbalance. Each alternative composition received a preference score of 1 to 3 depending on the rank order a child gave it. For the paired comparison study, each alternative composition was given a score based on the proportion of times it was chosen on its paired presentations. If an alternative was always chosen, its score was 1 whereas if it was never chosen its score was 0.

Provoked Composition Task

A classification taxonomy was applied to the children's placements; it was based on definitions of types of balance and imbalance presented earlier in this chapter. But a few other strategies emerged empirically when children discussed their placements. For example, when probed about a placement at the center of a composition some would simply say, "It needed something to fill the center." Such a strategy was called "centering." In other cases the center position was used to connect the two parts of the composition so that a block might be laid across the open space to touch the two halves. In that case, the strategy was called *connecting*. Most children's placements, however, fell broadly into the compositional forms de-

fined a priori. Children were always questioned about their placements and their responses were used to confirm a classification. Still
some children were less forthcoming and responded with "I don't
know." Unless a child's verbal response was directly disconfirming
(i.e., "filling the space"), a placement was classified in the most
appropriate category.

The general classificatory scheme then for the four problems included an *unbalanced category*, a *symmetrically balanced category*,
and an *asymmetrically balanced category* using either one (note this
could also be considered complex symmetry) or two dimensions for
balance. Other types of responses such as centering, connecting, or
local choices based on color (i.e., local color contrasts or a color
series of light to dark) were categorized separately.

Free Composition Task

Measurement of visual balance for the free compositions was a
challenge. Although it might have been possible to use the provoked
problem classification system, the great variety of compositions generated by this task would have led to unreliable classifications. A
better approach seemed to be for experts or "experts in training"
to evaluate each composition on several different relevant dimensions and to rely on their average evaluations for each dimension
to tap the constructs. This approach has been standard in aesthetics
research (Berlyne, 1974). Because there were so many compositions,
however, the evaluation task leant itself nicely to Q-sort techniques
even though visual stimuli have seldom been used as objects of a
Q sort and particularly for aesthetic judgments (but see Gauger &
Wyckoff, 1973; Stephenson, 1953). Therefore, using photographs
of the compositions "experts in training" and their teachers were
asked to sort them.

Except for the kindergarten children who only composed the blue
blocks, each child had produced four free compositions, two with
the blue and two with the gray blocks. One blue and one gray
composition were randomly chosen from the four and photographed in color. Compositions from all 32 elementary school children were photographed but only compositions from the 40
children who participated in middle school and again in high school
were photographed. Four Q sets were made from the photographed
compositions: two blue and two gray Q sets, one with the three-
block, and one with the five-block compositions. The blue three-

block Q set had 71 compositions, the gray three-block Q set had 55, and the blue and gray five-block Q sets each had 40, plus the 6 alternative compositions used in the picture selection task.

Students in two design classes at a local art college were used as the "experts in training." These classes were chosen because they had been studying principles of two-dimensional composition. The Q-sort task was given to them near the end of the semester. Their teachers also sorted one of the Q sets. Twenty-four students participated. Thirteen of the students were female and 11 were male. On the average, they were age 25 (range 19 to 41 years) and had 1.3 years of art school and three college art classes prior to the design class. Because of time constraints not all students were able to complete sorts of all four Q sets. On the average each Q set had 8 students who completed the sorts on four dimensions of composition: visual balance, static to dynamic, symmetry to asymmetry, and originality.

Before the students were asked to sort the photographs, I presented a brief review of the purpose of my study and discussed each of the four sort dimensions. The first three dimensions had also been explicitly discussed in their classes as part of the course curriculum. For the *visual balance* sort they were asked to use their eyes to look and apply all that they knew intuitively or formally about visual balance. For the *static to dynamic* sort, static compositions were defined as those that were at rest primarily by adhering strictly to an organization along the horizontal or vertical picture axes whereas dynamic compositions were those with movement and were likely to use the diagonal axes. They were encouraged, however, to improve on this view with their own thinking. For the *symmetry to asymmetry* sort, symmetry was defined as mirror images around a central axis whereas asymmetry implied marked deviations from symmetry. They were also told that visual balance could be achieved by either symmetry or asymmetry. A simple example of visual balance using asymmetry was described verbally. The final dimension was *originality*. Here they were exhorted to use their own feelings and perceptions but also to keep in mind that children had been limited by the materials provided and therefore judgments should be scaled within those limits. The students were provided with recording sheets that had brief anchors at each end and at the midpoint along a 7-point scale. They were asked to sort each Q set four times, once for each dimension.

TABLE 8.1a
SAMPLE IN MIDDLE SCHOOL

	Static/Dynamic	Symmetry/Asymmetry	Originality
Balance	−0.64	−0.91	−0.85
Static/Dynamic		0.77	0.83
Symmetry/Asymmetry			0.91

TABLE 8.1b
SAMPLE IN HIGH SCHOOL

	Static/Dynamic	Symmetry/Asymmetry	Originality
Balance	−0.21	−0.92	−0.61
Static/Dynamic		0.30	0.65
Symmetry/Asymmetry			0.73

Examining the agreement between the students' sorts led to eliminating the students who were outliers on the sort tasks. This meant that sorts from two raters were eliminated for each sort. The remaining students' interrater reliabilities (Kendall's W) for the different dimensions and composition types ranged from a low of .67 to a high of .88. The average across all dimensions and composition types was .78. Reliabilities for the gray compositions were slightly lower ($W = .77$) than for the blue compositions ($W = .80$) suggesting these may have been more difficult to judge. When the reliabilities for each dimension were averaged across composition types, originality ($W = .74$) was the lowest and symmetry to asymmetry ($W = .83$) was the highest. Balance ($W = .82$) was higher than the static to dynamic ($W = .75$) dimension.

The pattern of intercorrelations among the four dimensions for each type of composition suggested that students were judging compositions that were dynamic and asymmetrical as more original but less well balanced. Correlations for judgments on the middle school and high school samples are shown in Table 8.1a–b.

The teachers of the two classes had rated only one Q set, the gray five-block problem of the high school children. They showed the strongest agreement for symmetry to asymmetry ($r = .74$, $p < .01$), followed by visual balance ($r = .38$, $p = .01$) and originality ($r = .29$, $p = .05$). They did not agree on static to dynamic ($r =$

−.58, $p < .01$), which put one of them at odds with the pattern for the student ratings. The moderately strong correlation suggests that this teacher may have reversed the scale despite the anchors on the recording sheet. For one teacher, therefore, the pattern of intercorrelations among the dimensions was the same as for the students. The compositions judged as most well balanced were more static and symmetrical, and less original. The compositions judged more dynamic were judged asymmetrical and more original. In contrast, the other teacher's judgments showed no relationship between visual balance and static or dynamic and the most visually balanced compositions were judged more original and symmetrical. This teacher judged dynamic compositions as less asymmetrical and to a smaller extent less original.

Considering the judgments as a whole, there was a remarkable degree of consistency among all raters across the two samples. It suggests that the underlying constructs were approached in much the same way by the two classes, irrespective of the responses of one of their teachers. Given the stability of these judgments, developmental changes in the children's free compositions can be regarded as reflecting attributes of the compositions themselves. We now turn to the results of the studies.

9

THE COMPOSITIONS STUDIES

In the first chapter several predictions were laid out (Table 1.1) for two contrasting groups of hypotheses about development in talented children. The final predictions related to children's compositional abilities. It was predicted that if talented children primarily used operational reasoning for artistic composition, their advancements in composition would parallel developments in other conceptual areas, such as in logical or spatial reasoning. But if they largely relied on figurative abilities, their compositions could be quite sophisticated from a young age. Chapter 7 presented some exceptional examples of advanced composition strategies in the spontaneous drawings of young talented children. Nevertheless, one obstacle to evaluating spontaneous drawings for composition emerged from the developmental literature in composition. Past research acknowledged the confounding of composition strategies with thematic content and representational skills. An adequate study of normative development in composition that lacked these confounds did not appear to exist. Without such studies, it is difficult to know whether what is observed in drawings of talented children represents exceptional compositional competence or merely appears exceptional because of the advanced representational skills of talented children. Younger less talented children might be able to show the same sophistication when they do not have to draw. The studies presented in this chapter were designed to provide normative data on the development of composition skills by using tasks that do not depend on children's representational skills or thematic content of a composition. The studies were also designed to examine individual differences in compositional competence. If the hypotheses and model of talent proposed in this book are on the right track, there should be at least some children who are sophisticated in composition independently of their developmental level. The results from the studies described in chapter 8 are presented.

ANALYZING CHILDREN'S FREE COMPOSITIONS

Allowing children to compose nonrepresentational materials freely gives them an opportunity to be artistic and creative without imposing any external standards. The less structured the context, the more children can rely on their own values and standards. Even young kindergarten children appeared to understand the demands of this free task, although their compositions were often meant to be representational.

Development in Free Composition

The first question of interest was whether developmental trends in children's compositions could be detected. Compositions were judged by college art students using a series of four independent Q sorts on dimensions of *visual balance, static to dynamic, symmetrical to asymmetrical,* and *originality.* Seventy-two elementary and middle school children participated and 40 of the middle school students participated again in high school. Elementary and middle school children were given two three-block sets to compose and high school students were given two five-block sets. This meant that high school compositions had to be assessed separately from compositions of younger children.

Results for All Compositions. Looking broadly across the three-block compositions produced by children from kindergarten through middle school, a somewhat surprising result emerged. Children's ability to produce visual balance did not improve with age (or grade level) but was somewhat better in younger children. Younger children's compositions were judged as better balanced and more static and symmetrical. It appeared as if younger children were achieving better visual balance by relying on symmetry and horizontal and vertical alignments. The compositions of older children were judged as less well balanced but more dynamic, asymmetrical, and original, suggesting that older children used more sophisticated compositional strategies but at the expense of visual balance. Correlations for each rated dimension averaged across compositions with age and grade level are shown in Table 9.1. The mean ratings on each dimension are presented in Table 9.2.

In Figures 9.1 and 9.2, six arrangements composed by the grammar and middle school children are shown to exemplify the relationships described by these correlations. Arrangements in Figure 9.1a–c were composed by kindergarten, second/third-, and fifth-grade students, respectively. Ratings of visual balance ranged from 6.4 to 7, whereas ratings for static–dynamic were between 1.3 and 1.7. Ratings on symmetry–asymmetry were from 1.5 to 2.4 and those for originality between 1 and 2.7. These children produced compositions that were exceptionally well balanced but highly symmetrical and static and not very original. Contrast these with compositions by a sixth, a seventh, and an eighth grader in Figure 9.2 a–c, respectively. Ratings on visual balance for these compositions fell between 2 and 3.8; ratings on the static–dynamic dimension ranged between 4.6 and 5.8. Symmetry–asymmetry ratings were between 5.3 and 5.9 and originality ratings were between 5.7 and 6.5. These older children's arrangements were much more original, dynamic, and asymmetrical. But the children were unable to achieve a well-balanced composition.

The correlations for the high school students indicated that with the addition of more blocks, the younger students resorted to static and symmetrical arrangements to obtain visual balance. Older students, however, concentrated on producing more original composition, using dynamic and asymmetric arrangements that were difficult to compose in visual balance. In Figure 9.3a–c arrangements composed by two 10th graders and an 11th grader, respectively, are shown. Visual balance was rated as 7 in the compositions of the 10th graders with symmetry as 1 and originality as 2.3 and 2.8. Both were considered static with ratings close to 1. The composition of the 11th grader rated lower on visual balance (5.8) but was seen as highly symmetrical (1.6), more dynamic (5), and original (5.8). In Figure 9.4a–c are arrangements by two 11th graders and one 12th grader. These are more typical of the inverse relationship found between visual balance and asymmetry. In these compositions visual balance varied from 2.7 to 3.5 but asymmetry

TABLE 9.1
CORRELATIONS OF COMPOSITION DIMENSIONS AND GRADE
OR AGE

	Visual Balance	Static to Dynamic	Symmetry to Asymmetry	Originality
Grade				
K–8 ($n = 72$)	−0.26*	0.28**	0.31**	0.19
10–12 ($n = 40$)	−0.33*	0.15	0.36**	0.32*
	Visual Balance	Static to Dynamic	Symmetry to Asymmetry	Originality
Age				
5–14 ($n = 72$)	−0.28**	0.33**	0.33**	0.20*
15–18 ($n = 40$)	−0.42**	0.25	0.39**	0.36*

*$p \le .05$, **$p \le .01$.

ratings were between 5.1 and 5.9. Originality ratings were also high, between 4.6 and 6.5, and ratings on the dynamic dimension ranged from a low of 4.5 to a high of 6.7.

In order to understand more fully the compositions produced by children in each grade, the ratings for each of the four dimensions were correlated within a grade. Generally, the same pattern of associations was obtained, a pattern that very much expressed the correlations among the dimensions for the group as a whole. Compositions judged as more poorly balanced were also judged as more dynamic, asymmetrical, and original, whereas those judged as well balanced were rated as static, symmetrical, and less original. Nevertheless, there were some interesting differences in the strength of correlations between lower and upper grades.

Table 9.3 shows the pattern of correlations between visual balance and the other three dimensions for students in each grade. The initially strong association between visual balance and static arrangements declined as grade level increased. In the compositions of 11th graders there was no association and in those of 12th graders the association was small. The older high school students appeared not to be adhering strictly to the horizontal and vertical axes in order to achieve visual balance. Figure 9.5a shows a composition with the blue block set by an 11th-grade girl that received 5.8 on visual balance, 5.8 on dynamic, 5.4 on asymmetry, and 7

TABLE 9.2
MEAN ART STUDENT RATINGS FOR FREE COMPOSITION TASK

Grade	Visual Balance	Static/Dynamic	Symmetry/Asymmetry	Originality
Kindergarten[a] (n = 9)	5.10	2.59	2.98	3.54
Second/Third (n = 10)	5.10	2.85	2.75	3.45
Fifth (n = 12)	5.32	3.36	3.09	3.74
Sixth (n = 15)	5.10	3.01	2.85	3.28
Seventh (n = 14)	4.16	3.89	3.79	4.26
Eighth (n = 12)	4.06	3.73	4.37	4.40
Grammar & Middle School (N = 72)	**4.78**	**3.28**	**3.33**	**3.79**
Tenth (n = 15)	5.55	3.44	2.26	3.21
Eleventh (n = 12)	4.00	3.99	3.97	4.53
Twelfth (n = 13)	4.47	3.88	3.53	4.09
High School (N = 40)	**4.73**	**3.75**	**3.19**	**3.89**

[a]Kindergarten children did only a blue block composition.

Figure 9.1a. Composition by a kindergarten student.

Figure 9.1b. Composition by second/third-grade students.

Figure 9.1c. Composition by a fifth-grade student.

Figure 9.2a. Composition by a sixth grader.

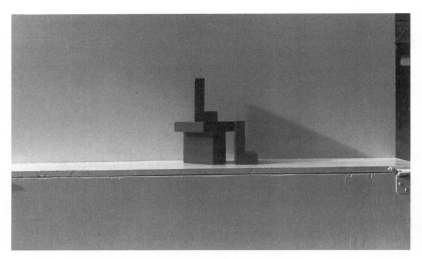

Figure 9.2b. Composition by a seventh grader.

Figure 9.2c. Composition by an eighth grader.

on originality. Generally, however, symmetry dominated as the major strategy for achieving visual balance regardless of grade level. The composition of a 12th-grade boy shown in Figure 9.5b is more typical of the older students' pattern. His composition received a 6.8 on visual balance and a 5.3 on dynamic but was still rated as highly symmetrical (1) and low on originality (3.8). Orig-

Figure 9.3a. Composition by a 10th grader.

Figure 9.3b. Composition by a 10th grader.

inality was inversely related to visual balance but originality and asymmetry were always positively related with correlations between a low of .45 and a high of .96 across the grades.

When the composition dimensions were examined for the two

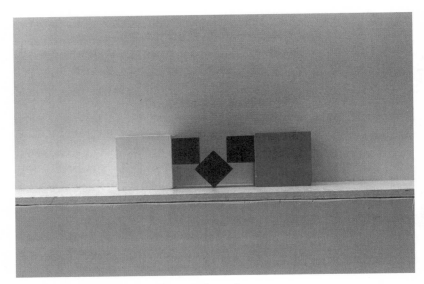

Figure 9.3c. Composition by an 11th grader.

Figure 9.4a. Composition by an 11th grader.

Figure 9.4b. Composition by an 11th grader.

Figure 9.4c. Composition by a 12th grader.

TABLE 9.3
CORRELATION OF VISUAL BALANCE WITH OTHER
DIMENSIONS BY GRADE FOR ALL FREE COMPOSITIONS

Grade Level	Static to Dynamic	Symmetry to Asymmetry	Originality
Kindergarten ($n = 9$)[a]	−0.60*	−0.92**	−0.83**
Grade 2 & 3 ($n = 9$)	−0.92**	−0.96**	−0.84**
Grade 5 ($n = 12$)	−0.77*	−0.93**	−0.88**
Grade 6 ($n = 15$)	−0.56*	−0.94**	−0.87**
Grade 7 ($n = 14$)	−0.53*	−0.86**	−0.90**
Grade 8 ($n = 12$)	−0.52*	−0.88**	−0.82**
Grade 10 ($n = 14$)	−0.53*	−0.94**	−0.68*
Grade 11 ($n = 12$)	−0.06	−0.97**	−0.48*
Grade 12 ($n = 12$)	−0.36	−0.89**	−0.78*

[a]Kindergarten children composed only the blue block set. * $p \leq .05$. ** $p \leq .01$.

block sets individually, associations between grade or age and dimension ratings were strongest for compositions with the gray block set. The direction of associations for both sets was the same, but only correlations for arrangements with the gray block set reached significance and associations were generally stronger for high school students than for younger children (Appendix 9.1). Some examples of the gray block compositions for high school students are shown in Figure 9.6. Figure 9.6 a–b shows two compositions by 10th graders that were rated as 6.3 and 4.8, respectively, on visual balance and 1.7 and 1 on asymmetry. These two dimension ratings can be contrasted with those for the compositions shown in Figure 9.7 a–b by an 11th and a 12th grader. These received a 2.4 and 2.8, respectively, on visual balance but a 6.1 and 4.7 on asymmetry. All these compositions, however, were between 4.2 (Figure 9.7a) and 6.2 (Figure 9.6b) on originality and with the exception of Figure 9.7a, above 4.5 on dynamic. The strict adherence to the horizontal and vertical axes of the composition in Figure 9.7a meant this composition was judged as quite static (2.5).

Summary. There was a strong covariation between visual balance and static symmetrical composition strategies in younger grammar school and middle school children. Eighth graders employed more asymmetrical and dynamic composition strategies but at

Figure 9.5a. Composition with the blue block set by an 11th-grade girl.

Figure 9.5b. Composition by a 12th grader.

Figure 9.6a. Composition by a 10th grader.

Figure 9.6b. Composition by a 10th grader.

Figure 9.7a. Composition by an 11th grader.

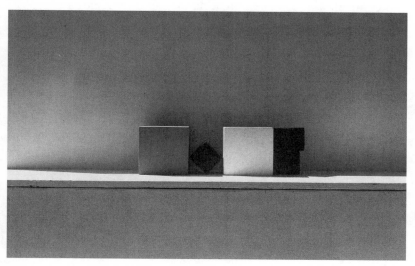

Figure 9.7b. Composition by a 12th grader.

the cost of producing less well balanced arrangements. A somewhat similar pattern was obtained when the high school children were given five blocks. Tenth graders were able to produce visually well-balanced arrangements, but they did so by using symmetry. Eleventh and 12th graders tried for more originality using asymmetrical composition strategies but again at the expense of visual balance.

ANALYZING THE PROVOKED COMPOSITIONS

The composition task that followed the free composition was designed to see whether children could be provoked to use more advanced composition strategies when they were asked simply to complete an almost finished composition. If a developmental trajectory toward use of increasingly more sophisticated forms of visual balance does exist, it could be more accessible with this type of task.

Accordingly, after a child finished freely composing a block set, the blocks were arranged in one of the artist's original compositions with one block left out. The block was given to the child to place and complete the composition. Completing the prepared compositions entailed including five blocks, even if a child had made the free composition with only three blocks. Two compositions were presented with the blue block set and two with the gray block set as shown in Figure 8.2. Each child was asked to demonstrate two ways to complete each composition.

Only middle and high school children participated in this task: 70 middle school children, including the 40 who were tested again, 3 years later, in high school. Although the provoked task was identical when repeated in high school, almost none of the children remembered it and most had only a vague recollection of being in the study at all. This is not surprising given the social and intellectual transitions that children undergo during this period of their lives.

Chapter 8 described some basic differences in the structure of the four provoked compositions. These are briefly reviewed here. By design the gray block problems were intentionally made more complex than the blue block problems. Whereas only mass and distance could be varied in the blue block problems, the gray block problems included tone as an element by using black, gray and white blocks. When specific composition strategies were contrasted for the blue and gray sets, differences in the middle school data suggested the gray block set may have been more difficult. Middle school children used significantly more centering and symmetry placements with the gray blocks and more one-dimensional balancing responses (complex symmetry) with the blue blocks. Other types of placements did not differ and no differences between problem types were found for high school students. The use of simpler composition strategies by younger children does suggest that the added dimensional attributes of the gray block problems made them more difficult to compose than the dimensionally less complex blue problems.

A second difference was in the use of negative space. As originally produced by the artists, one of the blue block and one of the gray block compositions had blocks tightly grouped together (*blue grouped* and *gray grouped*) whereas the other two compositions included open or negative space (*blue spaced* and *gray spaced*). This difference pulled for different solutions. The two open compositions were more suggestive of symmetry. In the case of the blue spaced problem, one potential solution was a true symmetry. In the case of the gray spaced problem, a true symmetry of mass could be achieved but this left the dimension of color unbalanced. These differences did appear to influence the strategies children used in balancing their compositions. In both the spaced problems the inclusion of open or negative space in the center of the composition was irresistible for most children; they placed the free block in the center. This bias was less pronounced in the high school students. They were better able to respond to the dimensional features of the problem and made more one-dimensionally balanced placements. In both middle and high school, children were significantly more likely to use complex symmetry and asymmetry to complete the grouped problems.

In order to simplify analyses, children's placements were grouped into four categories, (1) *unbalanced*, (2) *centering or symmetry*, (3) *balanced across one dimension* (complex symmetry), and (4) *balanced across two dimensions* (asymmetry). Frequencies were then examined by grade and problem type. Before discussing the results, a more detailed discussion of the variety of placements is presented.

Types of Provoked Placements and Explanations

Blue Grouped Block Problem (Figure 8.2a). Children could use one of several strategies to balance this composition visually. They could balance across one dimension, mass, by adding the missing block to the side with less mass to equalize mass on either side. They could also balance across two dimensions by trading off mass and distance with placements that compensated for the greater mass on one side with placements at a greater distance on the other. Placements in the central unfilled space were more complex. When they bridged the space and maintained visible mass in balance (as the original artist had; see Figure 8.1a), the results were judged as balanced across two dimensions. Children often said of such placement, "It follows the theme" or "It makes it look like one thing." Some children elaborated more, saying, as one middle school girl did, "It makes it a whole thing together. Each side looks balanced rather than one side having more to look at." But when central placements were used simply to fill the space, with little consideration for the whole, the response was judged as a centering strategy. Children were always questioned about their placements and this category was only scored when children explicitly stated they were filling the empty space. For example, one middle school child who placed the block upright in the center position with the L facing forward said, "There was a space there."

Blue Spaced Block Problem (Figure 8.2b). This problem was the only one that had a true symmetry solution. Beyond that, balance could be achieved by simply equating mass on either side of the composition. Balancing across two dimensions, mass and distance, could be achieved by recentering the composition on the right upside down T and placing the free block at a distance on the right that corresponded to the length of the open space of the left. Depending on the placement, putting the free block in the center might serve to balance the composition by giving an even distribution to mass or it might serve as a central anchor. If the block was placed as an L or upside down L in the center space, so that vertical and horizontal alignments were respected, it was considered a response that balanced mass. But if the block was placed with its broad side showing or at odd angles, it was scored as a central anchor placement. Verbal verification of the child's intention was always considered when assigning either of these scores.

Surprisingly, few children discovered the true symmetry solution (Figure 8.4e). On the average only 11% of the middle school or high school children used this solution. The greatest use was by eighth graders, 25% of whom used this in their second trial placement, and 11th graders, 25% of whom used symmetry in their first trial placement. The lowest percentage of children balancing with symmetry were the sixth and twelfth graders, for whom the averages were 3.5 and 6.5, respectively. Because it was infrequent, symmetry was combined with the centering strategy for analyses.

Gray Grouped Block Problem (Figure 8.2c). This problem included the possibility of balancing block size against tone or color. The three small blocks were black whereas the two large blocks were gray and white. The artist's original composition had equated across these two dimensions by balancing the large white block stacked on two small black blocks with one small black block stacked on the large gray block (Figure 8.1c). Placement of the white block to achieve the artist's composition was not uncommon, especially in the high school sample. Although it was rarely done, it was also possible to use distance and tone, aligning the large white block on the right side with the two black blocks but at a distance that compensated for the greater weight on the left hand side (height + dark tone) and recentered the composition on the two smaller stacked black blocks.

Another type of response was very close to the artist's original composition. It differed in that rather than resting the white block on the black stack in a way that compensated the two sides diagonally, the white block rested over to the left, touching the small black block on top of the gray block. The result was awkward and missed the elegant sense of balance achieved by the artist. These types of placements were considered a form of centering because the block was placed in a central position with respect to the whole.

Balancing across one dimension, mass, was possible by simply placing the white block on the same side as the two black blocks without using distance to balance. These types of placements varied; often the block was horizontally aligned and touched the small stack of black blocks, but it might also be rotated at an angle or shoved to the back of the composition. Some subjects seemed aware that the white block should be placed with the two stacked black blocks and stated that the gray and black blocks on the left were equal to the two blacks and white on the right. But other subjects were less clear, stating simply that it looked better on the right than on the left because there was "so much" on the left.

Unbalanced responses were generally of two kinds: In one case, the free white block was placed on the left side, usually stacked on top of the gray and black blocks (see Figure 8.5c), but it might also be placed adjacent to the gray block, recentering the composition on the gray block (see Figure 8.5b). This suggested a symmetry of mass but ignored balancing of tones. In the picture selection task, this position was used as the "symmetry" solution in contrast to the more blatantly unbalanced composition shown in Figure 8.5c. Interestingly, some of the subjects who used this symmetry of mass placement were actively aware of the colors and indicated they were making a color series from light to dark (white, gray, to black). The second kind of unbalanced placement was done to "hide" the white block behind the composition so that a little white showed through in the small center space. One subject summed up this response by saying that this "made a place to catch the attention of whoever was looking. Without it you look straight through the middle but with it you look at that instead." The effect, however, was to leave the composition as it was without the addition of the block, since the white background of the composition stage already could be seen through the small middle space.

Grey Spaced Block Problem (Figure 8.2d). Although a true symmetry solution was not possible for this problem, a symmetry of mass could be produced by placing the free small black block in a center position (see Figure 8.5e). Such a placement, however, ignored the imbalances in color or tone. In order to balance across the two dimensions of size and tone, the small black block needed to be placed adjacent to the large white block (see Figure 8.5d). When a child approximated this, the composition was considered balanced.

Distinguishing between placements that took into consideration the balance of the size of the blocks in relation to color and those that did not connect the relationship between the two attributes was difficult. Children's comments helped to make the distinction. Some examples in which children realized color was an additional compositional attribute follow: One sophomore aligned the free block on the left hand side of the white block. When asked about his placement he stated that the gray and black blocks on the left were equaled by the two black and one white block on the right. A senior girl aligned the block adjacent on the right hand side of the white block because the "left side is dark already. Two blacks (on right) balances color out." In contrast, children in the following examples appeared to have a vague sense of tone as an attribute of composition but not how it related to size of the blocks: A junior tried the block on either side of the composition and ended by putting it next to the white block on the inside of the composition because he did not like it next to the gray but could not say why. Another junior boy said, "No matter what side you put it on it will be unbalanced but it looks better with the white." Therefore, although all these placements were approximately equal, the first two responses were coded as balanced across two dimensions and the last two were coded as balanced across one dimension. Unbalanced placements were those that were put on the left hand or heavier side of the composition.

Children's Explanations for Their Placements. The rationales children used to explain why they made a particular placement not only helped to categorize ambiguous placements but also served as data that could be analyzed for development. Because of their complexity, the gray block problems appeared to provoke more thoughtfulness. Explanations given for placements in the blue block problems were much less varied but did follow the same general principles as those in the gray problems. Therefore, only children's explanations for the gray block compositions were formally analyzed by grade level. Table 9.4 describes five levels of verbal response.

At the simplest level, Level 1, children said, "I dunno," in describing the positions of the blocks or stated what the composition looked like to them, such as steps or a face. At the next level, Level 2, were explanations that considered local aspects of a placement, such as the need for the block in an empty space or the way it looked in relation to an adjacent block. At Level 3, children considered the composition as a whole, explaining their placements as attempts to connect or unify the piece or balance the whole. At Level 4, single dimensions of the whole such as the shape or distribution of mass across the whole were used. At the highest level, Level 5, children realized color was important to the whole either as a single dimension or in relation to size of the blocks.

Development in the Provoked Compositions

Results for Provoked Compositions. The mean frequencies by grade level for each type of placement summed across all compositions are presented in Table 9.5. Children most often completed these compositions with centering strategies, but they also used one-

TABLE 9.4
CODES FOR RATIONALES

Level 1: "Dunno"

1 = "I don't know"; "I like it; I don't like it"; "I like it better than first/I don't like it as much as first." Also if no comment and probes for color, side, and whole are negative.

2 = Representational, "It looks like"; Child describes the positions or names the colors of the blocks.

Level 2: Local Considerations

3 = A particular place seems to be the only or right place but no reason why is given. It is as if child sees the unfilled space and feels this is the only place. No reference to the whole is explicitly made: "It fills the middle"; "makes a point in the center"; "finishes it off"; "needed something there"; "there's a space for it"; "better than any other place"; "wouldn't fit anywhere else"; "looked right here"; "wouldn't look right anywhere else"; "that spot seemed kind of empty"; "didn't want to put it on side, looks better on top"; "interesting, don't expect it to be there [in that placement]"; "black looked like it was standing out by itself"; "needed an extra color there."

4 = Relating parts to other parts. Refers to some local aspect of the composition such as the way the colors contrast, liking the two colors together, the shadow the block casts, the angle of the placed block; the 3-D effect the block adds. Child can show this response by placing block at an odd angle and saying that she or he did this to make it different from the other blocks (child is focusing on the part as a contrast to the other parts). Putting block behind makes a background or place to look at. Also includes responses that made the composition taller (added height) or more geometric (suggesting specific placement adds these qualities to the other parts).

Level 3: Whole Considered

5 = "Connects" the two parts of the composition; closes up the space between the blocks; makes a triangle with the other black blocks. Makes a bridge between the two sides, "so it all fits together"; "makes a checkerboard [i.e., a pattern]." Included comments on overall design, "interesting design." Also included gradient of colors from light to dark, which suggests a way to connect the piece.

6 = Looks even, more complete, evens it out, makes a whole, balances the whole, makes it unity; symmetry. Included "balances out more on left than right – why? . . . the empty space on either side"; recognizes that putting block on top evens up height; implies an attempt to even up the whole rather than statement of local concerns. Also included: "It's a

TABLE 9.4 *(cont.)*

color thing – darkest in middle and two big ones on either side [a type of symmetry statement about the whole]."

7 = Child recognizes some imbalance in the composition; recognizes not centered with respect to width. "Couldn't put it on left; there's already a big block there." In symmetry of mass problem with side placement child states, "No matter where you put it it will unbalance it," in recognition of destroying symmetry.

Level 4: Single Dimension Considered in Relation to Whole

8 = Child cites the shape the piece achieves with the placement; the two sides are now opposites; "two big blocks look better facing each other diagonally." The whole now makes a square or larger shape; "two blacks make same height and then there's another on top and other side has one on top [child perceives relationship among the forms to make a shape]."

9 = Child discusses the space or distance of position in relation to the rest of the blocks. Child appears to realize that masses need to be equated. "Other side has a lot more so"; "there's so much over there"; "considering just space where eye hits."

Level 5: Color Is realized as a Dimension of Balance

10 = Child discusses the color equation. Varies from understanding use of color alone to an incomplete understanding of use of color with mass. Simple statements like "evens out the color"; "darkens the right side"; "you notice gray more than white so add black to make white more noticeable"; "black and gray together needs white"; "white could use more black, gray already has some black . . . putting black there balances it"; "black and white make gray – what about this little black one on top [of gray]? Oh yes black and white make gray." Child understands color equation with mass but not its use in the whole composition: i.e., "two black blocks and one white equals gray [incomplete]." These may be probed responses.

11 = Child discusses color and mass or space and distance equations. Very few of these, e.g., "two black blocks and one white equal one gray and one black."

Other

Child states deliberate attempt to achieve an unbalanced composition. "Everyone put it in center," so child deliberately places it off center, or "everyone expects it on right so I don't think it should be." Child places it on left. Only two children responded this way.

TABLE 9.5
MEAN RESPONSE FREQUENCY FOR ALL PROVOKED COMPOSITION TRIALS (N =8)

Grade	Centering	Balance One Dimension	Balance Two Dimension	Unbalanced	MANOVA Effects for Placements
Sixth (n = 27)	2.81	2.30	0.74	2.04	
Seventh (n = 19)	2.68	2.68	0.79	1.74	df = 3, 64
Eighth (n = 21)	3.00	2.00	0.90	1.90	
Middle School (N = 67)	2.84	2.31	0.81*	1.91	F = 55.07**
Tenth (n = 15)	3.13	2.73	0.87	1.27	
Eleventh (n = 11)	3.00	2.36	1.09	1.27	df = 3, 34
Twelfth (n = 13)	2.38	2.85	1.23	1.38	
High School (N = 39)	2.85	2.67	1.05*	1.31*	F = 41.85**

* $p \leq .05$. ** $p \leq .01$.

dimensional balancing strategies with almost the same frequency particularly in high school. Balancing across two dimensions was more difficult. Children only achieved this on about 10% to 13% of the trials, and the high school students had slightly more success than the middle school children. A bigger difference was observed in the unbalanced responses. Almost one-quarter of the children's placements were unbalanced in the middle school whereas approximately 16% of their placements were unbalanced in high school. However the difference in frequency of unbalanced placements in middle school and high school fell short of significance ($p = .07$).

When the distribution of placements within each sample was tested separately, grade level did not influence placements but the differences between the types of placements were significant (Table 9.5). In the middle school sample significantly fewer compositions were completed by balancing across two dimensions than by any other composition strategy, and unbalanced and one-dimensionally balanced placements were equally frequent. In high school, students made placements balanced across two dimensions almost as often as unbalanced completions but significantly less frequently than centering or one-dimensional balanced placements.

When the distribution of placements in the blue or gray problem was analyzed separately, the results were the same as for all compositions combined (Appendix 9.2). In middle school only two-dimensionally balanced placements were significantly less frequent than the other placement types, whereas in high school both unbalanced and two-dimensionally balanced placements were less frequent than the other types.

Overall the most frequent compositional strategies used for the blue block problems were one-dimensional balance and centering or symmetry. One-dimensional strategies dominated for the blue grouped problem and centering dominated for the blue spaced problem. Balancing across two dimensions was only attempted on 10% of the trials. Middle school children appeared more likely to use a strategy that resulted in an unbalanced composition than high school students, making these placements on almost one-quarter of the trials in contrast to 15% of the trials for high school children. This difference in frequency of unbalanced placements in middle school and high school was significant ($t = 2.02$, $df = 36$, $p = .05$).

As mentioned, middle school children may have found it more difficult to think in terms of the dimensional features of the gray block problems. Centering was more clearly the dominant strategy in these problems, but this was largely because of placements made for the gray spaced problem where the open central space pulled for a central placement. Comparisons of differences in mean frequencies for each placement type showed that across both compositions combined, two dimensionally balanced placements increased from middle to high school ($t = 2.06$, $df = 38$, $p = .05$).

Explanations for Placements. The frequency of explanations at each level for the gray block problems was analyzed in the same way as the placements by summing across all of the gray spaced and gray grouped block trials. Table 9.6 shows the mean frequencies for each of the five levels of explanation (see Table 9.4) by grade in school. Analysis by level of explanation (repeated factor) and grade level for the middle school students showed a significant effect for level of explanation but not for grade level or interaction of grade level with level of explanation. Contrasts between levels of explanation showed that only the highest-level explanations (mass and color) were significantly less frequent than other levels. In the high school sample, significant effects for level of explanation and interaction of level of explanation by grade were found but not for grade alone. Contrasts indicated that Level 2 (local) and Level 3 (whole) explanations were significantly more frequent than those at other levels.

Figure 9.8 shows the levels of explanation by grade for both samples. In the middle school sample there is no significant systematic pattern to the level of explanation used by children in different grade levels except that all children are very unlikely to use the highest levels. It is worth noting, however, that some eighth graders begin to use Level 2, or local explanations, over the other levels. This is interesting because in the high school sample there is a much more systematic pattern to the explanations used, one that is differentiated by grade in school. Most 10th graders used Level 2 explanations that stressed local considerations but 11th and 12th graders were more apt to use Level 3 explanations that emphasized the whole composition. Higher-level explanations that referred to dimensional features of a composition in relation to the whole were still used very infrequently but when they were used, it was the 12th graders who primarily invoked this level of explanation. Individual univariate analyses of variance for each level of explana-

TABLE 9.6
MEANS FOR LEVEL OF RATIONALE BY GRADE LEVEL[a]

Grade	Level 1 (Dunno)	Level 2 (Local)	Level 3 (Whole)	Level 4 (Mass)	Level 5 (Color)	MANOVA
Sixth ($n = 20$)	1.35	1.15	1.15	0.10	0.25	Level of Explanation
Seventh ($n = 14$)	1.14	1.21	1.28	0.14	0.14	$df = 3, 47$
Eighth ($n = 18$)	0.94	1.61	1.00	0.11	0.28	$F = 16.13**$
Middle School ($N = 52$)	**1.15**	**1.33**	**1.13**	**0.12***	**0.23***	
						Level of Explanation
						$df = 3, 24$
Tenth ($n = 10$)	0.70	2.20	0.60	0.10	0.40	$F = 8.28**$
Eleventh ($n = 11$)	1.09	1.00	1.64	0.00	0.18	Explanation by Grade
Twelfth ($n = 8$)	0.25	1.38	1.63	0.00	0.75	$df = 6, 46$
High School ($N = 29$)	**0.72**	**1.52***	**1.63***	**0.03**	**0.41**	$F = 2.39*$

[a]Levels 4 and 5 were summoned for analysis; * $p \leq .05$. ** $p \leq .01$.

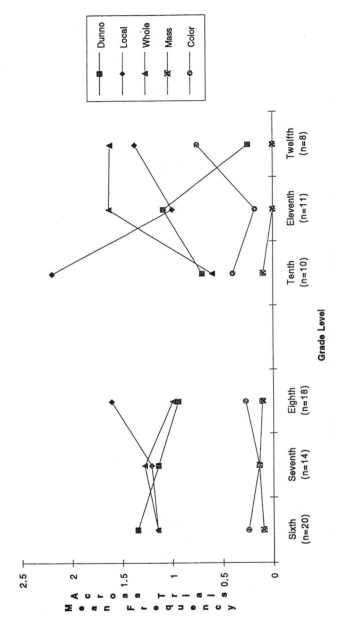

Figure 9.8. Levels of explanation used for placements in gray block provoked composition task (N = 4).

tion by grade confirmed that 10th graders made more frequent use of Level 2 explanations and 11th and 12th graders made more frequent use of Level 3 explanations. These results mark a shift from 10th to 11th grade in children's reasoning about their placement choices. The children in the upper grades were more likely to think of the compositions as a whole, whereas the younger high school students focused on the way particular parts of the arrangements looked.

The analyses reported suggested the pattern of explanations used changed during high school. But was there development between middle school and high school? To answer this question, the data from the subset of children who had participated in both the middle and high school samples were examined. Middle and high school levels of explanation were contrasted for each level of explanation (paired t-tests using the bonferroni correction). Only the frequency of Level 1 ($t = 3.22$, $df = 19$, $p = 005$) and Level 5 ($t = -2.94$, $df = 19$, $p = .008$) explanations changed from middle to high school. As Table 9.6 suggests, in middle school children more frequently resorted to Level 1 explanations whereas in high school students better understood the dimension of color in relation to balance.

Summary. When viewed through the lens of these four composition problems, children's compositional strategies appeared to develop somewhat more slowly from middle school through high school than one might anticipate when judging them against development in other domains. It is true that by high school unbalanced placements were less frequent and two-dimensionally balanced placements began to increase. But by and large, children completed their compositions by either centering the compositions or balancing them across a single dimension such as mass. The compositions that included more open space in the center were particularly prone to completion by centering, whereas those that were tightly grouped together pulled for placements where a single dimensional feature was put into balance. In the blue grouped composition, mass was almost always used over distance. In the gray grouped composition children used a greater variety of features. Of the 11% who balanced this problem by a single dimensional attribute, approximately one-quarter cited the block shapes, one-quarter cited distribution of mass, and almost half cited color as the single dimension put in balance. Thus rather than showing the influence of a developmental trajectory that was defined by an increasingly complex balancing strategy, the individual compositions themselves exerted the strongest influence on how they were completed.

Nevertheless, when children's explanations for their placements were examined, a progression that is consistent with an expectation of increasingly complex balancing strategies as children mature appeared. As children matured, explanations for their composition placements increasingly took first the parts and then the whole into account. The lowest-level explanation was predominantly used by lower-grade middle school children. At their best, children using this level explanation were able to describe what they saw in front of them. Sometimes this amounted to noting that the composition looked like something in the real world; at other times the relative positions of different blocks were described. Although middle school children in general showed few systematic preferences for one level of explanation over another, they did not appear to understand how particular dimensions such as mass or color related to balancing the whole. By the end of the middle school, there was some indication that children had made progress in defining the elements of a composition. More explanations that considered local relationships among parts were given by eighth graders. These kinds of explanations recognized the need to fill a specific gap in a piece or the local effects of color and shape of a placement. Local explanations persisted among 10th graders, suggesting that before children understand balance in relation to the whole, they must first isolate the local influences of parts. A marked shift occurred between 10th and 11th grades. High school children in the upper grades were primarily using Level 3 explanations that showed they were thinking of the composition as a whole and recognizing that where they placed the free block made a difference as to whether or not the whole piece would be balanced. Although generally infrequent, the highest level of explanation was more likely to be used by children in high school than middle school. At this level students discussed the part color or tone played in balancing the whole. It was largely the 12th graders who demonstrated this level of understanding.

Picture Selection Task

Once middle school and high school students completed their placements in the prepared compositions, they were asked to look at three pictures of how "other people had completed the composition" and to select the ones they considered best and second best. This produced a rank ordering among the three pictures. Similar data were obtained from two other samples of students taken from high school and university art classes. They were given the same compositions as projected slides in a series of paired comparisons. The picture selection data are summarized for each of the three picture types, asymmetrically balanced, "symmetrically" balanced, and unbalanced, across the four compositions in Table 9.7. The picture selection data are summarized as the mean rank for the sample. The paired comparison data are summarized as the proportion of times across all pairs a picture was selected as preferred to its contrast. When evaluating the picture selection task scores could vary between 1 and 3, with 1 as most preferred and 3 as least preferred, whereas the paired comparison data varied between 0 and 1 with 0 the least preferred and 1 the most preferred. Results from the middle school and high school picture selection task are discussed first.

The first question of interest was whether or not there was a developmental trend in children's picture selection from 6th through 12 grade. Table 9.7 shows the mean rank ordering of picture selection preferences for each grade level in the middle and high school samples. Across all samples the unbalanced pictures were least preferred. Analyses within each sample indicated that grade level did not influence preferences but in both middle and high school the unbalanced pictures were significantly less preferred to the other two compositions. In the middle school a more pronounced order to picture selection preferences was indicated. Children also preferred asymmetry to symmetry. High school students, although clear in their general distaste for the unbalanced pictures, showed an almost equal preference for the asymmetry and symmetry pictures. This was contrary to the expectation that children would develop an appreciation of more complex forms of balancing with age. Instead younger children appeared to show greater appreciation for this type of balance than older children.

In order to examine how children's preferences developed between middle and high school, preferences of students who participated at both times were analyzed for change. The results confirmed the differences between middle and high school preferences suggested by the within sample analyses. A significant change

TABLE 9.7
PICTURE SELECTION AND PAIRED COMPARISON TASKS BY
GRADE LEVEL

Total Sample	Unbalanced	Symmetry	Asymmetry	MANOVA
	Mean Preference for Picture Selections			
Sixth ($n = 27$)	2.29	2.08	1.63	
Seventh ($n = 19$)	2.14	1.99	1.87	
Eighth ($n = 21$)	2.28	1.96	1.76	$df = 2, 63$
Middle School ($N = 67$)	2.24*	2.02	1.74*	$F = 14.52*$
Tenth ($n = 15$)	2.65	1.53	1.65	
Eleventh ($n = 12$)	2.48	1.67	1.67	
Twelfth ($n = 13$)	2.46	1.71	1.62	$df = 2, 36$
High School ($N = 40$)	2.54*	1.63	1.64	$F = 63.05*$
	Mean Proportion of Choice for Paired Comparisons			
High School Paired Sample ($N = 47$)	0.24*	0.68*	0.58	$df = 2, 66$
College Paired Sample ($N = 22$)	0.23*	0.66	0.61	$F = 56.35*$

*$p \leq .01$.

from middle to high school (school level, $F_{1,37} = 20.04$, $p < .001$) and preference for some pictures over others (picture preference, $F_{2,36} = 26.85$, $p < .001$) was found. But of greatest interest was the finding that the order of preference was different in middle and high school (interaction between school level and picture preference, $F_{2,36} = 21.18$, $p < .01$). In the middle school, children showed a clear preference for the asymmetry pictures but in high school asymmetry and symmetry pictures were chosen first about equally and both were clearly preferred to the unbalanced pictures.

It had been predicted that students in the higher grades would have a marked preference for the artist's asymmetrically balanced compositions when compared to students in the lower grades. However, this was not the case. Instead it was the younger children who preferred the artists' compositions. When preferences for solutions to the individual compositions were examined it became apparent that when a true symmetry solution was offered, as in the compositions with open space, children chose symmetry over the more complex asymmetry composition. But when the symmetry solution was only a rough approximation, as in the grouped compositions, subjects chose asymmetry. When students were in middle school, the degree of preference for symmetry to asymmetry in the compositions with true symmetry was small. But in high school, preference for symmetry in these compositions was over three times as large. Therefore, when a true symmetry choice was available, it was unequivocally preferred by the high school children to unbalanced or asymmetrically balanced compositions.

The paired comparison task is probably a more sensitive indicator of picture preferences since judgments are made repeatedly for the same stimuli in paired combination with the other two choices. The combined paired comparison data from high school and college art class students confirmed and strengthened the results from the picture selection task. Unbalanced compositions were clearly least preferred. But a separate analysis showed the high school children also preferred symmetry to asymmetry, strengthening the conclusion from the analysis of the individual picture selection tasks that there is a shift to a greater preference for symmetry between middle and high school. When the responses to each of the four problems were examined separately, it became evident that as in the picture selection high school sample, these high school students' preference for symmetry was only apparent for the two compositions with true symmetry choices. In the other two problems, asymmetry was preferred. In the college sample, however, there was no clear preference for symmetry to asymmetry, although both were clearly preferred to the unbalanced composition. This college sample had taken almost twice as many art classes as the high school paired sample. The influences of training on composition performance are discussed at greater length in the next section.

The Effects of Training

Training, as measured by the number of art classes children had taken, did not appear to relate to middle school children's composition performance. Even a 3-week module specifically on composition given to sixth grade art classes had no effect when children were assessed before and after the module. By high school, however, the number of art classes a child had taken did relate to the child's composition performance. Data obtained from interviews with 25 of the high school students indicated that most students had taken close to four art classes (mode = 3.5; $M = 2.8$), approximately half of those during middle school. We might expect that students in upper grades would have had more art classes, but the association between grade level and number of art classes was near zero ($\rho = -.10$) for these students. This indicated that grade in school, the measure used in general for developmental level in the composition study, was not confounded with training. High school students who had taken more art classes produced more dynamic compositions in the free composition task ($\rho = .34$, $p = .05$). These students were also better able to balance their free compositions ($\rho = .33$, $p = .05$) and to produce symmetrical arrangements ($\rho = .33$, $p = .05$) with the gray block set. Originality did not relate to the number of art classes taken.

Performance on the provoked and picture selection tasks was not related to the number of art classes taken. But more surprising was the lack of association between the level of explanation used to justify a provoked composition placement and training in the arts. Most of the students interviewed about the art classes they had taken (64%) explained their placements with Level 3 reasoning that stressed balance across the whole composition. These students had taken an average of three art classes. The 20% who used higher-level explanations, in which color was related to balance of the whole, had taken an average of only two art classes.

Students in the two paired comparison samples had been sampled from art classes and therefore generally had more training in the arts than other high school students in the study. These two paired comparison samples also differed substantially from each other with respect to number of art classes taken (high school $M = 3.98$; university $M = 7.57$, $t = 2.78$, $df = 22.45$, $p < .01$) and age (high school $M = 15.87$ years, university $M = 23.14$, $t = 4.52$, $df = 21.75$, $p = .000$). In these samples the number of classes taken was confounded with grade ($r = .55$, $p < .01$) and in the high school sample it was confounded with age as well ($r = .49$, $p < .01$). Once grade level or age was partialed out, however, the results were consistent with those from the picture selection task. There was no relationship between training and choices in the paired comparison task.

Compositionally Sophisticated Children

One of the aims of the composition studies was to examine individual differences in children's compositional competence. It was expected that there would be some children who could be identified with greater sophistication in composition independently of developmental level and that their performance should be relatively consistent across the composition tasks. Chapter 7 identified important elements utilized by mature artists for successful compositions as visual balance attained through asymmetrical and dynamic balancing techniques. This standard has also been used by researchers who have studied the development of composition in children. These three aspects of composition, visual balance, asymmetry, and dynamism, were, therefore, used to identify compositionally sophisticated children. It is important to remember that visual balance was negatively correlated with asymmetry and dynamism in this study so children whose free compositions combined these three elements were indeed unique when compared to the other children.

The free composition task was used to identify the sophisticated group of children and their performance on the other composition tasks was analyzed for consistency. Children were identified in the sophisticated composition group on the basis of the sum of the ratings on visual balance, symmetry to asymmetry, and static to dynamic. Theoretically, the summed scores could range from a low of 3 (all 1s) to a high of 21 (all 7s). In practice, the range went from a low of 8.32 to a high of 15.41 for the middle school and 8.70 to 16.01 for the high school. The means and standard deviations of the two summed rating distributions were practically identical (middle school $M = 11.61$, SD $= 1.77$; high school $M = 11.66$, SD $= 1.71$). Children in the sophisticated group were defined as those in the top 25% of the distribution; those in the other 75% comprised a less sophisticated group.[1] This criterion identified 11 children in the sophisticated group of each sample. As one would expect, the summed rank means for the compositionally sophisticated groups within each sample were significantly higher than the mean for the other children. This mean difference was about 4 points in both samples.

1. There were six children in the grammar school sample who met the middle school criteria for the sophisticated group. Three were fifth graders, one was from the second/third-grade combination class, and the remaining two were kindergarten children. Since there were no data for this sample on the other composition tasks it was not possible to see how these younger children approached the other tasks. Nevertheless, it is interesting that some of the younger children fell into this group even when the score criterion for the older children was applied.

The sophisticated and less sophisticated groups of middle school children were equivalent in age but not in grade. The compositionally sophisticated group ($M = 7.36$ grade) was slightly more advanced in grade level than the other students ($M = 6.79$; $t = 2.37$, $df = 22$, $p = .03$). The two high school groups did not differ in age or grade. Compositionally sophisticated students, however, had taken an average of one more art class than their peers but this difference was not significant.

In order to examine whether or not performance of the two groups differed on the other composition tasks, multiple analysis of variance (MANOVA) analyses that equated subjects for grade level by using grade as a covariate were carried out. No differences in picture selection were found for the composition groups but placements in the provoked composition task did differ. Compositionally sophisticated students in both middle school and high school made significantly more balanced placements than less sophisticated students and less sophisticated students made more unbalanced placements than sophisticated students. These results are shown in Table 9.8. Although sophisticated students made more balanced placements overall, there were no significant differences by type of balanced placement. That is, compositionally sophisticated students were not more likely to use a particular type of balanced placement such as symmetry or one-dimensional balance than their peers.

Although these results suggested a degree of consistency in the performance of sophisticated and less sophisticated students, there was still a question as to whether or not their performance would be stable from middle to high school assessments. The correlation between students' relative summed rankings on the free composition task in middle and high school suggested that there was stability over the 4 years ($\rho = .36$, $p = .01$). Four of the 11 sophisticated students were still in the top 25% 4 years later, 1 dropped out of the study, and another 3 were within .50 point of the cutoff score. Of the high school subjects who had not been in the group in middle school but were now identified, 4 had scores in the middle school that put them only .30 point below the middle school criteria for the compositionally sophisticated group. Thus, although performance 4 years later was somewhat variable, approximately 70% of those identified as compositionally sophisticated in middle or high school performed consistently across the two points in time (see also regression analysis in Table 9.8).

TABLE 9.8
MANOVA AND MULTIPLE REGRESSION ANALYSIS FOR PROVOKED PLACEMENTS BY GROUP OF COMPOSITION SOPHISTICATION

	Total Balanced Placements Means (SD)	Unbalanced Placements Means (SD)	F Value
Middle School			
Sophisticated Group (n = 11)	7.00 (1.0)	1.00 (1.0)	
Less Sophisticated Group (n = 28)	5.70 (1.5)	2.20 (1.5)	Multivariate = 3.23*
High School			
Sophisticated Group (n = 11)	7.30 (1.0)	0.73 (1.0)	
Less Sophisticated Group (n = 29)	6.30 (1.2)	1.50 (1.0)	Multivariate = 2.84†

Predicting High School Performance: Results from Regression

	F Value	R^2	R
1. High School Unbalanced Placements	F = 5.24*	R = 0.13	0.36
2. Middle School summed ratings	Fchange = 4.44*	Rchange = 0.09	0.47

*$p \leq .05$. †$p = .07$.

Summary. When individual differences among children were examined, a group of children who were working at a sophisticated level in the free composition task could be identified. Their performance on the provoked task was highly consistent with their free composition performance. Children identified as compositionally sophisticated made more balanced placements than less sophisticated children and less sophisticated children made more unbalanced placements than sophisticated children. In addition, a child's performance on the free composition task in middle school was a good predictor of her or his high school performance, suggesting relative stability in ability over the 4 years between testings.

How Children Judge a Work of Art

The interview that explored the criteria children used when judging a work of art began by asking students which artistic dimensions they thought most important in a painting and what it was about paintings that caught their attention. Once children had discussed their criteria, they were probed about other artistic dimensions they had omitted. The entire list of criteria studied included subject matter, color, realism, three-dimensional qualities of a painting, originality, and visual balance. Two main considerations motivated the interview. One was an attempt to obtain information relative to some of the same aspects Parsons had captured in his interviews. A second was to probe the children specifically about visual balance: how they defined it and how important they thought it was. Since the interview was open-ended, the results summarize the primary dimensions children thought were important at a qualitative level.

Regardless of grade level, middle school children mentioned color, subject matter, and realism, in that order. Most said that what drew them to a painting was the color. Many preferred bright colors that stand out and quite a few mentioned that the colors should be appropriate for the subject matter. A number of eighth graders said they liked pastel colors best. When it came to subject matter there was a good deal more variety, as one would expect. Many children mentioned specific subject matter, like pictures of animals, people, flowers, or even airplanes. Other children used broader categories, like pictures about nature or peaceful things or, among the boys, pictures with action or about sports. Realism was definitely preferred to abstraction but a few children in each grade said they preferred abstract art or liked it as well as realistic art.

Only a very small number of middle school children mentioned the other dimensions spontaneously. Balance and originality were about three times more likely to be mentioned by eighth graders than by children in lower grades whereas the three-dimensional qualities of a picture were more likely to be mentioned by children in lower grades. Nevertheless, when the children were asked about each of these dimensions many responded that the dimension was important. Originality appeared to be most important; over half the middle school children said they did not like repetition of themes unless the themes were done in new or different ways. The three-dimensional qualities of a painting were important to a third of the children; most of them said they did not like flat depictions and some mentioned shadows and detail as imparting more dimensionality to a painting.

Visual balance was important to a little less than half the children and one-quarter said visual balance was not an important element in a picture. Children defined visual balance in different ways. A number of them defined it as organizing a picture so that things were evenly distributed across the picture. A few said it was symmetry or the centering of a picture. Others described it in negative terms, saying what it was not; for example, some children said they didn't like things all on one side of a painting. Another group seemed only vaguely aware of what visual balance was or admitted they did not know what it was.

High school students were easier to engage in the interview. They were more comfortable discussing art and appeared to have a better sense of what they were discussing. They also gave a greater variety of spontaneous answers. For example, a small percentage of children mentioned the feeling or mood a picture conveyed or the meaning the artist intended to convey as one of their primary criteria. Although the number of such children was small, most who mentioned these types of criteria were in 12th grade and only one was in 10th grade. Despite a broadening of perspective, most children regardless of grade gave color as the primary criterion, followed by subject matter and realism. Preferences were largely for bright colors, although some children mentioned earth tones or colors that were "toned down." Preferences for subject matter were much the same as those in middle school. Only a few children mentioned liking abstract art but two mentioned liking surrealism.

Almost none of the high school children mentioned the other criteria spontaneously and none mentioned visual balance. But once a criterion was brought up more of the high school children acknowledged its importance in a work of art than had in middle school. The children were almost twice as likely to maintain that originality and three-dimensional qualities of a painting were important when they were in high school as when they were in middle school. Again they eschewed repetition of themes but a number of them said that the originality of a work expressed something about the artist, about how the artist felt about the work, and that how the artist felt was important in their perception of the piece. Making a picture three-dimensional was seen as desirable, enhancing it and making it less distracting and "more fun to look at."

When probed, over half the high school students thought visual balance was important but a few children said they liked things that were off balance. The high school children gave much clearer definitions of visual balance and even if they didn't consider it a necessary artistic element, they appeared to know what it was. These definitions were not very different in their essence from those of middle school children, just better articulated and more definite. Most children pointed to the evenness of the distribution of elements in a picture. For example, one 10th grader said it was "evenness . . . not necessarily symmetry. In general I notice it, uneven feels awkward." A larger number of high school than middle school children mentioned symmetry as a way of defining visual balance. High school children still defined visual balance in terms of what it is not: "Lopsided looks goofy" or "Cluttered on one side or colors on one side look strange." A few older children appeared to realize that visual balance was important to the effectiveness of a piece. One 11th-grade girl said, "If it's all on one side it draws all the attention . . . it's easier to look at for long periods of time if it is balanced, easier to concentrate on the whole thing." A 12th-grade boy said, "If [a painting] is not balanced it won't please the eye . . . any artist won't want to do that."

Few of these children, regardless of whether they were now in high school or not, appeared to use criteria that were associated with Parsons's Stages 3 through 5 of aesthetic development explicitly. When Stage 3 criteria were employed, it was by high school children. Parsons found that training in the arts was a key factor in whether or not an individual had reached a higher stage of aesthetic development. It was not possible to analyze whether or not the children who were able to discuss the more advanced types of criteria had more training in art because data about the number of art classes were limited to a small subset of children. Nevertheless there were isolated cases of children who could score at Parsons's Stage 3 who had more training. One 10th-grade boy who had taken more art classes than his peers discussed a painting in terms of the feeling it imparts and was able to articulate the role of color in imparting feeling. An 11th-grade girl with more training mentioned the ideas and emotions that a piece conveyed as a key criterion. Another senior girl, who had more training than most, said that the mood a piece conveyed was an important criterion but she was careful to explain that she didn't like art that was disgusting or conveyed a depressing mood. One middle school boy who was recognized in high school as artistically talented mentioned that he liked an impressionist type of brush stroke in a painting. This might suggest a higher level of aesthetic appreciation but the criterion he mentioned first was the bright color of a piece, followed by whether it was realistic or abstract. Both were acceptable to him but his preference was for fantasy pictures. Consistent with this preference, he drew fantasy creatures when he was in high school. It is important to point out that many of the classes taken by these children were at the middle school rather than the high school level. At the time of the interview, most of the high school students were no longer taking any art classes. Training, therefore, as assessed in this study, was of a limited sort.

CONCLUSIONS

The studies presented in this chapter were carried out with the intent of looking at normative development in children's ability to compose an expressly artistic piece. Previous studies had indicated that children can appreciate aesthetic elements earlier than they can produce them. Studies had also suggested that the ability to compose a visually balanced piece depends on the development of certain cognitive operations such as part–whole or conservation operations. In contrast, a Gestalt view would assert that even younger children could successfully compose a piece by using the inherent bias of the perceptual system to regroup visual elements toward closure and stability. Drawings by talented children (see chapter 7) would support the Gestalt view in that even early drawings done by these children were often remarkably sophisticated in their composition.

It is not proposed that young talented children are able to plan sophisticated compositions, but rather that they continually monitor what they are doing during the drawing process and react to what they see by placing elements in locations that counterbalance elements already drawn to achieve a stable organization. This would help explain how at times, in their search for stable visual solutions to compensate for initial placement decisions, sophisticated compositions emerge. For example, Kate, who drew the juggler (Figure 7.1), may have first completed the main elements of the drawing and then observed that the high stack of pineapples disrupted the stability of the symmetrical organization. To regain organizational stability, she added extra lines to increase the density of the forms behind the juggler.

The studies presented in this chapter do not indicate a definitive answer as to whether or not children's composition skills emerge through conceptual development or by means of Gestalt principles of organization. Instead they suggest that both visual preferences and conceptual development are important to children's compositional ability. Results from the different tasks emphasize this interplay. Children's free compositions suggested that certain principles of composition were accessible to most school-age children. Even the grammar school children (kindergarten to fifth grade) were able to achieve visual balance by using symmetrical and static organizations. The nature of the task may have facilitated the discovery of stable symmetrical organizations. Unlike in a drawing, a child could freely vary the arrangement of elements until she was satisfied. In a drawing the only way a young child can achieve a similar effect is by being very attentive to and careful in each placement decision.

Older children in these studies were more experimental with their compositional choices, composing asymmetrical and dynamic arrangements with the blocks but at the expense of visual balance. It was interesting that despite these production choices, a number of the older children thought visual balance was important and even understood balance in terms of symmetry. At the same time, symmetry appeared to be rejected as a desirable element to produce and was often described by the older children as "too boring." One can speculate that once these children rejected symmetry and decided to be experimental with composition, they were at a loss as to how to produce a visually stable organization using asymmetrical and dynamic forms of organization.

Nevertheless in the picture selection study the high school students had a clear preference for true symmetry over asymmetrical balance and a general distaste for unbalanced compositions. Students' preferences were less decided when they were in middle school and almost as many of the younger children preferred asymmetrical balance as preferred true symmetrical balance. It appeared, therefore, that in terms of visual preference, children were first more appreciative of asymmetrical balance and later of symmetrical balance. The preference for true symmetry in the high school students appears to be a real development because it matched the results for the paired comparison study carried out with another group of high school and college students. Of equal importance was the shift away from selecting unbalanced compositions. Fewer of the older students preferred the unbalanced compositions. As they moved from middle to high school, children developed a greater visual preference for balanced compositions.

It was hoped that the provoked compositions, which offered children a task of intermediate complexity when compared with the free compositions and picture selection task, would produce clear developmental data. Instead, the results showed that the partial organization offered by each composition was the more compelling feature. Those compositions that presented an open organization appeared to pull overwhelmingly for a centering strategy whereas those that were more tightly grouped motivated children to complete them by balancing across one dimension. Despite this disappointment some interesting developmental sequences were apparent. Students were more likely to complete a composition by putting it in visual balance and were more able to articulate how the placements they had made worked to balance a piece when they were in high school than when they were in middle school. These changes over the 4 years between middle and high school testing, which paralleled the results for the preference study, strongly support the idea that conceptual development plays a role in children's ability to appreciate and produce visual balance.

It might be argued that many of these developments in composition abilities and preferences could just as easily be explained by increased training children received in the arts. In fact training as measured by the number of art classes did appear to influence the free composition task. High school students with more artistic training produced the more dynamic, symmetrical, and visually balanced compositions, suggesting that some principles of composition were learned in their art classes. Training, however, did not appear to affect children's placements on the provoked task nor improve their understanding of how a placement affected the composition as a whole. Training also did not appear to influence the visual preferences for compositions of the high school and adult samples. The measure of training was somewhat limited, especially in the high school sample, because class information was obtained from only a little over half the students. Information from all students and of a more detailed nature would help to clarify the relationship of training to development of composition skills.

The normative studies show a consistent pattern in their suggestion of a protracted period for the development of composition skills. Yet, it was noted that even some of the youngest children studied were able to produce visually balanced compositions by using symmetrical and static arrangements. This was consistent with the impression given by the drawings of the talented children that in some individual cases young children could successfully achieve a visually well-balanced work of art. Accordingly a number of analyses explored the idea that individual differences, like those observed between very young talented and less talented children, could be identified in this normative sample. By using the ratings on the free compositions and the responses to the provoked composition task a performance vector describing individual differences across tasks could be traced. Children who were identified as compositionally sophisticated by their combined ratings for visual balance, asymmetry, and dynamic organization of their free compositions were the most likely to produce balanced placements and least likely to produce unbalanced placements in the provoked task. This "sophisticated" composition group was also relatively stable, performing at the same relative levels in middle school and high school despite the intervening 4 years.

This consistency in composition performance for individual children stands in relief against the backdrop of an extended developmental progression. It is clear that much more research needs to be done in this complicated area of composition. Nevertheless, some speculations based on these preliminary studies are ventured. It is possible, as I have already suggested is true of artistic talent in general, that two developmental lines can be described for the emergence of composition skills. In the one case, conceptual development may play the strongest determining role. In this instance, children's ability to be successful with visual balance would depend on at least the development of concrete operations. These operations would allow children to deduce or anticipate the compensation relations between different parts of a picture or work of art and to relate the parts to the whole. Certainly, the rationales used by children in describing why they made a certain placement in the provoked task intimates the role of conceptual development. Middle school children were generally less able to explain why they chose a placement, and many simply did not know or could only describe the position of the blocks. In contrast, the high school students were much more consistent in relating the placement of a single element to the whole composition and some were even able to express the relationship of color/tone to visual balance. Puzzling, however, is the delay in children's ability to articulate this relationship. If concrete operations were all that was needed, most middle school children should have been able to articulate at least a Level 3 explanation that simply related the parts to the whole. This marked decalage immediately suggests one of two possibilities: the novelty of relating these operations to artistic composition, which few of these children have ever thought much about, or the necessity of formal operations to reflecting on or reasoning about artistic composition.

A second developmental line can be inferred from the data on individual differences. In this case, some children may be more visually attentive and instead of using their mind, use the "wisdom" of their eyes. These children would let their eyes organize a composition, achieving visual balance by manipulating the blocks until a stable form emerged. Certainly, the block tasks pulled for this kind of strategy since children were encouraged to use their eyes and keep trying different ideas until they were satisfied. Indeed, many were able to achieve a free composition that was rated on the balanced side of the rating scale (see Table 9.2) using compositionally simpler strategies like symmetry. But of greater interest was that a smaller number of children, even some in grammar school, were achieving visual balance by using asymmetrical and dynamic strategies, strategies that in terms of their development in the entire sample were very difficult to use successfully. The performance of these children was also remarkably consistent across the different tasks and across time. Although we cannot discount training in the arts as a factor in the ability of some of these older students, there were in fact no significant differences in the artistic training of sophisticated and less sophisticated groups in either the middle school or high school samples. The ubiquitousness of these composition skills in relation to age or developmental level suggests that these may be true individual differences that are not dependent on conceptual growth. Instead these more remarkable compositions may have been accomplished by the use of perception and visual attention to the task at hand.

10

TOWARD A MODEL OF
ARTISTIC DEVELOPMENT

In chapter 1 two groups of hypotheses were proposed about the origins of individual differences in artistic ability. The first contained two variants of the traditional farther faster hypothesis, that individual differences are a function of differences in developmental rate. The variants state that artistically talented children are accelerated because they are either intellectually gifted or precocious in spatial reasoning. The second group of hypotheses are the seeing, remembering, and doing, which are related to figurative thought with the claim that talent in the visual arts arises because visual information is better and more selectively encoded by talented children. *Seeing* speaks to the heightened visual sensitivity of talented children and their ability to overcome the object-centered perspective that dominates the perception of less talented children in order to see the world more directly in terms of visual surface features. *Remembering* identifies the superior visual memory of talented children that allows them to "call up" or reconstruct explicit visual images to serve as models for their drawings. *Doing* reflects the attention talented children direct to the act of drawing itself, which allows them to discover an effective denotation system and develop flexible drawing schemas very early in their artistic development. Simply stated, these hypotheses propose that talent in the visual arts arises out of differences in children's ability in figurative thought rather than differences in conceptual ability.

Although the studies presented in this book do not provide a decisive experimental test of these hypotheses certain predictions, if supported, would favor one group over another. If the farther faster hypotheses hold, most outcomes will have to do with developmental rate since these hypotheses assume that the same skills are developing in both groups of children but at different rates. Specifically as laid out in Table1.1 by the dimensions of observation, the farther faster hypotheses predicted that talented children would (1) use lines and shapes earlier but in much the same way as less talented children and (2) begin to rotate figures earlier but show the same range of orientations as less talented children. Since operational thought and/or spatial reasoning are developing at an accelerated rate in talented children, (3) spatial milestones such as occlusion and perspective would appear early in their drawings when compared to established norms. Spatial milestones in the drawings of less talented children should approximate the norms. Overall drawing development was predicted to be (4) faster in rate for talented children but not different in quality from that of less talented children. Finally, any differences in composition ability were again predicted to be the result of differences in rate of conceptual development and therefore (5) consistent with children's developmental level.

The second group of hypotheses, *seeing, remembering, and doing,* led to a different set of predictions. Underlying these hypotheses is the assumption that *what* develops is different in talented and less talented children. Therefore, if visual information is more selectively and better encoded in talented children including selective attention to the act of drawing itself, talented children should produce a more accurate correspondence between what they see and what they draw. This should cause talented children (1) to use lines and shapes to denote a different level of scene primitives than less talented children from the beginning of artistic development and (2) to favor visually realistic figure poses and orientations over canonical and formula-driven drawings. Since the appearance of spatial milestones in a drawing is still assumed to depend on spatial reasoning, (3) spatial milestones in the drawings of talented children should approximate the norms for the development of spatial concepts. Less talented children should also show some of these same milestones but may have greater difficulty mapping more complex spatial relationships onto a drawing. Overall drawing development would not simply be faster in talented children but (4) look different, as talented children would show a greater range and depth of skill in their drawings. Finally, if talented children selectively attend to the visual world, they should be able to use their eyes to regulate the two-dimensional form of their compositions. Therefore, (5) talented children should construct surprisingly skilled compositions at young ages, sooner than would be predicted from their conceptual stage of development.

What can we conclude relative to these five predictions from the studies presented? Table 1.1 is reproduced here as Table 10.1 with the actual results of the spontaneous drawing and composition studies in bold type. The results are summarized here. In chapter 3 children's use of line and shape was studied. Several key differences in the way talented and less talented children used lines and planes appeared to confirm the predictions made from the figurative hypotheses. Throughout their development talented children appeared to use a denotation rule that gave equal but separate weight to lines and the planes constructed with lines. When these children emphasized the plane at the expense of the line, it was to texture an animal's skin or decorate clothing. These techniques emphasized the surface features of the plane rather than its solidity. The dominance of a mapping rule that kept the denotation functions for line and plane separate suggested that talented children quickly caught on to the idea that a line should stand for an edge and a plane for a surface rather than a solid volume.

Less talented children did not use the same denotation rule throughout development. Younger less talented children often used line alone to represent higher-order scene primitives such as bodies. Older children constructed planes but filled them in solidly suggesting they were meant to express the solidity of a three-dimensional referent rather than its surface features. In addition, this technique merged the enclosing line with the plane so that the line could not serve an independent denotation function from the plane it enclosed. Nevertheless, by adolescence some of the less talented children used a denotation system that mapped edges onto lines and visual surfaces onto planes (see Figure 1.2.b but also see Figure 5.5b). It is possible that if older less talented adolescents had been sampled, more of these children would have shown this discovery.

The results from the analyses of figure drawing presented in chapter 4 were also consistent with predictions from the figurative hypotheses. These analyses showed that children of exceptional talent drew object-centered representations for a very short time in comparison to their less talented peers. Even before the talented children were able to construct a picture plane fully, the forms of

TABLE 10.1
SUPPORT FOR OPERATIVE AND FIGURATIVE HYPOTHESES[a]

Dimensions of Observation	Farther Faster Operative	Seeing, Remembering, and Doing Figurative
Elements: Line and Shape	T < LT in age of use	T uses differently than LT
Figure Rotations:		
Canonical	T ≈ LT in use	T < LT in use
Natural	T ≈ LT in use	T > LT in use
Spatial Milestones	T earlier than Norms	T ≈ Norms
	LT ≤ Norms	LT ≤ Norms
Overall Drawing Development	T rate faster than LT rate	T different from LT
Sophistication of Compositions	T ≈ Developmental Stage	T < Developmental Stage
	LT ≈ Developmental Stage	LT ≈ Developmental Stage

[a]T = talented, LT = less talented.

the figures they drew began to assume visually naturalistic poses (see Figures 1.4 & 3.8a). Soon after the appearance of a picture plane, talented children began to draw three-quarter rotations and foreshorten figure parts. The visual nature of their drawings was also indicated by the use of texture, shading, and shadow to create visual surfaces that suggested perspective even before techniques for geometric projection were applied. In contrast, less talented children of all ages primarily drew object-centered representations in which figures and objects assumed canonical poses. Even adolescents drew canonical views of the human figure (front views or profile views) and only a very few older children attempted foreshortening or indicated shading and shadow of surface features.

In chapter 5 the spatial relationships shown in a drawing were studied. A hypothesis of precocious conceptual development in talented children did not receive support from these observations. When the sequence of spatial concepts constructed in the drawings of talented children was compared with the norms, a close parallel was found (see Table 5.4). The progression from drawings that represented two-dimensional attributes to those that represented three-dimensional attributes was not observed until children reached the normative age range for the onset of concrete operations. Coordination of viewpoint was achieved later, at the age of late concrete operations, and quantification of 3-D drawings was not observed until even later, at the age of formal operations. Younger less talented children showed some of the same spatial milestones as talented children, but their appearance lagged a year or two behind. For example, all of the less talented children older than age 5 or 6 constructed the two-dimensional picture plane and most of the children age 7 to 8 constructed the three-dimensional picture plane by using vertical segregation or overlap. But as they got older, less talented children appeared to lose ground. Fewer were able to use projective drawing systems and only one less talented adolescent drew in perspective. This is consistent with the results of the analyses of line and plane for this group. As Willats (1992) suggests, having failed to arrive at a denotation rule that treats lines as edges and planes as visual surfaces, these children were unable to map the geometry of projected surfaces onto the picture plane.

In chapter 5 drawings by Alex, a talented autistic child, were presented. Alex provides an exemplar case in which conceptual ability apparently lagged markedly behind figurative ability. The wide gulf between figurative thought and conceptual development in this young boy appeared to facilitate an almost direct translation from perception to drawing schemas. Alex tested as very high on visual-spatial tasks but as delayed by several years on conceptual tasks. In this case, figurative thought appeared initially unconstrained by conceptual development. At age 4, he was already using line to denote contours and straight edges and by age 6 he was drawing single objects in perspective. Alex's approach to drawing was unique; he constructed his drawings by juxtaposing the apparent shapes of the parts rather than by first outlining the whole. His behavior toward objects, as described by his father, also suggested that he was seeing apparent visual surfaces and studying how these might change with changes in his position. Nevertheless, by age 8, as Alex made intellectual gains in school, his drawings became more conceptual and less visually realistic. They began to reflect a partial accommodation of drawing schemas to concepts that was totally absent in earlier drawings. He started to construct scenes in which the objects he formerly drew were related to other objects and to a ground. But even though he could still draw a single object in perspective, he did not adopt a single point of view across the scene. In fact, the interrelations of elements in his drawings suggested that he was as limited by his level of reasoning in this regard as other young talented children are. One can interpret these changes in Alex's drawings as signaling greater coordination between conceptual and figurative processes.

Overall drawing development was studied in chapter 6, which focused on developmental rate. On the basis of the literature, it was proposed that children who are developing at a faster rate would show greater variability in their drawing abilities. Variability was measured by the degree of variation above or below a child's modal level of performance. As predicted by the faster farther hypotheses, talented children did progress through the various levels of drawing development at a faster rate. But as the figurative hypotheses predicted, the *quality* of development also differed in the two talent groups. Less talented children showed greater variation below their modal level of performance whereas talented children showed greater variation above their modal level. In addition, the degree of variability in less talented children increased linearly with higher modal levels, reflecting the greater spread in ability as some children progressed and others did not. In contrast, talented children showed a nonlinear bimodal relationship with variability highest at modal Levels 2 and 4. This pattern suggested two specific points of growth during development.

In chapters 7, 8, and 9 children's composition abilities were studied. It was pointed out that there are few normative studies of composition ability and those there are, are flawed by being dependent on a child's representational skills. Given the representational skills of talented children, it is not surprising that a qualitative analysis of their early drawings revealed highly sophisticated composition strategies. For example, visual balance was achieved by equating color and size or direction of motion and mass. These strategies appeared at much earlier ages than similar strategies reported in the literature. Furthermore, if the appearance of spatial milestones is used as an index of cognitive stage, the appearance of asymmetrical balancing strategies in the drawings of these children was well in advance of conceptual advances in coordination of viewpoint. This is consistent with predictions from the figurative hypotheses of precocity in composition and suggests that when these children were considering the composition of a drawing they were focused on the two-dimensional picture plane.

Nevertheless, the dearth of studies in this area makes it difficult to know whether it is safe to assume that developments in composition ability should reflect conceptual development. Both groups of hypotheses in Table 10.1 make this assumption. The farther faster hypotheses assume it to be true for both talent groups whereas the figurative hypotheses assume it to be true for less talented artists. It is possible that both less talented and talented children use figurative abilities when composing a work of art. Less talented children may only seem more limited because their representational skills restrict the organization of their drawings. For these reasons, a normative study of composition that did not depend on representational skill was undertaken. It entertained two hypotheses: On the one hand, development of composition may rest on cognitive constructions universal to development; on the other, that development may rest on perceptual-motor abilities that allow perception to regulate the process of artistic production.

The results suggested that both conception and perception play a role. Many children, especially younger ones, produced visual symmetry as a way of balancing their free compositions, indicating that perceptual preferences were very influential. As a group, however, children showed development in composition ability throughout the protracted period of study. In the free compositions, older children attempted more sophisticated composition strategies than younger children and in the prepared compositions, unbalanced placements declined with the age of the children. These improvements suggested that conceptual development was influencing composition. Nevertheless, as the drawings of talented children indicated, some children used sophisticated strategies despite their stage of development. A small group of children who had achieved visual balance with asymmetrical and dynamic balancing strategies were identified. Their performance was highly stable across the composition tasks irrespective of grade in school. But even more compelling was the fact their performance was stable across time; this group's performance in high school could be predicted from their performance in middle school. These results strongly supported the qualitative observations of talented children in suggesting that some children, regardless of developmental stage, are much more attentive to visual balance.

In sum, there appears to be greater support for the predictions made from the figurative group of hypotheses than for those related to developmental rate. For some dimensions, however, it was difficult to know whether less talented children might eventually have shown the same quality of development. For example, if older children had been sampled, would more less talented children have arrived at the same denotation rules that talented children appeared to use from an early age? Although this is a possibility, it is unlikely that such a discovery in late adolescents would lead to the same improvement and quality of drawing. The flexible drawing procedures developed by talented children were a result of continual coordination of figurative abilities with conceptual progress and drawing schemas throughout their early development. These ideas will be expanded in the discussion of the proposed model of artistic development.

AN INTEGRATED MODEL OF ARTISTIC DEVELOPMENT

At the beginning of this book we reviewed three very influential approaches to drawing development. Although all have something important to contribute to our understanding of artistic development, none successfully incorporates the development of artistically gifted children. The first approach emphasizes conceptual development. It suggests why young children are limited in their drawing ability, but it does not explain why some children very quickly overcome these limits whereas most never progress much beyond their childish drawings. The second approach emphasizes perceptual factors. It suggests that progress in drawing is associated with learning to overcome the top down organization of the visual processing system that biases perception toward seeing phenomenal objects rather than visual surfaces. This approach implies arduous training for artistic development but does not illuminate why younger children are more limited than older children and adults or why talented children often progress with no training at all. The third approach stresses production difficulties. It suggests that the main problem young artists face is finding strategies that successfully translate three-dimensional properties of objects onto a two-dimensional picture surface. Although its proponents have elegantly demonstrated that young children's natural performance does not always match their true competence, the approach does not address individual differences in talent. At best it implies that talented children are those who have found better drawing strategies, but this does not tell us how or why they discovered these strategies.

My aim is not to dispense with these approaches but to demonstrate how each contributes to an understanding of individual differences in artistic development. The model of artistic development that I propose states that differences in talent arise from differences in the relative contributions of conceptual, figurative, and sensory-motor processes during periods critical to a child's semiotic development. These processes find a correspondence in each of the three approaches as concepts, perceptions, and production procedures. In particular there are differences in the degree of coordination between conceptual and figurative thought and their integration with sensory-motor drawing procedures. In less talented children, the coordination of conceptual and figurative schemes is only partial. Mental representations are always biased toward concepts and incompletely reflect visual characteristics of represented objects. Progress springs largely from a delayed translation of these incomplete coordinations to drawing procedures so that drawing schemas remain poorly integrated with conceptual and figurative schemes. At any given point less talented children's ability to generate an artistic idea and even mentally represent it may outstrip the drawing procedures in their artistic repertoire.

In talented children, the situation is the reverse. Talented children develop a large store of drawing schemas that can themselves provoke artistic development. The coordination between figurative and conceptual schemes and drawing schemas is immediate and much more complete. In chapter 6 the equilibration and disequilibration of mental schemes and drawing schemas during development were described in greater detail for talented children. We saw that typically new drawing schemas appeared to develop on the heels of evolving conceptual schemes, reflecting continual reciprocal assimilation and mutual accommodation between conceptual and figurative schemes and subordination of drawing schemas to this coordination process. But at times new drawing procedures appeared in advance of conceptual supports. In some cases a new procedure evolved in apparent response to a specific production difficulty whereas in others a child may have accessed and utilized a vivid episodic memory to generate a specific drawing.

In the sections that follow I try to demonstrate how individual differences in artistic development arise as a function of the different underlying contributions of conceptual, figurative, and sensory-motor processes during development.

Normative Development in the Visual Arts

In normative development, the early stages of conceptual development are determinative in drawing, even though young children appear to be dominated by figurative thought. This apparent paradox occurs in part because young children make only a global analysis of what they see. But it also results from the fact that young children draw by relying on memory, not by looking at their drawing subjects. In most young children, memory representations are also global and "filled in" by conceptual knowledge. Such a proposal is consistent with developmental data about the mental image in younger children (Childs & Polich, 1979; Dean et al., 1983; Kail et al., 1980; Piaget & Inhelder, 1971) and with research on memory systems that indicates an earlier developing implicit memory system that encodes global and invariant object-centered features and a later developing explicit memory system that encodes view-specific and episodic information. A description of normative development for drawing with special emphasis on the influence of conceptual development follows.

The beginning phase in children's drawing development arises out of sensory-motor activity. Chapter 3 described the pleasure 2-year-old children derive from the motor activity associated with making marks on paper and the process of assimilation that eventually gives meaning to these marks. A drawing becomes truly symbolic when the child repeats a certain schema and uses it consistently to stand for something in her world. These schemas derived from sensory-motor activity constitute the substrate on which global and imprecise intuitions of form and spatial relationships are imposed.

Children between the ages of 3 and 5 years make simple comparisons of things in the world in order to arrive at similarities and differences. They lack systematic strategies for perceptually exploring and reasoning about their world. Very young children, therefore, know the global shapes of objects and some of their more salient features (e.g., extension in two dimensions with pointed areas). On the basis of these elementary correspondences, children generate simple prototypic representations that respect certain denotation rules. For example, extendedness is the most basic perceptible property of shapes (Willats, 1992). Since arms and legs extend primarily in one direction, children don't use circles to stand for arms or legs; they use long lines ("sticks"). And because heads and bodies extend in two directions, they don't use lines to stand for heads and bodies; they use circles ("lumps"). Intrafigural topological relations such as whether a figure is closed or open and which of the internal parts are adjacent to each other are also roughly mapped onto a drawing. But children do not yet differentiate flat from round extensions or edges from surfaces.

Marr's and Gibson's theories of perception (see chapter 1) indicate that the bias of the visual system is to see the world from an object-centered perspective and to ignore the ephemeral specific view in which objects are embedded. In order to develop a denotation system that can represent specific features of the visual world, the natural object-centered bent of the visual system must be overcome. A great deal of art instruction is aimed at learning to see local viewer-centered visual primitives that reveal variations in light, texture, solidity, and perspective. But Willats (1985) notes that development itself also provides some access to view-specific features of a scene because children do progress from denotative rules that use "lumps" and "sticks" as natural analogues of extended areas to those that use these picture primitives as symbols for their lower-order dimensional scene equivalents, edges, and surfaces.

How do children discover these rules naturally? One answer lies in conceptual development. Chapter 1 reviewed some of the influences of conceptual development on children's ability to analyze what they see. One improvement in visual analysis results when children can impose more systematic looking strategies on their visual explorations (Piaget, 1969; Vurpillot, 1976). With better looking strategies, children are able to pay more attention to all parts of an object, to the relationship between parts and the whole, and to the correspondences between changes in the state of an object and the transformations it undergoes as its state changes (Piaget, Henriques & Ascher, 1992). Therefore, improved strategies for attending, looking, and seeing the world both pave the way for and result from conceptual progress. Another improvement results when children are better able to understand what it is that they are seeing. For example, even though a very young child can see and infer that an object is partially hidden, she does not understand that it is the occluding contour that indicates one object is in front of another object. This type of understanding appears to depend on conceptual development.

Initially conceptual progress produces a well-known contradiction in children's drawing behavior, drawings that are characterized primarily by their intellectual realism. In these types of drawings, children attempt to show their more elaborated conceptual knowledge but largely at the expense of visual realism. The contradiction comes about because at this stage of development, children are still strongly tied to figural thought and have great difficulty freeing themselves from the direct influences of a perceived configuration (e.g., preoperational conservation responses). Yet intellectually derived drawings dominate their artwork. This apparent discrepancy can be reconciled if it is assumed that intellectual knowledge dominates in part because children fail to look at their drawing models or at their drawings. Instead they draw from memory and since, as suggested before, their ability to analyze objects and their memory itself are still limited, the mental representation and drawing reflect only a rough qualitative correspondence to their real world equivalents. Therefore, concepts that at this point are largely qualitative categories exert the stronger influence over developing drawing procedures.

Children at this stage define objects by their salient visible features and by the properties and relations abstracted from their actions on objects. Such definitions lead to canonical representations that incorporate (a) features that invariably define an object's physical appearance, (b) a child's understanding of the relations among those features, and (c) features that define the object's function. For example, the apparent shape of a table becomes obscured by its known shape, the known relations among its sides, or its legs and the ground, and by its known function as a hard surface on which objects are placed. When young children include the handle of a cup in their drawings of a cup, it is not just because it is a salient physical feature but also because it has a salient function that defines it as a cup (holds hot liquids) instead of a glass. Likewise people are shown in rigid front poses even though such views are relatively rare in children's actual experience because front views unambiguously reveal the basic structure and attributes of a person. The point is that when young children's mental representations become laden with conceptual knowledge, the perceptual bias toward object-centered representations is further reinforced as children strive to define an object by its related concepts.

Conceptual influences, however, do not uniformly work toward producing intellectually derived drawings. The advent of operational reasoning in children allows a better understanding of the transformation of objects in motion and of the geometry of objects and their context. Improvements in children's reasoning allow them to begin to compose a system of comparisons that brings transformations and the resultant changes in the state of objects into correspondence and leads to more systematic strategies for visual exploration (Piaget et al., 1992). Accordingly, figurative thought as indexed by the mental image better expresses visual reality and the visual transformation that objects undergo with rotations or changes in position. As operational reasoning gains a stronger foothold, children can understand the more complex geometrical aspects of perspective and mentally represent objects as foreshortened and projected. With greater coordination of operational and figurative thought, children's drawings can move toward visual realism.

These improvements in conceptual understanding radically transform what children "see," allowing them to make a better visual analysis of both their world and their drawings. In less talented children, this often sounds the death knell for drawing. What they see when they look at their drawings is too discrepant with what they see when they look at the visual world and their drawing activity progressively drops off. One might wonder why children cannot simply modify their drawing schemas to correspond to their improved visual analysis. This consideration takes us full circle back to sensory-motor activity and its fundamental role in drawing.

Drawing schemas commence as sensory-motor procedures that are quickly influenced by figurative and conceptual thought as children develop. Yet it is always at the level of sensory-motor procedures that new and different ways of producing drawings are empirically tried out, errors corrected, and difficulties breached. Crucial here is learning to subjugate hand and drawing implement to one's intention, a process that for optimal performance requires visual monitoring of the activity as well as repeated practice of drawing schemas. When the sensory-motor procedures children have developed to produce drawings have accommodated to and been assimilated by conceptual thought but have remained relatively uncoordinated or unevenly coordinated with figurative thought, children develop drawing schemas that define or describe a topic conceptually. In most cases this involves few or no variations since one definition can work symbolically across contexts (e.g., a person at school or a person in the yard).

As children become capable of making a better visual analysis, they may be overwhelmed by trying to solve *how* to align their drawing with what they see by using the sensory-motor drawing schemas they have developed. Production strategies initially developed to resolve graphic dilemmas in favor of conceptual considerations need to be abandoned. New ones need to be invented that take into account the apparent shapes of projected objects. Children who have been content with habitually reproducing the same drawing may find it difficult to break down a drawing formula that has been schematized at the level of the whole (see chapter 5). The majority of less talented adolescents studied produced drawings using production strategies that from a representational level appeared to have been developed when they were younger. In drawings of the human figure, for example, few less talented adolescents attempted the distortions inherent in three-quarter rotations, sticking instead to flat depictions posed in either profile or front view. In geometric drawings, less than half of the adolescents used a projective drawing system. For these children, the difficulties of producing a visually realistic drawing appeared to remain paramount despite apparent normal development in other areas of functioning.

Development of Children Talented in the Visual Arts

When artistically talented children are tested, they usually score within the normal range for intelligence, but almost all demonstrate exceptional visual–spatial abilities including superiority in visual imagination and visual memory (see chapter 1). The visual-spatial superiority associated with artistic talent and with other kinds of giftedness has been explained as the result of biological differences in the organization of the brain (Winner, 1996). The normal dominance of the left hemisphere that is associated with language is replaced by a more nearly bilaterally symmetrical organization in which the right hemisphere, normally associated with visual-spatial skills, participates in left hemisphere tasks. Whatever the biological cause, children who develop artistic talent appear to start out in life with heightened figurative abilities, including heightened attention to visual configurations, when contrasted to other children (see Milbrath, 1995 and Winner, 1996).

Among individuals who have savant talent, such as Alex, heightened figurative abilities may go a long way in explaining the very early and remarkable visual realism in their drawings. In these cases brain dominance may be grossly asymmetrical since normal left hemisphere functions appear markedly immature. But figurative abilities alone cannot explain the artwork of talented children who are otherwise developing normally. Conceptual systems must also play a strong role. It is proposed that this type of artistic talent results when figurative and conceptual systems are continually coordinated throughout development. This coordination is much more complete than in less talented children because figurative thought is more salient for talented children. And although at first integration of the two systems appears to act as a brake on artistic ability, it later results in a powerful synergetic effect. Bamberger (1982) proposed a similar idea related to musical development; in the case of musically talented children integration between figural and conceptual systems was not always accomplished smoothly. The early excellence that resulted from heightened figurative abilities of young musicians did not always transfer to later development. In some gifted adolescents the emergence of formal strategies (e.g., analytical and compositional) interrupted well-practiced figural strategies (e.g., perceptual-motor musical representations) developed during their earlier years. The situation is somewhat different in the visual arts in that formal training is rarely provided for young visual artists. This means that *what* and *how* a child draws are usually left up to the child and this factor alone may promote a more seamless coordination between figurative and conceptual schemes throughout development.

Whereas less talented children, who attend to and remember fewer visual details, substitute concepts in their early drawings, talented children, who evidence heightened visual interests, construct precise correspondences between drawings and the real world even in their early drawings. The early appearance of recognizable forms in talented children is universally reported (Winner & Martino, 1993). Talented children studied in this book were drawing recognizable forms between the ages of 2 and 3. By the time these children were 4 years old, when most children begin to draw recognizable forms, the visual correspondence between two-dimensional forms and their referents was already quite striking. It is proposed that the correspondence is more precise because of the attention these children focus on the visual world. Whereas most young children make a visual correspondence between one or two salient features, these children succeed with half a dozen or more. Because talented children are better able to attend to visual configurations and to comparisons between real world referents and their drawings they are able to integrate conceptual and figurative schemes with their drawing procedures even during the earliest phases of drawing development.

Two issues related to this coordination process appear pivotal in launching talented children along the artistic superhighway; both have to do with the role of emerging drawing schemas in clarifying the correspondences children make. First, it is proposed that the act of drawing, which through action brings into correspondence what is seen (or represented in memory) with what is drawn, precociously moves the child toward a more refined analysis of what she sees. As a child attempts a point by point correspondence between real world referents and the drawing, the visual strategies applied to exploring these objects become more systematic. A better visual analysis in turn results in a better drawing, which in turn further facilitates visual analysis. Piaget (1979) demonstrated a related phenomenon in children's response to classical visual illusions. He found that if children were first asked to choose rods of equal length physically, they were able to "suppress" the strong illusionary effects of inequality when the rods were subsequently arranged in the Muller–Lyer or vertical illusion tests. Similarly, Pratt (1985) found that adult artists, who looked much more at drawing models than nonartists, created task-specific memory schemas that further facilitated the efficiency of information pick up.

Second, the act of drawing propels the child's conceptual understanding. Talented children in this study were demonstrating their understanding of spatial concepts in drawings at the youngest ages reported for these concepts in normative studies. Piaget (1974; 1979) suggested that conceptual understanding could be hastened by having children use actions to emphasize a correspondence. For example, he was able to train children precociously to conserve continuous matter using a clay ball by having them break off parts of the *ball* of clay and reattach the parts to produce the transformed *sausage* of clay. The children were able to see that what was taken away was isomorphic with what was added.

Nevertheless, just as Piaget was unable to push the youngest nonconservers to conserve, the developmental rate of spatial concepts in talented children was constrained by limits related to conceptual development. In other conservation training studies with normal children (Inhelder, Sinclair & Bovet, 1974) these constraints have been associated with whether or not a child shows transitional signs in stage development. Children who showed signs of transitional movement toward operatory thought, for example, empirical reversibility in conservation tasks, benefited from training but those below this level did not. In the talented children studied, conceptual development appeared to put a brake on the truly precocious development of perspective in their drawings.

The sequence of appearance of spatial milestones in the drawings of talented children argues for an immediate integration of developing spatial concepts with drawing schemas. Two aspects of development potentiated this integration. One was the drawing procedures talented children had already developed. Although some major conceptual shifts were indexed in the drawings of less talented children, many aspects of spatial reasoning never appeared in their drawings. A major impediment to this translation was the absence of flexible drawing procedures that could accommodate to a child's intention in this regard. In contrast, the rich variety of drawing schemas developed by talented children allowed an efficient integration at each new stage of conceptual development. As suggested in chapter 5, these were organized hierarchically and cross-indexed with each other so that they could be easily decomposed and recomposed as parts of a new type of drawing.

The second aspect to potentiate a near-seamless integration rests on talented children's figurative abilities. We have already discussed the manner in which heightened attention to the visual world in talented children could influence the development of drawing schemas. Coupled with a heightened visual interest is the unusually accurate visual memory found ubiquitously in artistically talented children. It is difficult to say whether this type of memory develops *because* of the initial visual bias these children have or whether its development is simply linked biologically with the type of brain organization that has been suggested to support artistic precocity (see Winner, 1996). In any case, it is clear that the ability to visualize a drawing subject accurately is a powerful aid in constructing a drawing.

Most of the talented children studied longitudinally indicated they were able to use their ability to visualize in drawing but not all depended on it. Since most of these children did not enter the study until age 8 to 10, it is difficult to assess whether they relied on visual memory early in their development. For example, Tara said that although she usually just drew she also used a picture in her mind of "real horses" she's known as models. Claire stated that she could use pictures in her head if she wanted to but "eighty percent of the time, I construct the picture on the paper." But the pictures in her head were usually better than her drawings. Peregrine also complained that the picture in her mind "is too complete. I can't copy it . . . I use it as an idea." In contrast Hondo reported drawing from a detailed picture in his mind: "I picture it in my mind and draw it out." Kate also stated that although it was not a conscious process for her, she did use a picture in her mind: "I set the picture up in my head. I see a person on a chair with clothes and then it comes out of my pencil."

It is interesting that these last two children who indicated the greatest reliance on a visual image were the ones who had the unprecedented drawings from age 4 (presented in chapter 1, Figures 1.4 and 1.5b). Because the drawings were such a departure from those that came before or after, it was suggested that these two drawings were based on recalling specific episodes. If true, it does demonstrate a very early heightened ability in talented children to construct a clear and accurate visual image and to utilize it to generate a drawing. Although these drawings appeared too novel to be immediately integrated into the children's repertoire, they likely opened up possibilities that pulled development forward (see chapter 6). In effect, later on when a child encounters a situation that upon analysis demands a similar drawing, she or he has already produced something that can be remembered and potentially integrated with her or his current level of conceptual development.

It must also be acknowledged that assuming these young talented children had access to veridical images from episodic memory is at odds with a constructivist view of memory. Such a view states that (a) memory is a construction, not a trace of what is seen, and (b) what can be constructed in memory is determined by a child's level of conceptual development. How can such young children represent in their minds or in their drawings figure poses that are several years in advance of what they themselves are consistently capable of producing or understanding? We do not have a clear understanding of how the saliency of specific visual configurations might influence the visual memory of young children with the type of figurative abilities suggested for talented children. In addition, other theories of memory take a different view of what develops. Some suggest that older children and adults remember better than younger children because they have more efficient strategies for accessing memory, greater available capacity in working memory, and a richer network of associations to support memory (Ackerman, 1988; Case, 1978; Kosslyn, 1980). The relative importance of figurative processes and how these processes change with conceptual development in artistically talented children are two areas that should be a central focus of further research.

APPENDIXES

2.1

Statistical Design and Computer Scoring for Drawings

LOGLINEAR ANALYSES

The full statistical model of interest for the cross-sectional sample was a 3 (age blocks 3–6, 7–10, 11–14 years of age) by 2 (talent groups) by N levels of dimension observed factor design. It is generally recommended that there be approximately 5 times the number of subjects per cell for these types of analyses and that there be no expected values less than 1. Ideally, then, if the full design included 3 levels of a dimension, it would require 90 subjects. Some dimensions, like figure rotation, included 4 or more levels of a dimension. In addition, children's drawing received scores on all the categories that could be observed in a drawing. For some drawings and categories obervations could not be made. For example, if there were no human or animal figures in a drawing, figure rotation could not be scored. This meant that the power to test the complete model in the same loglinear analysis was limited for a number of the analyses because insufficient samples were observed for some intersecting cells. In this case separate loglinear analyses, one for the effects of age and one for the effects of talent, were computed. A separate loglinear analysis was also calculated for the effects of age block in the less talented children alone ($N = 75$), so that the development with age of less talented children could be studied alone and contrasted with results for the longitudinal sample. There were too few subjects in the talented cross-sectional sample to carry out statistical analyses for the effects of age.

Loglinear analysis was also used for the longitudinal study data. Using loglinear models for repeated measures analyses has become an accepted practice for conditional and lagged sequential analyses with qualitative time series data (Bakeman & Adamson, 1989; Gottman & Roy, 1990). The longitudinal data presented special problems, however, because although there were many drawings per child, there were only 8 children in the sample. A single score per repeated measure for a subject would result in too few data points for robust analysis. Some difficulties have been successfully solved for single subject and small group factor analyses by use of the chained-p technique. *Chaining* here refers to using repeated scores for a single subject within a measurement unit. This increases the data points available for each unit of measurement and for the overall analysis, and as long as the number of scores contributed to each measurement unit is equal or at least proportional to what it would have been without the multiplication, the procedure is assumed valid. This procedure was followed for the longitudinal analyses by using four observations for every subject within each repeated measurement unit. The repeated unit consisted of three age blocks (3–6, 7–10, 11–14). Therefore, there is one data point for each year for a subject. Data were not available for all 8 subjects for every year of the study. At age 3 only 5 subjects had data, at age 4 only 6 subjects, and at age 14 only 7 subjects; at all other ages data were available for all 8 subjects. As a result 90 data points instead of 96 (4 observations by 3 age blocks by 8 subjects) were used across the 12 years of study.

Data analysis was based either on the single drawing or on an "average" score obtained when multiple drawings were used. Since scoring was based on categorical codes the "average" score was the proportion of drawings for a child that contained a given code. Proportions were then transformed back to a binary score of 0 or 1. A child got credit for *simple presence* if 25% of the drawings had the score; this usually amounted to at least one drawing that included the category. When the *predominance* of a category type was of interest, a higher criterion of greater than one-third of the drawings was used. Although 51% might seem the most natural criterion for predominance, in actual fact category codes were often split among three or more codes. For example, line orientation could be uncontrolled, straight single or parallel, or paired with either contour lines or vertical, horizontal, or oblique orientations.

Computer Algorithms

The computer algorithms uniquely assigned each child a scale value based on *the highest scale score* achieved at a given age. Therefore, if a child had several different drawings for a given year or several different codes within a single drawing, each scoring at a different level, the child was always given the score at the highest level. This single score for a child at each age was then used in loglinear analyses. Each algorithm is presented.

Line Orientation. The data analyzed for these comparisons were judgments as to whether or not a particular type of line *dominated* a drawing rather than whether it was simply present or absent (see Milbrath, 1982). Only a single category was assigned to a subject's drawing; it was based on a hierarchical algorithm that specified the following levels: Level 1, *scribble*, if no other frequent category was present with scribble; Level 2, *single straight line*, if one of the single straight lines was dominant (horizontal, vertical, etc.) but no other frequent category was present; Level 3, *parallel lines*, if frequent parallel lines were present either alone or with frequent single straight or contour lines; and Level 4, *contour lines* if frequent contour lines were present alone or with no other frequent lines. The validity of this simple inclusion hierarchy was based on the first appearance of these types of lines in the normative sample (see chapter 3).

Active Line, Active Plane, Shape, and Symmetry. The data used for the algorithms for active line, active plane, symmetry, and shapes were also based on dominant or frequent use of one of the categories rather than simple presence or absence (see Milbrath, 1982). Three scales were constructed: (1) a seven-category line activity scale that assigned categorical scores based on *all observed* combinations of high active line, active line/plane (line and plane in visual equality), and high active plane; a category was only assigned if it had been scored as frequent or in high use; (2) a three-category scale that included all possible combinations of the individual categories such as high use of symmetry, high use of asymmetry, and use of both together, that is, there were drawings that were judged to be high in both symmetrical and asymmetrical elements; and (3) a similar three-category scale for the modular use of shapes: high use of circles, high use of triangles/angles, and high use of both together.

Figure Rotation. A four-point scale based on the literature and the development of the different figure rotations in the samples studied was constructed from the originally judged categories described in Milbrath (1982). The scale also appeared sound in terms of a logical analysis of the complexity and the technical skill a child would need to accomplish the figure rotations at each level. The drawings were assigned to one of the following four levels on the basis of the presence or absence of a rotation: Level 1, front views; Level 2, profiles and front and profile mixes; Level 3, three-quarter mixed with front or profile views; and Level 4, pure three-quarter views. A drawing always received the score of the highest level rotation present in the drawing.

Picture Plane. Each figure was originally judged as described in Milbrath (1982) for the construction of a ground line or plane in a drawing. A child was scored positive for the appearance of a category on the basis of simple presence or absence. A single scale was then constructed from the categorically coded data. Four levels of *picture plane* were determined by a computer algorithm that uniquely assigned a child to a level based on the following criteria: Level 1, the absence of any ground indicator; Level 2, ground indicated by a line; Level 3, ground indicated by both a line and a plane; or Level 4, ground indicated by a plane alone.

Positioning Devices. Positioning categories were partitioned into four levels by constructing an algorithm that employed the following criteria based on simple presence or absence: Level 1, the exclusive use of horizontal segregation and/or transparency; Level 2, the use of vertical segregation or of overlaps with transparencies; Level 3, the use of both vertical segregation and overlap with no transparencies; Level 4, the exclusive use of overlap with no transparencies. Exclusivity, however, did not pertain to horizontal segregation because this type of positioning device is ubiquitous in spontaneous drawings and therefore could occur with any of the other higher level categories. Definitions for the individual categories are given in Milbrath (1982).

Drawing Systems. This scale was based on research by Willats (1977) that showed a developmental progression in children's use of drawing systems. The individual categories are defined in Milbrath (1982). Only drawings that represented geometric objects such as buildings or trucks were coded with drawing systems. Roads, although not "objects," are included. Three types of projective drawing systems were assigned hierarchically to the most advanced level present in a child's drawings on the basis of the computer algorithm. The algorithm followed the criterion of simple presence or absence to assign the following hierarchy: Level 1, the absence of a projective system as either elevation or plan drawings; Level 2, oblique projective systems; Level 3, naive and/or linear perspective systems.

Perspective Indicators. The scale for perspective indicators was based on combinations of the three perspective indicators, foreshortening, modeling, and shading or shadow, as defined in Milbrath (1982). A computer algorithm uniquely assigned each child a score based on the presence or absence of no, one, two, or all three types of perspective indicators in her or his drawings. Use of all three was considered the most advanced level.

APPENDIX 3.1
REPEATED MEASURES ANALYSIS OF VARIANCE FOR
FREQUENT LINE USE IN TALENTED LONGITUDINAL
SAMPLE

Line Type	Mean Proportion of Drawings			F Value
	Ages 3 to 6	Ages 7 to 10	Ages 11 to 14	
Contour	.69**	.85	.83	$F_{3, 5} = 89.01$**
Oblique parallel	.16**	.26	.33	$F_{3, 5} = 6.16$*
Horizontal parallel	.20†	.24	.26	$F_{3, 5} = 9.62$*

*$p < .05$. **$p < .01$. †$p = .06$.

APPENDIX 3.2

TOTAL CROSS-SECTIONAL SAMPLE: LOGLINEAR
ANALYSIS FOR AGE BLOCKS ON FREQUENT LINE TYPE

Factor	Observed Count & Percentage	Expected Count & Percentage	Adjusted Residual
Line Scribble			
Ages 3 to 6	10.00 (32.26)	3.25 (10.48)	4.72
Ages 7 to 10	1.00 (2.63)	3.98 (10.48)	−1.98
Ages 11 to 14	.00 (.00)	3.77 (10.48)	−2.53
Line Single			
Ages 3 to 6	5.00 (16.13)	2.66 (8.57)	1.79
Ages 7 to 10	1.00 (2.63)	3.26 (8.57)	−1.64
Ages 11 to 14	3.00 (8.33)	3.09 (8.57)	−.06
Line Parallels			
Ages 3 to 6	9.00 (29.03)	16.53 (53.33)	−3.23
Ages 7 to 10	29.00 (76.32)	20.27 (53.33)	3.56
Ages 11 to 14	18.00 (50.00)	19.20 (53.33)	−.49
Line Contour			
Ages 3 to 6	7.00 (22.58)	8.56 (27.62)	−.75
Ages 7 to 10	7.00 (18.42)	10.50 (27.62)	−1.59
Ages 11 to 14	15.00 (41.67)	9.94 (27.62)	2.33

$L^2 = 34.88.$ $df = 6.$ $p < .001.$

LONGITUDINAL SAMPLE: LOGLINEAR ANALYSIS FOR
THE EFFECT OF AGE BLOCK ON USE OF MODULAR
SHAPES

Factors	Observed Count & Percentage	Expected Count & Percentage	Adjusted Residual
No Modular Elements			
Ages 3 to 6	3.00 (10.71)	10.58 (37.78)	−3.56
Ages 7 to 10	14.00 (43.73)	12.09 (37.78)	.86
Ages 11 to 14	17.00 (56.67)	11.33 (37.78)	2.61
Circles			
Ages 3 to 6	22.00 (78.57)	12.76 (45.56)	4.22
Ages 7 to 10	11.00 (34.38)	14.58 (45.56)	−1.58
Ages 11 to 14	8.00 (26.67)	13.67 (45.56)	−2.54
Circles & Triangle/Angle			
Ages 3 to 6	1.00 (3.57)	1.87 (6.67)	−.79
Ages 7 to 10	4.00 (12.50)	2.13 (6.67)	1.65
Ages 11 to 14	1.00 (3.33)	2.00 (6.67)	−.89
Triangle/Angle			
Ages 3 to 6	2.00 (7.14)	2.80 (10.00)	−.61
Ages 7 to 10	3.00 (9.38)	3.20 (10.00)	−.14
Ages 11 to 14	4.00 (13.33)	4.00 (10.00)	.75

$L^2 = 22.52.$ $df = 6.$ $p = .001.$

CROSS-SECTIONAL SAMPLE: LOGLINEAR ANALYSIS
FOR TALENT GROUPS ON ACTIVE LINE, ACTIVE PLANE

Factors	Observed Count & Percentage	Expected Count & Percentage	Adjusted Residual
Active Line			
Less Talented	3.00 (4.00)	2.14 (2.86)	1.11
Talented	.00 (.00)	.86 (2.86)	−1.11
Active Plane			
Less Talented	20.00 (26.67)	18.57 (24.76)	.72
Talented	6.00 (20.00)	7.43 (24.76)	−.72
Active Line/Plane			
Less Talented	19.00 (25.33)	27.14 (2.86)	−3.66
Talented	19.00 (63.33)	10.86 (2.86)	3.66
Combined Active Line & Active Plane			
Less Talented	5.00 (6.67)	3.57 (4.76)	1.45
Talented	.00 (.00)	1.43 (4.76)	−1.45
Combined Active Line & Active Line/Plane			
Less Talented	8.00 (10.67)	5.71 (7.62)	1.86
Talented	.00 (.00)	2.29 (7.62)	−1.86
Combined Active Plane & Active Line/Plane			
Less Talented	18.00 (24.00)	15.71 (20.95)	1.21
Talented	4.00 (13.33)	6.29 (20.95)	−1.21
All Three in Combination			
Less Talented	2.00 (2.67)	2.14 (2.86)	.19
Talented	1.00 (3.33)	.86 (2.86)	−.19

[a] $L^2 = 20.19.$ $df = 6.$ $p = .001.$

TOTAL CROSS-SECTIONAL SAMPLE: LOGLINEAR
ANALYSIS FOR THE EFFECT OF AGE BLOCK ON ACTIVE
LINE, ACTIVE PLANE

Factors	Observed Count & Percentage	Expected Count & Percentage	Adjusted Residual
Active Line			
Ages 3 to 6	2.00 (6.45)	.89 (2.86)	1.43
Ages 7 to 10	1.00 (2.63)	1.09 (2.86)	−.10
Ages 11 to 14	.00 (.00)	1.03 (2.86)	−1.27
Active Plane			
Ages 3 to 6	3.00 (9.68)	7.68 (24.76)	−2.32
Ages 7 to 10	15.00 (39.47)	9.41 (24.76)	2.63
Ages 11 to 14	8.00 (22.22)	8.91 (24.76)	−.44
Active Line/Plane			
Ages 3 to 6	11.00 (35.48)	11.22 (36.19)	−.10
Ages 7 to 10	13.00 (34.21)	13.75 (36.19)	−.32
Ages 11 to 14	14.00 (38.89)	13.03 (36.19)	.42
Combined Active Line & Active Plane			
Ages 3 to 6	5.00 (16.13)	1.48 (4.76)	3.54
Ages 7 to 10	.00 (.00)	1.81 (4.76)	−1.73
Ages 11 to 14	.00 (.00)	1.71 (4.76)	−1.66
Combined Active Line & Active Line/Plane			
Ages 3 to 6	4.00 (12.90)	2.36 (7.62)	1.32
Ages 7 to 10	.00 (.00)	2.90 (7.62)	−2.22
Ages 11 to 14	4.00 (11.11)	2.74 (7.62)	.97
Combined Active Plane & Active Line/Plane			
Ages 3 to 6	5.00 (16.13)	6.50 (20.95)	−.79
Ages 7 to 10	8.00 (21.05)	7.96 (20.95)	.02
Ages 11 to 14	9.00 (25)	7.54 (20.95)	.74
All Three in Combination			
Ages 3 to 6	1.00 (3.23)	.89 (2.86)	.15
Ages 7 to 10	1.00 (2.63)	1.09 (2.86)	−.10
Ages 11 to 14	1.00 (2.78)	1.03 (2.86)	−.03

$L^2 = 29.93$. $df = 12$. $p = .003$.

LOGLINEAR ANALYSIS FOR CROSS-SECTIONAL
TALENT GROUPS ON ROTATION

Factor	Observed Count & Percentage	Expected Count & Percentage	Adjusted Residual
Front Views			
Less Talented	17.00 (43.59)	13.00 (33.33)	2.1243
Talented	5.00 (18.52)	9.00 (33.33)	−2.1243
Profile & Profile Front Mixes			
Less Talented	15.00 (38.46)	13.00 (33.33)	1.0622
Talented	7.00 (25.93)	9.00 (33.33)	−1.0622
Three-Quarter Front & Profile Mixes			
Less Talented	4.00 (10.26)	7.68 (19.70)	−2.3177
Talented	9.00 (33.33)	5.32 (19.70)	2.3177
Pure Three-Quarter Views			
Less Talented	3.00 (7.69)	5.32 (13.64)	−1.6912
Talented	6.00 (22.22)	3.68 (13.64)	1.6912

$L^2 = 10.69$. $df = 3$. $p = .014$.

TOTAL CROSS-SECTIONAL SAMPLE: LOGLINEAR
ANALYSIS FOR AGE BLOCK ON ROTATION

Factor	Observed Count & Percentage	Expected Count & Percentage	Adjusted Residual
Front Views			
Ages 3 to 6	10.00 (55.56)	6.00 (33.33)	2.3452
Ages 7 to 10	6.00 (25.00)	8.00 (33.33)	−1.0856
Ages 11 to 14	6.00 (25.00)	8.00 (33.33)	−1.0856
Profile & Profile Front Mixes			
Ages 3 to 6	7.00 (38.89)	6.00 (33.33)	.5863
Ages 7 to 10	11.00 (45.83)	8.00 (33.33)	1.6284
Ages 11 to 14	4.00 (16.67)	8.00 (33.33)	−2.1712
Three-Quarter Front & Profile Mixes			
Ages 3 to 6	1.00 (5.56)	3.55 (19.70)	−1.7689
Ages 7 to 10	5.00 (20.83)	4.73 (19.70)	.1755
Ages 11 to 14	7.00 (29.17)	4.73 (19.70)	1.4623
Pure Three-Quarter Views			
Ages 3 to 6	.00 (.00)	2.45 (13.64)	−1.9768
Ages 7 to 10	2.00 (8.33)	3.27 (13.64)	−.9490
Ages 11 to 14	7.00 (29.17)	3.27 (13.64)	2.7792

$L^2 = 19.13$. $df = 6$. $p = .004$.

LONGITUDINAL TALENTED SAMPLE: LOGLINEAR
ANALYSIS FOR AGE BLOCK ON ROTATION

Factor	Observed Count & Percentage	Expected Count & Percentage	Adjusted Residual
Front Views			
Ages 3 to 6	8.00 (33.33)	3.08 (12.82)	3.6126
Ages 7 to 10	.00 (.00)	3.59 (12.82)	−2.5345
Ages 11 to 14	2.00 (7.69)	3.33 (12.82)	−.9579
Profile & Profile Front Mixes			
Ages 3 to 6	12.00 (50.00)	6.15 (25.64)	3.2846
Ages 7 to 10	8.00 (28.75)	7.18 (25.64)	.4435
Ages 11 to 14	.00 (.00)	6.67 (25.64)	−3.6672
Three-Quarter Front & Profile Mixes			
Ages 3 to 6	1.00 (4.17)	2.15 (8.97)	−.9904
Ages 7 to 10	3.00 (10.71)	2.51 (8.97)	.4023
Ages 11 to 14	3.00 (11.54)	2.33 (8.97)	.5603
Pure Three-Quarter Views			
Ages 3 to 6	3.00 (12.50)	12.62 (52.56)	−4.7240
Ages 7 to 10	17.00 (60.71)	14.72 (52.56)	1.0787
Ages 11 to 14	21.00 (80.77)	13.67 (52.56)	3.5275

$L^2 = 46.37.$ $df = 6.$ $p < .001.$

APPENDIX 5.1
TOTAL CROSS-SECTIONAL SAMPLE: LOGLINEAR
ANALYSIS FOR AGE BLOCK ON GROUND SCALE

Factor	Observed Count & Percentage	Expected Count & Percentage	Adjusted Residual
No Ground Indicated			
Ages 3 to 6	17.00 (54.84)	6.79 (21.90)	5.2811
Ages 7 to 10	2.00 (5.26)	8.32 (21.90)	−3.1050
Ages 11 to 14	4.00 (11.11)	7.89 (21.90)	−1.9316
Ground Line			
Ages 3 to 6	5.00 (16.13)	3.54 (11.43)	.9798
Ages 7 to 10	5.00 (13.16)	4.34 (11.43)	.4195
Ages 11 to 14	2.00 (5.56)	4.11 (11.43)	−1.3663
Ground Line & Plane			
Ages 3 to 6	5.00 (16.13)	8.56 (27.62)	−1.7044
Ages 7 to 10	18.00 (47.37)	10.50 (27.62)	3.4087
Ages 11 to 14	6.00 (16.67)	9.94 (27.62)	−1.8131
Ground Plane			
Ages 3 to 6	4.00 (12.90)	12.10 (39.05)	−3.5542
Ages 7 to 10	13.00 (34.21)	14.84 (39.05)	−.7651
Ages 11 to 14	24.00 (66.67)	14.06 (39.05)	4.1902

$L^2 = 43.40.$ $df = 6.$ $p < .001.$

LONGITUDINAL TALENTED SAMPLE: LOGLINEAR
ANALYSIS FOR AGE ON GROUND SCALE

Factor	Observed Count & Percentage	Expected Count & Percentage	Adjusted Residual
No Ground Indicated			
Ages 3 to 6	6.00 (21.43)	2.49 (8.89)	2.8092
Ages 7 to 10	.00 (.00)	2.84 (8.89)	−2.2010
Ages 11 to 14	2.00 (6.67)	2.67 (8.89)	−.5238
Ground Line			
Ages 3 to 6	7.00 (25.00)	2.49 (8.89)	3.6093
Ages 7 to 10	1.00 (3.13)	2.84 (8.89)	−1.4272
Ages 11 to 14	.00 (.00)	2.67 (8.89)	−2.0953
Ground Line & Plane			
Ages 3 to 6	10.00 (35.71)	6.22 (22.22)	2.0690
Ages 7 to 10	9.00 (28.13)	7.11 (22.22)	1.0005
Ages 11 to 14	1.00 (3.33)	6.67 (22.22)	−3.0478
Ground Plane			
Ages 3 to 6	5.00 (17.86)	16.80 (60.00)	−5.4843
Ages 7 to 10	22.00 (68.75)	19.20 (60.00)	1.2586
Ages 11 to 14	27.00 (90.00)	18.00 (60.00)	4.1079

$L^2 = 47.50.$ $df = 6.$ $p < .001.$

LOGLINEAR ANALYSIS FOR CROSS-SECTIONAL
TALENT GROUPS ON POSITION SCALE

Factor	Observed Count & Percentage	Expected Count & Percentage	Adjusted Residual
Horizontal Segregation and/or Transparency			
Less Talented	22.00 (33.85)	16.42 (25.26)	2.8339
Talented	2.00 (6.67)	7.58 (25.26)	−2.8339
Vertical Segregation or Overlap with Transparency			
Less Talented	15.00 (23.08)	14.37 (22.11)	.3359
Talented	6.00 (20.00)	6.63 (22.11)	−.3359
Vertical Segregation and Overlap without Transparency			
Less Talented	15.00 (23.08)	22.58 (34.74)	−3.5134
Talented	18.00 (60.00)	10.42 (34.74)	3.5134
Overlap without Transparency			
Less Talented	13.00 (20.00)	11.63 (17.89)	.7880
Talented	4.00 (13.33)	5.37 (17.89)	−.7880

$L^2 = 15.57$. $df = 3$. $p < .001$.

TOTAL CROSS-SECTIONAL SAMPLE: LOGLINEAR
ANALYSIS FOR AGE ON POSITION SCALE

Factor	Observed Count & Percentage	Expected Count & Percentage	Adjusted Residual
Horizontal Segregation and/or Transparency			
Ages 3 to 6	14.00 (60.87)	5.81 (25.26)	4.5142
Ages 7 to 10	8.00 (22.22)	9.09 (25.26)	−.5328
Ages 11 to 14	2.00 (5.56)	9.09 (25.26)	−3.4531
Vertical Segregation or Overlap with Transparency			
Ages 3 to 6	7.00 (30.43)	5.08 (22.11)	1.1058
Ages 7 to 10	10.00 (27.78)	7.96 (22.11)	1.0408
Ages 11 to 14	4.00 (11.11)	7.96 (22.11)	−2.0172
Vertical Segregation and Overlap without Transparency			
Ages 3 to 6	2.00 (8.70)	7.99 (34.74)	−3.0129
Ages 7 to 10	15.00 (41.67)	12.51 (34.74)	1.1081
Ages 11 to 14	16.00 (44.44)	12.51 (34.74)	1.5523
Overlap without Transparency			
Ages 3 to 6	.00 (.00)	4.12 (17.89)	−2.5718
Ages 7 to 10	3.00 (8.33)	6.44 (17.89)	−1.8992
Ages 11 to 14	14.00 (38.89)	6.44 (17.89)	4.1700

$L^2 = 45.01.$ $df = 6.$ $p < .001.$

LONGITUDINAL TALENTED SAMPLE: LOGLINEAR
ANALYSIS FOR AGE BLOCK ON POSITION SCALE

Factor	Observed Count & Percentage	Expected Count & Percentage	Adjusted Residual
Horizontal Segregation and/or Transparency			
Ages 3 to 6	7.00 (25.00)	2.20 (7.87)	4.0684
Ages 7 to 10	.00 (.00)	2.52 (7.87)	−2.0653
Ages 11 to 14	.00 (.00)	2.28 (7.87)	−1.9163
Vertical Segregation or Overlap with Transparency			
Ages 3 to 6	10.00 (35.71)	4.40 (15.73)	3.5082
Ages 7 to 10	4.00 (12.50)	5.03 (15.73)	−.6272
Ages 11 to 14	.00 (.00)	4.56 (15.73)	−2.8337
Vertical Segregation and Overlap without Transparency			
Ages 3 to 6	11.00 (39.29)	16.99 (60.67)	−2.7986
Ages 7 to 10	22.00 (68.75)	19.42 (60.67)	1.1686
Ages 11 to 14	21.00 (72.41)	17.60 (60.67)	1.5763
Overlap without Transparency			
Ages 3 to 6	.00 6(.00)	4.40 (15.73)	−2.7615
Ages 7 to 10	6.00 (18.75)	5.03 (15.73)	.5863
Ages 11 to 14	8.00 (27.59)	4.56 (15.73)	2.1357

$L^2 = 45.21. \ df = 6. \ p < .001.$

APPENDIX 5.6

LOGLINEAR ANALYSIS FOR CROSS-SECTIONAL
TALENT GROUPS ON DRAWING SYSTEMS

Factor	Observed Count & Percentage	Expected Count & Percentage	Adjusted Residual
No Projection System			
Less Talented	33.00 (82.50)	28.85 (72.13)	2.4928
Talented	11.00 (52.38)	15.15 (72.13)	−2.4928
Oblique Projection Systems			
Less Talented	6.00 (15.00)	6.56 (16.39)	−.4057
Talented	4.00 (19.05)	3.44 (16.39)	.4057
Perspective Systems			
Less Talented	1.00 (2.50)	4.59 (11.48)	−3.0355
Talented	6.00 (28.57)	2.41 (11.48)	3.0355

$L^2 = 9.86$. $df = 2$. $p < .007$.

APPENDIX 5.7

TOTAL CROSS-SECTIONAL SAMPLE: LOGLINEAR
ANALYSIS FOR AGE ON DRAWING SYSTEMS

Factor	Observed Count & Percentage	Expected Count & Percentage	Adjusted Residual
No Projective System			
Age 3 to 6	18.00 (99.99)	12.98 (72.13)	3.1410
Ages 7 to 10	21.00 (72.41)	20.92 (72.13)	.0469
Ages 11 to 14	5.00 (35.71)	10.10 (72.13)	−3.4623
Oblique Projective Systems			
Ages 3 to 6	.00 (.00)	2.95 (16.39)	−2.2376
Ages 7 to 10	6.00 (20.69)	4.75 (16.39)	.8628
Ages 11 to 14	4.00 (28.57)	2.30 (16.39)	1.4022
Perspective Systems			
Ages 3 to 6	.00 (.00)	2.07 (11.48)	−1.8194
Ages 7 to 10	2.00 (6.90)	3.33 (11.48)	−1.0681
Ages 11 to 14	5.00 (35.71)	1.61 (11.48)	3.2417

$L^2 = 21.45$. $df = 4$. $p < .001$.

LONGITUDINAL TALENTED SAMPLE: LOGLINEAR
ANALYSIS FOR AGE ON DRAWING SYSTEMS

Factor	Observed Count & Percentage	Expected Count & Percentage	Adjusted Residual
No Projective System			
Age 3 to 6	18.00 (81.82)	8.25 (37.50)	5.3003
Ages 7 to 10	6.00 (28.57)	7.87 (37.50)	−1.0311
Ages 11 to 14	.00 (.00)	7.87 (37.50)	−4.3305
Oblique Projective Systems			
Ages 3 to 6	4.00 (18.18)	6.19 (28.13)	−1.2805
Ages 7 to 10	8.00 (38.10)	5.91 (28.13)	1.2398
Ages 11 to 14	6.00 (28.57)	5.91 (28.13)	.0555
Perspective Systems			
Ages 3 to 6	.00 (.00)	7.56 (34.37)	−4.1905
Ages 7 to 10	7.00 (33.33)	7.22 (34.37)	−.1226
Ages 11 to 14	15.00 (71.43)	7.22 (34.37)	4.3615

$L^2 = 47.89$. $df = 4$. $p < .001$.

LOGLINEAR ANALYSIS FOR CROSS-SECTIONAL
TALENT GROUPS ON PERSPECTIVE INDICATORS

Factor	Observed Count & Percentage	Expected Count & Percentage	Adjusted Residual
No Perspective Indicators			
Less Talented	62.00 (82.67)	51.43 (68.57)	4.9193
Talented	10.00 (33.33)	20.57 (68.57)	−4.9193
One Perspective Indicator			
Less Talented	8.00 (10.67)	9.29 (12.38)	−.8433
Talented	5.00 (16.67)	3.71 (12.38)	.8433
Two Perspective Indicators			
Less Talented	4.00 (5.33)	7.86 (10.48)	−2.7208
Talented	7.00 (23.33)	3.14 (10.48)	2.7208
Three Perspective Indicators			
Less Talented	1.00 (1.33)	6.43 (8.57)	−4.1891
Talented	8.00 (26.67)	2.57 (8.57)	4.1891

$L^2 = 29.59$. $df = 3$. $p < .001$.

TOTAL CROSS-SECTIONAL SAMPLE: LOGLINEAR
ANALYSIS FOR AGE BLOCK ON PERSPECTIVE
INDICATORS

Factor	Observed Count & Percentage	Expected Count & Percentage	Adjusted Residual
No Perspective Indicators			
Ages 3 to 6	30.00 (96.77)	21.26 (68.57)	4.0292
Ages 7 to 10	28.00 (73.68)	26.06 (68.57)	.8499
Ages 11 to 14	14.00 (38.89)	24.69 (68.57)	−4.7325
One Perspective Indicator			
Ages 3 to 6	.00 (.00)	3.84 (12.38)	−2.4931
Ages 7 to 10	4.00 (10.53)	4.70 (12.38)	−.4345
Ages 11 to 14	9.00 (25.00)	4.46 (12.38)	2.8358
Two Perspective Indicators			
Ages 3 to 6	.00 (.00)	3.25 (10.48)	−2.2688
Ages 7 to 10	3.00 (7.89)	3.98 (10.48)	−.6505
Ages 11 to 14	8.00 (22.22)	3.77 (10.48)	2.8388
Three Perspective Indicators			
Ages 3 to 6	1.00 (3.23)	2.66 (8.57)	−1.2665
Ages 7 to 10	3.00 (7.89)	3.26 (8.57)	.1865
Ages 11 to 14	5.00 (13.89)	3.09 (8.57)	1.4059

$L^2 = 32.88$. $df = 6$. $p < .001$.

LONGITUDINAL TALENTED SAMPLE: LOGLINEAR
ANALYSIS FOR AGE BLOCK ON PERSPECTIVE
INDICATORS

Factor	Observed Count & Percentage	Expected Count & Percentage	Adjusted Residual
No Perspective Indicators			
Ages 3 to 6	23.00 (82.14)	8.40 (30.00)	7.2542
Ages 7 to 10	4.00 (12.50)	9.60 (30.00)	−2.6910
Ages 11 to 14	.00 (.00)	9.00 (30.00)	−4.3916
One Perspective Indicator			
Ages 3 to 6	4.00 (14.29)	13.07 (46.67)	−4.1380
Ages 7 to 10	23.00 (71.88)	14.93 (46.67)	3.5606
Ages 11 to 14	15.00 (50.00)	14.00 (46.67)	.4482
Two Perspective Indicators			
Ages 3 to 6	.00 (.00)	3.11 (11.11)	−2.2540
Ages 7 to 10	3.00 (9.38)	3.56 (11.11)	−.3893
Ages 11 to 14	7.00 (23.33)	3.33 (11.11)	2.6089
Three Perspective Indicators			
Ages 3 to 6	1.00 (3.57)	3.42 (12.22)	−1.6838
Ages 7 to 10	2.00 (6.25)	3.91 (12.22)	−1.2848
Ages 11 to 14	8.00 (26.67)	3.67 (12.22)	2.9583

$L^2 = 68.50$. $df = 6$. $p < .001$.

APPENDIX 9.1
CORRELATIONS FOR COMPOSITION DIMENSIONS
WITH GRADE LEVEL AND AGE

	Balance	Static to Dynamic	Symmetry to Asymmetry	Originality
	Blue Block Problems			
Grade K–8 ($N = 71$)	−.20	.19	.17	.09
Ages 5–14	−.19	.19	.22	−.20
Grade 10–12 ($N = 39$)	−.16	.22	.20	.19
Ages 15–18	−.17	.22	.20	.19
	Gray Block Problems			
Grade 2/3–8 ($N = 55$)	−.25	.18	.32*	.21
Ages 7–14	−.20	.22	.30*	.21
Grade 10–12 ($N = 38$)	−.35*	−.05	.34*	.23
Ages 15–18	−.32	−.01	.30	.21

*$p \leq .05$.

MEAN RESPONSE FREQUENCY FOR BLUE AND GRAY BLOCK
PROVOKED COMPOSITION TRIALS (N = 4)

Grade	Centering/ Symmetry	Balance One Dimension	Balance Two Dimension	Unbalanced
	Blue Block Compositions			
Sixth ($n = 28$)	1.14	1.43	0.29	1.11
Seventh ($n = 19$)	1.21	1.63	0.42	0.74
Eighth ($n = 21$)	1.43	1.00	0.48	1.00
Middle School ($N = 68$)	**1.25**	**1.35**	**0.38**	**0.97**
Tenth ($n = 15$)	1.60	1.40	0.40	0.60
Eleventh ($n = 11$)	1.36	1.18	0.55	0.73
Twelfth ($n = 13$)	1.15	1.85	0.38	0.46
High School ($N = 39$)	**1.38**	**1.49**	**0.44**	**0.59**
	Gray Block Compositions			
Sixth ($n = 30$)	1.70	0.93	0.40	0.87
Seventh ($n = 19$)	1.47	1.05	0.37	1.00
Eighth ($n = 21$)	1.57	1.00	0.43	0.90
Middle School ($N = 70$)	**1.60**	**0.99**	**0.40**	**0.91**
Tenth ($n = 15$)	1.53	1.33	0.47	0.67
Eleventh ($n = 12$)	1.58	1.25	0.58	0.50
Twelfth ($n = 13$)	1.23	1.00	0.85	0.92
High School ($N = 40$)	**1.45**	**1.2**	**0.63**	**0.7**

BIBLIOGRAPHY

Ackerman, B. (1988). Cued recall for category, thematic and ad hoc classified events in children and adults. *Journal of Experimental Child Psychology, 45,* 88–118.

Allik, J., & Laak, T. (1985). The head is smaller than the body: But how does it join on? In N. H. Freeman & M. V. Cox (Eds.), *Visual Order* (pp. 266–286). Cambridge: Cambridge University Press.

Arnheim, R. (1969). *Visual thinking.* Berkeley: University of California Press.

Arnheim, R. (1974). *Art and visual perception: A psychology of the creative eye.* Berkeley: University of California Press.

Arnheim, R. (1988). *The power of the center.* Berkeley: University of California Press.

Bailystock, E., & Olson, D. (1987). Spatial categories: The perception and conceptualization of spatial relations. In Steven Harnad (Ed.), *Categorical perception: The groundwork of cognition* (pp. 511–531). New York: Cambridge University Press.

Bakeman, R., Adamson, L. B., & Strisik, P. (1989). Lags and logs: Statistical approaches to interaction. In M. H. Bornstein & J. Bruner (Eds.), *Interaction in human development.* Hillsdale, NJ: Lawrence Erlbaum.

Bamberger, J. (1982). Growing up prodigies: The midlife crisis. In D. H. Feldman (Ed.), *Developmental approaches to giftedness and creativity* (pp. 61–77). San Francisco: Jossey-Bass.

Barnhart, E. N. (1942). Developmental stages in compositional construction in children's drawings. *Journal of Experimental Education, 11*(2), 156–184.

Barret, M. D., & Light, P. H. (1976). Symbolism and intellectual realism in children's drawings. *British Journal of Educational Psychology, 46,* 198–202.

Bedard, J., & Chi, M. H. (1992). Expertise. *Current Directions in Psychological Science, 1,* 135–139.

Berlyne, D. E. (1974). *The new experimental aesthetics*. Washington, D.C.: Hemisphere.

Berman, P. W. (1976). Young children's use of the frame of reference in construction of the horizontal, vertical and oblique. *Child Development, 47*, 259–263.

Berman, P. W., Cunningham, J. G., & Harkulich, J. (1974). Construction of the horizontal, vertical and oblique by young children: Failure to find the oblique effect. *Child Development, 45*, 474–478.

Berman, P. W., & Golab, P. (1975). Children's reconstruction of the horizontal, vertical and oblique in the absence of a rectangular frame. *Developmental Psychology, 11*, 117.

Biskup-Meyer, K., & Siegel, B. (1995). *Gestalt spatial problem solving skills in autistic and normal children*. Paper presented at the European Academy of Child Psychiatry, Utrecht, Netherlands, July.

Blakeslee, S. (1996, November 26). Workings of split brain challenge notions of how language evolved. *New York Science Times*.

Blank, P., Massey, C., Gardner, H., & Winner, E. (1984). Perceiving what paintings express. In R. Crozier & A. Chapman (eds.), *Cognitive processes in the perception of art* (pp. 127–143). Amsterdam: North-Holland.

Bremmer, G., & Moore, S. (1984). Prior visual inspection and object naming: Two factors that enhance hidden feature inclusion in young children's drawings. *British Journal of Developmental Psychology, 2*, 371–376.

Bretherton, I. (1984). *Symbolic play: The development of social understanding*. New York: Academic Press.

Bryant, P. E. (1969). Perception and memory of the orientation of visually presented lines by children. *Nature, 224*, 1331–1332.

Bryant, P. E. (1974). *Perception and understanding in children*. London: Methuen.

Callahan, T. (1993). Structure in the process of seeing and drawing. In B. Burns (Ed.), *Percepts, concepts and categories* (pp. 149–171). Amsterdam: North-Holland.

Cantor, N., & Mischel, W. (1979). Prototypes in person perception. In L. Berkowitz (Ed.), *Advances in experimental and social psychology* (pp. 3–52). San Diego: Academic Press.

Carothers, T., & Gardner, H. (1979). When children's drawings become art: The emergence of aesthetic production and perception. *Developmental Psychology, 15*, 570–580.

Case, R. (1978). Intellectual development from birth to adulthood: A neo-Piagetian investigation. In R. S. Siegler (Ed.), *Children's thinking: What develops?* (pp. 37–71) Hillsdale, NJ: Lawrence Earlbaum.

Case, R. (1992). Neo-Piagetian theories of intellectual development. In Beilin, H., & Pufall, P. (Eds.), *Piaget's theory: Prospects and possibilities* (pp. 61–104). Hillsdale, NJ: Lawrence Erlbaum.

Case, R., Okamoto, Y., Griffin, S., McKeough, A., Bleiker, C., Henderson, B., & Stephenson, K. (1996). The role of central conceptual structures in the development of children's thought. *Monographs of the Society for Research in Child Development, 61*(1–2, Serial no. 246).

Chi, M. T. H. (1978). Knowledge structures and memory development. In R. S. Siegler (Ed.), *Children's thinking: What develops?* (pp. 73–96) Hillsdale, NJ: Lawrence Erlbaum.

Childs, M., & Polich, J. M. (1979). Developmental differences in mental rotation. *Journal of Experimental Child Psychology, 27,* 339–351.

Chipp, H. B. (1968). *Theories of modern art.* Berkeley: University of California Press.

Clark, A. B. (1897). The child's attitude toward perspective problems. In E. Barnes (Ed.), *Studies in Education,* Vol. 1 (pp. 283–294). Stanford, CA: Stanford University Press.

Clark, G. (1989). Screening and identifying students talented in the visual arts: Clark's drawing abilities test. *Gifted Child Quarterly, 33*(3), 98–105.

Cooper, L. A. (1991). Dissociable aspects of the mental representation of visual objects. In R. H. Logies & M. Denis (Eds.), *Mental images in human cognition* (pp. 3–34). Amsterdam: North-Holland.

Costall, A. (1985). How meaning covers the traces. In N. H. Freeman & M. V. Cox (Eds.) *Visual Order* (pp. 17–30). Cambridge: Cambridge University Press.

Cox, M. V. (1981). One thing behind another: Problems of representation in children's drawings. *Educational Psychology, 1,* 275–287.

Cox, M. V. (1985). One object behind another: young children's use of array-specific or view-specific representations. In N. H. Freeman & M. V. Cox (Eds.) *Visual Order,* (pp. 188–201). Cambridge: Cambridge University Press.

Cox, M. V. (1986) *The child's point of view.* London: The Harvester Press.

Cox, M. V., & Parkin, C. E. (1986). Young children's human figure drawing: Cross-sectional and longitudinal studies. *Educational Psychology, 6*(4), 353–368.

Crook, C. (1985). Knowledge and appearance. In N. H. Freeman & M. V. Cox (Eds.), *Visual order* (pp. 248–265). Cambridge: Cambridge University Press.

Csikszentmihalyi, M., Rathunde, K., & Whalen, S. (1993). *Talented teenagers: The roots of success and failure.* New York: Cambridge University Press.

Csikszentmihalyi, M., & Robinson, R. E. (1986). Culture, time and the development of talent. In R. J. Sternberg & J. E. Davidson (Eds.),

Conceptions of giftedness (pp. 264–284). New York: Cambridge University Press.

Cupchik, G. C. (1992). From perception to production: A multilevel analysis of the aesthetic process. In G. C. Cupchik & J. Laszio (Eds.), *Emerging visions of the aesthetic process* (pp. 83–99). New York: Cambridge University Press.

Davis, A. M. (1985). The canonical bias: young children's drawings of familiar objects. In N. H. Freeman & M. V. Cox (Eds.), *Visual order* (pp. 202–213). Cambridge: Cambridge University Press.

Dean, A., Duhe, D. A., & Green, D. A. (1983). The development of children's mental tracking strategies on a rotation task. *Journal of Experimental Child Psychology, 36*, 226–240.

Dennis. S. (1992). Stage and structure in the development of children's spatial representations. In R. Case (Ed.) *The mind's staircase: Exploring the conceptual underpinnings of children's thought and knowledge* (pp. 229–245). Hillsdale, NJ: Lawrence Erlbaum.

Deregowski, J. B., Parker, D. M., & Dziurawiec, S. (1996). The role of typical contours in object processing by children. *British Journal of Developmental Psychology, 14*, 425–440.

Deregowski, J. B., & Strang, P. (1986). On the drawing of a cube and its derivatives. *British Journal of Developmental Psychology, 4*, 323–330.

DiLeo, J. (1970). *Young children and their drawings.* New York: Brunner-Mazel.

Downs, R. M. (1981). Maps and mappings as metaphors for spatial representation. In L. S. Liben, A. H. Patterson, & N. Newcombe (Eds.), *Spatial representation and behavior across the life span: Theory and application* (pp. 143–166). New York: Academic Press.

Dubery, F., & Willats, J. (1972). *Drawing systems.* London: Studio Vista.

Duthie, R. K. (1985). The adolescent's point of view: studies of forms in conflict. In N. H. Freeman & M. V. Cox (Eds.), *Visual order* (pp. 101–120). Cambridge: Cambridge University Press.

Edwards, B. (1979). *Drawing on the right side of the brain.* Los Angeles: J. P. Tarcher.

Eng, H. (1957) *The psychology of child and youth drawings.* London: Routledge.

Feldman, D. H. (1980). *Beyond universal in cognitive development.* Norwood NJ: Ablex.

Feldman, D. H. with Goldsmith, L. (1986). *Nature's gambit.* New York: Basic Books.

Fisher, K., Bullock, D., Rotenberg, E., & Raya, P. (1993). The dynamics of competence: How context contributes directly to skill. In R. Wozniak & K. Fischer (Eds.), *Development in context* (pp. 93–117). Hillsdale, NJ: Lawrence Erlbaum.

Fiske, S. (1982). Schema-triggered affect: Applications to social perception. In M. S. Clark & S. T. Fiske (Eds.), *Affect and cognition: The 17th Annual Carnegie Symposium on Cognition* (pp. 55–78). Hillsdale, NJ: Lawrence Erlbaum.

Flavell, J. (1990). Perspective on perspective taking. H. Beilin & P. Pufall, (Eds.), *Piaget's theory: Prospects and possibilities* (pp. 107–139). Hillsdale, NJ: Lawrence Erlbaum.

Flavell, J., & Wohlwill, J. F. (1969). Formal and functional aspects of cognitive development. In D. Elkind (Ed.), *Studies in cognitive development: Essays in honor of Jean Piaget* (pp. 67–120). New York: Oxford University Press.

Freeman, N. H. (1972). Process and product in children's drawings. *Perception, 1,* 123–140.

Freeman, N. H. (1975). Do children draw men with arms coming out of the head? *Nature, 254,* 416–417.

Freeman, N. H. (1980). *Strategies of representation in young children.* London: Academic Press.

Freeman, N., Chen, M., & Hambly, M. (1984). Children's different use of alignment cues when encoding and when producing a match-to-target. *British Journal of Developmental Psychology, 2,* 123–138.

Freeman, N. H., & Hargreaves, S. (1977). Directed movements and the body-proportion effect in preschool children's drawing of the human figure drawing. *Quarterly Journal of Experimental Psychology, 29,* 227–235.

Freeman, N., & Janikoun, R. (1972). Intellectual realism in children's drawings of a familiar object with distinctive features. *Child Development, 43,* 1116–1121.

Furth, H., Ross, B., & Youniss, J. (1974). Operative understanding in children's immediate and long-term reproductions of drawings. *Child Development, 45,* 63–70.

Gardner, H. (1973). *The arts and human development.* New York: Wiley.

Gardner, H. (1980). *Artful scribbles: The significance of children's drawings.* New York: Basic Books.

Gardner, H. (1983). *Frames of mind.* London: Heinemann.

Gardner, H., Winner, E., & Kircher, M. (1975). Children's conceptions of the arts. *Journal of Aesthetic Education, 9,* 60–77.

Garfunkel, G. (1980). *The development of compositional balance in children's drawings.* Paper presented at the annual meeting of the American Educational Research Association, Boston.

Gauger, W., & Wyckoff, D. (1973). Aesthetic preferences for water resource projects: An application of Q methodology. *Water Resources Bulletin, 9*(3), 522–528.

Gesell, A., & Armatruda, C. (1941). *Developmental diagnosis.* New York: Hoeber.

Getzels, J. W., & Csikszentmihalyi, M. (1976). *The creative vision: A longitudinal study of problem-finding in art.* New York: Wiley.

Gibson, J. J. (1954). A theory of picture perception. *Audio-Visual Communication Review, 1,* 3–23.

Gibson, J. J. (1966). *The senses considered as perceptual systems.* Boston: Houghton Mifflin.

Gibson, J. J. (1971). The information available in pictures. *Leonardo, 4,* 27–35.

Gibson, J. J. (1978). The ecological approach to the visual perception of pictures. *Leonardo, 11,* 227–235.

Gibson, J. J. (1979). *The ecological approach to visual perception.* Boston: Houghton Mifflin.

Gobbo, C., & Chi, M. (1986). How knowledge is structured and used by expert novice children. *Cognitive Development, 1,* 221–237.

Golomb, C. (1992). *The creation of a pictorial world.* Berkeley: University of California Press.

Goodenough, F. (1926). *Measurement of intelligence by drawings.* New York: Harcourt, Brace & World.

Goodman, N. (1968). *Languages of art.* Indianapolis, IN: Bobbs-Merill.

Goodnow, J. (1977). *Children drawing.* Cambridge, MA: Harvard University Press.

Goodnow, J. J., & Friedman, S. (1972). Orientation in children's human figure drawings: An aspect of graphic language. *Developmental Psychology, 7,* 10–16.

Gottman, J. M., & Roy, A. K. (1990). *Sequential analysis: A guide for behavioral researchers.* New York: Cambridge University Press.

Graham, F. K., Berman, P. W., & Ernhart, C. B. (1960). Development in preschool children of the ability to copy forms. *Child Development, 31,* 339–359.

Greenfield, P. (1966) On culture and conservation. In J. S. Bruner, R. R. Olver, & P. Greenfield (Eds.), *Studies in cognitive growth* (pp. 225–256). New York: Wiley & Sons.

Gridley, P. F. (1938). Graphic representation of a man by four-year-old children in nine prescribed drawing situations. *Genetic Psychology Monographs, 20,* 183–350.

Haberman, S. J. (1978). *Analysis of qualitative data* (Vol. 1). New York: Academic Press.

Hagen, M. (1985). There is no development in art. In N. H. Freeman & M. V. Cox (Eds.), *Visual order* (pp. 59–77). Cambridge: Cambridge University Press.

Harris, D. B. (1963). *Children's drawings as measures of intellectual maturity*. New York: Harcourt, Brace & World.

Harris, P. L. (1977). The child's representation of space. In G. Butterworth (Ed.), *The child's representation of the world* (pp. 83–93). New York: Plenum.

Hermelin B., & O'Conner, N. (1986). Spatial representation in mathematically and in artistically gifted children. *British Journal of Educational Psychology, 56,* 150–157.

Higgins, T. (1981). Role taking and social judgment: Alternative developmental perspectives and processes. In J. Flavell & L. Ross (Eds.), *Social cognitive development: Frontiers and possible futures.* New York: Cambridge University Press.

Hochberg, J. (1978). Visual arts and the structures of the mind. In S. S. Madeja (Ed.), *The arts, cognition and basic skills.* St Louis, MO: CEMREL.

Huttenlocher, J., & Presson, C. (1973). Mental rotation and the perspective problem. *Cognitive Psychology, 4, 277–299.*

Ibbotson, A., & Bryant, P. E. (1976). The perpendicular error and the vertical effect. *Perception, 5, 319–326.*

Ingram, N. (1985). Three into two won't go: Symbolic and spatial coding processes in young children's drawings. In N. H. Freeman & M. V. Cox (Eds.), *Visual order* (pp. 231–247). Cambridge: Cambridge University Press.

Inhelder, B., & Piaget, J. (1964). *The early growth of logic in the child.* New York: Basic Books.

Inhelder, B., Sinclair, H., & Bovet, M. (1974). *Learning and the development of cognition.* Cambridge, MA: Harvard University Press.

Ives, W. (1980). Preschool children's ability to coordinate spatial perspectives through language and pictures. *Child Development, 51,* 1303–1306.

Ives, W., & Rovet, J. (1979). The role of graphic orientations in children's drawings of familiar and novel objects at rest and in motion. *Merrill-Palmer Quarterly, 24(4),* 281–292.

Jahoda, G. (1981). Drawing styles of schooled and unschooled adults: A study in Ghana. *Quarterly Journal of Experimental Psychology, 33,* 133–143.

Kail, R., Pelegrino, J., & Carter, C. (1980). Developmental change in mental rotation. *Journal of Experimental Child Psychology, 29,* 102–116.

Karmiloff-Smith, A. (1990). Constraints on representational change: Evidence from children's drawings. *Cognition, 34,* 57–83.

Katz, D. (1935). *The world of colour.* London: K. Paul, Trench, Trubner.

Kellman, P. K. (1988). Theories of perception and research in perceptual development. In Yonas, A. (Ed.), *Perceptual development in infancy:*

The Minnesota symposia on child psychology (Vol. 20, pp. 276–299). Minneapolis: University of Minnesota Press.

Kellogg, R. (1979). *Analyzing children's art.* Palo Alto, CA: National Press Books.

Kemler, D. G. (1983). Exploring and reexploring issues of integrality, perceptual sensitivity and dimensional salience. *Journal of Experimental Child Psychology, 36,* 365–379.

Kennedy, J. J. (1992). *Analyzing qualitative data.* New York: Praeger.

Kennedy, J. M. (1993). *Drawing and the blind: Pictures to touch.* New Haven, CT: Yale University Press.

Kerschensteiner, G. (1905). *Die entwicklund der zeichnerschen begabung* (Development of drawing aptitude). Munich: Druck and Verlag von Carl Gerber.

Klaue, K. (1992). The development of depth representation in children's drawings: Effects of graphic surface and visibility of the model. *British Journal of Developmental Psychology, 10,* 71–83.

Klee, P. (1978). *Paul Klee notebooks, Vol. 1. The thinking eye.* J. Spiller (Ed.) London: Lund Humphries.

Koenig, O., Reiss, L. P., & Kosslyn, S. (1990). The development of spatial relation representations: Evidence from the studies of cerebral lateralization. *Journal of Experimental Child Psychology, 50,* 119–130.

Koffka, K. (1963). *Principles of Gestalt Psychology.* New York: Harcourt, Brace & World.

Koppitz, E. M. (1968). *Psychological evaluation of children's human figure drawings.* London: Grune & Stratton.

Kosslyn, S. (1980). *Image and mind.* Cambridge, MA: Harvard University Press.

Kosslyn, S., Margolis, J., Barrett, A., Goldknopf, E., & Daly, P. F. (1989). Age differences in imagery abilities. *Child Development, 61,* 995–1010.

Krascum, R., Tregenza, C., & Whitehead, P. (1996). Hidden-feature inclusions in children's drawings: The effects of age and model familiarity. *British Journal of Educational Psychology, 14,* 441–455.

Lange-Keuttner, C., & Reith, E. (1995). The transformation of figurative thought: Implications of Piaget's and Inhelder's developmental theory for children's drawings. In C. Lange-Keuttner & G. V. Thomas (Eds.), *Drawing and looking: Theoretical approaches to pictorial representation in children.* London: Harvester Wheatsheaf.

Langer, S. (1953). *Feeling and form: A theory of art.* New York: Scribner.

Lark-Horovitz, B., Lewis, H., & Luca, M. (1973). *Understanding children's art for better teaching.* Columbus, OH: Charles F. Merrill.

Lewis V., & Boucher, J. (1991). Skill, content and generative strategies in autistic children's drawings. *British Journal of Developmental Psychology, 9*(3), 393–416.

Liben, L. (1974). Operative understanding of horizontality and its relation to long-term memory. *Child Development, 45,* 416–424.

Liben, L. (1975). Long-term memory for pictures related to seriation, horizontality and verticality concepts. *Developmental Psychology, 11,* 795–806.

Liben, L. S., & Downs, R. M. (1991). The role of graphic representations in understanding the world. In R. M. Downs, L. S. Liben, & D. S. Palmero (Eds.), *Visions of aesthetics, the environment and development: The legacy of Joachim F. Wohlwill* (pp. 139–180). Hillsdale, NJ: Erlbaum.

Light, P. (1985). The development of view-specific representation considered from a socio-cognitive standpoint. In N. H. Freeman & M. V. Cox (Eds.), *Visual order* (pp. 214–230). Cambridge: Cambridge University Press.

Light, P., & Humphrey, J. (1981). Internal spatial relationships in young children's drawings. *Journal of Experimental Child Psychology, 31,* 521–530.

Light, P., & MacIntosh, E. (1980). Depth relationships in young children's drawings. *Journal of Experimental Child Psychology, 30,* 79–87.

Light, P., & Simmons, B. (1983). The effect of a communication task upon the representation of depth relationships in young children's drawings. *Journal of Experimental Child Psychology, 35,* 81–92.

Luquet, G. H. (1935). *Le dessin enfantin.* Paris:Alcan.

Machotka, P. (1966). Aesthetic criteria in childhood: Justifications of preference. *Child Development, 37*(4), 877–885.

Marr, D. (1982). *Vision: A computational investigation into the human representation and processing of visual information.* San Francisco: W. H. Freeman.

Marr, D., & Nishihara, H. K. (1978) Representation and recognition of the spatial organization of three-dimensional shapes. *Proceedings of the Royal Society London B, 200,* 269–294.

Milbrath, C. (1982). *Coding Manual for Spatial Relationships in Drawings.* Unpublished manuscript (available from the author).

Milbrath, C. (1987). Spatial Representations of Artistically Gifted Children: A Case of Universal or Domain Specific Development? *Genetic Epistemologist, XV,* 3–4.

Milbrath, C. (1995). Germinal motifs in the work of a gifted child artist. In C. Golomb (Ed.), *The development of artistically gifted children: Selected case studies* (pp. 101–134). Hillsdale, NJ: Lawrence Erlbaum.

Milbrath, C., & Seigel, B. (1996). Perspective taking in the drawings of a talented autistic child. *Visual Arts Research, 22,* 56–75.

Millar, S. (1975). Visual experience or translation rules? Drawing the human figure by blind sighted children. *Perception, 4,* 363–371.

Milner, B., Corkin, S., & Teuber, H. L. (1968). Further analysis of the hippocamla amnesic syndrome. *Neuropsychologia, 6,* 215–234.

Mitchelmore, M. C. (1985). Geometrical foundations of children's drawings. In N. H. Freeman & M. V. Cox (Eds.), *Visual order* (pp. 289–309). Cambridge: Cambridge University Press.

Molnar, F. (1992). A science of vision for visual arts. In G. C. Cupchik & J. Laszlo (Eds.), *Emerging visions of the aesthetic process,* (pp. 100–117). New York: Cambridge University Press.

Moore, V. (1987). The influence of experience on children's drawings of familiar and unfamiliar objects. *British Journal of Educational Psychology, 5,* 221–229.

Morra, S., Moizo, C., & Scopesi, A. (1988). Working memory (or the M operator) and the planning of children's drawings. *Journal of Experimental Child Psychology, 46,* 41–73.

Munro, T., Lark-Horovitz, B., & Barnhart, E. N. (1942). Children's art abilities: Studies at the Cleveland Museum of Art. *Journal of Experimental Psychology, 11*(2), 97–160.

Naeli, H., & Harris, P. (1976). Orientation of the diamond and square. *Perception, 5,* 73–78.

Nash, H., & Harris, D. B. (1970). Body proportion in children's drawing of a man. *Journal of Genetic Psychology, 117,* 85–90.

Nelson, K. (1992). Emergence of autobiographical memory at age 4. *Human Development, 35*(3), 172–177.

Nicholls, A. L. (1993). *Developing and understanding of projection rules for drawing.* Paper presented at the American Psychological Convention, August, Toronto, Ontario.

Nicolaides, K. (1969). *The natural way to draw: A working plan for art study.* Boston: Houghton Mifflin.

Norman, D. A. (1983) Some observations on mental models. In D. Gentner & A. Stevens (Eds.), *Mental models* (pp. 7–14). Hillsdale, NJ: Lawrence Erlbaum.

O'Conner N., & Hermelin, B. (1983). The role of general and specific talents in information processing. *British Journal of Developmental Psychology, 1,* 389–403.

Olson, D. R. (1970). *Cognitive development: The child's acquisition of diagonality.* New York: Academic Press.

Palmer, S., Rosch, E., & Chase, P. (1981). Canonical perspective and the perception of objects. In J. Long & A. D. Baddeley (eds.), *Attention and Performance IX.* Hillsdale, NJ: Lawrence Erlbaum

Parsons, J. (1987). *How we understand art: A cognitive developmental account of aesthetic experience.* New York: Cambridge University Press.

Pascual Leone, J. (1988). Organismic processes for neo-Piagetian theories:

A dialectical causal account of cognitive development. In A. Demetriou (Ed.), *The neo-Piagetian theories of cognitive development: Toward an integration* (pp. 531–570). Amsterdam: North-Holland.

Pascual Leone, J. (1995). Learning and development as dialectical factors in cognitive growth. *Human Development, 38,* 338–348.

Perner, J., Kohlmann, R., & Wimmer, H. (1984). Young children's recognition and use of the vertical and horizontal in drawings. *Child Development, 55,* 1637–1645.

Phillips, W. A., Hobbs, S. B., & Pratt, F. R. (1978). Intellectual realism in children's drawings of cubes. *Cognition, 6,* 15–33.

Piaget, J. (1951) *Play dreams and imitation.* London: Heinemann.

Piaget, J. (1969). *The mechanisms of perceptions.* New York: Basic Books.

Piaget, J. (1974). *Experiments in contradiction.* Chicago: University of Chicago Press.

Piaget, J. (1977). The role of action in the development of thinking. In W. F. Overton & J. M. Gallagher (Eds.), *Knowledge and development* (Vol. 1, pp. 17–42). New York: Plenum.

Piaget, J. (1979). Correspondences and transformations. In F. B. Murray (Ed.), *The impact of Piagetian theory on education philosophy, psychiatry and psychology* (pp. 17–27). Baltimore: University Park Press.

Piaget, J. (1985). *The equilibration of cognitive structures.* Chicago: University of Chicago Press.

Piaget, J., Henriques, G., & Ascher, E. (1992) *Morphisms and categories.* Hillsdale, NJ: Lawrence Erlbaum.

Piaget, J., & Inhelder, B. (1956/1967). *The child's conception of space.* New York: Norton.

Piaget, J., & Inhelder, B. (1969). Mental images or intellectual operations and their development. In P. Fraisse & J. Piaget (Eds.), *Experimental psychology its scope and method* (Vol. 7, pp. 87–164). London: Routledge & Kegan Paul.

Piaget, J., & Inhelder, B. (1971). *Mental imagery in the child.* New York: Basic Books.

Piaget, J., Inhelder, B., & Szeminska, A. (1960). *The child's conception of geometry.* New York: Basic Books.

Pillow, B. H., & Flavell, J. (1986). Young children's knowledge about visual perception: Projective size and shape. *Child Development, 57,* 125–135.

Pinto, G., & Bombi, A. S. (1996). Drawing human figures in profile: A study of the development of representative strategies. *Journal of Genetic Psychology, 157*(3), 303–321.

Pratt, F. (1985). A perspective on traditional artistic practice. In N. H. Freeman & M. V. Cox (Eds.), *Visual order* (pp. 32–58). Cambridge: Cambridge University Press.

Radkey, A., & Enns, J. T. (1987). Da Vinci's window facilitates drawing of total and partial occlusion in young children. *Journal of Experimental Child Psychology, 33*, 222–235.

Reid, D. Kim (1978) Genevan theory and the education of exceptional children. In Gallagher & Easley (Eds.), *Knowledge and development,* Vol. 2 (pp. 199–241). New York: Plenum.

Reith, E. (1988). The development of use of contour lines in children's drawings of figurative and non-figurative three-dimensional models. *Archives de Psychologie, 56*, 83–103.

Reith, E. (1994). *Using a da Vinci window to study children's ability to measure and represent visual projection.* Paper presented at the Annual Symposium of the Jean Piaget Society, June, Chicago.

Reith, E., & Lui, C. H. (1995). What hinders accurate depiction of projective shape? *Perception, 24,* 995–1010.

Reith, E., Steffan, C., & Gellieron, C. (1994). Children's drawing of water level: Operatory knowledge, attention to visual image, and depiction skills. *Swiss Journal of Psychology, 53*(2), 86–97.

Rosenblatt, E., & Winner, E. (1988). Is superior visual memory a component of superior drawing ability? In L. Ober & D. Fein (Eds.), *The exceptional brain: Neuropsychology of talent and superior abilities* (pp. 341–363). New York: Guilford.

Rosensteil, A. K., Morison, P., Silverman, J., & Gardner, H. (1978). Critical judgment: A developmental study. *Journal of Aesthetic Education, 12*(4), 95–100.

Rosser, R. A. (1981). The emergence of spatial perspective taking: An information-processing alternative to egocentrism. *Child Development, 54*, 660–668.

Saenger, E. (1981). *Drawing systems: A developmental study of representation.* Unpublished Ph. D. thesis, Department of Social Psychology, Harvard University.

Schacter, D. L. (1990). Perceptual representation systems and implicit memory. In A. Diamond (Ed.), *The development and neural basis of higher cognitive functions.* New York: New York Academy of Sciences.

Schacter, D. L., Chiu, C. Y., & Ochsner, K. N. (1993). Implicit memory: A selective review. *Annual Review of Neurosciences, 16*, 159–182.

Sedgwick, H. A. (1980). The geometry of spatial layout in pictorial representation. In M. A. Hagen (Ed.), *The perception of pictures* (Vol. 1, pp. 32–89). New York: Academic Press.

Selfe, L. (1977). *Nadia: A case of extraordinary drawing ability in an autistic child.* New York: Academic Press.

Selfe, L. (1983). *Normal and anomalous representational drawing ability in children.* London: Academic Press.

Selfe, L. (1995). Nadia reconsidered. In C. Golomb (Ed.), *The development of artistically gifted children: Selected case studies* (pp. 197–236). Hillsdale, NJ: Lawrence Erlbaum.

Sheppard, J. (1991). *Realistic figure drawing.* Cincinnati: North Light Books.

Silk, A. M., & Thomas, G. V. (1986). Development and differentiation in children's figure drawings. *British Journal of Psychology, 77,* 399–410.

Silk, A. M., & Thomas, G. V. (1988). The development of size scaling in children's figure drawings. *British Journal of Developmental Psychology, 6,* 285–299.

Simon, D. P., & Simon, H. A. (1978). Individual differences in solving physics problems. In R. S. Siegler (Ed.), *Children's thinking: What develops?* (pp. 325–348) Hillsdale, NJ: Erlbaum.

Smith, L. B. (1989). A model of perceptual classification in children and adults. *Psychological Review, 96,*125–144.

Snyder, S. S., & Feldman, D. H. (1984). Phases of transition in cognitive development: Evidence from the domain of spatial representation. *Child Development, 55,* 981–989.

Spelke, E., Breinlinger, K., Jacobson, K., & Phillips, A. (1993). Gestalt relations and object perception: A developmental study. *Perception, 22,* 1483–1501.

Squire, L. R. (1987). *Memory and brain.* New York: Oxford University Press.

Squire, L. R., Knowlton. B., & Musen, G. (1993). The structure and organization of memory. *Annual Review of Psychology, 44,* 453–495.

Stacy, J. T., & Ross, B. M. (1975). Scheme and schema in children's memory of their own drawings. *Developmental Psychology, 11,* 37–41.

Stephenson, W. (1953). *The study of behavior: Q-technique and its methodology.* Chicago: University of Chicago Press.

Sullivan, M. W., Rovee-Collier, C. K., & Tynes, D. M. (1979). A conditioning analysis of infant long-term memory. *Child Development, 50,* 152–162.

Taunton, M. (1980). The influence of age on preferences for subject matter, realism, and spatial depth in painting reproductions. *Studies in Art Education, 21,* 40–52.

Taunton, M. (1982). Aesthetic responses of young children to the visual arts: A review of the literature. *Journal of Aesthetic Education, 16,* 93–107.

Taylor, M., & Bacharach, V. R. (1982). Constraints on the visual accuracy of drawings produced by young children. *Journal of Experimental Child Psychology, 34,* 311–329.

Temkin, A. (1987). Klee and Avant-Garde 1912–1940. In C. Lanchner (Ed.), *Paul Klee*. New York: Museum of Modern Art.

Thomas, G. V., & Silk, A. M. J. (1990). *An introduction to the psychology of children's drawings*. New York: New York University Press.

Thomas, G., & Tsalimi, A. (1988). Effects of order of drawing head and trunk on their relative sizes in children's human figure drawings. *British Journal of Developmental Psychology*, 6(2), 191–203.

Thouless, R. H. (1931). Phenomenal regression to the real object. *Journal of Psychology,* 21(4), 339–359.

Trautner, H. M. (1996). Drawing procedures in children's free drawing, copying, and tracing of the human figure. Poster presented at the Piaget Centennial Conference, *The growing mind*. Geneva, Switzerland.

Turiel, E. (1969). Developmental processes in the child's moral thinking. In P. Mussen, J. Langer, & M. Covington (Eds.), *Trends and issues in developmental psychology*. New York: Holt.

Uzgiris, I., & Hunt, M. McV. (1975). *Assessment in infancy: Ordinal scale of psychological development*. Urbana: University of Illinois.

Van Sommers, P. (1984). *Drawing and cognition*. Cambridge: Cambridge University Press.

Vurpillot, E. (1976). *The visual world of the child*. New York: International Universities Press.

Walk, R. D., Karusaitos, K., Lebowitz, C., & Falbo, T. (1971). Artistic style as concept formation for children and adults. *Merrill-Palmer Quarterly*, 17, 347–356.

Willats, J. (1977). How children learn to draw realistic pictures. *Quarterly Journal of Experimental Psychology*, 29, 367–382.

Willats, J. (1981). What do the marks in the picture stand for? The child's acquisition of systems of transformation and denotation. *Review of Research in Visual Arts Education*, 13, 18–33.

Willats, J. (1985). Drawing systems revisited: The role of denotation systems in children's figure drawings. In N. H. Freeman & M. V. Cox (Eds.), *Visual order* (pp. 78–100). Cambridge: Cambridge University Press.

Willats, J. (1987). Marr and pictures: An information processing account of children's drawings. *Archives de Psychologie*, 55, 105–125.

Willats, J. (1992). The representation of extendedness in children's drawings of sticks and discs. *Child Development*, 63(3), 692–710.

Winner, E. (1996). *Gifted children*. New York: Basic Books.

Winner, E., Blank, P., Massey, C., & Gardner, H. (1983). Children's sensitivity to aesthetic properties of line drawings. In D. Rogers & J. A. Sloboda (Eds.), *The acquisition of symbolic skills* (pp. 97–104). New York: Plenum.

Winner, E., & Martino, G. (1993). Giftedness in the visual arts and music.

In K. Heller, F. Monks, A. H. Passow (Eds.), *International handbook of research and development of giftedness and talent.* Elmsford, NY: Pergamon Press.

Winner, E., Rosenblatt, E., Windmueller, G., Davidson, L., & Gardner, H. (1986). Children's perception of 'aesthetic' properties of the arts: Domain-specific or pan-artistic? *British Journal of Developmental Psychology* , 4, 149–160.

INDEX